NEWBORNS AT RISK

Medical Care and Psychoeducational Intervention

Gail L. Ensher, EdD

Associate Professor of Special Education
Syracuse University
Syracuse, New York

David A. Clark, MD

Associate Professor of Pediatrics
New York Medical College
Valhalla, New York

AN ASPEN PUBLICATION®
Aspen Publishers, Inc.

1986

Rockville, Maryland
Royal Tunbridge Wells

Contributors

Salome A. Arenas, MS
Division of Special Education and
    Rehabilitation
Syracuse University

Debra A. DeSocio, MS
Division of Special Education and
    Rehabilitation
Syracuse University

Evelyn S. Stevens, MSW
School of Social Work
Syracuse University

Photographic Contributions

by

Alix Lawson-Board, Newhouse School of Public
Communications, Syracuse University

Andrejs Ozolins, BA, Division of Special Education and
Rehabilitation, Syracuse University

NEWBORNS AT RISK

Medical Care and Psychoeducational Intervention

Library of Congress Cataloging in Publication Data

Ensher, Gail L.
Newborns at risk.

Includes bibliographies and index.
1. Infants (Newborn)—Diseases—Treatment. 2. Child development. 3. Sick children—
Education. I. Clark, David A. II. Title.
RJ254.E57   1986   618.92'01   86-14156
ISBN: 0-87189-389-4

Editorial Services: Ruth Bloom

Library of Congress Catalog Card Number: 86-14156
ISBN: 0-87189-389-4

Printed in the United States of America

2 3 4 5

To

Kimberly Elizabeth,

Darlene, Jenny, Kim, and Mindy

Table of Contents

Foreword

Newborns at Risk: Medical Care and Psychoeducational Intervention paints a picture of neonatology and early childhood intervention strikingly at odds with the tumult and drama surrounding America's most famous "neonates"—Baby John Doe, Baby Jane Doe, and Baby Faye. The point is not that the book concerns infants other than those who drew national attention, but that the authors approach their topic in thoughtful, not stereotyped ways. In every aspect, this is a book about newborns at risk; it concerns babies of exceedingly low birthweight, infants who have suffered the insult of the birthing process or various diseases and syndromes, and infants abused by chemicals or by parental smoking and drinking. It concerns infants injured by their social origin, by insufficient nutrition, perinatal care, and environmental hazards. It speaks to the needs of infants disabled by a host of other physical and psychological occurrences. Yet, throughout this book, the authors convey a sense of optimism. They never reveal the hopelessness that so characterizes many of our public discussions of at risk and disabled infants, nor do they communicate a feeling of special charity toward newborns whose prospects for normal development have been jeopardized. Through the authors' eyes we come to see infants at risk as fully valued and valuable children.

Drs. Ensher and Clark make no effort to shield us from the devastating effects on children of adult society's failures (e.g., exposure to environmental dangers, insufficient nutrition) or from science's limitations (e.g., the absence of cures for Tay-Sachs disease or Down syndrome or, for that matter, the absence of guarantees for the extremely premature newborn). What the authors *do* communicate is a careful, inquiring spirit. We learn with them, as they explain what they believe is now known, the areas of certainty in infant care (e.g., how particular assessment instruments bias us in one way or another, how medicine *can* respond effectively to head injuries and degrees of asphyxia at birth). They also show us uncertainties, for example the near impossibility of predicting the prospects for any child's development, whether of extremely low or typical birthweight, whether disabled or not, whether at risk or not.

Matter-of-factly, the authors lead us through a varietal teach-in on a whole host of medical conditions and treatments as well as educational and psychological program strategies. The orientation is forever optimistic and developmental. As the authors communicate so well, all children are at risk. One can hardly read the passages on normal childbirth without feeling a bit in awe as to how any youngsters survive with what we might call typical or normal prospects. At the same time, this book never underestimates extreme needs for dramatic, consistent, and persistent intervention, whether medical or educational, to enhance the lives of those children who have experienced the greatest insults.

In many ways, this is a book that owes its life to the remarkable developments in neonatology and public education during the last decade. All states now sponsor comprehensive, Level Three, neonatal units, which can respond to the most unusual medical crises of infants. This fact reflects a priority within social policy and medical practice toward aggressive infant care. It also suggests a national commitment to lowering persistently high levels of infant mortality. At the same time, *Newborns at Risk: Medical Care and Psychoeducational Intervention* never communicates a Pollyannish view of the current state of social policy for infants. In the very first chapter, for instance, we learn of inadequate prevention services, such as prenatal care, despite modest increases in the national birthrate. Further, the authors frequently remind us that many of the important strides in medical treatment have been unevenly available to infants born into low and middle or high socio-economic groups. Their perspective on this problem is clear; all infants deserve aggressive, state-of-the-art medical care.

Professionals have experienced a similar revolution over the last decade and a half. In 1971 special educators Burton Blatt and Ignacy Goldberg took a dramatic step in their conceptualization of the educational process for youngsters with disabilities. Testifying before a federal court judge in the landmark PARC case, these experts declared all children to be educable. In making the claim that all children could benefit from an education, they set the stage for legislation of Public Law 94–142, the Education for All Handicapped Children Act (1975). That act provided the impetus for a dramatic expansion in the availability of infant and preschool programming for at risk and disabled children. It is quite clear that experts who testified on universal educability broke with an existing tradition, at least in many professional circles, of seeing some children as learners and other children as incapable of learning. Today, educators express near unanimity on the educability question. That is, most individuals, including the research community, believe that all people, no matter how disabled, are capable of learning. Indeed, we have no alternative. There are two reasons that undergird this belief. First, educators have been able to demonstrate learning by nearly every youngster. We have not, through our failure with a particular child, proven that education is impossible with that child, but only that our techniques or approaches to date have been unsuccessful. Second, this admittedly optimistic perspective grows out of the knowledge that were educators to adopt an educability/noneducability model for approaching youngsters with severe and profound disabilities, they would by definition consign certain infants and young students to custodial care. In view of the dramatic gains that have been made in our ability to educate seriously impaired children and in light of our consistent inability to accurately predict individual developmental progress, this appears an extremely imprudent and indeed immoral position to take. Hence, educators have opted instead for the educability imperative. *Newborns at Risk* reflects this relatively new but nevertheless powerful tradition.

It is no accident that Ensher and Clark not only affirm the importance of providing quality medical treatment and education/early intervention to at risk infants, but also believe we should integrate these two realms of service. In their view, education and medicine are inextricably linked. In making this point, the authors provide us the latest knowledge on methods of implementing what professionals have come to see as essential. Note, for example, the policy declaration of the Association for Persons with Severe Handicaps concerning medical treatment and social intervention:

> The Association reaffirms the right to equal medical treatment for all infants in accordance with the dignity and worth of these individuals, as protected by the Constitution and Bill of Rights of the United States of America ....

> The Association for People with Severe Handicaps acknowledges the obligation of society to provide for life-long medical, financial, educational support to handicapped persons to extend to them opportunities to achieve potential, equal and equivalent, to those opportunities offered other/all members of our society. (The Association for People with Severe Handicaps.) (*TASH Newsletter*, Policy Statement of the Critical Issues Committee, June 1983, p.1)

In a multiplicity of ways, Ensher and Clark's book provides us a blueprint for implementing the programmatic implications of that national declaration.

One of the most satisfying qualities of this text is its articulation of key principles that underlie the delivery of quality medical and developmental programs to at risk infants. These beliefs, while never articulated by the authors in list form, pervade the text and can be summarized as follows:

- All infant intervention—whether medical, educational, or related human service—must be provided in a manner consistent with the belief that all children deserve the most aggressive, considered treatment that a society can make available. In other words, the authors give no audience to those who would provide some youngsters with aggressive treatment while consigning others to the dangers of custodialism or nontreatment.

- Parents are important. Few professionals articulate such a clear vision of professional and parent cooperation as Ensher and Clark. Time and again, through rich examples of children and families at risk, the authors reveal the unique benefits that derive when parents and professionals collaborate in responding to the needs of a youngster. This book assumes that professionals can and must take families seriously.

- Professionals must communicate effectively with each other, with their various publics, and with parents. One cannot read this book without having an enormous appreciation for the authors' ability to articulate complex and difficult-to-understand knowledge in a simple, straightforward, and informative fashion. They have shown the behavior they presumably expect from their fellow professionals.

- We probably cannot improve the lives of at risk infants if we hold on to uninformed stereotypes about these children and about treatment strategies. Professionals, parents, and all other interested parties have an obligation to look beyond stereotyped notions of disability and treatment strategies. We must not be afraid to explore the complexities of child development and professional practice.

- All services should reflect a fundamental belief in the individual's capacity for change. The question for professionals—whether medical personnel, educators, or other human service specialists—is not whether a youngster can develop, but rather how professional practice can improve the opportunities for a child's development.

- Social policy can improve life circumstances for at risk infants. While most of this book focuses on intervention strategies for the individual at risk baby, the authors continually remind us of the impact of social policy, social funding, and broad programmatic decisions on the promotion or diminution of particular treatment strategies. The authors show, for example, implicitly as well as explicitly, a persistent and troubling imbalance between the high technology of early medical intervention and the still nearly universal inadequacy of family support and educational intervention programs.

- Quality services demand a spirit of inquiry. Ensher and Clark share with us those areas of medical and educational intervention in which they themselves are engaged in research. For example, in a marvelous chapter on high risk infant development, the authors reveal their struggles to develop an early childhood assessment instrument that would compare preterm baby development against typical child development, thus providing families and professionals additional measures for understanding the normal course of development for children born at risk.

- The future of educational and medical intervention suggests a fuller integration of people with disabilities into the mainstream of society. Throughout this book the authors implicitly call for a policy of normalization with respect to intervention strategies. Parents and families are seen walking through and spending countless hours in intensive care units. At risk and severely disabled infants are seen being served by public school and mainstream early intervention programs. Parents are pictured bringing their youngsters home from the hospital, often with an array of hospital equipment, thus maximizing the fullest and earliest integration of the high risk or disabled infant into the life of the family and community.

The last principle is emblematic of the book and the changes that have recently occurred in the field. The idea that a person's choices for services occur in the context of mainstream social institutions, such as regular hospitals and public schools, reflects a growing awareness that people with disabilities—whether infants, young children, adolescents, or adults—are gaining fuller acceptance within society than was ever previously thought possible. Nowhere in this book do we find any suggestion that high risk and clearly disabled youngsters should be consigned to institutions. The authors correctly assume that children, however disabled, should have increasingly diverse opportunities to develop in natural community settings. In its indominable and yet totally sensible optimism, this book promotes the assumption that all children can develop, all children can benefit from treatment or education, and all children have a right to participate in society. And it goes a long way toward demonstrating how professionals can best facilitate these goals.

Douglas P. Biklen
Director
Division of Special Education
and Rehabilitation
Syracuse University

Preface

This book first developed from very special interests and experiences during the course of a three-year contract awarded in August 1979 to Syracuse University's School of Education by the New York State Office of Mental Retardation and Developmental Disabilities. The project was funded with the particular purpose of delivering home-based intervention services to markedly premature and other high risk infants discharged from an intensive care nursery in Crouse-Irving Memorial Hospital, Syracuse, New York. It was to be carried out under the unified direction of cross-disciplinary specialists.

Notwithstanding the varied physical, developmental, and educational needs of many infants and young children, genuine collaborative efforts continue to be in short supply. Occasional interaction among professions has centered almost exclusively on medical issues. Thus, we have designed this book to accomplish the following objectives:

1. to offer an easily understood, scholarly text that discusses prenatal and perinatal events, routine newborn care, and major medical conditions of high risk infants

2. to provide a text that ties major medical and psychosocial conditions of newborns to probable developmental outcome

3. to offer a critique of past and contemporary models of parent-infant intervention in intensive care nursery, home, center-based, and school settings

4. to present a cross-disciplinary framework for future intervention efforts with high risk newborns, parents, medical staff, and other human service professionals.

The integration of medical and psychoeducational concepts, philosophy, research, and clinical practice represents a perspective heretofore virtually absent from the professional literature. In our view, this text will have achieved a primary purpose if it facilitates greater insight and knowledge among students of several disciplines concerning the medical care and educational prevention of disability in infants born at risk. Second, we hope that the book may be modestly successful in orienting narrowly trained professionals to a new concept of role that diminishes rivalries, heightens the personalization with which service is delivered, and helps to focus attention on the family unit as the responsible agent in the development of the child. To a large extent we designed the text to serve the practitioner working with infants and families and the graduate student training in the areas of early childhood and special education.

The book is organized into four parts, each of which covers a different aspect of the medical and psychoeducational prevention of developmental problems in high risk newborns. To provide an introductory view, the first chapter discusses the historical context and contemporary perspectives on the medical treatment and early intervention with vulnerable infants and their families.

Part I, *From Conception to Discovery of the World*, covers material relating to high risk pregnancies, perinatal events, initial medical concerns and problems of the newborn, and the sensory motor and psychological development of preterm and other high risk babies.

Part II, *Clinical Issues: Insult, Identification, Assessment, and Prognosis*, discusses major medical insults to the newborn including jaundice, respiratory distress, nutritional and metabolic disorders, abnormal physical development, and infection. The initial chapter of this section describes the basic neurology of the newborn, and the concluding chapter takes a look at past, present, and future strategies for developmental assessment.

Part III, *Intervention: Process and Practical Application*, focuses on the needs of families of high risk and handicapped infants and subsequently describes early intervention endeavors in hospital, home, center-based, day-care, and public school settings.

Last, Part IV, *A Framework for the Future*, considers areas of need within our systems of service delivery and, drawing upon the expertise and experiences of parents, concludes with a chapter on future directions for enhancing the potentials of high risk infants, families, and professionals.

Gail L. Ensher
David A. Clark

Acknowledgments

This book would not have been written without the help of many people. Our first and greatest appreciation goes to our families: to Kimberly Elizabeth and to Darlene, Jenny, Kim, and Mindy, who have taught us the real meaning of parenting and child development; and to our own parents, who have given so unstintingly of their love and support over the years.

Several colleagues have made a very special difference in our professional lives. These include the late Burton Blatt and Margaret Williams, who were always present to offer wisdom and encouragement to go on; and Douglas Biklen, Katharine Butler, Harold Herber, Ernest Kraybill, and Albert Murphy, who have been faithful mentors, friends, and examples of the very best in our respective fields.

A number of people have contributed to the writing of this book. We owe a sincere debt to those families who opened their homes, allowed us to visit week after week, and wrote personal, heartfelt stories. They are Henry and Effie Buie, Gary and Margaret Brockway, Pamela and William Corrigan, Michael and Beth Daly, Fred and Sarah Edelman, Linda and Patrick Fullan, Nicholas and Carol Marsella, and Robert and Ann Pratt. We also wish to thank our Master's students, Salome Arenas, Debra DeSocio, and Evelyn Stevens, who shared in the toils of creating this manuscript.

We deeply appreciate the time and efforts of those who have been responsible for preparing other aspects of this book: for the beautiful photographs taken by Alix Lawson-Board and Andrejs Ozolins; for the countless library articles that were reviewed by Lori Brooks, Joanne Hopkins, and Judith Witkin; and for the endless typing of this manuscript in its various stages by Alix Lawson-Board, Anne Luke, and Patricia Felice.

Finally, we would like to thank all of those graduate students and families of high risk babies who have listened to our thoughts and ideas along the way and who were genuinely responsible for the initial conception of this work.

Part I

FROM CONCEPTION TO DISCOVERY OF THE WORLD

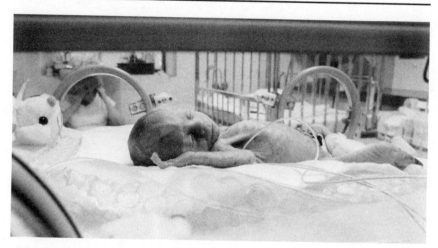

A National Natality Survey conducted in 1980 revealed 3,612,000 births in the United States (Singh, Torres, & Forrest, 1985). This figure remained relatively stable between 1980 and 1982, increasing by approximately one percent each year. At the same time, the proportion of women receiving prenatal care during this period declined. These figures specifically reflected higher incidences of inadequate service among expectant mothers who were least educated, unmarried, younger than 18, and black. These trends are troubling in light of known evidence that the well-being of the newborn begins long before birth and is intimately connected to the welfare and nutrition of the mother, and in view of the growing mass of data linking prematurity and other risk factors to the above groups. Research in the field of neonatology over the past 20 years has been responsible for vast improvements in mortality rates and has perceptively enhanced the prospects for normal developmental outcome, even among extremely low birthweight populations. Yet, progress toward the prevention of developmental problems could be further advanced were this country to meet the U.S. Surgeon General's call for an increase in services by 1990 such that 90 percent of women across all ethnic, economic, and age groups are receiving appropriate prenatal care beginning within the first trimester.

REFERENCE

Singh, S., Torres, A., & Forrest, J.D. (1985). The need for prenatal care in the United States: Evidence from the 1980 national natality survey. *Family Planning Perspectives, 17,* 118–124.

1

The High Risk Infant: Historical Context and Contemporary Perspectives

Today there is a growing realization that developmentally delayed and other at risk infants are less fragile than previously supposed. This awareness has opened new opportunities for conveying to the child a sense of love and care through physical contact and other means of stimulation essential to the psychological well-being of infants and parents. Compatible with adequate medical precautions, for example, newborns in intensive care units commonly are handled and talked to by nursery personnel, and babies are removed from incubators at the earliest possible time. Moreover, with the exceptions of extreme damage or very negative environmental influence, expanding evidence seems to indicate that normal development is a likely outcome. Thus, we have in the newborn a potent ally in support of early intervention.

As the number and variety of infant and preschool programs increase, many basic questions remain. One problem is that we know too little about how impairment or prematurity affects parent and family and, consequently, too little about the impact of the differential treatment accorded such children. In part, the task, not well addressed in early childhood, is how to separate limitations imposed by physical and cognitive delays from those that arise from diverse interactions with the high risk infant and young child. The birth of preterm and at risk children into families of poverty and sociocultural deprivation often presages developmental disabilities at a later age (Sameroff, 1981; Sameroff & Chandler, 1975). To what extent this predictive effect is the result of family lives on the edge of inadequacy and easily susceptible to disruption and failure is presently unclear. In the long range, the influence of such factors likely determines the success of early intervention.

Realistically, we do not need a superficial regeneration of enthusiasm for early education, but rather the assurance that present high interest fulfills its obligation (Caldwell, 1970, p. 725) in research, training, and service. The charge is a formidable one in light of the need for more defined measures of child and family growth, more defined program goals, greater understanding of the notion of risk, broader perspectives in early intervention, and longitudinal data on program effectiveness.

VULNERABILITY AND RISK IN NEWBORNS

The *neonatal period* includes the first four weeks of life and, despite recent scientific progress, remains the time of greatest mortality in childhood, with the risk highest within the first 24 hours of life. *Perinatology* is a broader term used to designate the time extending from the twelfth week of gestation through the neonatal period. The high incidence of death and disease during the perinatal period makes it essential to identify as early and rapidly as possible those at risk and to intervene whenever possible. The goal, therefore, becomes not only reduction in mortality but decrease in the incidence of handicapping conditions.

Some Historical Considerations in Neonatal Care

As defined by the late Alexander Schaffer, neonatology is the "art and science of diagnosis and treatment of disorders of the newborn infant." Pierre Budin, a French obstetrician, was the first individual recognized as having articulated and published a set of guidelines for medical care of the newborn. In 1892 he established "a special department for weaklings" in a Parisian maternity hospital. He used the weight of 2,500 grams or less (454 grams = one pound) as a definition for prematurity. This statement subsequently was adopted by the American Academy of Pediatrics in 1935 and by the World Health Organization in 1950. Advances during that 50 years focused primarily on prevention of infection and on early nutrition for sick newborns. Dr. Julius Hess established the first premature infant center in Chicago just after World War I. Meanwhile, significant strides in understanding the growth, nutrition, physiology, and pathology of newborns was achieved by European researchers in Finland, Germany, and France. Unfortunately, as a consequence of the two World Wars and the great economic depression of the 1930s, much of this information was slow to be transmitted to the United States.

A major contributor to the field of neonatology in this country was Ethel Dunham. With an appointment in the Department of Pediatrics at Yale, she then worked as the director of the Division of Research in Child Development of the Children's Bureau in Washington, D.C. Between 1919 and 1940 she compiled information on premature infants and subsequently published that material as a book entitled *Premature Infants: A Manual for Physicians*. This work not only provided guidelines but also generated interest in the care of newborns. By the 1950s, much research on the physiology and treatment of the neonate was being initiated. Concurrent with these developments, major changes were occurring in adult medicine, especially in the fields of cardiology and hematology. The American Cancer Society and the American Heart Association were founded during this time, and funding for research was being allocated to diseases that affected adults. Thus, it was not until the

1960s that more government and business money finally was made available for research on the problems and care of the newborn. Since that time, there has been rapid growth both in the understanding of newborns and in the status of current technology. Prematurity during this era was redefined to include criteria of birthweight as well as indication of physical and neurologic maturity. As a result of these changes in classification, morbidity associated with variations of intrauterine growth then could be identified more precisely and addressed within this same time frame. Technological advances with smaller and more accurate pieces of equipment to monitor and treat the newborn were made, a benefit of research carried out during the early NASA space exploration programs.

Throughout the 1960s, numerous studies were done to analyze various causes of neonatal mortality and morbidity. In states such as Wisconsin and Massachusetts, regional perinatal centers were developed to provide for the unique needs of the complicated obstetrical patient and the sick newborn. The reduction in mortality demonstrated by these facilities became the impetus for the establishment of perinatal centers across the country.

Organization of Perinatal Care

Careful delineation of risk factors that could be life-threatening in mothers or that might result in problems in newborns helped immeasurably to determine where services of medical intervention should best be made available. Medical facilities within given geographic regions varied markedly in their ability to offer perinatal care, with differences reflecting population density of the area, the size and financial help of the institution, experience and skill of the medical-nursing staff, proximity to larger facilities, and available equipment. Hence, it became quite natural that institutions within specific localities needed to join together in order to afford optimal care.

In the United States, three basic levels of treatment have emerged. A Level One service is the community hospital that generally has fewer deliveries and is designed primarily for the mother and baby with no risk factors. These institutions still must have available the equipment and personnel for competent emergency service prior to transport of the mother or child when the need arises.

A Level Two facility is the hospital that has larger maternity and nursery services. These institutions usually are located in urban and suburban areas and are capable of giving service to selected mothers and newborns with problems. However, there is considerable diversity among such institutions, depending on resources and the skills of their personnel.

The Level Three facility can handle the full range of complications of pregnancy and of sick newborns. Most, but not all, of these facilities are associated with medical schools. They provide for the care of newborns with severe respiratory distress, cardiac diseases, and various surgical problems. Consultation of subspecialists in various areas of pediatrics must be readily accessible. Many of these facilities have been designated as regional perinatal centers, which have responsibility for developing systems of patient transport, setting the standard for care within a given location, and improving the level of service in the referring institutions by outreach education. The impact of this approach has led to a decrease of nearly 50 percent in infant mortality over the last ten years. There also has been a concomitant decrease in the percentage of infants with residual handicapping conditions.

Stresses of Medical Care

While new scientific approaches have altered dramatically what can be done for sick infants, may tensions surrounding the care of these newborns have surfaced. Some of these are social issues, such as the increased number of pregnancies in adolescence, legalization of abortions, the working mother, and the dissolution of families. Added to these considerations are the often unrealistic expectations of parents for completely healthy children. One very specific problem for both the family and society is the cost of this highly technical care. A baby born 12 weeks prematurely, with an uncomplicated course, may be expected to be hospitalized for a minimum of two months, and the more involved infant may be hospitalized six months or longer. The cost per day exceeds $500 and in a sick newborn may approach several thousands of dollars. Thus, hospital bills of $30,000 or more for a sick, small newborn are not uncommon. Annually, the estimated cost for neonatal intensive care in this country is approximately $1.5 billion. For the most part, this expenditure is being borne by state financial aid and by private insurance companies.

Although social and financial pressures are considerable, even greater are the increasing legal and ethical obligations for newborn care. Who decides what technology should be used and for how long in the case of an individual baby with little or no hope of survival, let alone meaningful existence? Recently, three infants who received national publicity have brought to light some of these specific concerns: Baby John Doe, Baby Jane Doe, and Baby Faye. Baby John Doe was an infant with Down syndrome, born in the Midwest; he was missing a portion of his esophagus. Although this condition was surgically correctable, the family and medical staff chose not to intervene and the baby died. While this was common practice 30 years ago, it is highly unlikely that such a child would not have surgery today.

A second child, Baby Jane Doe, was a little girl born in New York with hydrocephalus and a large open myelomeningocele. While prognosis for long-term survival is very tenuous, the typical care is supportive, with the closing of the myelomeningocele and a decompression of the abnormally large head filled with excessive cerebrospinal fluid. The parents and medical staff elected not to pursue this route; yet the baby did not expire as rapidly as predicted by the medical staff. This information subsequently was given to a "right-to-life" lawyer who pursued a court order for certain medical services. Baby Jane Doe then became a pawn in the much larger national conflict. The ensuing situation was very costly financially and emotionally to the family, medical staff, and institution in which the child was receiving care. Considerable debate has followed, with Surgeon General C. Everett Koop taking a leading role in the courts, now requiring extensive care of neonates with handicapping conditions.

Superimposed upon these two cases was the widely publicized baboon heart transplant of Baby Faye in California in 1984. The infant had a form of congenital heart disease for which no existing surgical technology other than a transplant was available. The medical staff responsible for her care presented an overly optimistic picture of the potential for success of their procedure and, in fact, predicted less than 48 hours before she died that this child might live to 21 years. While complications and her body's rejection of the baboon heart initially were concealed, the physician staff now has been criticized for an overzealous and highly experimental approach to this particular child.

Taken together, the three cases described above barely scratch the surface of moral and legal dilemmas facing the families and the medical-nursing staffs within intensive care nurseries. The majority of neonatologists are overwhelmingly committed to the ancient principle of medicine that human life is worth saving. Toward that end, the regionalization of perinatal care and technology has improved the survival and outcome of babies within the last 30 years. Issues now confronting intensive care nurseries are less technical and more ethical, as neonatologists seek to define those fine lines between salvaging a life, prolonging death, and enhancing the quality of life.

Defining the Parameters of Risk

Concepts of vulnerability and risk in infants and young children for years have formed the fabric of research and service in early childhood. Recently, professionals in education, psychology, pediatrics, and related clinical fields have focused their energies on evaluation of children particularly within specified categories of risk for impairment and developmental delay (Fitzhardinge & Pape, 1981; Keogh & Kopp, 1978; Solnit & Provence, 1979; Thoman & Becker, 1979; Tjossem, 1976). While groups have been defined in terms of broad and narrow parameters of child and family characteristics, basically these factors have been attributed to one or a combination of three sources:

1. environmental influences such as restricted or aberrant patterns of interaction between primary caretaker and child, which may adversely impact on later school performance
2. biological conditions, which have been associated consistently with mental retardation or other developmental disorders, e.g., Trisomy 21 (Down syndrome)
3. medical conditions, such as severe respiratory distress requiring periods of extensive medical support, which often in the past have been related to later impairment.

Such categories are by no means mutually exclusive but may interact to promote additional developmental problems beyond initial insult. Indeed, in the ways that handicapped and high risk infants are perceived, there may be differences so ordinary or so subtle as to belie the probable magnitude of their real effect.

In large measure, educational programs for infants and young children until recently have been organized around the premise that discrete deficits could be identified in the early months and appropriate therapy and treatment employed in the name of prevention or amelioration. This has proven to be an unworkable assumption. Developmental screening techniques for assessing newborns are, at best, gross in estimating current functioning, and they largely have fallen short of the goal of predicting greatest need or future potential. The large number of children leaving intensive care nurseries who have eluded early identification yet later manifested moderate to severe disabilities confirms that, even in the face of significant impairment, evidence most often is tentative and outcome uncertain. Any valid risk indices appropriate to the newborn period must encompass both biomedical criteria relative to the child and environmental conditions of the family and the community. In the long run, there is no substitute for astute clinical acumen in the early identification process. Criteria carefully drawn but applied without attention to individual child and family characteristics may prove to be of little benefit, leading to neglected opportunities and eventual untoward developmental consequences.

Finally, because potentially handicapping conditions are not discerned readily in many preterm and other high risk infants, professionals need to conceptualize a network of services for all youngsters suspect of developmental insult or delay. Specifically, with the prominence of neonatal medicine and the emerging focus on infants as a national priority, early identification of children and families who meet certain eligibility criteria should become a routine and financially recognized practice. The strategy is not without problems. Attempts at implementation in the past have been disappointed by errors of overreferral or inadequate detection of handicapping conditions. Accurate screening during the newborn period and early months of life is a considerable undertaking, which requires multiple samplings of behavior, taken over extended periods of time, that are based on a broad spectrum of risk parameters and measures of child development. This prevention approach thus allows for the monitoring of behavioral and developmental milestones without recourse to labeling or the early stigmatizing of child and family. Among the total risk population, the main goal is to determine which infants and families are in greatest jeopardy. With research and commitment to a new philosophy, some medical and educational centers now are combining resources to achieve this purpose.

DIRECTIONS IN INFANT AND EARLY CHILDHOOD EDUCATION

Past and Present Approaches

Early childhood education over the past 20 years has witnessed noteworthy changes in focus and format. In large part, these are a reflection of contemporary society and the evolution of major socioeconomic, political, and philosophical forces impacting on life in the American family. The decade of the sixties saw the rise of idealism and "unprecedented interest" in preschool, compensatory education, which culminated in the national adoption of Project Head Start and the "war on poverty" (Winschel, 1970; Zigler & Valentine, 1979). Invested with a faith that the cycle of social and intellectual delays often observed among economically disadvantaged youngsters could be prevented, the program served 500,000 impoverished children during its first year. The decade from 1960 to 1970 also laid claim to numerous federally supported demonstration projects for the two- to five-year-old (Blatt & Garfunkel, 1969; Hodges, McCandless, & Spicker, 1967; Karnes, 1969; Klaus & Gray, 1968; Levenstein, 1970; Weikart, 1967). Like Project Head Start, these programs were rooted in the concept of the educability or modifiability of intelligence and a firm belief that intervention could make a difference in producing long-term gains and circumventing later school failure. Contrary to high hopes and widespread conviction, this prophecy remained largely unfulfilled, and the efficacy of education in the early years was opened to scrutiny, doubt, and controversy. Analyses, ranging from unrealistic prediction to errors of interpretation and methodological problems, abound in search of answers. Years later with experience and hindsight to our advantage, researchers and service providers have acknowledged the folly of our assumptions and our limited vision of the requisites for effecting enduring change within vulnerable families. The national debate on compensatory education proceeded, and at least in the short term, the unbridled idealism and promising expectations of the decade were tempered in response to the doubting and dissident.

The period that followed gave pause for reflection and reexamination of program goals and target populations. The late sixties and early seventies were a boon to intervention with infants and younger children of low income and disadvantaged families. The hope—in the hearts and minds of many— was that earlier stimulation, for longer periods, with active parent participation, might yield the enduring developmental gains that had not been witnessed with the older preschool child. Educators sought answers both within and outside the home, and research took form in several models of intervention. Underlying all of these early projects was the overriding goal of identifying those conditions most instrumental in the development of the young child. In retrospect, one must ask whether the concept and mode of implementation were sufficiently bold to counter the prevailing tide of biosocial influence for a sizeable proportion of our population. The burning controversies of effectiveness remained. But despite the new wave of funding, overwhelming investments of interest and time, public sympathy, and program expansion, interventions for the most part continued to be "broad band," nonspecific, and "directed at infants with widely differing risk conditions" (Keogh & Kopp, 1978, p. 533).

Programs for the severely handicapped, which received impetus during this time from parents with the passage of Public Law 94–142 (*Federal Register*, 1977) and the slowly emerging, concurrent focus on the biologically involved infant, were little solace to the educator plagued with ambiguity and imprecision of the art. The pioneering work of Provence and Lipton (1962) and others on evaluation and follow-up of infants in institutions seemed to offer ample rationale for preventing custodial care and its adverse developmental consequence. Also, burgeoning contemporary programs such as those initiated for preschool children with Down syndrome at the Experimental Education Unit of the University of Washington's Child Development and Retardation Center (Hayden & Dmitriev, 1975; Hayden & Haring, 1976) reported convincing, short-term progress.

Entering the 1980s, the literature is replete with labels of dysfunction, short-term solutions, inadequately explained contradictions, and lingering controversy. Rapid changes in society, political paradoxes, newborn technologies, spiraling family problems, and economic constraints have made it nearly impossible for educational systems to keep pace with demands. The scope of the infant education effort can no longer be confined to issues of curriculum content, type of setting, mode of evaluation, nature of disability, and orientation of trained personnel—concerns that have occupied researchers of the past and present. As we look forward to early education in the decade ahead, educators and other human service professionals will need to assume a more imaginative posture toward the direction of research and implementation, especially with the high risk newborn.

There is much to learn about intensive care nurseries and, given the necessary limitations of study in these settings, understanding what happens to hospital staff, parents, and infants in the face of critical care will not be easy. To date, a great deal of what we do in terms of psychosocial and developmental intervention with infants and families lacks a solid empirical base. Yet, researchers are beginning to raise pertinent and timely questions. We need to know, for example, what kinds of stimulation are growth promoting for what kinds of infants and parents. Do some babies experience excessive or inappropriate stimulation in hospital units, and if so, are there ways to mitigate short-term adverse effects? What kinds of intervention and interaction in-hospital with parents carry the potential for maximizing later healthy relationships with their children, and how do these vary with the stage of crisis, educational background, and ages of the parents? Should we even attempt to implement developmental infant programs in intensive care nurseries? Under what circumstances do long-term hospitalizations and extended separation of child from parent have negative developmental impact? What are the underlying processes of early parent-infant attachment, and what transitions from hospital to home are needed by parents and infants?

Based on available information and speculation, we at best can draw inferences about these questions. Furthermore, many factors influence parents and children over time, with considerable variation and inconsistency along the way. The broader, ecological view of human development offers promise for gaining such insight about high risk and handicapped infants.

Continued Research

Over the past three decades, the fields of early childhood and human development have seen many changes in methodologies of study, target populations, assessment techniques, and strategies for intervention, as well as in the theoretical constructs for understanding infant development. By the same token, many of the same basic questions raised by pioneers in early intervention research persist as variations on a central theme. We have erred at both ends of the continuum in our quest for data and explanation, examining minute pieces of behavior only to lose sight of the larger picture, or conceptualizing global issues to the neglect of the finer subtleties of individual difference. Still, the rationale for continued research and interest among professionals has not been diminished by such obstacles. If anything, it has been intensified.

In a sense, we again stand at a turning point, with opportunities for setting new directions and priorities in research and the delivery of services to the very young who have suffered medical insult. Unfettered by conventions of the past, the task minimally will call for research

- grounded in an unswerving commitment to the development of human potential
- carried out in diverse hospital, home, and school environments
- implemented over long periods of time
- applied with different caretakers
- designed to evaluate the nature of medical and educational interventions at varying ages
- offered in response to the individual and frequently unexplained needs of high risk infants and their families.

An understanding of vulnerable newborns is a compelling incentive, and the potential for prevention is a mandate that cannot be denied.

REFERENCES

Blatt, B., & Garfunkel, F. (1969). *The educability of intelligence: Preschool intervention with disadvantaged children*. Washington, D.C.: The Council for Exceptional Children.

Caldwell, B.M. (1970). The rationale for early intervention. *Exceptional Children, 36,* 717–726.

Federal Register. (August 23, 1977). Washington, D.C.; U.S. Government Printing Office.

Fitzhardinge, P.M., & Pape, K.E. (1981). Follow-up studies of the high risk newborn. In G.B. Avery (Ed.), *Neonatology: Pathophysiology and management of the newborn* (2nd ed.) (pp. 350–367). Philadelphia: J.B. Lippincott.

Hayden, A.H., & Dmitriev, V. (1975). The multidisciplinary preschool program for Down's Syndrome children at the University of Washington model preschool center. In B.Z. Friedlander, G.M. Sterritt, & G.E. Kirk (Eds.), *Exceptional infant: Assessment and intervention* (Vol. 3, pp. 193–221). New York: Brunner/Mazel.

Hayden, A.H., & Haring, N.G. (1976). Early intervention for high risk infants and young children: Programs for Down's Syndrome children. In T.D. Tjossem (Ed.), *Intervention strategies for high risk infants and young children* (pp. 573–607). Baltimore: University Park Press.

Hodges, W.L., McCandless, B.R., & Spicker, H.H. (1967). *The development and evaluation of a diagnostically based curriculum for preschool psychosocially deprived children*. Washington, D.C.: U.S. Office of Education.

Karnes, M.B. (1969). *Research and development program on preschool disadvantaged children: Final report*. Washington, D.C.: U.S. Office of Education.

Keogh, B.K., & Kopp, C.B. (1978). From assessment to intervention: An elusive bridge. In F.D. Minifie & L.L. Lloyd (Eds.), *Communicative and cognitive abilities—Early behavioral assessment* (pp. 523–547). Baltimore: University Park Press.

Klaus, R.A., & Gray, S.W. (1968). The early training project for disadvantaged children: A report after five years. *Monographs of the Society for Research in Child Development, 33,* (4, Serial #126).

Levenstein, P. (1970). Cognitive growth in preschoolers through verbal interaction with mothers. *American Journal of Orthopsychiatry, 40,* 426–432.

Provence, S., & Lipton, R.C. (1962). *Infants in institutions.* New York: International Universities Press.

Sameroff, A.J. (1981). Psychological needs of the mother in early mother-infant interactions. In G.B. Avery (Ed.), *Neonatology: Pathophysiology and management of the newborn* (2nd ed.) (pp. 303–321). Philadelphia: J.B. Lippincott.

Sameroff, A.J., & Chandler, M.J. (1975). Reproductive risk and the continuum of caretaking casualty. In F.D. Horowitz, M. Hetherington, S. Scarr-Salapatek, & M. Siegel (Eds.), *Review of child development research* (Vol. 4, pp. 187–244). Chicago: University of Chicago Press.

Solnit, A.J., & Provence, S. (1979). Vulnerability and risk in early childhood. In J.D. Osofsky (Ed.), *Handbook of infant development* (pp. 799–808). New York: John Wiley.

Thoman, E.B., & Becker, P.T. (1979). Issues in assessment and prediction for the infant born at risk. In T.M. Field, A.M. Sostek, S. Goldberg, & H. H. Shuman (Eds.), *Infants born at risk: Behavior and development* (pp. 461–483). New York: SP Medical & Scientific Books.

Tjossem, T.D. (1976). Early intervention: Issues and approaches. In T.D. Tjossem (Ed.), *Intervention strategies for high risk infants and young children* (pp. 1–33). Baltimore: University Park Press.

Weikart, D.P. (1967). *Preschool intervention: A preliminary report of the Perry Preschool Project.* Ann Arbor, MI: Campus Publishers.

Winschel, J.F. (1970). In the dark . . . Reflections on compensatory education 1960–1970. In J. Hellmuth (Ed.), *Disadvantaged child—Compensatory education: A national debate* (Vol. 3, pp. 3–23). New York: Brunner/Mazel.

Zigler, E., & Valentine, J. (Eds.). (1979). *Project Head Start: A legacy of the war on poverty.* New York: The Free Press.

2

Before Birth

FETAL-MATERNAL INTERACTION

The importance of prenatal life was perhaps best expressed by Samuel Taylor Coleridge when he wrote, "The history of man in the nine months preceding his birth would probably be far more interesting and attain events of greater moment than all the three score and ten years that follow it" (Coleridge, 1968). Put in another way, the threat to intact physical and mental survival of a human being starts long before birth and is tied directly to the well-being of the mother. If professionals are to understand the high risk infant, this is where we must begin our discussion.

Conception

It is now well recognized that the general health and nutrition of the mother may limit or enhance her ability to conceive and maintain a pregnancy (Anderson, Jenss, Moshier, Randall, & Marre, 1965; Rantakallio, 1969). In the past 15 to 20 years, multiple advances in medicine have allowed mothers with diseases such as diabetes to conceive and maintain pregnancies, resulting viable newborns (Gabbe et al., 1977). At the same time, infants born to mothers with chronic illnesses often are premature and have specific risks relating to their mothers' conditions. Recently, too, research has demonstrated that exposure of fathers to various chemicals may limit the reproductive capability of couples (Joffe, 1979). Specifically, lead and anesthetic agents increase first trimester spontaneous abortions in mothers and, in addition, cause a higher percentage of low birthweight infants. Cigarettes and anesthetic agents are associated with a greater incidence of congenital anomalies (Ad Hoc Committee on the Effect of Trace Anesthetics on the Health of Operating Room Personnel, 1974; Soyka & Joffe, 1980).

Several agents may cause an increased rate of multiple gestation pregnancies, but frequently not without problems. Fertility drugs (e.g., Clomid) tend to result in superovulation, with a greater chance of fertilization and multiple gestation. Similar effects also are seen in mothers who have been on birth control pills. When they wish to become pregnant and stop using oral contraception, there is a tendency among women to superovulate for several months. However, in such situations, although the mother may be able to conceive, it is less likely that she will carry the pregnancy to term (DeGeorge, 1970).

Table 2–1 illustrates the significant numbers of previously unrecognized early fetal losses. Within the last several years, a very sensitive assay test (radioimmuno assay) for detection of human Chorionic Gonadotropin (hCG) in blood has been developed. This hormone, produced by very early fetal tissue, is the chemical measured in the typical urine pregnancy test. The radioimmuno assay allows for detection of hCG in blood in very small quantities. Using this technique, researchers have found that in a population of women of childbearing age followed monthly approximately 50 percent more pregnancies were identified than could be recognized by any other technique (Simpson, 1980). These additional pregnancies all terminated spontaneously in the first four to five weeks.

Fetal Wastage

The human gestational period is 40 weeks, with the full-term infant born between 38 and 42 weeks. The first trimester of pregnancy is an especially hazardous time. In addition to fertilization of the egg and implantation of the developing embryo in the uterus, placental tissue must be established rapidly to maintain fetal growth. Failure of the placenta to develop leads to spontaneous abortion. Not all these fetuses are chromosomally abnormal, but there is a disproportionate number of first trimester spontaneous abortions that may be associated with such abnormalities (Kerr, 1976). The first trimester of pregnancy is also the period when the embryo and fetus grow quickly and many crucial cell divisions take place. Drugs, maternal infections, or any other agents that may cause malformations exert their greatest effect at this time (Heinonen, Slone, & Shapiro, 1977). Although a few generalizations may be made with respect to fetal wastage in the first trimester, the vast majority of spontaneous abortions have no known medical cause.

Table 2–1 Outcome per 1,000 Pregnancies

Number	Outcome
320	Early Unrecognized Fetal Loss
100	Fetal Wastage
8	Perinatal Loss
10	Neonatal Death
562	Surviving Newborns

The Placenta

The placenta has two basic functions. The first is to provide a means by which essential nutrients can be transferred from the mother's blood to the fetus and the second, to serve as a mechanism for clearing waste products from fetal blood (Mead Johnson Symposium on Perinatal and Developmental Medicine, 1981). Since the fetus has a very high metabolic rate, it burns calories quickly and produces a number of waste products. For example, carbon dioxide, once transferred across the placenta, is excreted by the mother's lungs. Breakdown products of protein such as urea, when cleared across the placenta, are excreted by the maternal kidneys. Likewise, bilirubin, formed by the decomposition of red blood cells, crosses the placenta and then is cleared through the mother's liver.

All basic nutrients necessary for fetal growth must be transferred from the mother to the baby. These include simple sugars, proteins, fats, minerals, and vitamins. In the human placenta initially there are only thin layers of cells in the connective tissue between the maternal and fetal blood circulations. As pregnancy proceeds, the placenta increases in both weight and diameter, allowing increased surface area for transfer of nutrients to the fetus and excretions of wastes from the fetus (Flexner, 1955).

On the maternal side, many factors affect the rate at which nutrients cross the placenta. The first of these is the mother's blood supply to the placenta. Diseases such as hypertension may limit the blood flow to the placenta, thereby decreasing fetal nutrients and potentially restricting elimination of fetal waste products (Boyd & Hamilton, 1970). This condition obviously is undesirable for the fetus and, if severe enough, may lead to spontaneous abortion. Malformations of the placenta may lead to inefficient mixing of maternal blood, offering a poor gradient for nutrient release to the fetus. Similarly, the area of the membrane across which diffusion occurs may be limited in some situations, e.g., multiple gestation. In particular, since the tissues between the fetus and mother have a very high protein and fat content, the materials diffusing across these membranes may be restricted by their size, their electrical charge, and their fat and protein solubility. These problems tend to retard fetal growth.

On the fetal side, factors such as the flow characteristics of blood from the newborn's heart to the placenta and total blood volume of the fetal-placental unit may affect uptake of nutrients. Numerous experiments have been performed, examining the transport of nutrients from the mother to the fetus. Some substances, such as glucose, have a specific transport system, and stereospecific forms of amino acids may be transferred preferentially (Crompler, Dent, & Lindon, 1950). Of necessity, most of our knowledge in these areas has been gained from animal experiments and thus may have only narrow application.

Another very important placental function is the protection of the fetus from maternal rejection. Since half of the fetal genes are from the father, there are proteins produced in the baby that are foreign to the mother. In other situations, such as heart and kidney transplants, when foreign proteins are placed in an individual that recipient may reject the organ. The placenta creates a barrier that is, in part, physical and perhaps immunologic, which minimizes the mixing of fetal and maternal blood and may block the mother's immune response, thus allowing her to tolerate the foreign proteins (Anderson, 1971).

The placenta is also an endocrine organ, and during a pregnancy many hormones, such as human Chorionic Gonadotropin (hCG), placental lactogen, progesterone, and estrogens, are synthesized by the placenta (Ryan, 1962). These secretions aid in establishing the appropriate hormonal milieu for maintenance of the pregnancy. In addition, they encourage increased blood supply to the uterus and prevent the cyclic shedding of the endometrium. Thus, all of these functions of the placenta—nutritive, excretory, and protective—are vital to the newborn throughout the 40-week gestational period.

Amniotic Fluid

The amniotic fluid surrounding the infant obtains its name from the innermost layer of the membranes, the *amnion*. In early pregnancy, the fluid is derived primarily from the membrane, but in later pregnancy a significant proportion of the substance comes from fetal urine and from fetal pulmonary secretion, as well as a transudate across the fetal skin and umbilical cord (Plentl, 1966).

The amniotic fluid has numerous roles (Ostergard, 1970). One of the most important is the mechanical protection of the infant against trauma. The fluid also allows for a gravity-free environment in which delicate structures, such as the hands, feet, and facial structures, can grow without compression from a strong, muscular uterus.

Circulation in the amniotic fluid has other functions. The fetus may swallow as much as one pint of liquid daily (Plentl, 1966). As the amniotic fluid contains some protein, there is an early induction of enzymes to digest protein in the fetal intestinal tract. Too little amniotic fluid may be present if there are no kidneys or if these organs are formed abnormally. This situation may lead to compression of the fetus and, frequently, to maldevelopment of the lungs. On the other hand, an excess amount of amniotic fluid suggests the possibility of obstruction to the fetal intestinal tract or perhaps fetal neurologic disease, which often is manifested as poor sucking. Finally, perhaps most familiar to pregnant women are the samples of amniotic fluid that may be taken to assess fetal maturity, chromosomes, and metabolic abnormalities, in order to test for fetal well-being.

HIGH RISK PREGNANCY

A high risk pregnancy implies jeopardy both to the mother and to the fetus. If the mother has a serious health problem such as congenital heart disease, the pregnancy may be life-threatening to her. More typically, however, the term *high risk pregnancy* is used to imply some maternal problem that may lead to perinatal mortality and morbidity. Approximately

15 to 20 percent of women account for over 50 percent of the fetal and neonatal deaths. For this reason, physicians have suggested that careful attention to the needs of mothers would bring about the greatest impact on fetal and neonatal well-being (Committee on Perinatal Health, 1976).

Fetal Growth

The growth of the fetus is dependent on maternal nutrition before as well as throughout the pregnancy. Mothers with a prepregnancy weight of less than 100 pounds have more than twice as many infants of low birthweight than mothers with a prepregnancy weight of 120 pounds or greater (Eastman & Jackson, 1968). Moreover, women who either do not gain or lose weight during the pregnancy have a threefold increase in low birthweight infants beyond those who gain the recommended 24 pounds during the entire gestation (Eastman & Jackson, 1968). A normal weight gain generally can be accomplished by approximately 300 additional calories per day (Emerson, Saxena, & Pomdexter, 1972). About one-third of the increase during pregnancy represents fetal weight, with the placenta, amniotic fluid, and uterus each accounting for approximately 8 to 10 percent of the additional gain. An increase in fluid and blood volume in the mother contributes another 15 percent of weight; breast enlargement makes up about 5 percent, and the remaining 10 to 15 percent of the increase is the result of fat and other maternal stores held in reserve in anticipation of breast-feeding (Babson & Benson, 1975).

In recent years, there have been many changes in our information about maternal-infant growth during pregnancy. The older concept that the fetus is parasitic in terms of the mother and develops at the expense of maternal nutrition has not proven valid. Various experiments have demonstrated this notion to be extremely simplistic. For example, on a magnesium-deficient diet, a mother may show no ill effect, but the fetus usually is runted and very ill (Dancis, Springer, & Cohlan, 1971). No easy generalizations can be made about all of the nutrients required by the fetus. Each nutriment seems to be handled individually, and fetal growth and welfare may be only minimally affected, if at all. Close spacing of pregnancies too may deplete maternal body stores, resulting in a higher incidence of low birthweight infants in the subsequent pregnancies. With all that we have said, it is important to emphasize that the health of the fetus and mother depend not simply on the quantity of food but also on adequate quality of the nutrients required for fetal growth.

Fetal development is assessed in several ways during the pregnancy. The most obvious of these methods is carried out by the monitoring of progressive uterine enlargement. If uterine growth lags behind that expected by the date of the mother's last menses, then fetal growth retardation may be at fault, the result of either fetal or maternal disease. At the other end of the continuum, if the uterus is growing more rapidly than expected, excess amniotic fluid, an overgrown fetus, or multiple gestation may be responsible. Presently, the growth of the individual fetus can be best documented with the use of ultrasound. In this technique, sound waves allow visualization of the fetal head, and the transverse or biparietal diameter provides a good estimate of fetal growth (Kohorn, 1967). In those instances where mothers are known or suspected to be at risk for any of the above disorders, it is essential that monitoring be conducted on a routine basis. To do less may jeopardize mother and baby.

Fetal Maturity

Fetal maturity cannot be based on estimated weight, head size, uterine size, or expected delivery date alone. An older method of determining fetal age was an x-ray of the fetus. Examination of the long bones of the legs for the sites of calcification used to be done to obtain a rough estimate for fetuses greater than 36 weeks gestation (Christie, 1949). This technique has been abandoned because of the potential hazard of fetal radiation. Today, it is well recognized that the most important index of fetal maturity is the determination of whether or not the lungs have matured biochemically. As the fetal lungs mature, an increased concentration of the substance lecithin is shed from the fetal lung fluid through the trachea, into the amniotic fluid. Sphingomyelin, another fat in the amniotic fluid, remains at fairly constant levels throughout the pregnancy. Thus, the ratio of the lecithin to sphingomyelin in the amniotic fluid serves as an important index of fetal lung maturity. If this ratio is two or greater, the risk of premature lung disease (hyaline membrane disease) is very low (Donald, Freeman, Goebelsmann, Chan, & Nakamura, 1973). Such assessments of fetal lung maturity can be used to allow the delivery of an infant prior to term, when continuation of the pregnancy may be harmful either to the mother or to the fetus.

Maternal Characteristics and Conditions Affecting the Fetus

Numerous high risk maternal characteristics or conditions may lead to increased fetal mortality and neonatal mortality and morbidity. Some of these factors are social; others relate to specific anatomic variations in the mother; still others deal with reproductive histories or medical problems preexisting or acquired during the pregnancy (Aubry & Nesbitt, 1969). For years, there has been more than ample evidence that maternal ages of less than 15 years or greater than 40 years, especially the first for the older mother, may result in vulnerability to mother and/or newborn. Low socioeconomic groups have a disproportionately greater number of low birthweight infants. Unwed mothers frequently have severe social and emotional problems during pregnancy that may impinge upon appropriate nutrition and may even, through denial, limit obtaining prenatal care. In different ways, obesity, malnutrition, and short stature may impact adversely on fetal well-being and the ability of the mother to carry the pregnancy to term.

Physical problems are a large concern among high risk pregnancies. Abnormalities of the maternal genital tract, such as incompetent cervix and malformation of the uterus, may prevent the pregnancy from reaching term. Mothers who have had two previous abortions, either induced or spontaneous, or those who have had stillborn, premature, or overgrown infants are likely to repeat the experience, unless there is determination of the problem and intervention. Women with high blood pressure, severe renal disease, severe heart disease, diabetes, cancer, sickle cell disease, drug addiction or alcoholism, pulmonary disease, or various surgical problems also are at great risk for not maintaining the pregnancy and may produce a premature or growth-retarded fetus (Anderson, Jenss, Moshier, Randall, & Marre, 1965; Gold, 1968). Early in pregnancy, drug exposure or transplacental infections may lead to fetal malformations, and severe anemia in the mother may result in poor fetal oxygenation and spontaneous abortion. Later, abnormal position or premature separation of the placenta may cause fetal demise or premature delivery. In addition, a prolonged gestation may result in severe fetal distress as a result of placental aging and, thus, inability of the placenta to provide appropriate nutrients and eliminate waste products. Toxemia of pregnancy, which is characterized by maternal edema, high blood pressure, and protein in the urine, threatens both fetal survival and maternal health.

On the social side, the detrimental effect of maternal smoking is one of the more pressing problems that recently has been brought to light (Witter & King, 1980). Multiple studies of the outcome of pregnancies of smoking mothers have shown a reduction in the birthweight of the fetus of approximately five to eight ounces when compared with fetuses of non-smoking mothers. In addition, there is a 20 to 35 percent increase in perinatal mortality as a result of maternal cigarette smoking. Obviously, every effort should be made to discourage the mother from smoking during pregnancy.

Last, we should point out that while it is apparent that many factors correlate with compromised fetal growth and development, the picture is much more optimistic than it might seem. Relatively few mothers suffer from these conditions.

Primary Fetal Disease

Certainly, not every problem of the fetus and newborn can be attributed to maternal health, nutrition, or adverse pregnancy factors. There are a number of pathologies that may best be described as *primary fetal diseases*. Largest among these are conditions dealing with fetal genetic disorders, aberrant chromosomal or inherited diseases, or malformations with no known specific predisposition. More particularly, early embryonic and fetal development may be altered drastically by the presence of additional genetic material or the absence of essential chromosomal material. The most common and obvious example of the aforementioned is Trisomy 21 (Down syndrome), resulting from the acquisition of an additional number 21 chromosome (Penrose & Smith, 1966). These infants have a characteristic facial appearance, often congenital heart disease, and variable mental retardation. Although in recent times there seems to be an increased incidence of neonates with Down syndrome with advanced maternal age, no specific other factor that results in this condition has been identified. Other diseases have a specific genetic inheritance, and these have variable developmental effects on the newborn. Many metabolic diseases, e.g., phenylketonuria, Tay-Sachs disease, or galactosemia, usually are not immediately evident in the newborn period. With such disorders, damage to the central nervous system, which ultimately leads to mental retardation, often is a result of abnormal metabolism and the inability to clear toxic products from the body. Prior to birth, the placenta provides an efficient mechanism for clearing these toxic materials. Yet, after delivery, these chemicals begin to accumulate and, in the instance of phenylketonuria, can cause severe developmental delays in the absence of medical intervention and dietary control.

Finally, infants may have malformations leading to their demise that have either no genetic base or a variable origin. These include intestinal anomalies, defects of the abdominal wall (e.g., omphalocoele), and deformities of the lungs. The etiologies of other fetal diseases such as cleft lip and palate, neural tube defects (e.g., myelomeningocele), and certain genital and kidney diseases are not always clear; they may or may not have a genetic predisposition.

In conclusion, it is clear that future efforts need to be directed toward the prevention of those conditions—both social and medical—that are within our realm of anticipation. We predict that with specific attention to these problems that affect mother and child it would be possible, by the year 2000, to reduce the current morbidity statistics by at least 25 to 30 percent. We know enough now to make such a commitment of time and funding toward this end. Accomplishing the goal would require the assistance of a variety of disciplines in hospitals, clinics, high schools, and even home settings in order to educate and follow potential parents before conception and throughout gestation.

REFERENCES

Ad Hoc Committee on the Effect of Trace Anesthetics on the Health of Operating Room Personnel. (1974). *Anesthesiology, 41,* 321–340.

Anderson, U.M., Jenss, R., Moshier, W., Randall, C., & Marre, E. (1965). High risk groups—Definition and identification. *New England Journal of Medicine, 273,* 308–313.

Anderson, J.M. (1971). Transplantation—Nature's success. *Lancet, 2,* 1077–1082.

Aubry, R.H., & Nesbitt, R.E.L. (1969). High risk obstetrics, Part 1. Perinatal outcome in relation to a broadened approach to obstetric care for patients at special risk. *American Journal of Obstetrics and Gynecology, 105,* 241–248.

Babson, S.G., & Benson, R.C. (Eds.). (1975). Standard prenatal care and identification of risk factors. *Management of high risk pregnancy and intensive care of the neonate* (pp. 6–21). St. Louis: C.V. Mosby.

Boyd, J.D., & Hamilton, W.J. (1970). Uteroplacental circulatory system. *The human placenta* (pp. 18–46). Cambridge, MA: W. Heffer & Sons.

Christie, A. (1949). Prevalence and distribution of ossification centers in the newborn infant. *American Journal of Diseases of Children, 77,* 355–361.

Coleridge, S.T. (1968). In M.B. Strauss (Ed.), *Familiar medical quotations* (p. 179). Boston: Little, Brown.

Committee on Perinatal Health. (1976). *Toward improving the outcome of pregnancy: Recommendations for the regional development of maternal and perinatal health services.* White Plains, NY: The National Foundation March of Dimes.

Crompler, H.R., Dent, C.E., & Lindon, D. (1950). The amino-acid pattern in human fetal and maternal plasma at delivery. *Biochemical Journal, 47,* 223–227.

Dancis, J., Springer, D., & Cohlan, S.Q. (1971). Fetal homeostasis in maternal malnutrition: II. Magnesium deprivation. *Pediatric Research, 5,* 131–136.

DeGeorge, F.V. (1970). Maternal and fetal disorders in pregnancies of mothers of twins. *American Journal of Obstetrics and Gynecology, 108,* 975–978.

Donald, I.R., Freeman, R.K., Goebelsmann, U., Chan, W.H., & Nakamura, R. M. (1973). Clinical experience with the amniotic fluid lecithin/sphingomyelin ratio. *American Journal of Obstetrics and Gynecology, 115,* 547–550.

Eastman, N.J., & Jackson, E. (1968). Weight relationships in pregnancy. *Obstetrical and Gynecological Survey, 23,* 1003–1025.

Emerson, J.K., Saxena, B., & Pomdexter, E.L. (1972). Caloric cost of normal pregnancy. *Obstetrics & Gynecology, 40,* 786–794.

Flexner, L.B. (Ed.). (1955). *Gestation, transaction of first conference.* New York: Corlies, Macy.

Gabbe, S.G., Mestman, J.H., Freeman, R.K., Goebelsmann, U.T., Lowensohn, K.I., Nochimson, D., Cetrulo, C., & Quilligan, E.J. (1977). Management and outcome of pregnancy in diabetes mellitus, Classes B to R. *American Journal of Obstetrics and Gynecology, 129,* 723–728.

Gold, E.M. (1968). Identification of the high risk fetus. *Clinical Obstetrics & Gynecology, 11,* 1069–1080.

Heinonen, O.P., Slone, D., & Shapiro, S. (1977). *Birth defects and drugs in pregnancy.* Littleton, MA: Publishing Sciences.

Joffe, J.M. (1979). Influence of drug exposure of the father on perinatal outcome. *Clinics in Perinatology, 6,* 21–36.

Kerr, M.G. (1976). Chromosome studies of spontaneous abortions. In J.J. Kellar (Ed.), *Modern trends in obstetrics and gynecology* (pp. 114–136). London: Butterworth.

Kohorn, E.I. (1967). An evaluation of ultrasonic fetal cephalometry. *American Journal of Obstetrics and Gynecology, 97,* 553–559.

Mead Johnson Symposium on Perinatal and Developmental Medicine. (1981). *Placental Transport, 18,* 3–34.

Ostergard, D.R. (1970). The physiology and clinical importance of amniotic fluid, a review. *Obstetrical & Gynecological Survey, 25,* 297–319.

Penrose, L.S., & Smith, G.F. (1966). *Down's anomaly.* Boston: Little, Brown.

Plentl, A.A. (1966). Formation and circulation of amniotic fluid. *Clinical Obstetrics & Gynecology, 9,* 427–439.

Rantakallio, P. (1969). Groups at risk in low birthweight infants and perinatal mortality. *Acta Paediatrica, Supplement, 193,* 5–71.

Ryan, K.J. (1962). Hormones of the placenta. *American Journal of Obstetrics and Gynecology, 84,* 1695–1713.

Simpson, J.L. (1980). *Suboptimal outcome of pregnancy.* New York, March of Dimes Birth Defects Conference.

Soyka, L.F., & Joffe, J.M. (1980). Male medicated drug effects on offspring. In R.H. Schwarz & S.J. Yaffe (Eds.), *Progress in clinical and biological research: Drugs and chemical risks to the fetus and newborn* (pp. 49–66). New York: Allan R. Liss.

Witter, F., & King, T.M. (1980). Cigarettes and pregnancy. In R. H. Schwarz & S.J. Yaffe (Eds.), *Progress in clinical and biological research: Drugs and chemical risks to the fetus and newborn* (pp. 83–92). New York: Allan R. Liss.

3

Perinatal Events

While many high risk characteristics can be identified among pregnant women before labor begins, most adverse perinatal factors arise *intrapartum* without warning. Through careful monitoring of the fetus, perinatologists are attempting to identify some of these unforeseen problems in order to improve management of pregnancy and, therefore, medical and developmental outcome. This chapter will deal with the events surrounding labor and delivery and the subsequent problems that may ensue for high risk infants as a result of complications during those processes.

LABOR AND DELIVERY

Labor is defined as the onset of regular uterine contractions (Friedman, 1981; Pritchard & MacDonald, 1985). At the least, it is a complex process, where physiologic and hormonal developments still are not fully understood. Furthermore, although we do not have information about all of the changes that finally initiate this sequence of events, sufficient technology is presently available to enhance or inhibit the process respectively by the use of oxytocin or tocolytic agents (Hemminki & Starfield, 1978).

The initial stage of labor is called the *latent phase* and is so termed because little of consequence seems to be happening. However, subclinically, uterine contractions are becoming more coordinated and organized. The cervix has not yet begun to dilate; yet its consistency changes in preparation for dilatation and fetal descent. The latent phase for a first pregnancy averages approximately 6.5 hours and only rarely exceeds 20 hours. In the second or subsequent pregnancies, the average time of the latent phase is 4.8 hours and seldom exceeds 14 hours (Babson, Benson, Pernoll, & Benda, 1980).

The *active phase* of labor starts when the cervix begins to dilate. This process takes place at 1.2 to 1.5 centimeters per hour and usually is completed at 9 to 10 centimeters within a six-hour period. As the cervix expands, it also thins and retracts and fetal descent begins. This course reaches its maximum rate once the cervix is fully dilated, and can be traced by examining the relationship of the leading edge of the fetus (usually the head) to the bony prominences on the maternal pelvis called the *ischial spines*. Descent of the fetus is more rapid in the *multiparous* than in the *primiparous* (first delivery) mother but in either case should exceed one to two centimeters per hour (Babson, Benson, Pernoll, & Benda, 1980; Friedman, 1981; Pritchard & MacDonald, 1985).

Effect of Labor on the Fetus

The mechanical energy of the contracting uterus during labor constitutes a significant stress to the fetus. Prior to the rupture of the membranes, the amniotic fluid provides a cushion that helps to distribute the intrauterine pressure quite evenly across the fetus. In the second stage of labor, intrauterine pressure increases to approximately 5 to 8 times that of the resting phase; and if the mother "bears down," this may rise to 12 to 15 times the quiet state (Sureau, 1974). There is, of course, considerable variation from mother to mother regarding the intensity, frequency, and duration of uterine contractions. Once the membranes have been ruptured and the amniotic fluid escapes, however, the fetus typically orients in preparation for delivery. The fetal body part then nearest the cervix begins to descend into the maternal pelvis and is said to be *engaged*. In 90 percent of pregnancies, the head is the presenting body part. On the other hand, if the buttocks or feet are engaged first, this is a *breech presentation.* In either case, with the cushion of amniotic fluid lost, the greatest pressure then is exerted on the presenting part, which is located in the narrowest portion of the uterus, at its outlet toward the cervix (Lindgren, 1972). At this point in the delivery, problems may arise. In some newborns, pressure is transmitted to the skull and may be responsible for intracranial hemorrhage. Compression of the infant's head by uterine contractions also may result in a transient lowering of the fetal heart rate. In most instances, this reaction does not seem to be deleterious if the duration is short and if there is a prompt return to normal levels once the contraction has ceased (Schifrin, 1982).

In addition to the above changes, uterine contractions also place pressure on the placenta and interfere with placental blood flow. This situation is of some consequence to the fetus since nutrients and waste products must be exchanged through the placenta. Thus, fetal oxygen tension is less during labor and carbon dioxide, a waste product, is higher. Because oxygen is crucial for normal tissue metabolism and carbon dioxide interferes with these processes (partly by lowering the blood pH), a prolonged labor can lead to severe metabolic stress for the infant (Sureau, 1974).

Although difficult to quantitate, labor is traumatic for the fetus. In general, the healthy newborn can tolerate this unavoidable stress. Consequently, the goal of modern obstetrics is the identification of those fetuses with reduced tolerance, such as the preterm infant, who should be carefully monitored to avoid serious complications.

Monitoring the Fetus

As we have already discussed in this chapter, the general health and development of the fetus is evaluated throughout pregnancy by measuring the progress of uterine growth (Tropper & Fox, 1982). While many maternal illnesses (e.g., diabetes or toxemia of pregnancy) may result in chronic fetal distress, unplanned events just prior to or during labor in otherwise healthy mothers can lead to acute fetal distress. These conditions include premature separation of the placenta (placental abruption), compression or prolapse of the umbilical cord through the cervix, or the acute onset of maternal illness such as pneumonia, which may impair the mother's blood oxygenation and therefore, secondarily, that of the fetus who is dependent on the mother. In each case, by assessing the well-being of the fetus a decision can be made as to whether an infant has a better chance for survival in an intensive care nursery. Understandably, these decisions become very difficult when the fetus is more than ten weeks premature (Babson, Benson, Pernoll, & Benda, 1980).

Obviously, the fetus cannot be monitored through direct access. Its well-being must be ascertained indirectly by several techniques. As mentioned previously, one parameter that can be watched fairly carefully is the fetal heart rate pattern. This can be measured by an external monitor or, once the membranes have been ruptured, a fetal scalp electrode may be employed. By such methods, several different patterns of fetal heart rate abnormalities have been described. In general, if the fetal heart rate slows and quickens in response to various stresses, there is the assurance that the fetus is not compromised. On the other hand, when fetal *tachycardia* (rapid heart rate) or *bradycardia* (low heart rate) is observed, these signs indicate severe distress, requiring immediate intervention on behalf of the newborn (Hon & Koh, 1981). In response to severe intrauterine stress, infants of greater than 34 weeks gestation may pass meconium (the contents of the fetal bowel) into the amniotic fluid (Miller, Sacks, & Yeh, 1975). This material is sterile, viscous, and green, and contains many proteins and chemicals from the developed gastrointestinal tract. It should prompt careful evaluation of fetal well-being—even if the heart rate, up to that time, has been considered normal. Finally, one additional means of monitoring the fetus, once the membranes have been ruptured, consists of the sampling of fetal blood, usually from the scalp of the engaged head. By assessing the blood pH, determinations can be made as to whether the newborn is compensating metabolically (Miller, 1982). Certainly, the strategies discussed above will not resolve all of the problems that may arise during labor and delivery; however, they do offer some guidelines for the modern obstetrician to manage these events in order to afford the best possible outcome for mother and child.

Birth Trauma

Just as labor is stressful, vaginal delivery is traumatic to nearly every baby. Virtually every healthy newborn will have molding of the head, commonly with edema of the scalp. Newborns also may acquire cephalohematomas, caused by bleeding under the outer surface of the bones of the lateral skull that scrape across the pelvic ischial spines. Cephalohematomas usually enlarge within several days after birth as additional fluid is drawn into the area in response to breakdown of the red blood cells. They then resolve slowly by calcifying around the outer edges until a firm mass is formed. As the infant's head grows during the first year, the skull remolds and the lump on the side of the head becomes less obvious and finally resolves (Behrman & Mangurten, 1977).

Other injuries to the head are possible as a result of delivery, including paralysis of the seventh cranial nerve, which is termed the *facial nerve*. This nerve may be damaged by pressure, especially with the application of forceps near the point where the nerve emerges from the skull and the jaw articulates with the skull. Such trauma frequently leads to a paralysis of the involved muscles. Clinically, when the infant cries the mouth is drawn to the normal side and there tends to be drooping and loss of wrinkles on the affected side. The child also may have difficulty closing the eyelid on the affected side. The majority of facial palsies begin to diminish spontaneously within several days, but total recovery may require several weeks to months (Manning & Adour, 1972).

Any prominence from the head may be traumatized during delivery. The eyes and eyelids may become edematous with bruising; there may be hemorrhage in the sclera of the eye; and corneal abrasions can occur. In addition, the ears are prone to abrasions, hematomas, and occasional lacerations, which require cleansing and suture. The majority of these insults clear over the first several weeks with little residual effect.

Most serious are injuries that tend to occur in the area of the neck. For example, the lateral neck swelling seen in newborns may result from bleeding into the belly of the sternocleidomastoid muscle (Sanerkin & Edwards, 1966), which connects the sternum and the clavicle (cleido-) to the mastoid area of the skull. Contraction of this muscle allows for turning of the head. A hematoma in this muscle, as it resolves, frequently causes scarring and foreshortening of the muscle leading to torticollis (a stiffening of the neck). If this condition is not recognized early and appropriate physical therapy initiated, it becomes a severe problem.

The nerves of the neck are especially susceptible to impairment. The *brachial plexus* includes the nerves that extend from the neck to innervate the arm. An *Erb's palsy*, which is a paralysis of the shoulder and upper arm, results from injury to the fifth and sixth cervical nerve roots. A *Klumpke's or lower arm paralysis* results from injury to the eighth cervical and the first thoracic nerve root (Eng, Koch, & Smokvina, 1978). In most cases, such problems follow a prolonged and very difficult labor. Quite commonly, the infant is large, has had severe fetal distress, and the increased pressure applied to the head and shoulders to assist delivery may result in trauma. The principal treatment for these difficulties is the maintenance of an appropriate range of motion for the affected joints. This course may be accomplished by partial immobilization, followed by an active physical therapy program by seven to ten days of age. If the nerve roots are intact, return of function may appear within several days as local edema and hemorrhage recede. Although the rate of recovery varies with the degree of injury, most infants return to normal function within three to six months. An occasional infant with severe injury, however, may show continued improvement over a period of several years. In particular, paralysis of the lower arm has a poor prognosis, with the possibility of developing a claw deformity of the hand (Behrman & Mangurten, 1977). Similarly, several other nerves in the neck may be affected. The *phrenic nerve* that innervates the diaphragm may be disrupted, resulting in a paralyzed diaphragm and asynchronous respiration. In addition, there may be trauma to the *recurrent laryngeal nerve* that leads to unilateral vocal cord paralysis, often associated with respiratory distress.

Further potential birth injuries include a fractured clavicle or extremity, rupture of the liver or spleen, hemorrhage into the adrenal gland, and in the case of infants in a breech presentation, trauma to the genitalia. The prognosis in each of these events varies considerably, but fortunately most are treatable with good return of function in a relatively short period of time. Of course, whenever a form of birth trauma has been identified, it is important to examine the infant carefully for other injuries and to treat these expectantly (Behrman & Mangurten, 1977).

EVALUATION, STABILIZATION, AND TRANSITION

Apgar Score

Prior to 1953, there were no objective assessments at birth for the condition of the newborn. Subsequent to this time, Virginia Apgar, an anesthesiologist, proposed a scoring system examining five characteristics of the infant that were thought to correlate with recovery from intrauterine stress (Apgar, 1953). The five parameters are *heart rate, color, reflex irritability, respiratory effort,* and *muscle tone.* Each of these variables is scored on a zero-to-two basis. More specifically, *zero* is given for the complete absence of a response; for instance, no heart rate, no respiratory effort, and blue color. A *two* is given for the best response, such as a heart rate of greater than 100, a regular respiratory effort, and a totally pink color. These scores are assigned at one and five minutes. Although there has been considerable debate about interpretation, many physicians would agree that the one-minute Apgar score is a relatively accurate reflection of the severity of the intrauterine distress and is an indication of how well the infant has responded. The five-minute Apgar score is thought to be more predictive of morbidity and mortality (Drage, Kennedy, & Schwarz, 1964). Over the last 30 years, some authors have attempted to modify the original evaluations by weighting the parameters that seem to be more important; i.e., heart rate and respiratory effort. By and large, the more precise evaluations are being used as research tools rather than as aids to clinical practice.

There are serious difficulties with the use of the Apgar score as a prediction of outcome. Many infants who are born with distress may not be evaluated in the heat of the resuscitation effort. Also, it is a common belief among obstetricians that pediatricians tend to give lower one-minute and higher five-minute Apgar scores than do obstetricians. Despite the simplicity of the measure, the Apgar has been very helpful in offering a general description of the state of the newborn. Yet it is essential to remember that this score in no way replaces an accurate recording of the sequence of resuscitation and timeliness of the infant's response in order to assess accurately the degree of asphyxia.

Resuscitation

Resuscitation is the process of stabilizing an acutely compromised individual, in this instance, the neonate. The process has three phases, including the anticipation of problems, proper recognition, and appropriate treatment (Fisher & Paton, 1979). As mentioned in Chapter 2, there are multiple prenatal and perinatal factors that may place an infant at risk. Approximately 90 percent of the newborns who have low Apgar scores are predictable prior to birth. In these situations, an appropriate resuscitation team should be available to address the specific needs of the baby. At birth, the neonate is very wet and loses heat rapidly. Therefore, the child needs to be quickly dried and placed under a radiant form of heat. The newborn is stimulated to cry, not by hanging the infant by the ankles and slapping the buttocks but by a gentle flicking of the feet or stimulation to the chest. A stethoscope is used to assure that there is an adequate heart rate and respiratory effort. If there is a good respiratory effort with a heart rate greater than 100, a simple clearing of the airway with a bulb syringe to remove mucous generally is all that is necessary. On the other hand, if the respiratory effort is compromised, the child may require oxygen, occasionally including manual ventilation with a mask over the face. In the event that this attempt is unsuccessful, the infant then may demand intubation and manual ventilation through the trachea. If the heart rate begins to fall, cardiac massage is often necessary. The relatively few newborns who do not respond to this combination of efforts may show improvement with the addition of medications.

Some newborns have a low blood pressure and may respond to expansion of the blood volume with protein, blood, or a salt solution. Following this treatment, correction of the low blood pH with sodium bicarbonate, as long as respiration is being supported, may be beneficial. Additionally, a cardiac stimulant such as epinephrine may be useful.

After resuscitation of a newborn with birth asphyxia, many biochemical alterations may occur. These may include a continued acidosis (a disturbance in the acid balance of the body), which needs correction. Since this is a very stressful period, available calories may have been consumed and these infants thus are prone to *hypoglycemia* (a deficiency of sugar in the blood). There may be excessive potassium loss from cells, with the blood calcium becoming inappropriately low 24 to 48 hours after birth (Phibbs, 1981).

The potential for problems does not end with the aforementioned. There are many other sequelae of asphyxia that must be anticipated. Among these are:

- pulmonary problems, such as increased respiratory distress, pulmonary hemorrhage
- cardiovascular difficulties, such as congestive heart failure, enlarged heart
- renal disorders—blood or protein in the urine, failure to produce urine
- central nervous system problems, as evidenced by cerebral edema, hemorrhage, seizures, irritability, or tremulousness

- gastrointestinal conditions, such as poor intestinal motility, hemorrhage, and ulcers.

All of these consequences should be expected and recognized in a timely fashion so that prompt treatment can be given to assure minimum future compromise.

Temperature Control

Prior to birth, the temperature of the fetus always is slightly over one degree Fahrenheit greater than that of the mother. Heat in the fetus is a waste product and results from a very high metabolic rate in comparison with the mother's. Heat is transferred across the placenta to the mother and dissipated. This occurrence may explain why many women in their third trimester are very flushed. At the time of birth, there is an abrupt temperature decrease in the newborn as a result of evaporative heat loss. This is one of several mechanisms thought to be responsible for the initiation of respiration. For this reason, infants who are placed in a warm water bath at birth may stop breathing and have a reduction in heart rate as a consequence of poor blood oxygenation (Oliver, 1965).

In intensive care nurseries, temperature control is one of the most important therapies carried out by the medical-nursing staff (Silverman, Fertig, & Berger, 1958). The goal is maintenance of newborns in their *neutral thermal environment*, which is defined as the point where body temperature is normal and the baby is burning the least amount of oxygen (oxygen consumption), thus reflecting a low, conservative caloric consumption (Hill & Rahimtulla, 1965; Oliver, 1965).

There are two levels or types of heat loss. The *internal gradient* is a term used for describing how neonates fail to conserve heat. Babies who are premature or undergrown have little subcutaneous fat as insulation, and internally generated heat is readily lost to the skin. These infants frequently have a large surface-area-to-body-mass ratio and are less able to conserve heat (Klaus, Fanaroff, & Martin, 1979). The *external gradient* refers to the process whereby heat is dissipated from the skin surface. Radiant heat loss, which is the most common form for humans, refers to heat energy that escapes directly into the environment; e.g., the sun radiating heat over long distances. Evaporative heat loss is the amount of heat required to dissipate a specific amount of water. Generally, this factor is important for neonates primarily in the delivery room. Convective heat loss is the equivalent of a windchill factor; infants in a draft or those exposed to excessive manipulation are less able to maintain the unstirred layer of warm air close to the skin. Conductive loss refers to heat transferred from one solid body to another; e.g., from a baby to a cold blanket or cold stethoscope (Klaus, Fanaroff, & Martin, 1979).

All of the above forms of heat loss are addressed in some way in an intensive care nursery. There are two primary pieces of equipment used for doing so. The first of these is the radiant warmer (See Figure 3–1), which affords compensating radiant heat to maintain body temperature. This treatment is used more frequently with very ill neonates, where ready access for therapeutic maneuvers is critical. The hazard of the radiant warmer is excessive fluid loss, frequently 50 percent greater than that of infants placed in an incubator device (Williams & Oh, 1974).

The second device used to prevent heat loss is an incubator, where blankets, walls, and equipment are warmed to near the body temperature of the infant. In the isolette, convective heat loss is minimized because the infant is shielded from drafts, and radiant heat loss is diminished because the inner surface of the incubator is warmed. As a consequence, the first gradient of radiant heat loss from the baby to the inner surface of the incubator reduces the neonate's loss (Oliver, 1965).

Failure to maintain a proper thermal environment may be fatal to the newborn. Studies published as late as 1964 reveal a 50 percent or greater increase in mortality in infants nursed at room temperature versus those fed in a warmed environment (Buetow & Klein, 1964; Day, Caliguiri, Kamenski,

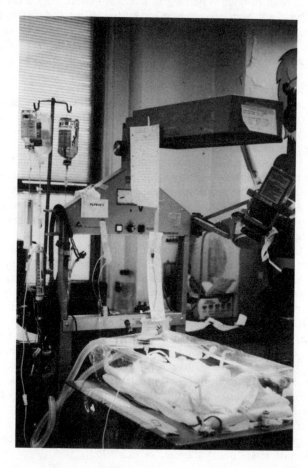

Figure 3–1 Radiant Warmer

& Ehrlich, 1964; Silverman & Agate, 1964). Secondly, it is well known that children with respiratory distress frequently require additional oxygen, as their rate of caloric expenditure is higher. Body resources that have been used excessively to maintain body temperature, therefore, are not available for tissue repair and growth. Such babies require longer stays in intensive care nurseries.

Physiology and Behavior during Transition

Transition from the intrauterine to extrauterine existence is one of the most traumatic periods experienced in our lives. The baby is cut loose from his/her life support system and must make a very rapid transference to air breathing with major changes in the circulatory system. Virtually every body system now must adapt to this hostile environment. The lungs, which have been filled with fluid, must expel or absorb the fluid to allow adequate exchange of oxygen and carbon dioxide. The central nervous system now must deal with stimuli that have not been present or were muted within the uterus, including touch, smell, taste, vision, and hearing. The kidneys begin to concentrate and dilute to rid waste products. The gastrointestinal system must digest food properly to provide appropriate nutrition for the baby in a very rapid growth phase.

Among these changes, one of the most profound is the rapid transition of the circulatory system. Prior to birth, less than five percent of the blood pumped by the heart enters the lungs. Blood returning from the placenta has sufficient oxygen for fetal needs. As it enters the right side of the heart, this blood either may cross directly to the left side and travel to the body, or may be pumped by the right muscle chamber (ventricle) out toward the lungs. Most of this blood bypasses the lung through a vessel called the patent ductus arteriosis, connecting the pulmonary and systemic circulations. At birth, the lungs expand rapidly and blood flow must match the lung expansion for the baby to survive. Resistance in the lung blood vessels drops precipitously over the first 24 to 48 hours, and thus there may be backflow of small amounts of blood from the systemic toward the now lower-pressure pulmonary circulation. An increase in the blood oxygen level typically leads to contraction of muscles in the wall of the patent ductus arteriosis and histologic obliteration within one week after birth. However, many preterm infants are incapable of closing this patent ductus arteriosis, and heart failure may result (Smith & Nelson, 1976).

In closing, we would like to turn the reader's attention to the behavior of the newborn during the transition period. Specifically, there are three phases: A first reactive phase, a sleep phase, and a second reactive phase. The first reactive phase begins at birth or shortly thereafter, and may last as long as six hours. The neonate is alert and exploratory, and responds quickly to various stimuli. The second phase is a sleep state, which may last from three to six hours. A second reactive phase follows, by which time the healthy infant has established good control of respiration and circulation (Desmond, et al., 1965; Desmond, Franklin, Vallbona, et al., 1963).

Table 3–1 Transitional Period Behavior of the Newborn

	First Period of Activity *(alerting, exploratory behavior)*	*Unresponsive Interval* *(sleep phase)*	*Second Period of Reactivity*
Age	Birth - 1 hour	2-3 hours	3-4 hours
Color	Transient cyanosis, flushing with cry	Pink	Swift color changes
Heart Rate	Tachycardia (180) decreasing over 15 min to 140	Slow 100-120	Wide swings in rate
Respiration	Flaring, grunting, retracting common first 15 minutes then rapid	Shallow, regular	Irregular brief apneic pauses
Activity	Intense activity—eyes open, sucking, spontaneous reflexes	Occasional brief startle during sleep	Variable
Tone	Increased tone, especially upper extremities	Relaxed	Variable
Bowel	Sounds heard after 15 minutes	Frequent visible peristalsis	Frequent meconium passage

Sources: From "The Relation of Maternal Disease to Fetal and Neonatal Morbidity and Mortality" by M. Desmond et al., 1961, *Pediatric Clinics of North America, 8,* pp. 421-440. Copyright 1961 by W.B. Saunders Company; "The Clinical Behavior of the Newly Born: The Term Baby" by M. Desmond et al., 1963, *Journal of Pediatrics, 62,* pp. 307-325. Copyright 1963 by The C.V. Mosby Company; and "The Transitional Care Nursery: A Mechanism for Preventive Medicine in the Newborn" by M. Desmond et al., 1966, *Pediatric Clinics of North America, 13,* pp. 651-668. Copyright 1966 by W.B. Saunders Company.

On delivery, if the infant is vigorous and reactive to the experience of being born, a characteristic series of changes in vital signs and clinical appearance take place. These include a first period of reactivity, a relatively unresponsive interval, and a second period of reactivity (see Table 3–1).

> During the first period of reactivity changes ... include tachycardia, rapid respiration, transient rales, grunting, flaring and retraction, a falling body temperature, hypertonus and alerting exploratory behavior. ... Bowel sounds become evident during the first 15 minutes, and oral mucus may be visible.
>
> After the first period of reactivity, heart and respiratory rates decline while diffuse motor activity reaches a peak and then diminishes. General responsiveness declines and the infant sleeps. After sleep, the infant enters a second period of reactivity. Oral mucus may again become evident, the infant becomes more responsive to exogenous and endogenous stimuli, and heart rates become labile. The bowel is cleared of meconium. In some infants the secondary reactivity period results in waves of heightened autonomic activity. Wide swings in heart rate (bradycardia to tachycardia) occur along with the passage of meconium stools, the handling of mucus, vasomotor instability, and irregular respiration with apneic pauses. (Desmond, Rudolph, & Phitaksphraiwan, 1966, pp. 655–656)

Not surprisingly, there is marked variability in the behavior of the newborn during transition. Failure to respond in accordance with the described patterns does not suggest that the infant is brain damaged, or even temporarily compromised. It should be clear from our discussion in this chapter that labor and delivery pose an especially stressful time for the infant. However in most instances, the anticipation of potential problems and their correction lead to a smooth transition of the fetus from intrauterine existence to the hostile outer world.

REFERENCES

Apgar, V.A. (1953). A proposal for a new method of evaluation of the newborn infant. *Anesthesia and Analgesia, 32*, 260–267.

Babson, S.G., Benson, R.C., Pernoll, M.L., & Benda, G.I. (1980). Assessment of fetal health in high-risk labor. In S.G. Babson & R.C. Benson (Eds.), *Management of high risk pregnancy and intensive care of the neonate* (pp. 22–41). St. Louis: C.V. Mosby.

Behrman, R.E., & Mangurten, H.H. (1977). Birth injuries in neonatal-perinatal medicine. In R.E. Behrman (Ed.), *Neonatal-perinatal medicine* (pp. 70–94). St. Louis: C.V. Mosby.

Buetow, K.C., & Klein, S.W. (1964). Effect of maintenance of "normal" skin temperature on survival of infants of low birthweight. *Pediatrics, 34*, 163–170.

Day, R.L., Caliguiri, L., Kamenski, C., & Ehrlich, F. (1964). Body temperature and survival of premature infants. *Pediatrics, 34*, 171–181.

Desmond, M.M., Franklin, R., Blattner, R., & Hill, R.M. (1961). The relation of maternal disease to fetal and neonatal morbidity and mortality. *Pediatric Clinics of North America, 8,* 421–440.

Desmond, M.M., Franklin, R., Vallbona, C., Hill, R.M., Plumb, R., Arnold, H., & Watts, J. (1963). The clinical behavior of the newly born: The term baby (I). *Journal of Pediatrics, 62,* 307–325.

Desmond, M.M., Rudolph, A.J., & Phitaksphraiwan, P. (1966). The transitional care nursery: A mechanism for preventive medicine in the newborn. *Pediatric Clinics of North America, 13,* 651–668.

Drage, J.S., Kennedy, C., & Schwarz, R.K. (1964). The Apgar score as an index of neonatal mortality. *Obstetrics & Gynecology, 24,* 222–230.

Eng, G.D., Koch, B., & Smokvina, M.D. (1978). Brachial plexus palsy in neonates and children. *Archives of Physical Medicine and Rehabilitation, 59,* 458–464.

Fisher, D.E., & Paton, J.B. (1979). Resuscitation of the newborn infant. In M. Klaus & A. Fanaroff (Eds.), *Care of the high-risk neonate* (pp. 23–44). Philadelphia: W.B. Saunders.

Friedman, E.A. (1981). The labor curve. *Clinics in Perinatology, 8,* 15–25.

Hemminki, E., & Starfield, B. (1978). Prevention and treatment of premature labour by drugs: Review of controlled clinical trials. *British Journal of Obstetrics and Gynaecology, 85,* 411–417.

Hill, J., & Rahimtulla, K. (1965). Heat balance and the metabolic rate of newborn babies in relation to environmental temperature; and the effect of age and of weight on basal metabolic rate. *Journal of Physiology, 180,* 239–265.

Hon, E.H., & Koh, K.S. (1981). Management of labor and delivery in neonatology. In G.B. Avery (Ed.), *Neonatology: Pathophysiology and management of the newborn* (2nd ed.) (pp. 120–131). Philadelphia: J.B. Lippincott.

Klaus, M., Fanaroff, A., & Martin, R.J. (1979). The physical environment. In M. Klaus & A. Fanaroff (Eds.), *Care of the high-risk newborn* (pp. 94–112). Philadelphia: W. B. Saunders.

Lindgren, L. (1972). The engagement of the foetal head in the uterus when the vertex presents. *Acta Obstetrica and Gynecology Scandinavia, 51,* 37–45.

Manning, J., & Adour, K. (1972). Facial paralysis in children. *Pediatrics, 49,* 102–109.

Miller, F.C., Sacks, D.A., & Yeh, S.Y. (1975). Significance of meconium during labor. *American Journal of Obstetrics and Gynecology, 122,* 573–577.

Miller, F.C. (1982). Prediction of acid-base values from intrapartum fetal heart rate data and their correlation with scalp and funic values. *Clinics in Perinatology, 9,* 353–361.

Oliver, T.K., Jr. (1965). Temperature regulation and heat production in the newborn. *Pediatric Clinics of North America, 12,* 765–779.

Phibbs, R.H. (1981). Delivery room management of the newborn. In G.B. Avery (Ed.), *Neonatology: Pathophysiology and management of the newborn* (2nd ed.) (pp. 182–201). Philadelphia: J. B. Lippincott.

Pritchard, J.A., & MacDonald, P.C. (1985). The physiology of labor. In J.A. Pritchard & P.C. MacDonald (Eds.), *Williams obstetrics* (pp. 295–321). Norwalk, CT: Appleton-Century-Crofts.

Sanerkin, N.G., & Edwards, P. (1966). Birth injury to the sternocleidomastoid muscle. *Journal of Bone and Joint Surgery, 48B,* 441–447.

Schifrin, B.S. (1982). The fetal monitoring polemic. *Clinics in Perinatology, 9,* 399–408.

Silverman, W., & Agate, F. (1964). Variation in cold resistance among small newborn animals. *Biology of the Neonate, 6,* 113–119.

Silverman, W., Fertig, J., & Berger, A. (1958). The influence of the thermal environment upon the survival of newly born premature infants. *Pediatrics, 22,* 876–886.

Smith, C.A., & Nelson, N.M. (1976). *Physiology of the newborn infant* (4th ed.). Springfield, IL: Charles C Thomas.

Sureau, C. (1974). The stress of labor. In S. Aladjem & A. Brown (Eds.), *Clinical perinatology* (pp. 291–335). St. Louis: C. V. Mosby.

Tropper, P.J., & Fox, H.E. (1982). Evaluation of antepartum fetal well-being by measuring growth. *Clinics in Perinatology, 9,* 271–284.

Williams, P.R., & Oh, W. (1974). Effects of radiant warmer on insensible weight loss in newborn infants. *American Journal of Diseases of Children, 128,* 511–514.

4

The Newborn

Prior to the early 1960s, newborns weighing less than 2,500 grams (five and one-half pounds) arbitrarily were classified as premature infants, whereas those greater than 2,500 grams were identified as full-term. In 1961, the World Health Organization discarded this definition of preterm infants. Newborns weighing less than 2,500 grams subsequently were termed *low birthweight*, irrespective of the duration of gestation. Following these changes, birthweight alone was no longer used as a measure of the maturity of the newborn and an independent assessment of growth (including weight, length, and head circumference) thus was considered in relation to determinations of gestational age (Colman & Rienzo, 1962; Gruenwald, 1963; Warkany, Monroe, & Sutherland, 1961). Moreover, new information led to a characterization of infants based upon appropriateness of intrauterine growth for newborn gestational age. Today, according to present criteria, a *full-term infant* is considered to be 38 to 42 weeks gestation (37 to 41 weeks by World Health Organization standards). Babies born prior to this period are considered *premature*, and babies born beyond this time frame are judged *post-term*. The purpose of this chapter for the early childhood educator and clinician is to describe the various dimensions of *sizing* and *routine newborn care*, and the various implications of both for treatment and outcome of the neonate. It should become obvious, as we progress through this discussion, that certain conditions in particular predispose infants toward a higher degree of risk and vulnerability than do others. In terms of subsequent follow-up, we need to be alert to babies with such medical histories.

SIZING

Gestational Age Assessment

Intrauterine assessment of gestational age is difficult to ascertain. X-rays for bone growth and sonograms for head development may be extremely inaccurate if the fetus is growth-retarded. Although maternal dates are useful, irregular menstrual periods, hemorrhage especially in the first trimester, and abnormal fetal size also may confuse the issue. Thus, several methods based

35

on physical and neurologic characteristics of the newborn have been developed to assess gestational age.

External Physical Characteristics

Many external physical characteristics of newborn infants progress in an orderly fasion during gestation (Farr, Kerridge, & Mitchell, 1966; Farr, Mitchell, & Neligan, 1966; Usher, McLean, & Scott, 1966). Table 4–1 presents representative physical characteristics for neonates born at 28, 32, 36, and 40 weeks gestation. The first of these indicators is the vernix caseosa, a cheese-like material that initially appears at approximately 24 weeks of gestation. It covers the body of the fetus and begins to diminish at approximately 36 weeks gestation. In the full-term infant, it is scant and found generally only in the creases.

The skin of the very preterm infant is thin and translucent. Blood vessels are prominent and are most easily seen over the abdomen. With increasing gestation, vessels become less apparent as a result of deposition of fat and thickening of the skin. The *lanugo*, which is the fine hair of the fetus, covers the entire body as early as 22 weeks gestation. It begins to vanish from the face only three to four weeks prior to birth and still can be seen on the shoulders of most newborns.

The third characteristic, the nipple and the surrounding tissue (areola), are not visible or are barely evident in the very premature infant. It is only at 34 weeks gestation that the areola begins to raise. In response to maternal hormones and with good nutrition, fat deposits in the breast and, by term, a five to six millimeter nodule can be felt.

The ear in the full-term infant has a well-defined incurving of the outer edge. It is firm with developed cartilage and stands erect from the head. By comparison, the ear of the very preterm infant is flat, somewhat shapeless, and does not spring back when it is folded, a result of little cartilage.

Development of genitalia is another indicator of gestational age. The maturity of males, in part, can be traced by descent of the testes, which begin as intra-abdominal organs, first appearing at the beginning of the inguinal canal at approximately 28 weeks gestation. The testes then descend into the scrotum and are pendulous at term. In response to this development, the scrotum manifests increased folds and becomes progressively more pigmented. In the female, deposition of fat again plays a role. In the severely preterm infant, the clitoris is very prominent and the labia majora (outer lips) are small and widely separated. As the fetus approaches term, there is fatty deposition in the labia majora and, by term, the labia minora (inner lips) and clitoris are covered completely.

The sole or plantar creases are entirely absent on the feet of the severely premature baby. Faint red marks appear over the anterior half of the foot by about 30 to 31 weeks, and a definite anterior sole crease can be seen by 32 weeks gestation. Generally, by 36 weeks creases cover the anterior two-thirds of the foot, and the entire sole by full-term.

Another recently described physical characteristic, which aids in the assessment of gestational age, is the sequential regression of vessels in the

Table 4–1 Physical Characteristics for Gestational Age

Gestational Age (Weeks)

Physical Finding	28	32	36	40
Vernix	Covers body	Covers body	Diminishing	Scant in creases
Skin	Thin, translucent prominent vessels	Thicker, vessels less apparent	Pink, few vessels	Early desquamation
Lanugo	Covers entire body	Covers body	Vanishes from face	Present on shoulders
Breast	No palpable tissue	No palpable tissue, areola visible	Areola raised, 1–2 mm nodule	5–6 mm nodule
Ear				
Form	Flat	Flat	Incurving upper 2/3	Well defined, incurving
Cartilage	Stays folded	Scant, unfolds slowly	Thin, springs from folding	Firm, erect from head
Genitalia				
Male	Testes not palpable or at inguinal canal inlet	Testes in inguinal canal	Testes in upper scrotum	Testes in lower scrotum
Female	—	Prominent clitoris; labia majora small	Clitoris nearly covered by labia minora	Labia minora and clitoris covered
Sole				
Creases	Smooth, no creases	1–2 anterior creases	Creases anterior 2/3 of sole	Creases entire sole

Source: From "Assessment of Gestational Age and Development at Birth" by L.O. Lubchenco, 1970, *Pediatric Clinics of North America, 17*, 125-145.

anterior capsule of the lens of the eye. At 27 to 28 weeks, these vessels cross the entire lens. By 29 to 30 weeks, there is central clearing, which continues until only small remnants can be seen on the periphery at 33 to 34 weeks gestation (Hittner, Hirsch, & Rudolph, 1977).

In general, the physical characteristics described above should be examined within the first 24 hours. With the predictable loss of extracellular fluid, the characteristics of the skin and the appearance of the sole creases otherwise may be altered. Once the infant is cleaned, vernix also is no longer useful for gestational age assessment.

Neurologic Assessment

While determination of gestational age by physical criteria should be performed immediately after birth, the neurologic evaluation needs to be completed later, when the infant is quiet. With the events of transition, this assessment usually cannot be done until the end of the first day or possibly the second or third day. Numerous perinatal factors may affect the neurologic assessment including asphyxia, maternal anesthesia, maternal medications, and various illnesses and syndromes that may afflict the newborn. Neurologic development of the fetus during the last trimester is characterized, normally, by an increase in muscle mass and tone as well as by changes in reflexes and joint mobility in the extremities. Dutch and French neurologists first provided the details of the neurologic examination by gestational age (Amiel-Tison, 1968; Prechtl & Beintema, 1964). Current neurologic evaluation after birth focuses more specifically on examination of muscle tone (both passive and active), joint mobility, and primitive reflexes.

Infants born at 28 weeks gestation or less have very poor muscle tone and evidence a resting posture that is hypotonic, with full extension of the arms and legs. Flexor tone begins to appear at 30 weeks gestation, increasing in the lower extremities before the upper extremities. Characteristically, a 35- to 36-week infant has good muscle tone quality in the lower extremities, but only partial bending in the arms. By full-term, the resting posture should include full flexion at the joints of both upper and lower extremities. The severely preterm infant does not resist various passive maneuvers, such as the heel-to-the-ear or the scarf sign. Likewise, active tone may be seen as early as 30 weeks when the infant extends his/her leg in response to stimulation of the soles of the feet. At 32 weeks gestation, the baby straightens his/her legs when placed in a standing position. By 36 weeks, the neck extensors and flexors begin to function and, by 38 weeks, most infants can hold their heads for a few seconds when pulled to a sitting position.

Trunk tone can be measured by ventral suspension (Figure 4–1). With the infant prone, chest resting on the examiner's hand, the baby is lifted off the examining surface and body position is noted. Very premature infants have poor trunk tone and will appear to be draped over the hand. By 32 to 34 weeks, the back is straightened and, by full-term, the head rises above the straightened back.

Joint mobility or flexibility with respect to gestational age may be examined in the wrist and ankle. With the square window sign, the hand is

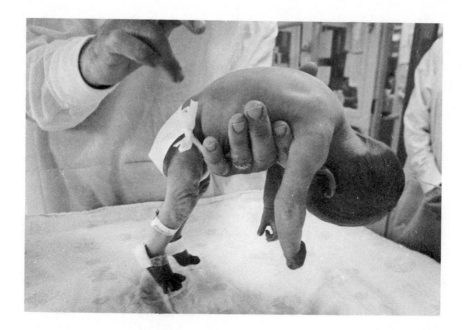

Figure 4–1 Ventral Suspension of a Moderately Premature Infant

flexed at the wrist and the angle between the hand and wrist is measured (Figure 4–2). In ankle dorsiflexion, the foot is flexed at the ankle with sufficient pressure for maximum change. The angle between the dorsum of the foot and the anterior leg then is measured. In the 28-week infant, the wrist does not flex beyond 90 degrees. By 36 weeks, the angle is 45 degrees and, at term, the hand touches the arm. Ankle dorsiflexion reflects a similar pattern of development. The preterm infant generally has an angle of greater than 45 degrees, which progresses to zero by term. In both cases of wrist and ankle mobility, the relatively stiff joints of early gestation become more relaxed at term.

Primitive reflexes—e.g., sucking, rooting, grasping, galant, Moro, (Figure 4–3), crossed extension, pupillary reflex, glabellar tap, tonic neck reflex (ATNR) (Figure 4–4), and neck righting—also have been used to determine gestational age. Prior to 32 weeks, virtually all of these reflexes are absent or, at best, are very weak. By term, all are well established. Furthermore, with progressive development of the central nervous system over the first year of life, these reflexes generally disappear. Persistence may occur in infants with central nervous system damage.

Gestational age assessment of newborns now is accomplished most commonly with the use of a combination of both physical and neurologic findings. This current trend first was initiated in 1970 by Dubowitz and his colleagues (Dubowitz & Dubowitz, 1977; Dubowitz, Dubowitz, & Goldberg, 1970), who developed a scoring system that utilized neurologic measures

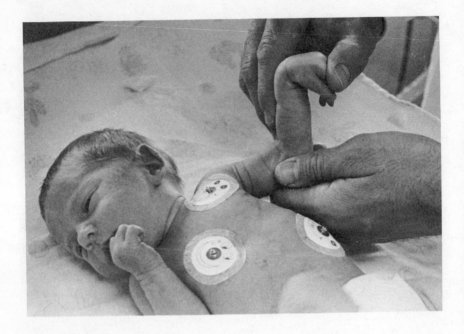

Figure 4–2 Square Window Sign

paralleling those of Amiel-Tison and the physical characteristics described by Farr and others. Accordingly, 10 neurologic and 11 physical characteristics were weighted, with a higher score assigned for more mature characteristics. A total score could then be obtained and the gestational age determined by means of a graph. Many abbreviations of this assessment have appeared recently. Overall, these are briefer versions that correlate well with the more sophisticated scoring systems. Such examination also allows for less handling and exposure of the acutely ill preterm infant.

Most recent measures of gestational age now encompass examination of the ear, breast tissue, plantar (sole) creases, and lens vessels as described in Table 4–2. An infant of 28 weeks typically scores no more than one. A full-term infant, on the other hand, achieves 14 points or more according to this system. The evaluation is accurate plus or minus 11 days, which is within the scoring range of the Dubowitz scoring system (Narayanan et al., 1982).

Growth for Gestational Age

Once gestational age of the newborn has been established, growth characteristics of the child can be examined to determine whether intrauterine growth has been appropriate. Unfortunately, there is no uniform definition of infants who are *small-for-gestational age* (SGA) or *large-for-gestational age* (LGA). Designations of "normal" have been arbitrary. Limits of less than the third percentile, less than the tenth percentile, and less than

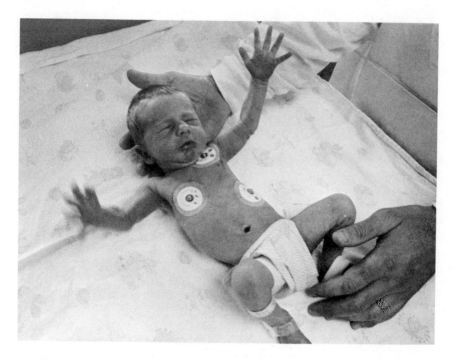

Figure 4-3 The Moro Response

---

two standard deviations from the mean all have been used in reference to the SGA infant. For the large-for-gestational age infant, the limits of "appropriate" variously have been set at greater than the ninety-seventh percentile, greater than the nintieth percentile, and greater than two standard deviations from the mean. In addition, the measurements used for these comparisons have differed considerably, including birthweight, length, head circumference, and length-to-head circumference ratio (Cassady, 1981). As a result of such inconsistencies within the medical literature, comparisons and contrasts of the outcome of premature, low birthweight, small-for-gestational age, and large-for-gestational age infants are problematic and difficult to understand (see Figure 4-5).

Neonatal Morbidity by Birthweight and Gestational Age

Lubchenco and several colleagues carefully documented the increased mortality risk by birthweight, as matched to gestational age (Lubchenco, Delivoria-Papadopoulos, & Searls, 1972). The group at lowest risk for death in the newborn period (0.1 percent or 1 per 1000 live births) not surprisingly are those infants born term and appropriate for gestational age. On the other hand, neonates born preterm or post-term show an increased incidence of neonatal mortality, which is exaggerated by abnormally small or large fetal

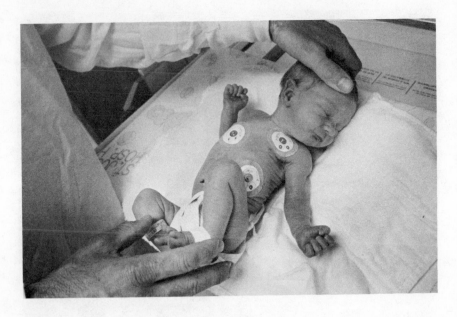

Figure 4–4 The Asymmetrical Tonic Neck Reflex (ATNR)

growth. For example, term infants born large-for-gestational age may have a neonatal mortality rate as high as 1 percent (or 1 per 100 live births), a tenfold increase above infants born term and appropriate for gestational age. The mortality risk for the growth-retarded newborn is much greater and may reach as high as 9 percent (or 9 per 100 live births), a ninetyfold increase over appropriately grown term newborns. As birthweight and gestational age decrease, infant mortality increases dramatically to virtually 100 percent for infants born less than 26 weeks gestation and weighing less than 700 grams (approximately one and one-half pounds). Morbidity statistics parallel figures on neonatal mortality (Lubchenco, 1976).

Despite confusion in the nomenclature and diverse standards of norm, high risk subgroups (SGA and LGA) have been the focus of much attention, the small-for-gestational age infant having received the greatest amount of interest. This latter group is extremely heterogeneous, with many subpopulations. Numerous causes have been associated with the growth-retarded newborn.

As Table 4–3 shows, many *fetal factors* may result in decreased growth potential. Just as there is a large variation in the birthweight of healthy, full-term infants between populations (Meredith, 1970), familial trends for low birthweight infants have been noted, implying a genetic basis (Johnstone & Inglis, 1974). The identification of racial and ethnic differences in expected birthweight has suggested additional inherited influences that may alter growth potential (Barron & Vessey, 1966; Ounsted & Ounsted, 1973).

Table 4–2 Rapid Assessment of Gestational Age

Criteria	Score				
	0	1	2	3	4
Ear Firmness (palpate upper pinna and note recoil after folding)	Pinna extremely soft, foldable into bizarre shapes with no recoil	Pinna soft along the edge, easily folded with slow recoil	Pinna with some cartilage, but thin at places, "ready recoil"	Pinna stiffened by cartilage up to periphery, immediate recoil	—
Breast Nodule (pick up breast tissue with thumb and forefinger)	No breast tissue palpable	Nodule on one or both sides less than 0.5 cm.	Nodule on one or both sides 0.5–1.0 cm.	Nodule on one or both sides more than 1.0 cm.	—
Plantar Creases	No creases	Faint red marks over anterior 1/2	Reddish marks over anterior 1/2. Definite creases over anterior 1/3	Creases over more than anterior 1/3	Creases all over. Deep indentations over anterior 1/3
Lens Vessels (ophthalmoscope set on +12 diopters)	Vessels completely covering the lens	Area central clearing <1/4 total lens diameter	Area central clearing 1/4–1/2 total lens diameter	Small vessel loops at periphery, >1/2 of lens clear	Lens clear except occasional faint loop or vessel remnant

Source: From "A Simple Method for Assessment of Gestional Age in Newborn Infants" by I. Narayanan et al., 1982, *Pediatrics, 69*, pp. 27-32. Copyright 1982 by American Academy of Pediatrics.

Congenital infections that have gained access to the fetus prior to birth may interfere with intrauterine fetal growth (Lubchenco, 1976). Chapter 12 will discuss these infections in detail—among the most common are rubella, cytomegalovirus, syphilis, toxoplasmosis, and herpes. These infectious diseases impair the development of genetically normal cells, and such infants may be born growth-retarded, with microcephaly, deafness, cataracts, hepatosplenomegaly, pneumonia, hepatitis, and other evidence of multiple organ infection. Excessive or insufficient chromosomal material may cause a

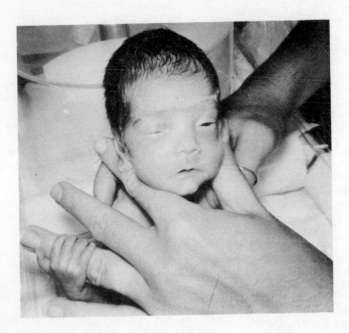

Figure 4–5 Preterm Baby Girl, 26 Weeks Gestation, Birthweight of 750 Grams

number of chromosomal syndromes (e.g., Trisomy 21, Trisomy 18, and Turner's syndrome), all of which may be associated with growth retardation. Moreover, even in the absence of specific chromosomal abnormalities, congenital anomalies such as microcephaly result in SGA newborns. For instance, metabolic errors in the handling of nutrients crucial to tissue growth is known; yet in many instances, the precise sequence of events leading to them still is not well understood.

A second series of factors associated with *inadequate health of the placenta* can result in poor development of the newborn. One such condition is a decreased placental mass that may provide insufficient nutrients for fetal growth and poor clearance of waste products. These conditions often are seen with placental abruption or infarction, and with the rapidly aging placenta of the mother who has delivered post-term. In addition, growth retardation has been intrinsic and often linked to several placental factors including malformations, vascular disease, and poor implantation site (DiGaetano & Gabbe, 1983).

The third large category of factors associated with growth retardation may be classified as *maternal variables*. Reduced uteroplacental blood flow with concomitant decreases in nutrient transfer to the fetus underlies many other examples of various growth-retarded newborns. Maternal vascular disease including advanced diabetes, chronic hypertension, and hypertension associ-

Table 4–3 Factors Associated with Growth-Retarded (SGA) Newborns

FETAL—Decreased Growth Potential

- Genetics—Population
- Congenital Infection
- Chromosomal Syndromes
- Congenital Anomalies
- Metabolic Errors

PLACENTAL

- Decreased Placental Mass
- Intrinsic Placental Disease

MATERNAL

- Reduced Uteroplacental Blood Flow
- Decreased Nutrient Availability
- Decreased Oxygen Availability
- Drugs
- Multiple Gestation

Sources: Neonatology: Pathophysiology and Management of the Newborn, 2nd ed. (pp. 262-286), by G.B. Avery (Ed.), 1981, Philadelphia: J.B. Lippincott Company. Copyright 1981 by J.B. Lippincott Company; and "Intrauterine Growth Retardation" by A.F. DiGaetano and S.G. Gabbe, 1983, Current Problems in Obstetrics and Gynecology, 6, pp. 7-30. Copyright 1983 by Year Book Medical Publishers, Inc.

ated with toxemia all have been associated with impaired fetal growth (Gruenwald, 1966; Long, Abell, & Beischer, 1980). Decreased nutrient availability to the fetus may be seen in mothers with poor nutrition or gastrointestinal disease, and in women who smoke. In a similar fashion, decreased oxygen availability to the newborn curtails fetal metabolism. The two most common examples are mothers residing at high altitudes and, again, those who smoke. More unusual causes are evidenced among mothers with cyanotic heart disease and a hemoglobinopathy such as sickle cell disease.

Drugs have been shown to impair fetal growth through a variety of mechanisms. Twenty years ago thalidomide produced congenitally abnormal babies with short limbs and reduced body weight. Head growth usually was spared (McBride, 1961). In addition, there is well-documented evidence that alcohol results in fetal growth impairment and mental retardation, along with multiple anomalies of the face, eyes, cardiovascular, and musculoskeletal systems (Clarren & Smith, 1978). Maternal narcotic addiction too has been associated with poor newborn development.

Last, twin gestation is another important consideration among those factors determining growth. Over the years, many cases have been cited. In 1966, Gruenwald observed that the growth rate of twins followed that of a singleton fetus until approximately 32 weeks gestation, after which there was a progressive falling off in the development of twins (Gruenwald, 1966). In a recent study, an incidence of growth retardation in twins was documented to be as high as 17.5 percent (Houlton, Marivate, & Philpott, 1981). Twins, in addition, may be discordant in their weights (see Figure 4–6), with one weighing considerably more than the other and placental asymmetry affording insufficient nutrients to the smaller twin.

Typically, the impact of growth retardation on the newborn is varied and pervasive. In general, head growth, disproportionate to restricted weight and length, tends to be spared (Lubchenco, 1976). More often than not these babies have clinical problems, even at term, which are quite similar to those of children born prematurely (Sweet, 1979). For instance, *hypoglycemia* in both groups is a result of decreased body stores of glycogen, a polymer of

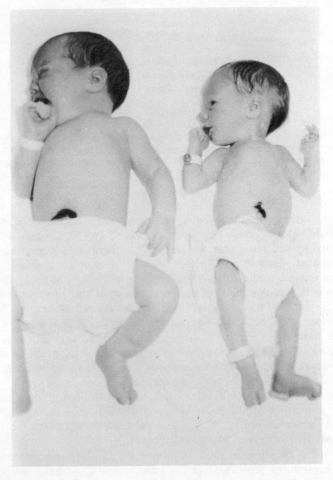

Figure 4–6 Discordant Twins

glucose normally stored in the liver (Cornblath, Wybregt, Baens, & Klein, 1964). Essentially, the stress of adaptation to extrauterine life results in increased glucose utilization with little caloric reserve. Thus, hypoglycemia usually occurs within the first 12 hours after birth and can be treated with intravenous glucose or an early feeding regimen. Both preterm and SGA infants are prone to hypothermia. Their surface area-to-body mass is decreased, and heat is dissipated more readily. Thus, such newborns have little subcutaneous fat to conserve heat and, with a poor caloric reserve, heat generation is impaired (Sweet, 1979). Often, growth-retarded infants suffer from problems that arise from increased total numbers of red blood cells (polycythemia). While the etiology of this condition is not known, it has been theorized that intrauterine hypoxia (reduced oxygen content and oxygen tension) results in elevated red blood cell production, probably a form of compensation (Gruenwald, 1963). These polycythemic infants are usually asymptomatic but, if the fraction of red blood cells in the blood exceeds 70 percent, they may show symptoms of respiratory distress, cardiac failure, hypoglycemia, seizures, and increased jaundice. The benefits of treatment are controversial; however, excess red blood cells can be removed, while care is taken to preserve the blood volume by replacement of plasma.

In conclusion, we should point out that while maternal and fetal disease may account for abnormalities of growth in many newborns, not every excessively large or small newborn is the result of a pathologic process. Quite obviously, tall and heavy parents tend to produce large babies, and small, thin parents have small babies.

Our discussion has focused mainly on the small-for-gestational age baby. Problems of equal seriousness may arise among infants born large-for-gestational age, who generally tend to be more homogeneous than populations of smaller neonates. Commonly, fetal hyperinsulinism is an underlying factor for excessive fetal growth, and this condition most frequently is prompted by maternal diabetes. The maternal pancreas fails to produce quantities of insulin sufficient to prevent the blood glucose of the mother from rising. This maternal hyperglycemia, in turn, results in fetal hyperglycemia. Subsequently, the elevated serum glucose in the newborn provokes excess insulin production and secretion from the fetal pancreas, resulting in overgrowth, especially of fatty tissue, heart, liver, and the adrenal gland. Brain weight is not affected, as evidenced by studies of gestational age matched controls (Naeye, 1965). At birth, these infants remain hyperinsulinemic; however, the glucose supply that originally stimulated the insulin release is withdrawn, resulting in *hypoglycemia*. Fetal hyperinsulinemia also inhibits lung maturation, causing an increased incidence of respiratory distress in the newborn period (Robert, Neff, Hubbell, Taeusch, & Avery, 1976).

Congenital anomalies are more frequent among large-for-gestational age infants born to diabetic mothers. These disorders include cardiac defects, gastrointestinal malformations, spinal anomalies, and the caudal regression syndrome (a malformation of the pelvic region and lower extremities). Pedersen compared infants of diabetic mothers with nondiabetic controls and discovered a twofold increase in congenital anomalies with mild to moderate maternal diabetes, and a fourfold increase in neonatal congenital anomalies with the more severe forms of maternal diabetes (Pedersen, 1977). The large fetal size also predisposes these infants to birth trauma, especially cephalohematomas, brachial plexus injuries, and fractured clavicles as discussed in Chapter 3.

Other etiologies associated with excessive fetal growth include the *Beckwith syndrome* and *Rh isoimmunization*. Beckwith syndrome is a clinical disorder consisting of macroglossia (increased size of the tongue), gigantism (abnormal development of the body or parts), large organs, and neonatal hypoglycemia (related to hyperinsulinemia in approximately one-half of the patients). Many newborns have accompanying congenital anomalies, but most evidence normal chromosomes. The neonatal mortality is high, and many babies have residual developmental disabilities (Beckwith, 1969). Rh isoimmunization, which will be covered in detail in Chapter 8, has been associated with fetal hyperinsulinemia. Commonly, such infants are overgrown and hypoglycemic (Barrett & Oliver, 1968).

Long-Term Outcome As a Function of Gestational Age

Data on long-term outcome of neonates is very difficult to evaluate. Reports frequently reflect not only the interests but also the biases of the investigators. Variables included in analyses of children with handicaps often are study specific, making comparisons complex and not infrequently ambiguous. Racial, ethnic, social, and economic factors repeatedly are ill-defined or hard to interpret. Many follow-up investigations have been conducted retrospectively with poor case controls and, even in the few prospective projects, important information may have been missed and the sample size for follow-up may have been incomplete (Lubchenco, 1976). Ultimately, prognosis for development hinges on gestational age and intrauterine growth and development, as well as on perinatal problems, early childhood illnesses, family dynamics, and other environmental factors much too subtle and complex to quantitate properly.

Most reports of long-term outcome study children only for the first several years of life; rarely are data available beyond five years. Intellectual and motor function are virtually always the primary focus, with little attention paid to behavioral and emotional development. To this time, problems in funding and a mobile society have inhibited the duration and completeness of longitudinal follow-up studies.

ROUTINE NEWBORN CARE

Following resuscitation and stabilization of the newborn and an appropriate gestational age assessment, each infant receives specific *prophylactic* health care. This involves proper identification, care of the umbilical cord, eye care, administration of vitamin K, and newborn metabolic screening. In general, such treatments are designed to prevent infection or other adverse conditions.

Newborn Identification

Before the newborn leaves the delivery room, two identical bands indicating the mother's admission number and the sex of the infant are placed on the baby's wrist and ankle. The accuracy of identifiers is checked prior to the baby's leaving the delivery room and again upon admission to the nursery. Later, the mother must verify the information on the identification bands both prior to feedings and as a condition of discharge from the hospital (American Academy of Pediatrics and American College of Obstetricians and Gynecologists, 1983).

Although newborns are still being footprinted for identification, this technique recently has been deemed basically unreliable. Widely available sophisticated blood-typing techniques appear to be much more accurate and, concomitantly, cost effective (Thompson, Clark, Salisbury, & Cahill, 1981).

Cord Care

At delivery, the cord is clamped to prohibit blood loss. It then dries and, in approximately 7 to 10 days, is shed. Since this area is a site of potential infection, much attention has been paid to preventing colonization of the cord. Methods presently used include local application of triple dye and various antimicrobial agents such as Bacitracin. Although alcohol may hasten drying of the cord, probably it is not very effective in the healing process (American Academy of Pediatrics and American College of Obstetricians and Gynecologists, 1983).

Eye Prophylaxis

Ophthalmia neonatorum (conjunctivitis of the newborn) may be caused by many infectious agents. Approximately 100 years ago, Crede initiated the use of silver nitrate in newborn eye care, and this prophylaxis markedly reduced the incidence of *gonorrheal ophthalmia neonatorum*. The most recent revision of the American Academy of Pediatrics guidelines (1983) directed toward preventing neonatal ophthalmia include: (1) Installation of a prophylactic agent in the eyes of all newborns; and (2) A choice of prophylactic agents including 1 percent silver nitrate solution, 0.5 percent erythromycin ophthalmic ointment or drops, and 1 percent tetracycline ophthalmic ointment or drops. While all three of these are potent against gonococcal disease, only erythromycin and tetracycline are effective against *chlamydia*, a less serious eye infection that includes a purulent discharge that limits vision. For those few infants unfortunate enough to develop ophthalmia neonatorum, the specific infectious agent must be identified and treatment administered to prevent loss of vision.

Vitamin K

Hemorrhagic disease of the newborn was described first in 1894 as a generalized bleeding that occurred in the first week of life in otherwise healthy infants (Townsend, 1894). It is now known to be caused by a severe depression of the clotting *Factors II, VII, IX,* and *X,* secondary to a deficiency of vitamin K. Thus, all newborn infants, as a part of routine care, receive a single dose (0.5 to 1.0 milligrams) of natural vitamin K1 oxide within one hour of birth. Although this prophylaxis generally is given intramuscularly, oral administration is also effective (American Academy of Pediatrics and American College of Obstetricians and Gynecologists, 1983; Hathaway & Bonnar, 1978).

Metabolic Screening

Numerous metabolic diseases presently can be diagnosed within the early newborn period. These include *phenylketonuria* (PKU) and *congenital hypothyroidism,* two of many diseases that may result in retarded growth and development. Identification of these infants and dietary or therapeutic intervention have been shown to minimize the consequences of these inherited conditions. A blood sample should be obtained from every neonate prior to discharge. Small amounts of blood taken by heel-stick are placed on testing cards that then are analyzed in centralized laboratories in each state. All infants identified with abnormal results in the screening program subsequently must be tested by more sophisticated means. Although screening programs are expensive, the long-term cost to the state for infants with developmental delay far exceeds the outlay for screening programs.

In conclusion, while we will be returning to this topic of developmental outcome in much greater detail in Chapter 6, several generalizations are appropriate at this point in our discussion.

1. Overall, lower birthweight infants have a greater likelihood of a poor prognosis (Fitzhardinge & Ramsay, 1973; Kitchen et al., 1980; Lubchenco, 1976).
2. Small-for-gestational age neonates are more prone to poor neurological and developmental outcomes (Lubchenco, Delivoria-Papadopoulos, & Searls, 1972; Nickel, Bennett, & Lamson, 1982).
3. Neonates with severe respiratory distress or intracranial hemorrhage and seizures in the newborn period are at greater risk for neurologic and intellectual deficits (Desmond & Wilson, 1980; Ruiz, LeFever, Hakanson, Clark, & Williams, 1981).

Finally, the long-term developmental prognosis for an individual child only rarely can be predicted with sufficient accuracy to counsel parents with full certainty. However, continuous evaluation of high risk infants and children is helpful, and early intervention should allow high risk infants to reach their potential.

REFERENCES

American Academy of Pediatrics and American College of Obstetricians and Gynecologists. (1983). *Guidelines for perinatal care.* Evansville, IN: American Academy of Pediatrics & American College of Obstetricians and Gynecologists.

Amiel-Tison, C. (1968). Neurological evaluation of the maturity of newborn infants. *Archives of Disease in Childhood, 43,* 89–93.

Barrett, C.T., & Oliver, T.K., Jr. (1968). Hypoglycemia and hyperinsulinism in infants with erythroblastosis fetalis. *New England Journal of Medicine, 278,* 1260–1263.

Barron, S.L., & Vessey, M.P. (1966) Birthweights of infants born to immigrant women. *British Journal of Preventive and Social Medicine, 20,* 127–134.

Beckwith, J.B. (1969). Macroglossia, omphalocele, adrenal cytomegaly, gigantism, and hyperplastic visceromegaly. In D. Bergsma (Ed.), *The clinical delineation of birth defects* (Vol. 5, pp. 188–196). New York: National Foundation—March of Dimes.

Cassady, G. (1981). The small for date infant. In G.B. Avery (Ed.), *Neonatology: Pathophysiology and management of the newborn* (2nd. ed.) (pp. 262–286). Philadelphia: J.B. Lippincott.

Clarren, S.K., & Smith, D.W. (1978). The fetal alcohol syndrome. *New England Journal of Medicine, 298,* 1063–1067.

Colman, H., & Rienzo, J. (1962). The small term baby. *Obstetrics & Gynecology, 19,* 87–91.

Cornblath, M., Wybregt, S., Baens, G., & Klein, R. (1964). Symptomatic neonatal hypoglycemia: Studies of carbohydrate metabolism in the newborn infant. *Pediatrics, 33,* 388–402.

Desmond, M.M., & Wilson, G.S. (1980). The very low birthweight infant after discharge from intensive care: Anticipatory health care and developmental course. *Current Problems in Pediatrics, 10,* 1–59.

DiGaetano, A.F., & Gabbe, S.G. (1983). Intrauterine growth retardation. *Current Problems in Obstetrics and Gynecology, 6,* 7–30.

Dubowitz, L.M.S., & Dubowitz, V. (1977). *Gestational age of the newborn.* Menlo Park, CA: Addison-Wesley.

Dubowitz, L.M.S., Dubowitz, V., & Goldberg, C. (1970). Clinical assessment of gestational age in the newborn infant. *Journal of Pediatrics, 77,* 1–10.

Farr, V., Kerridge, D., & Mitchell, R. (1966). The value of some external characteristics in the assessment of gestational age at birth. *Developmental Medicine and Child Neurology, 8,* 657–660.

Farr, V., Mitchell, R., & Neligan, G. (1966). The definition of some external characteristics used in the assessment of gestational age of the newborn infant. *Developmental Medicine and Child Neurology, 8,* 507–511.

Fitzhardinge, P., & Ramsay, M. (1973). The improving outlook for the small prematurely born infant. *Developmental Medicine and Child Neurology, 15,* 447–459.

Gruenwald, P. (1963). Chronic fetal distress and placental insufficiency. *Biology of the Neonate, 5,* 215–265.

Gruenwald, P. (1966). Growth of the human fetus: II. Abnormal growth in twins and infants of mothers with diabetes, hypertension, or isoimmunization. *American Journal of Obstetrics and Gynecology, 94,* 1120–1132.

Hathaway, W.E., & Bonnar, J. (1978). Bleeding disorders in the newborn. In W.E. Hathway & J. Bonnar (Eds.), *Perinatal coagulation* (pp. 115–169). New York: Grune & Stratton.

Hittner, H., Hirsch, N., & Rudolph, A. (1977). Assessment of gestational age by examination of the anterior vascular capsule of the lens. *Journal of Pediatrics, 91,* 455–458.

Houlton, M.C.C., Marivate, M., & Philpott, R.H. (1981). The prediction of fetal growth retardation in twin pregnancy. *British Journal of Obstetrics and Gynaecology, 88,* 264–273.

Johnstone, F., & Inglis, L. (1974). Familial trends in low birth weight. *British Medical Journal, 3,* 659–661.

Kitchen, W.H., Ryan, M.M., Rickards, A., McDougall, A.B., Billson, F. A., Keir, E. H., & Naylor, F. D. (1980). A longitudinal study of very low-birthweight infants: IV. An overview of performance at eight years of age. *Developmental Medicine and Child Neurology, 22,* 172–188.

Long, P.A., Abell, D.A., & Beischer, N.A. (1980). Fetal growth retardation and preeclampsia. *British Journal of Obstetrics and Gynaecology, 87,* 13–16.

Lubchenco, L.O. (1970). Assessment of gestational age and development at birth. *Pediatric Clinics of North America, 17,* 125–145.

Lubchenco, L.O. (1976). *The high risk infant.* Philadelphia: W.B. Saunders.

Lubchenco, L.O., Delivoria-Papadopoulos, M., & Searls, D. (1972). Long-term follow-up studies of prematurely born infants: II. Influence of birth weight and gestational age on sequelae. *Journal of Pediatrics, 80,* 509–512.

McBride, W.G. (1961). Thalidomide and congenital abnormalities. *Lancet, 2,* 1358.

Meredith, H.V. (1970). Body weight at birth of viable human infants: A worldwide comparative treatise. *Human Biology, 42,* 217–264.

Naeye, R.L. (1965). Infants of diabetic mothers: A quantitative morphologic study. *Pediatrics, 35,* 980–988.

Narayanan, I., Dua, K., Gujral, V., Mehta, D.K., Matthew, M., & Prabhakar, A. (1982). A simple method for assessment of gestational age in newborn infants. *Pediatrics, 69,* 27–32.

Nickel, R.E., Bennett, F.C., & Lamson, F.N. (1982). School performance of children with birthweights of 1000 grams or less. *American Journal of Diseases of Children, 136,* 105–110.

Ounsted, M., & Ounsted, C. (1973). On fetal growth rate: Its variations and their consequences. *Clinics in Developmental Medicine* (No. 46). Philadelphia: J.B. Lippincott (Spastics International Medical Publications).

Pedersen, J. (1977). *The pregnant diabetic and her newborn.* Baltimore: Williams & Wilkins.

Prechtl, H.E.R., & Beintema, D. (1964). The neurological examination of the full term newborn infant. *Clinics in Developmental Medicine* (No. 12). Philadelphia: J.B. Lippincott (Spastics International Medicine Publications).

Robert, M.F., Neff, R.K., Hubbell, J.P., Taeusch, H.W., & Avery, M. E. (1976). Association between maternal diabetes and the respiratory distress syndrome in the newborn. *New England Journal of Medicine, 294,* 357–360.

Ruiz, M.P., LeFever, J.A., Hakanson, D.O., Clark, D.A., & Williams, M.L. (1981). Early development of infants of birth weight less than 1000 gms. with reference to mechanical ventilation in the newborn period. *Pediatrics, 68,* 330–335.

Sweet, A.Y. (1979). Classification of the low-birthweight infant. In M. Klaus & A. Fanaroff (Eds.), *Care of the high risk neonate* (pp. 63–93). Philadelphia: W.B. Saunders.

Thompson, J.E., Clark, D.A., Salisbury, B., & Cahill, J. (1981). Footprinting the newborn infant: Not cost effective. *Journal of Pediatrics, 99,* 797–798.

Townsend, C.W. (1894). The haemorrhagic disease of the newborn. *Archives of Pediatrics, 11,* 559–565.

Usher, R., McLean, F., & Scott, K. (1966). Judgement of fetal age: II. Clinical significance of gestational age and an objective method for its assessment. *Pediatric Clinics of North America, 13,* 835–848.

Warkany, J., Monroe, B., & Sutherland, B. (1961). Intrauterine growth retardation. *American Journal of Diseases of Children, 102,* 249–279.

5

Drugs

The use of drugs is a timely subject in contemporary society. Justifiably, there is widespread concern among patients and medical personnel alike over the potential harmful effects during pregnancy. These worries, in turn, extend to the newborn for possible jeopardies incurred by drugs given inadvertently to the infant by breast-feeding or administered intentionally in the course of specific medical treatment. While it is not possible here to present a comprehensive discussion on the influence of drugs, we believe that the topic does deserve special attention in terms of its impact on the fetus, therapies in the newborn, and adverse effects through breast-feeding.

INFLUENCE OF DRUGS

Prenatal Effects

During the early 1960s, obstetricians and pediatricians identified an alarming epidemic of congenital malformations associated with the use of the drug thalidomide. This substance was originally synthesized in Germany in 1956 and was prescribed for its sedative effects. Routine administration increased the incidence of newborn malformations of arms and legs and, on a world-wide basis, approximately 10,000 neonates suffered anomalies connected with maternal ingestion of the drug. This experience, which led to early disuse of the medication, kindled intense interest in the effects of such agents on the developing fetus and newborn.

Thalidomide is one of a few medications where the teratogenicity (capacity for inducing malformations) has been firmly established (Sucheston & Cannon, 1973). Methotrexate, a cancer chemotherapeutic agent, similarly is well recognized for its risk in causing abnormalities in the fetus. In both cases, appropriate decisions can be made to balance potential harm to the mother versus the neonate. Unfortunately, for most drugs the information is not as clear-cut (Abdul-Karim, 1981). Data regarding possible changes in metabolism as a result of pregnancy are lacking for a large majority of medications. In addition, other side effects, of as yet unknown magnitude, need to be considered, including fetal death, growth retardation, disturbances of fetal metabolism, disabilities that become manifest in later life, decreased longevity, predisposition toward malignancies, and drug dependence (Abdul-Karim & Clark, 1982).

There are many reasons why the risk of fetal toxicity of a drug cannot be readily estimated. Much of the work on drug effects has been done in animals, and no single animal species, including primates, can be used as an adequate substitute for the human. The impact of a drug varies widely with the amount given, as well as with the means and rate of administration. In general, the drug levels in the body are proportionate to the ability of that individual to metabolize and excrete the medication. If there is impairment in liver or kidney function, the effects may be more severe. For specific drugs such as thalidomide, the substance itself is not the critical factor, but rather a breakdown product produced in the liver. Since the metabolic pathway that alters thalidomide is found only in rabbits and in humans and varies from individual to individual, a particular constellation of conditions ultimately was responsible for the resulting impairments, a pregnant mother receiving the medication and metabolizing it to the lethal breakdown product at the critical embryonic developmental stage of four to six weeks gestation. Even in the susceptible mother, babies exposed to the breakdown product after six weeks into the pregnancy had no obvious developmental abnormalities (Aranda, Hales, & Gibbs, 1983). Other difficulties in determining degrees of toxicity include the less obvious delayed effects of the medication. Behavioral or mental disorders that, theoretically, could arise from an early drug insult are very difficult to quantitate. There is virtually no animal model that is adequate, and it is also impossible to apportion the contribution of various factors such as genetics, perinatal history, and environmental and social deprivation. A further concern is the prevalence of multiple drug use during pregnancy. If vitamins and minerals are included, nearly all pregnant women receive one or more medications. Even if these substances are excluded from categories of risk, the pregnant woman still consumes many other prescribed and nonprescribed drugs. These include antihistamines, analgesics (e.g., aspirin), antibiotics, tranquilizers, and antiemetics to prevent vomiting. Also, it is difficult to sort out the influence of alcohol, cigarettes, and illicit drugs such as marijuana (Doering & Steward, 1978; Hill, Craig, Chaney, Tennyson, & McCulley, 1977). For the interested reader, several current reviews examine the effects and potential risks of antibiotics, anticoagulants, and medications used to treat epilepsy (Cohlan, 1980; Hill, 1979).

In addition to medications that cause malformations, others are nonteratogenic but still may have marked negative consequences for the newborn. Analgesics may interfere with coagulation. Anesthetic agents may result in depressed respiration in the neonate. The antibiotic sulfonamides (sulfa drugs) may produce accelerated red blood cell destruction in certain susceptible newborns. Antihistamines may result in rapid heart rate, vomiting, and jitteriness, and diazepam (Valium), which crosses the placenta, may effect neonatal hypothermia, irregular breathing, prolonged hypotonia, and a poor sucking reflex (Abdul-Karim & Clark, 1982; Hill, 1979).

In summary, medications administered to the mother in the first trimester have greater potential for producing fetal malformation. Medications given to the mother in the third trimester may produce a nonteratogenic effect in the newborn, most commonly central nervous system depression with failure to adapt properly to extrauterine existence. The second most common effect is behavioral, including feeding difficulties, hypotonia, and withdrawal symptoms. There are relatively few data on subtle drug effects and, presently, no easy means by which these data can be obtained.

Drugs Used in the Neonate

In the past, drug dosage for newborns was extrapolated from available information on rates of metabolism in adults and older children. However, such research failed to account for the delayed elimination of many medications in the newborn. Studies over the last decade have gone a long way toward providing a much better understanding of the diverse factors that can affect absorption, distribution, and excretion of drugs. As a result, safe and effective guidelines for medications in the neonate now have been established.

The following discussion will afford the reader some appreciation of the delicate and subtle balance that needs to be maintained throughout the often long course of medical intervention with the high risk infant. For example, premature infants with restricted fat digestion and absorption generally are less able to absorb fat soluble vitamins (Bell, Brown, Milner, Sinclair, & Zipursky, 1979).

Once absorbed, drugs are distributed in the body. Some are primarily water soluble and others are basically fat soluble. Dosages in the infant vary, depending upon the nature of these medications. In the newborn with a total body water content greater than that of adults and older children, water soluble drugs have a greater volume of distribution and often have to be given in larger amounts for therapeutic benefit. By comparison, the fat content of babies, especially preterm children, is lower and, therefore, the lipid soluble drugs have a smaller volume of distribution, usually requiring reduced drug doses to maintain appropriate therapeutic levels (Marselli, 1976; Roberts, 1984).

Another set of concerns involves the liver and kidneys, major organs for the excretion of drugs. The newborn liver, for instance, has a restricted ability to metabolize medications such as Valium and phenobarbital, and thus the rate of elimination is prolonged. On the other hand, phenobarbital induces the production of hepatic (liver) enzymes that rapidly increase the clearance of the drug. Understandably, such anticonvulsants must be monitored carefully in order to avoid subtherapeutic levels. Renal (kidney) function gradually improves after birth and reaches adult values at approximately one year of age. Therefore, medications must be adjusted to lower doses to prevent toxic accumulation (Kauffman, 1981).

Basically, four major groups of drugs are used commonly in the newborn. These are antibiotics, cardiovascular medications, anticonvulsants, and medications to stimulate respiration. Each is used for a specific indication and only for a limited period of time, with careful attention to side effects and toxicities. If adverse symptoms do arise, the drug is stopped and alternatives prescribed. As is evident in the following discussion, all medications serve necessary purposes but may cause substantial impairment in the newborn.

Drugs classified as antibiotics are used to assist the immune defenses of the infant against bacteria (McCracken & Nelson, 1977; McIntosh, 1984). In general, they are divided into two groups; i.e., *bacteriostatic* and *bactericidal* medications. Penicillin and penicillin-like drugs such as ampicillin fall into the latter category and serve the function of disrupting the cell walls of susceptible bacteria. By contrast, bacteriostatic antibiotics limit bacterial multiplication. Each of these groups has identified toxicities. For instance, elevated blood levels of some of the bacteriostatic drugs may result in damage to the kidneys or the inner ear.

Cardiovascular medications are a heterogeneous group of drugs employed to control heart rate, to improve cardiac function, and to control blood pressure. To the layperson, the most familiar form is digitalis; the specific variety used in children is called *digoxin* (Wettrell & Andersson, 1977). In neonates, the drug is short-acting and is helpful in treating congestive heart failure and very rapid heart rates. Toxicities of elevated blood levels of digoxin include vomiting, poor feeding, and arrythmic heart patterns. Furthermore, for a number of the cardiovascular therapies, toxicities result in conditions that are the converse of problems being treated. For example, agents used for high blood pressure may produce an abnormally low blood pressure (Adelman, 1978), and medications for low pressure may have an opposite effect. Drugs prescribed to slow or speed the heart, in contrast, may create an opposing abnormal rhythm at toxic levels. For the most part, the majority of cardiovascular medications have no direct demonstrable impact on the central nervous system but indirectly may cause complications by restricting adequate quantities of blood to the brain (Roberts, 1984).

Pulmonary respiratory drugs are stimulants prescribed for apnea of prematurity, the two primary medications being theophyline and caffeine. Initially, these are given in small doses and then maintained while blood levels are monitored. Any beneficial effects of reducing the severity of apnea at prematurity are seen within a day or two of the start of the medication. Side effects of each medicine frequently are jitteriness and gastrointestinal symptoms, including abdominal distension and vomiting (Aranda, Grandin, & Sasyniuk, 1981).

Anticonvulsant drugs are given to control seizures in the newborn period. Because of its effectiveness and its rate of metabolism in the neonate, phenobarbital is the medication of choice for infants. Blood levels are readily achieved and therapeutic ranges are relatively easily titrated. The major detriment of acute phenobarbital excess is lethargy, sometimes associated with respiratory depression. Alternatively, Dilantin is a potent seizure medication; however, the oral absorption of this drug is incomplete and somewhat unreliable. Other medications such as paraldehyde and Valium, may be effective in the newborn, but rarely are indicated and may have significant pulmonary respiratory toxicities (Johnson & Freeman, 1981; Roberts, 1984; Volpe, 1977).

BREAST-FEEDING AND DRUGS

Human milk is uniquely suited to the nutritional needs of the full-term infant. However, within the past 20 years, numerous investigators have shown that maternal medications and environmental contaminants may pass into breast milk, resulting in harmful effects in the newborn. Thus, it is not always easy to decide whether or not a mother should nurse while she is taking a particular medication. Much of the information available regarding specific contraindications has been derived from individual case reports of affected infants. There are relatively few data on specific risks to a given infant when its mother is taking a particular drug.

Again, many factors determine the presence of a compound in a mother's milk. The maternal drug level, the time of administration of the medicine, the volume and time of feeding, and the breast milk composition all are important to the degree of absorption. Secondly, toxicities are influenced by the extent to which the drug is soluble, the size of the molecule, and its binding to maternal proteins, both within the mother's blood and her milk. The intestinal tract of the newborn, too, may limit the amount of drug that is metabolized (Anderson, 1979; Levy, Granit, & Laufer, 1977).

Few medications are absolutely incompatible with breast-feeding. Those that are include drugs that are tissue poisons used in cancer chemotherapy and in the treatment of goiters. Chloramphenicol (an antibiotic), even in small concentrations, may produce an exaggerated response wherein the bone marrow of the newborn fails to produce red cells. Isoniazid, a medication used to treat tuberculosis, is secreted into breast milk and may result in liver toxicity in the infant. A number of environmental chemicals, such as DDT, PCB, and PBB may be concentrated in the milk and therefore pass to the baby. Lithium, a successful therapeutic agent for manic-depressive illness, can cause high blood levels in the infant, altering the sensorium (Abdul-Karim & Clark, 1982; Giacoia & Catz, 1979). Other medications that need to be used for the health of the mother should be given only with caution. Most of these are sedatives, antipsychotic and anticonvulsive agents, which may produce decreased responsiveness in the newborn. In addition, aspirin in the breast milk can cause bleeding tendencies in the infant by interfering with platelet function, although this risk is minimized if the mother takes it just after nursing (Aranda, Hales, & Gibbs, 1983).

Last, there are several drugs thought to be very harmful in humans for which there are presently no data. Most of these are illicit substances such as heroin, cocaine, and LSD. Opiates are detectable in small quantities in breast milk, but it is unlikely that in these amounts they would produce addiction in the newborn (Abdul-Karim & Clark, 1982).

In general, drugs should be avoided during lactation. Medications frequently are prescribed for the nursing mother, with only marginal indications. If a maternal drug is necessary and there is a known hazard in the newborn, often a more innocuous therapy can be prescribed. Ultimately, the physician must consider every time a drug is recommended whether benefits to the mother outweigh dangers to the infant. Regrettably, problems arise inadvertently when mothers do not realize that they are pregnant. Also, while increasing numbers of elementary and high schools are instituting drug education programs, much more needs to be done with young people who are unaware of the devastating effects of drugs and alcohol.

REFERENCES

Abdul-Karim, R.W. (1981). *Drug usage during pregnancy.* Philadelphia: G.F. Stickley.

Abdul-Karim, R.W., & Clark, D.A. (1982). Drugs and pregnancy outcome. *Advances in Clinical Obstetrics and Gynecology, 1,* 75–94.

Adelman, R.D. (1978). Neonatal hypertension. *Pediatric Clinics of North America, 25,* 99–110.

Anderson, P.O. (1979). Drugs and breast-feeding. *Seminars in Perinatology, 3,* 271–276.

Aranda, J.V., Grandin, D., & Sasyniuk, B.I. (1981). Pharmacologic considerations in the therapy of neonatal apnea. *Pediatric Clinics of North America, 28,* 113–133.

Aranda, J.V., Hales, B.F., & Gibbs, J. (1983). Developmental pharmacology. In A.A. Fanaroff & R.J. Martin, (Eds.), *Neonatal-perinatal medicine* (pp. 150–173). St. Louis: C.V. Mosby.

Bell, E.F., Brown, E.J., Milner, R., Sinclair, J.C., & Zipursky, A. (1979). Vitamin E absorption in small premature infants. *Pediatrics, 63,* 830–832.

Cohlan, S.Q. (1980). Drugs and pregnancy. In B.K. Young (Ed.), *Perinatal medicine today* (pp. 77–96). New York: Alan R. Liss.

Doering, P.L., & Steward, R.B. (1978). The extent and character of drug consumption during pregnancy. *Journal of the American Medical Association, 239,* 843–846.

Giacoia, G.P., & Catz, C.S. (1979). Drugs and pollutants in breast milk. *Clinics in Perinatology, 6,* 181–196.

Hill, R. M. (1979). *Perinatal pharmacology: Maternal drug ingestion and fetal effect* (pp. 1–18). Evansville, IN: Mead Johnson.

Hill, R.M., Craig, J.P., Chaney, M.D., Tennyson, L.M., & McCulley, L.B. (1977). Utilization of over-the-counter drugs during pregnancy. *Clinics in Obstetrics and Gynecology, 20,* 381–393.

Johnson, M.V., & Freeman, J.M. (1981). Pharmacological advances in seizure control. *Pediatric Clinics of North America, 28,* 179–194.

Kauffman, R.E. (1981). The clinical interpretation and application of drug concentration data. *Pediatric Clinics of North America, 28,* 35–45.

Levy, M., Granit, L., & Laufer, N. (1977). Excretion of drugs in human milk. *New England Journal of Medicine, 297,* 789.

Marselli, P.L. (1976). Clinical pharmacokinetics in neonates. *Clinical Pharmacokinetics, 1,* 81–86.

McCracken, G.H., & Nelson, J.D. (1977). *Antimicrobial therapy for newborns: Practical application of pharmacology to clinical usage.* New York: Grune and Stratton.

McIntosh, K. (1984). Bacterial infections of the newborn. In M.E. Avery & H. W. Taeusch, (Eds.), *Diseases of the newborn* (5th ed.) (pp. 729–747). Philadelphia: W.B. Saunders.

Roberts, R.J. (1984). Principles of neonatal pharmacology. In M.E. Avery, & H.W. Taeusch, (Eds.), *Diseases of the newborn* (5th ed.) (pp. 950–968). Philadelphia: W.B. Saunders.

Sucheston, M.E., & Cannon, M.S. (Eds.). (1973). Thalidomide syndrome. *Congenital malformations* (pp. 233–239). Philadelphia: F.A. Davis.

Volpe, J.J. (1977). Neonatal seizures. *Clinics in Perinatology, 4,* 43–63.

Wettrell, G., & Andersson, K.E. (1977). Clinical pharmacokinetics of digoxin in infants. *Clinical Pharmacokinetics, 2,* 17–25.

6

Sensory, Motor, and Psychological Development of the High Risk Infant

With recent technological advances in neonatal care, the survival of preterm and other high risk infants has improved greatly. These changes, however, have raised many questions about the development of seriously ill newborns. Very low birthweight infants between 500 and 750 grams, who would have died five years ago, now are being treated throughout the course of multiple insults and prolonged hospital stays. While longitudinal studies are under way, it will be several years before the data are in and results for such children determined. One especially pressing issue with smaller and sicker populations is that we may be saving more lives of premature infants overall and that among certain groups of newborns the numbers of severely delayed youngsters may be on the rise; e.g., babies suffering chronic lung disease with long periods of mechanical ventilation. A second, related problem that has influenced our knowledge of the developmental status of the preterm and high risk infant is the gap between the effects of current treatments and data reported in our journals. Essentially, we always are dealing with a five to ten year delay. Last, although the technology of newborn care has changed decidedly for the better, practices still vary from center to center relative to numbers of deliveries at regional Level Three hospitals, the sophistication of transport systems, and capacities for involving parents. Such disparities make it difficult to generalize across facilities. With all considered, however, most recent studies indicate that the prognosis for newborns treated in intensive care nurseries is quite optimistic.

In this chapter we will look at the sensory, motor, language/cognitive, and psychosocial development of the high risk infant as reflected in research carried out over the past ten years. In particular, we will focus on improvements in neonatal outcome, conditions that still consistently tend to be associated with delayed or impaired development, and educational implications of our knowledge.

SENSORY AND PERCEPTUAL SKILLS

Vision

Any discussion of vision and eye diseases of the newborn needs to be based upon a firm grasp of the function of the eye, which resembles the operation of a camera. There is an outermost layer termed the *conjunctiva*. The most anterior portion of the eye, through which we see, is the *cornea*, and immediately behind this is a layer of fluid termed the *aqueous humor* that separates the cornea from the lens. The *pupil* or *lens* is surrounded by the iris, the colored portion of the eye, and also is attached to a circular muscle that modifies the shape of the pupil to allow for the focusing of light in the back of the eye. Behind the lens is another, more viscous fluid called the *vitreous humor*. Last, the posterior area of the eye consists of the *retina*, which has two major types of sensing cells, the *rods* for distinguishing light from dark and the intensity of light and the *cones* that are color sensitive. These cells, in turn, send impulses to the posterior portion of the brain, where they are received and interpreted. Therefore, much like a camera, light entering the eye is focused by the lens, its intensity is controlled by the aperture (pupil size), and subsequently it strikes the sensitive material of the retina. Any interference with the transmission of light from the anterior portion of the eye to the retina or with neuron transmission to the brain results in visual impairment. At birth, the newborn who has been living in a light deprived environment is capable of processing complex visual information. The term infant responds to objects that are bright, with high degrees of contrast, and can fix on and track an object over a limited distance. Although visual acuity is difficult to determine, recent evidence suggests that newborns are able to focus up to approximately ten inches. They respond to human faces, shiny objects, and preferentially to the color red. To date, this work has been done nearly exclusively with populations of full-term healthy infants and virtually no data are available on small premature neonates.

Despite our lack of research in some areas of newborn capability, vision and hearing losses associated with prematurity have been a longstanding concern of pediatricians and neonatologists. Some historical perspective helps us to comprehend the current problem. The term *retrolental fibroblasia*, for example, first was used to describe the clinical appearance of damaged eyes of preterm infants with a vascularized membrane or overgrowth of fibrous tissue behind the lens of the eyes. Later, it was discovered that this membrane was, in actuality, the totally detached retina (McCormick, 1977, p. 4). Terry was the first ophthalmologist to recognize the condition. So extensive were such insults that by 1945, 12 percent of all premature infants with birthweights of 1,300 grams or less suffered from the disease (McCormick, 1977). By 1950, oxygen had been identified tentatively as an offending agent and, in 1951, a new and more appropriate name was coined to refer to the condition—*retinopathy of prematurity* (ROP). Today, these labels commonly are heard and casually used by the general public, who still largely hold to the belief that ROP is caused exclusively by the administration of oxygen. In fact, the damage emerges with increased blood oxygen levels beyond the physiologic range, in combination with elevated blood carbon dioxide levels. At present, several trends have been illuminated; however, predictive patterns unfortunately are yet to be discovered. Many very immature babies receiving oxygen by mechanical ventilation fail to develop the disease, and other severely premature newborns who never have had supplemental oxygen manifest the problem. Despite conditions requiring intense ventilatory support, ROP rarely is seen in the full-term baby.

Classification systems have now been created in order to describe the abnormal development of the immature retina. While this portion of the eye in babies at full-term is nearly complete, infants born at approximately 28 weeks gestation (12 weeks premature) are still in the formative stages of their growth, with only 50 to 60 percent of the retina fully developed. In such instances, continued appropriate blood vessel growth and nutrients are essential to assure proper maturation. To the experienced ophthalmologist, the retinal lesion (*Stage 1*) first appears as a severe constriction of the peripheral vessels, a condition rarely seen before four to six weeks after birth. In the subsequent stage, there is evidence of dilation and tortuosity with peripheral *new* blood vessel ingrowth. This impairment then may progress to *Stage 2*, where hemorrhage in the retina occurs. By *Stage 3*, blood vessels proliferate into the vitreous humor and there may be localized detachment of the retina. Thus, any light that strikes the detached retinal tissue cannot be converted into an electrical impulse in the brain, and vision is lost. Complete detachment obviously results in total blindness. At any stage of the disease, there may be resolution of the abnormal vascular process; however, wherever scarring is present, this leads to a distortion of the retina.

In 1981, Phelps projected that approximately 2,100 infants would be affected annually by this troublesome disease. These numbers unfortunately have shown little or no improvement over the past three to four years. In 1983, Hunt and Deddish noted a marked increase in the incidence of strabismus in preterm infants, particularly among babies with birthweights of less than 1,500 grams. Including all grades of retinopathy of prematurity, the incidence is approximately 30 to 35 percent for the infant under 1,500 grams. About 1 percent of this very low birthweight population suffers blindness, and another 3 to 4 percent have significant visual impairment (myopia). Hunt and Deddish also concur with other physicians that the prevalence of ROP recently has grown with improved survival rates of infants with birthweights of less than 1,100 grams. These figures are quite disappointing in light of the high level of technology in intensive care nurseries in the United States.

Recent aggressive monitoring of the blood oxygen levels of newborns with respiratory distress has minimized the role of oxygen in the pathogenesis of this illness. Also, there are suggestive data, not yet fully confirmed, that early administration of supplemental vitamin E may decrease the severity of the disease, although the treatment is not yet reflected in any changes in the incidence of such insults. Moreover, once the disease is present, relatively little can be done. New experimental techniques in surgical or laser fixation of the retina show some promise. However, even with apparent resolution of the illness, these children are in the long-term more prone to retinal detachment and to amblyopia (roving eye).

Many other abnormalities of the eyes have been reported in the newborn period. Infants may be born with no eyes or abnormally small eyes. The iris may be missing, have little pigment (albinisim), or be not fully formed. The lens may be absent or dislocated. Tumors such as hemangiomas (an abnormal growth of blood vessels) may disrupt or distort the developing eye. Retinoblastoma, an aggressive tumor arising in the retina, is found in approximately 1 in 20,000 births and usually is first recognized beyond one year of age. Without prompt management in cases of retinoblastoma, including removal of the affected eye, the mortality rate is 100 percent.

Cataracts, opacities affecting the lens of the eye, occur in several forms. About one-third of the newborns with these anomalies have no apparent systemic illness. On the other hand, cataracts may be traumatic or associated with chromosomal disorders such as Trisomy 18 and Trisomy 13, and approximately 50 percent of the infants with rubella syndrome are thus affected. A number of metabolic diseases, most notably galactosemia, have been characterized by cataracts. Neonates with this latter disorder are able to digest the primary milk sugar lactose for its components, glucose and galactose. However, the body then is unable to convert galactose to utilizable glucose, and complexes of the excess carbohydrate deposit within the lens, impairing vision. Since cataracts interfere with light stimulation of the retina, they should be removed surgically as early as possible in order to promote appropriate development of the retina and, secondarily, the central nervous system.

Last, unlike adult *glaucoma*, increased anterior chamber (aqueous humor) pressure is rare in the newborn. Whenever the condition does emerge as a congenital problem, there frequently is excessive tearing and light sensitivity, and the increased pressure in the anterior chamber of the eye stretches the cornea and results in blurred vision. Glaucoma is associated with a number of syndromes; it is seen with transplacental infections, but also may arise as an isolated defect. Surgery can be performed to reestablish adequate drainage of the anterior chamber.

Visual perception, as distinguished from sensory skills, has been studied by looking at tracking, visual attentiveness, and visual preference during the neonatal period. While this area has been widely investigated with respect to the development of the term baby, less has been done relative to the premature infant. The following studies are illustrative of the types of work that have been conducted to the present time. In an evaluation of typical and neurologically impaired preterm and full-term babies, Morante, Dubowitz, Levene and Dubowitz (1982) found that the visual acuity in low risk preterm infants at 33 to 34 weeks was comparable to that of full-term infants on 60 percent of the tasks, but pattern preference capacities were less well developed. This research was based on the visual discrimination of four different pairs of patterns, and visual perception was assessed by abilities of neonates to distinguish black and white stripes of different widths. The study, in addition, analyzed the performance of neurologically impaired term and preterm infants at 36 and 40 weeks gestation and disclosed that, as might be expected, abnormal preterm infants showed poorer pattern preference abilities and were not as adept on visual acuity tasks. Further, compared with other preterm babies with known neurological impairment, premature infants with intraventricular hemorrhage revealed even greater problems with visual perception.

In a similar study, Dubowitz, Dubowitz, and Morante (1980) examined the visual performance of the preterm infant by using the tracking techniques of Brazelton's neonatal scale and the pattern preference and fixation strategies of Fantz. Following infants from 28 to 37 weeks gestation, the authors demonstrated visual discrimination only after 30 weeks, with maturity equal to that of the full-term infant by 34 weeks. Babies less than 30 weeks gestation, with one exception, showed no fixation or tracking. By 40 weeks gestation, such delays appeared to be resolved, with the few preterm infants included in the sample able to function as well as their full-term counterparts, and in some situations better.

These findings coincide closely with the results of other studies of visual perception. Ruff and her colleagues (Ruff, Lawson, Kurtzberg, McCarton-Daum, & Vaughan, 1982) compared the visual following skills of term and preterm infants at 40 weeks postconceptual age. In general, the preterm infants did not differ from the term infants. There were, however, delays evident among those premature babies who showed other early signs of atypical learning and responsiveness. Likewise, Paine, Pasquali, and Spegiorin (1983) investigated the visually directed prehension of 227 infants in relation to gestational age and intrauterine growth. They also found early developmental delays among preterm and small-for-date infants as compared with full-term infants. Yet, for the majority of premature babies, such problems no longer were apparent by four to five months chronological age. Finally, based on their research on the visual attending of term and preterm infants, Fantz and Fagan (1975) reported that responsiveness to size and number of pattern details differed markedly for both groups as a function of age during the first six months. Second, the development of the preterm infant varied clearly from that of the term infant by age from birth, but not by age from conception.

Overall, the results of the above studies seem to confirm our analyses (Ensher, Bobish, Michaels, Gardner, & Butler; in press) of visual attentiveness to patterns and faces and visual tracking of preterm infants. This research has been carried out during the standardization of a developmental scale and is based on six years of work with over 1,000 evaluations of full-term and preterm infants. We, too, have found delays in the early visual skills of premature infants who, by three to five months chronological age, begin to follow typical patterns of term babies. The very few exceptions to this large majority are those newborns in whom other impairments are evident within the first four to eight weeks after birth. Notably, while the number of infants at 26 to 28 weeks gestation was small, the visual performance of this group at six months chronological age has approached the normal limits of their healthier, full-term counterparts. The results are very encouraging.

Hearing

Unlike vision, the development of the auditory system may be stimulated by sounds reaching the fetus in utero. In normal hearing, sound waves strike the ear drum (tympanic membrane). This energy then is transmitted through three small middle ear bones, the hammer (malleus), anvil (incus), and stirrup (stapes). Vibrations along this bony chain lead to stimulation of a membrane that, in turn, transmits energy to stimulate small hairlike extensions of nerve cells in the inner ear. This energy subsequently travels, via electrical nerve impulses, into the temporal portion of the brain where sound is differentiated and interpreted. Recently, it has been found that full-term newborns are able to discriminate a wide range of frequencies and intensities of auditory stimulation. They also have capacities to habituate, accommodate, and block out repetitive loud stimuli.

The causes of hearing loss in early childhood are numerous, and the mere fact that an infant has been admitted to a special care nursery increases the likelihood of impairment from 1 chance in 1,000 to 1 chance in 50 (Poland, Wells, & Ferlauto, 1980, p. 31). More particularly, Bergstrom (1980) has reported that "recently developed intensive neonatal detection methods find that 1 in 600 to 800 otherwise normal neonates has a profound congenital hearing loss and that 1 in 60 of the infants in neonatal intensive care units has such a loss" (p. 23). Other statistics worth noting suggest that approximately 25 percent of the cases of hearing loss are of a genetic etiology, another 42 percent have a nongenetic origin, and about 33 percent are of unknown causes (Bergstrom, 1980). Most nongenetic hearing impairments occur either during the nine months of pregnancy or within the first six months after birth.

In 1972, a Joint Committee on Hearing Screening developed a high risk register for screening infants with potential hearing impairment. The committee cited five indicators including a family history of childhood deafness, maternal rubella during pregnancy, or other intrauterine factors such as cytomegalovirus infections, hyperbilirubinemia, maxillofacial anomalies, and a birthweight of 1,500 grams or less. To this list of criteria that have documented associations with early hearing loss, some authors (Poland, Wells, & Ferlauto, 1980) have added the problems of anoxia and acidosis. Today, asphyxia and intracranial hemorrhage seem to be the leading determinants of impaired hearing. While many special care nurseries still lack early screening procedures, educators and child development specialists are emphasizing the need for systematic identification programs. (Cox, Hack & Metz, 1981; Salamy, Mendelson, Tooley, & Chaplin, 1980). Every year pediatricians identify numbers of preschool children with significant disabilities, who have gone undetected. If associated with prematurity, usually such losses occur in the high frequency range, with total deafness being rare.

Over the past ten years, two methods of early identification have been used fairly effectively in intensive care units. The *Crib-O-Gram* records infant reflex responses to narrow-band noise. A motion-sensitive transducer is placed beneath the crib mattress, and the level of arousal of the newborn is scored. This process is repeated several times in order to obtain a reliable assessment. It is estimated that the possibility for false negatives is about 4 percent and false positives about 15 percent (Poland, Wells, & Ferlauto, 1980). The *brainstem-evoked response* is another tool that has been used with the preterm baby (Cox, Hack, & Metz, 1981; Salamy, Mendelson, Tooley, & Chaplin, 1980; Schulman-Galambos & Galambos, 1975). Reportedly, this is one of the most reliable and objective techniques available to assess neonatal auditory functioning. Until now, it has been very difficult to obtain evaluations of young children of less than two to three years. Brainstem-evoked response audiometry, one of the newly developed electrophysiological tests, measures sensory functioning in the subcortical portions of the auditory pathway and allows for objective measurement of peripheral and brainstem auditory acuity (Cox, Hack, & Metz, 1981, p. 53). Schulman-Galambos and Galambos (1975) have emphasized the important advantages of this method, indicating that responses are not subject to fatigue or habituation with continued stimulation and are not influenced by stages of sleep (p. 462). Thus, it is possible to elicit consistent responses in the newborn, an area of considerable difficulty in the past with the high risk infant. Commenting on the detection of hearing loss in infancy, Poland, Wells, and Ferlauto (1980) have noted:

> It is expensive and does require a person with considerable special training if the technique is to be used reliably. Brainstem-evoked potentials, however, are probably the single most powerful tool that can be used in evaluating the hearing acuity of the hard-to-test child. The method can be used effectively for estimating the learning threshold in babies younger than six months and is also the best method available for determining the symmetry of an already established hearing loss in the child who will not wear earphones. (p. 44)

NEUROMOTOR DEVELOPMENT

Neuromotor patterns of behavior constitute the most widely investigated area of development in the premature and high risk infant. There are obvious reasons for this level of interest. Neuromotor responses comprise the largest repertoire of early observable and well documented behavior of the newborn. Consequently, infant scales and evaluation instruments include a fairly extensive collection of items to assess this dimension of development. In addition, evaluation of this range of responses generally offers the educator, clinician, and pediatrician an immediate basis for determining the current status of the preterm infant in the special care nursery, equally applicable to the very low birthweight baby and to the larger neonate with other medical problems.

As we have indicated in earlier chapters, the increasing survival of smaller infants has generated much research, and this has been particularly focused on short- and long-term neuromotor behavior. It is well recognized that babies born at less than 30 weeks gestational age, weighing less than 1,500 grams, manifest delays. The critical questions then for us to answer are: For how long do these problems persist; are babies following just slower but typical patterns of development; when should we become concerned; and are there certain medical insults that seem to predispose babies toward lasting handicaps? These are the issues that we will attempt to address relative to the very low birthweight infant and the larger preterm baby.

Outcome for Infants Weighing 1,500 Grams or Less

Follow-up of the premature infant has shown that very low birthweight continues to be a critical factor relative to significant neuromotor problems (Bennett, Chandler, Robinson, & Sells, 1981; Nickel, Bennett, & Lamson, 1982; Saigal, Rosenbaum, Stoskopf, & Milner, 1982). To be sure, the prevalence of major handicapping conditions has declined dramatically within the past 20 years, dropping from an incidence of 50 to 70 percent in the 1960s to present figures of 5 to 15 percent (Vohr & Hack, 1982). Yet, among this group of the tiniest infants, certain insults tend to be more common and often are associated with poor prognoses. Most frequently cited are problems of perinatal asphyxia, bronchopulmonary dysplasia, and intracranial hemorrhage—events where the severity and occurrence are directly and inversely related to extremely low birthweight and gestational ages of less than 30 weeks (Hunt & Deddish, 1983; Vohr, Bell, & Oh, 1982; Vohr & Hack, 1982). Most recent studies on infants of 1,000 grams or less consistently bear out these patterns. For example, reporting on a study in Melbourne, Australia, Orgill, Astbury, Bajuk, & Yu (1982) confirmed that

> in a 4-year period the neonatal survival rate for 26 infants weighing 501–750 gm was 42% and for 81 infants weighing 750–1,000 gm it was 61%. All 59 surviving infants have been assessed at follow-up; 39 were at least 2 years old (corrected for prematurity) and data from the remaining 20 were derived from assessment at 1 year corrected age. Five children had cerebral palsy, 4 had multiple handicaps, 4 each had a sensory handicap, 2 had developmental delay, and 1 had a dilated right ventricle without clinical hydrocephalus. Twelve of the 16 children with defined handicaps were considered to have significant functional handicaps. Therefore, of the 107 infants in this series, 48 (45%) died, 12 (11%) survived with significant functional handicaps, and 47 (44%) were considered to be developing within the normal range. (p. 823)

Similarly, Hirata and several colleagues investigated the outcome of 60 infants with birthweights of 501 to 750 grams admitted to the special care nursery of Children's Hospital of San Francisco and the University of California. They noted that

> the infants who died had a significantly increased incidence of intracranial hemorrhage, and their mothers had a significantly decreased use of tocolytic drugs and betamethasone. Of the 24

survivors, two died after discharge, leaving 22 long-term survivors. Of these, 18 (82%) were observed until 20 months to 7 years of age . . . . Two infants (11%) had neurologic sequelae, 12 (67%) were completely normal, and four (22%) were functional and of borderline or below average intelligence. (Hirata et al., 1983, p. 741)

As with many of these studies, the numbers are very small upon which to base any firm developmental conclusions, and it is nearly impossible to predict, at the outset, the particular course that any given baby will take. For parents, educators, and physicians, most are "wait and see" situations.

In addition to the above findings correlating with gestational age and birthweight, poor head growth appears to be another characteristic closely correlated with less advantageous developmental outcome (Eckerman, Sturm, & Gross, 1985; Gross, Kosmetatos, Grimes, & Williams, 1976; Lipper, Lee, Gartner, & Grellong, 1981). In particular, some researchers now make a distinction between very low birthweight babies who are merely small-for-gestational age and infants who also show small head circumference and later delayed neurodevelopmental outcome. Lipper and her colleagues have pointed out that often "smaller birthweight in relation to gestational age" has been associated with a poor prognosis (p. 505). The authors suggest, however, that perhaps the key predictor is head growth retardation.

Based on numerous statistics and studies on preterm and high risk newborns, it would be reasonable to assume that the astute clinician should be able to identify those babies who will have long-term and/or severe neuromotor problems. Such is not the case initially, with the exception of the most extreme impairments. For this reason, babies falling within the realm of severe prematurity (1,500 grams or less) and having documented high risk medical complications need to be followed on a periodic schedule for evaluation of neuromuscular development. In line with this course of thinking, experts in the field have attempted to describe typical patterns of behavior of the preterm infant and significant ways in which these differ from the full-term baby (Carter & Campbell, 1975; Fox & Lewis, 1982; Illingsworth, 1983; Kurtzberg, Vaughan, & Daum, 1979; Palmer, Dubowitz, Verghote, & Dubowitz, 1982; Prechtl, Fargel, Weinmann, & Bakker, 1979; Saint-Anne Dargassies, 1966, 1972). Palmer, Dubowitz, Verghote, and Dubowitz (1982) have pointed out the difficulties associated with attempting to arrive at such generalizations.

The variability of response of preterm infants was apparent in this study and has been commented on by several authors (Parmelee, 1975; Prechtl et al., 1979; Touwen, 1980). Many studies comparing preterm and full-term infants have attempted to characterize the neurological development of the preterm infant as accelerated or retarded (Finnstrom, 1971; Parmelee, 1975; Kopp et al., 1975). Because of the specific problems of preterm birth and the large number of variables affecting the preterm infant we consider it impossible to characterize the preterm infant as more or less neurologically mature than the full-term but rather as different in several important respects. (p. 188)

Why differences persist among some infants of similar gestational age and not among others continues to be a puzzlement. Allowing for variation in length of hospitalization and the nature of medical insult, many severely low birthweight infants initially exhibit several of the following patterns of neuromotor development that seem to continue into the third and fourth months after birth. Asymmetries of the trunk, shoulders, arms, and legs often are seen with the head turned to the right or left side. Usually, there is a high incidence of random movement, characterized by a jerky and arrhythmic quality. Similarly, these babies startle frequently in response to any change in position or external stimulation such as the ringing of a bell or twirling of a red ring within visual range. The asymmetrical tonic neck reflex predominates, with the head turned toward the extended arm and leg, the opposite arm and leg observed in flexed positions. Often there is the presence of an exaggerated Moro response, with extension and abduction of the arms to 180 degrees. One frequently sees the infant, supine or prone, in a position of full flexion of the arms and legs so that two or more extremities are off the floor. When babies are moved through the passive range of motion, there often is a maximal resistance of both arms and legs, with only limited mobility possible. Immediate and full flexion in response to recoil of the arms and legs generally is present. In a prone position, infants are able to lift their heads only to a 5 to 10 degree angle, so as to clear the nose in turning from one side to the other. As might be expected, there is no evidence of weightbearing or weightshifting, as is seen within the first month or two in a full-term baby. In response to ventral suspension (the Landau reaction), these babies remain in a draped position, with the head, arms, and legs well below the horizontal plane. Hands in the prone position, as in supine, are held most of the time in a fisted position, with thumbs flexed inside the palm. When pulled to a sitting position, infants are unable to maintain the range and their heads passively hang backward. Moreover, in sitting with support these babies make no attempt to bring their heads to an upright position, even momentarily, but passively hang forward.

By the fourth month chronological age, most of the above behaviors are being integrated into more typical and directed activity, and the majority of the newborn responses are seen less than 50 percent of the time or not at all. Yet, other significant milestones remain delayed. For instance, purposeful reaching, hands-to-midline, and hand regard, which ordinarily appear in the fourth and fifth month, may not be readily evident until six or seven months chronological age, and the skill of independent sitting for indefinite periods of time may be established only as the baby approaches the ninth or tenth month (See Figures 6–1 and 6–2).

Within the full-term population, the typical range for the development of reciprocal crawling lies between 6 and 9 months of age. The severely premature baby may not reach this milestone until 10 to 12 months of age. Transitions from and into sitting usually are beginning to emerge for the full-term baby between 7 and 10 months. The preterm youngster still may have

Figure 6–1 Prone Position of an Eight-Month Old Baby Girl, Born at 28 Weeks Gestation

difficulty with falling at 12 months of age, and backward protective responses may not be available to these babies until a still later age of 13 to 14 months. There is much variability among full-term babies in the development of walking, some starting at an early 9 months, with others taking their first steps at 13 to 14 months. For the severely premature baby, it is not uncommon for independent walking to be delayed until sometime around 16 to 17 months. Once the skill is developed, on the other hand, many babies are as coordinated as their full-term counterparts.

Being able to determine problems that are surfacing requires an experienced and sensitive educator or child development specialist. For still unknown reasons, many severely premature babies between six and eight months seem to manifest higher tone than is normally found among full-term youngsters. Such symptoms naturally bear careful watching. Yet, if other skills appear to be evolving regularly within the time frame of adjusted age and without the presence of concerning or obviously atypical behavior, often these children perform well within the range of typical development by the time they reach their second birthday. Further, whether this group of children later will show signs of more subtle difficulties once in school is a subject of keen interest in a number of current follow-up programs (Astbury, Orgill, Bajuk, & Yu, 1985; Ford et al., 1985; Pape, Buncie, Ashby, & Fitzhardinge, 1978; Peacock & Hirata, 1981; Teberg et al., 1982).

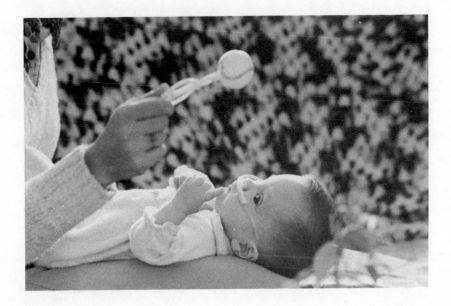

Figure 6–2 Reaching Activity of a Seven-Month Baby Boy Born at 32 Weeks Gestation, Weighing 1,240 Grams

Developmental Outcome of the Borderline to Moderately Premature Infant

The infant weighing more than 1,500 grams and/or delivered at 32 weeks gestational age responds very differently from the smaller and shorter-term newborn and, in general, carries a far better prognosis for a healthy developmental outcome (Bennett, Chandler, Robinson, & Sells, 1981; Drillien, 1972; Palmer, Dubowitz, Verghote, & Dubowitz, 1982; Saint-Anne Dargassies, 1966, 1979). The "evolutionary patterns to normalization" (Saint-Anne Dargassies, 1979) are more immediate, more direct, and less guarded. Usher (1981) has commented:

> The many physiologic handicaps of the infant born 1 to 2 months prematurely can be dealt with effectively using modern therapeutic techniques. Rare prematurity-related deaths are the result of specific disease entities, either respiratory distress syndrome or severe infection. (p. 230)

Initially, babies born at 32 weeks or later may have difficulty feeding as a result of a poor suck (Figure 6–3) and may manifest other problems of anemia, metabolic disorders, and hyperbilirubinemia, but usually they do not suffer the severe complications seen in the extremely premature infant. Thus, in terms of their neuromotor behavior, typically the quality and rate of development within the first 18 months is much less adversely affected than that of the extremely low birthweight infant (Figure 6–4). Notably, the baby delivered between 32 and 37 weeks gestation is not troubled with the excessive random and tremulous movement and extremes in flexion and extension tone that are markedly apparent with the severely premature baby. Major milestones such as reaching, transferring objects, rolling, sitting, crawling, and standing may be delayed, but often—without other significant complications—these lag by shorter periods of four to six weeks. Obviously, the earlier the gestational age and lower the birthweight, the greater the gap between the observed and the normal. In addition, typical newborn behaviors such as the Moro, asymmetrical tonic neck reflex, fisted hands, and the placing foot response may be a bit more exaggerated in the initial stages and persist by two to four weeks longer than what is seen in a typical population of full-term babies. However, in our experience, by six to eight months chronological age, premature youngsters delivered at 34 to 37 weeks gestation reveal no greater variation than do those infants born at 38 to 41 weeks. Saint-Anne Dargassies (1979) has suggested:

> The pediatrician who is responsible for the developmental follow-up of children born prematurely, must know that normalization is seldom rapid (only 16%), or belated (i.e., at the age of 3 years). Normalization occurs between age one and age two in 64% of cases. But the preliminary signs should be known; the child must begin to emerge from its pathological condition at about 6 months in some cases, more often at about 9 months. (p. 243)

MENTAL DEVELOPMENT

Data on the long-term effects of prematurity on mental development do not lead to clear-cut conclusions. Furthermore, accurate predictions about future development in the areas of language and cognition are difficult to make because they are a function of so many factors. Today, despite the overwhelming medical problems of preterm and high risk infants, profession-als who work with and follow such groups often agree that the home experiences after discharge, in most situations, far outweigh the impact of hospitalization and initial impairment. One needs only to spend time with families and young children in order to understand why this is the case. Some parents constantly talk to their babies, encouraging them to attend, to survey their environment, to vocalize, to explore, and to problem-solve. Within the first year to 18 months, these mothers, fathers, and siblings are well involved in looking at books, reading, and sampling the rich experiences of words and the symbolic world with their newest family member. Other parents are more subdued in their approach—sometimes stifling the young inquiring mind or not knowing how to help it grow toward fulfillment. In a lifetime, these differences make a difference, and the data on language and cognitive development exemplify this observation.

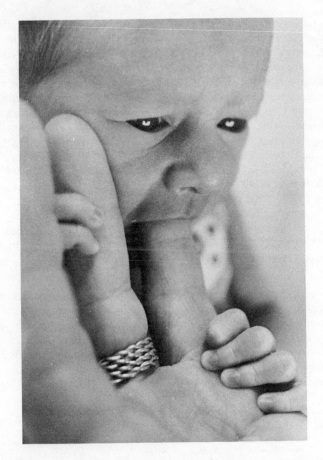

Figure 6–3 Sucking Response of a Premature Baby, 34 Weeks Gestational Age

Language of the High Risk Infant

In the normal course of events, infants very early develop a diverse repertoire of behavior for communicating with their immediate environment. They cry in order to make their needs known. Usually within the first month, they smile to familiar faces, particularly those of the primary caregiver, and to soft talking. They can be soothed and quieted by being held, walked, and patted, or by the voice of a significant family member, frequently the mother. Their vocalizations may increase or decrease in response to external stimulation such as a schematic or doll face or in response to soft talking of a familiar person. While attending to an object or person, sucking patterns may be interrupted for brief periods of high interest and scanning. Typically, they react by eye blinking, eye widening, or startle to the ringing of a bell, and by their fifth and sixth month are able to localize such sounds from side to side.

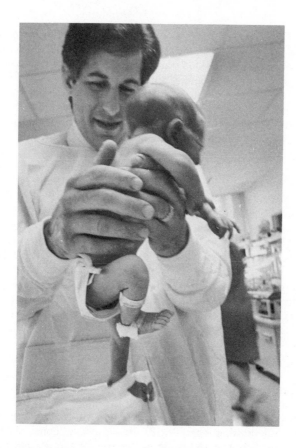

Figure 6–4 Placing Foot Response of a Moderately Premature Infant

Cooing and differentiated short vowel sounds begin to appear within the first two months, and later are followed by initial consonants such as "g," "b," "d," "p," "m" and "n." Vocal play with repetitive sounds increases throughout the first six months, although there is much variability in the amount and type of vocalization among babies. Some are spontaneously verbal when alone, while others respond more directly to personal interaction. By seven months, babies are beginning to make two-syllable repetitions such as "da-da" and "ma-ma," and as they reach 12 to 14 months they should be using one or two of these words in appropriate context. Often at this age, also, babies want to sit with a book to look at pictures, jabbering and pointing as they turn pages.

Between 15 and 24 months, typical development of speech and language accelerates. Toddlers begin to involve themselves in a great deal of symbolic play with dishes, dolls, and other favorite toys. They can follow one direction by 19 months, and often say "bye-bye" when putting on a hat and coat. Some children even have a gross sense of time at this age, and begin to look for

Mommy or Daddy at a certain hour of the day in day-care or babysitting situations. By 19 months too, they should have an expressive vocabulary of 20 to 35 words. They point to body parts on themselves and on a doll, and can name pictures or familiar people in a photograph. By 19 to 20 months, babies typically are beginning to put together two-word sentences such as "more juice" or "juice all gone." As he or she approaches the second birthday, the child should be able to select two or three objects correctly from a familiar series such as a ball, shoe, spoon, and cup.

Research on the development of speech and language in the very low birthweight baby seems to bear out consistent delays (Fitzhardinge, 1976; Fitzhardinge & Pape, 1981; Knobeloch & Kanoy, 1982; Parmelee, 1981; Rubin, Rosenblatt, & Salow, 1973; Siegel et al., 1982). Undoubtedly, problems stem from different factors at varying stages. Initially, the effects of prematurity and other medical-related variables such as the length of intubation or the occurrence of apnea and asphyxia may bear more heavily on the rate of development. It is common, for example, for the extremely low birthweight baby to evidence little discrimination of sounds beyond high-pitched crying up to the fourth or fifth month, and to experience frequent periods of irritability so that it is difficult to assess differentiation of the infant's needs. The social smile in response to the familiar voice of the mother may not appear until the fourth month, which proves somewhat frustrating to parents.

The maturation of single and two-syllable repetitive sounds—in the absence of obvious pathology—usually follows a typical pattern of development, but both the onset and frequency of vocalizations often are depressed. This situation appears to be especially prevalent with boys. Moreover, without the direct attention and intervention of the parents or primary caretakers in facilitating these skills, babies may continue to manifest significant delays up to or following 24 months of age. Perhaps the latter is one of the reasons that, in our experience, neuromotor lags typically seem less persistent over the first three years, even among the smallest preterm infants, in comparison with the emergence of communicative skills.

The point at which an early intervention program should be initiated is a difficult clinical judgment. Professionals should not overreact, and certainly if a toddler is beginning to use familiar words appropriately at about 20 months—though they might be few—there is justification for cautious expectations that the child will achieve a normal range of performance by three years. Such hopes probably are warranted if delays are uncomplicated by symptoms of excessive drooling, feeding difficulties, tongue thrusting, hearing impairment, or other obvious abnormalities. On the other hand, if a child appears frustrated in not being able to communicate, does not appear to understand what is said, and lacks a minimal level of comprehendable expressive language of a few words, assistance before age three is indicated. There are, of course, differing points of view on these issues, some professionals taking a conservative approach and waiting "for the best." We differ with this position because language is so crucial to later learning and school performance. If the cooperation of parents can be enlisted in the face of early developmental lags, frequently problems can be ameliorated or at least greatly minimized. We have seen dramatic changes in young children born at risk, given the benefit of formal programming and family support. In order to make reasonable judgments about these matters, we have followed this guide: To evaluate the quality and level of home interaction with the child and offer directed guidance to parents. If gains in orderly patterns of communication begin to surface, perhaps further intervention is not necessary. If this is not the outcome, however, we usually suggest that families seek additional assistance. The optimistic side of this discussion is that while many very low birthweight children at 24 months reveal serious speech and language delays, studies indicate that "for a good proportion of children, the speech defect is temporary and is not apparent by school age" (Fitzhardinge & Pape, 1981, p. 359).

Cognitive Skills of the Preterm Infant

By far, the overwhelming numbers of studies on cognitive development of preterm populations have been based on general evaluative measures such as the *Brazelton,* the *Denver,* the *Gesell Scales,* and the *Bayley Scales* (Commey & Fitzhardinge, 1979; Field et al., 1978; Pape, Buncie, Ashby & Fitzhardinge, 1978; Rothberg et al., 1981) or, at later ages, on standardized tests such as the *Stanford-Binet* or *Wechsler Intelligence Scale for Children* (Dunn et al., 1980; Stewart, Turcan, Rawlings & Reynolds, 1977). Efforts to analyze specific components of cognitive competence are beginning to emerge (Rose, 1981; Rose, Gottfried, & Bridger, 1979), and these investigations are sorely needed in order to gain a better understanding of the wide range of abilities that constitute infant cognition and their long-term implications. Hunt (1981), for example, has suggested the importance of examining "functional discontinuities" seen across ages among typical populations and looking at their relevance to children at risk for handicapping conditions (p. 350).

In the areas of language, motor, and sensory skills development we have discussed the fact that the preterm infant initially and sometimes thereafter may differ significantly from the full-term baby. Our experience has led us to similar conclusions with respect to cognitive functioning. During the first 12 months of life, infants ordinarily make remarkable progress toward knowledge of the world about them. This process starts with the objects and the people closest at hand and takes place through mutual and regular daily interaction. Babies by four months of age (Olson, 1981) learn to distinguish their parents and siblings from other individuals. They tend to smile more in response to the familiar face of their mother and can be soothed by her comforting when all other attempts prove unsuccessful. Within the first two to three months, infants are especially attracted to bright contrasting colors such as yellow and red, and gaze for sustained periods of two minutes or more at novel patterns and schematic faces. By four months, babies are beginning to reach for rattles and other attractive objects held at midline and may make gross attempts to grasp. However, the skill of following objects held and dropped or looking for partially covered playthings will not be acquired until the fifth or sixth month. Typically, babies become more socially interactive at this stage—laughing and gaining enjoyment from games such as "Peek-A-Boo." They become increasingly aware that objects can be manipulated, transferred, and banged, and do so with spoons, blocks, rattles, and other materials small enough to hold. Also at this age, they begin to search for objects that are partially covered and understand that toys can be pulled toward them with an attached string.

The period from 6 to 12 months is a stage of rapid physical growth, active exploration, and the appearance of several critical milestones. By 7 to 8 months babies are capable of responding to hand clapping, with imitation or on verbal command to "Pat-A-Cake." They can be taught to throw a ball reciprocally and are interested in more independent hand-to-mouth activities such as self-feeding with Cheerios and other table foods. Two months later, the skill of object permanence is well established. Babies search for toys dropped or completely hidden. They play with containers, taking out and putting objects into canisters or dishes. Some children at 9 to 10 months are beginning to develop a basic cause-effect relationship with pop-up and musical toys. Finally, the child near his or her first birthday begins to evidence simple problem-solving skills. For example, if Cheerios are hidden behind a plexiglass screen, the 12-month-old is able to figure out how to retrieve these attractive bits successfully. Likewise, if raisins are placed in toy milk cartons, the child typically attempts several strategies by probing, dumping, or pouring. Basic round block recognition too is seen at this age, although for some youngsters this skill is not evident consistently until 13 to 14 months.

From 15 months to the end of the second year, the development of language and cognition are closely intertwined. These abilities, coupled with an emerging social autonomy, dramatically change the ways in which the now skillful toddler relates to the immediate environment. The child makes his or her needs known by telling someone. Most youngsters at this age have a desire to feed and dress themselves and like to play dress-up. They know their own names well and those of friends with whom they associate daily. They can demonstrate the utility of many common objects such as a toothbrush, comb, tissues, or play dishes. They have a basic comprehension of how puzzles fit together and can place two or three pieces successfully. Light switches and other gadgets are a great fascination and wonderful source of amusement. With amazing dexterity, the 20- to 24-month-old understands how to get to what is wanted, whether or not an object is within apparent grasp. In part, this last capacity is a result of new opportunities opened to the toddler, as he or she develops a firmer grasp of cause and effect relationships. The world has now become a place where the child can act independently in the environment without repeated demonstration.

The preterm infant and toddler present a very different pattern of behavior, especially if the child has sustained an insult of prematurity of less than 30 weeks gestation. Wide variations from the norm are seen in initial capacities of the severely low birthweight baby to attend to any stimuli, which frequently prove disruptive. The simple task of focusing on a directed object or face for a period of one to five seconds may elude the infant within the first two to three months of life. As a result, it is not surprising that such a child does not actively survey the immediate surroundings, as the full-term baby does at six to eight weeks. Likewise, any attempts to search for partially or fully covered objects or efforts to attain pull-toys by means-ends are considerably delayed by several weeks. Some of this disparity may be a function of physical limitations; however, even among babies of 34 to 35 weeks gestation who are sitting at six months, the lack of awareness of objects once out of sight is not uncommon.

How young children manipulate objects tells us a great deal about their cognitive level of understanding. Instead of interest in playing with two or more toys, banging, or attention to detail—milestones usually evident between five and six months—the preterm baby may be content beyond the eighth to ninth month only to hold and mouth. Play with cars, books, and problem-solving toys such as pop-up and musical boxes similarly may be reduced to mouthing and no schemes of purposeful behavior. These observations often accompany delays in symbolic language development. Finally, the constructive placing and stacking of nesting or concentric cups, discriminating of round block shapes, and scribbling with crayons typically appears four to six months later in the severely premature toddler than is expected of the 11- to 12-month-old. Taking the place of more refined skills, banging is the primary source of play and satisfaction.

The cognitive development of the premature baby raises a number of critical issues and remains to date a fertile area for study. In the total pattern of growth and later school performance, delays of six to eight weeks may not be significant enough to upset the timetable of acquisition and organization on a permanent basis. Within the normal population, full-term children without insult vary widely in skill development, and we should expect no less among babies at risk. On the other hand, we know that the severely preterm infant is unable to focus on and interact in a sustained and coherent way with persons and surroundings, often for extended periods of several weeks or months. As long as this condition persists, milestones such as object permanence, cause and effect relationships, problem-solving, and other dimensions of cognition will continue to be delayed.

Much research is now being done (see Chapter 15) in medical centers across the country to determine the effect and appropriateness of early stimulation in intensive care nurseries. Perhaps studies of this nature in the future will shed light on the development of cognition in the premature baby by gestational age, birthweight, and varying medical conditions. Thus far, the results are sparse and inconclusive. Presently in question are such issues as the substance of effective intervention, optimal gestational ages and duration for stimulation, the impact on various aspects of infant behavior, and effective ways of intervening with parents of high risk babies in home settings. As we begin to answer a few of these questions prospectively, some of the concerns and enigmas about cognitive development in the high risk infant—in terms of why some children do well and others do not—can be examined more closely. Certainly, we know from the substantial body of research on "disadvantaged" youngsters that a large part of that puzzle will involve parents, the nature of their interactions, and the ways that they offer appropriate stimulation for their babies.

PSYCHOSOCIAL DEVELOPMENT

Within the first few hours of life, babies begin to interact with persons of their immediate environment in ways that are mutually satisfying to infant and caregiver. The subsequent unfolding of these relationships thus becomes the building block of infant social cognition and later personality development. The crying newborn can be brought to a quiet state by one or both parents almost instantly. In response to a familiar voice, the infant typically reacts with a noticeable change in activity level, some babies becoming very still and others showing a dramatic increase in their rate of movement. By three to six months, the alert and socially attentive baby plays and skillfully anticipates parental interaction by smiling, cooing, and expressing obvious excitement. Sometime between the sixth and ninth month, babies clearly become distressed by the presence of a nonfamily member or by separation of any kind from mother or father. The degree to which such stranger anxiety persists is variable in duration and intensity and frequently is difficult to cope with; yet it is a healthy sign in the overall schema of psychosocial development and usually diminishes by the beginning of the tenth month.

The period extending from the first to the second year is marked by a growing awareness of the child's affective world and social autonomy. The youngster, for instance, may cry in reaction to verbal reprimands or expressions of anger directed toward others or self. Playful teasing with games of "Hide and Seek" is common; and some time after the end of the first year, the child learns well the meaning and use of the word "No." Usually, toddlers look to their mothers and fathers for reinforcement and censoring of their behavior. Indeed, before "the act," many children seem fully aware that their behavior may draw a negative response, and appear *intent* on testing the limits of their freedom. In a similarly positive fashion, the 21-month-old may reveal innermost desires of acquisition by responding "Thank you" before claiming an attractive object. Finally, the 24-month-old understands and uses, at will, the giving or withholding of affection with people, as well as with toy dolls and favorite animals. The toddler is able to delay immediate wants, if only for a few seconds, and with some verbal reassurance comprehends the fact that the parent will return before long. The child now is prepared to interact more fully with peers and adults and to meet the world with an unbridled curiosity and quest for learning that brings new knowledge and insight day by day. As a whole, the development of motor abilities, language, cognition, and psychosocial skills has superbly equipped the young child to accomplish this task.

For the high risk infant, the course of psychosocial development is as variable as within full-term populations. Yet as we have discussed elsewhere in this text, distinguishing trends repeatedly are cited in the literature. These discussions primarily have centered around the earliest patterns of social awareness and interaction of the preterm and high risk infant upon hospital discharge. In this context, irritability and inattentiveness have commonly characterized behaviors of the premature newborn. Moreover, certain medical centers have carried out follow-up programs and have found that the incidence of child abuse reportedly is quite high. Speculations are that such events may be closely linked to problems of attachment and extraordinary child care demands in the first weeks at home. Examination of existing studies and our own research, however, seem to bear out the conclusion that, given time, these initial disruptions in parent-child interactions and differences in psychosocial development are resolved with no long-term negative effects.

To be sure, as we have visited and worked with families, we too have observed stress and sometimes discord between parent and child. It is not uncommon for these difficulties to persist throughout the first five months. On the other hand, our evaluations of a comparison group of full-term babies has rendered us a firm basis for a second judgment, and by no means is this latter group free from problems of frequent irritability which may occur from six to a dozen times per day or continuously from afternoon into the evening hours. More importantly, for both high risk and full-term babies, these troublesome events usually have passed by six months of age. Continuation of such behavior beyond this point may—although not always—suggest other underlying medical or environmental contributors that require closer scrutiny.

Socially and emotionally, as we might expect, we do see delays in the preterm baby that parallel the milestones in other areas of development. Thus, for example, we have frequently observed strong anxiety reactions among babies of less than 32 weeks gestation becoming manifest around the ninth and tenth month or later and lasting until the first birthday. Again, in our two-year follow-up program with selected babies we have not seen persistent negative effects. What *is* certain are the pervasive hazards of some environments and the acceleration of these difficulties throughout the preschool years. Further, as our research has taken us into homes over the past five years, we have been truly impressed with the consistency of psychosocial patterns within families among siblings who were not even the target of our study. Our work has led us to believe that the progress of social and emotional growth is much more inherent in the child's home setting than contingent on the early prematurity or the nature of the particular medical insult. The togetherness of families, the affection expressed toward children, the consistency of behavioral management, the use of positive rather than negative discipline, and the appropriateness of parental expectations are a few of the factors—irrespective of income or educational level—that influence psychosocial development in negative or positive directions.

In summary, there is a wealth of information currently available on the sensory, motor, and psychological development of the preterm and high risk infant. At present, the data suggest a higher incidence of developmental problems among infants weighing less than 1,500 grams or born at less than 32 weeks gestation. However, noteworthy among these studies are prevalent exceptions and the candid acknowledgement of researchers that it is very difficult at the earliest stages of treatment and recovery to make unqualified predictions. There are few medical conditions where the type and severity of developmental difficulty can be specified unquestionably. In the process of growing, environment and experience make the critical difference—especially for the young born early. In part, there is a lasting frustration that parents share because they want guarantees. There are none. On the other hand, families consistently are revealing great hope for the tiniest and most critical newborns. Should impairments surface with some of these children of the 1980s, we have the secure knowledge that such variations are not as limiting as they might have been, given a loving home with parents who care and know how to spend quality time with their babies.

REFERENCES

Astbury, J., Orgill, A.A., Bajuk, B., & Yu, V.Y.H. (1985). Neonatal and neurodevelopmental significance of behaviour in very low birthweight children. *Early Human Development, 11,* 113–121.

Bennett, F.C., Chandler, L.S., Robinson, N.M., & Sells, C.J. (1981). Spastic diplegia in premature infants. *American Journal of Diseases of Children, 135,* 732–737.

Bergstrom, L. (1980). Causes of severe hearing loss in early childhood. *Pediatric Annals, 9,* 23–30.

Carter, R.E., & Campbell, S.K. (1975). Early neuromuscular development of the premature infant. *Physical Therapy, 55,* 1332–1341.

Commey, J.O.O., & Fitzhardinge, P.M. (1979). Handicap in the preterm small-for-gestational age infant. *The Journal of Pediatrics, 94,* 779–786.

Cox, C., Hack, M., & Metz, D. (1981). Brainstem-evoked response audiometry: Normative data from the preterm infant. *Audiology, 20,* 53–64.

Drillien, C.M. (1972). Aetiology and outcome in low birthweight infants. *Developmental Medicine and Child Neurology, 14,* 563–574.

Dubowitz, L.M.S., Dubowitz, V., & Morante, A. (1980). Visual function in the newborn: A study of preterm and full-term infants. *Brain & Development, 2,* 15–27.

Dunn, H.G., Crichton, J.U., Grunau, R.V.E., McBurney, A.K., McCormick, A.G., Robertson, A.M., & Schulzer, M. (1980). Neurological, psychological and educational sequelae of low birthweight. *Brain & Development, 2,* 57–67.

Eckerman, C.O., Sturm, L.A., & Gross, S.J. (1985). Developmental courses for very-low-birthweight infants differing in early head growth. *Developmental Psychology, 21,* 813–827.

Ensher, G.L., Bobish, T.P., Michaels, C.A., Gardner, E.F., & Butler, K.G. (in press). *Syracuse scales of infant development and home observation.* Syracuse, NY: Syracuse University Press.

Fantz, R.L., & Fagan, J.F., III (1975). Visual attention to size and number of pattern details by term and preterm infants during the first six months. *Child Development, 46,* 3–18.

Field, T., Hallock, N., Ting, G., Dempsey, J., Dabiri, C., & Shuman, H.H. (1978). A first-year follow-up of high risk infants: Formulating a cumulative risk index. *Child Development, 49,* 119–131.

Fitzhardinge, P.M. (1976). Follow-up studies on the low birthweight infant. *Clinics in Perinatology, 3,* 503–515.

Fitzhardinge, P.M., & Pape, K.E., (1981). Follow-up studies of the high risk newborn. In G.B. Avery (Ed.), *Neonatology: Pathophysiology and management of the newborn* (2nd ed.) (pp. 350–367). Philadelphia: J.B. Lippincott.

Ford, G.W., Rickards, A.L., Kitchen, W.H., Lissenden, J.V., Keith, C.G., & Ryan, M.M. (1985). Handicaps and health problems in 2-year old children of birthweight 500 to 1500 g. *Australian Paediatric Journal, 21,* 15–22.

Fox, N., & Lewis, M. (1982). Motor asymmetrics in preterm infants: Effects of prematurity and illness. *Developmental Psychobiology, 15,* 19–23.

Gross, S.J., Kosmetatos, N., Grimes, C.T., & Williams, M.L. (1976). Newborn head size and neurological status: Predictor of growth and development of low birthweight infants. *American Journal of Diseases of Children, 132,* 753–756.

Hirata, T., Epcar, J.T., Walsh, A., Mednick, J., Harris, M., McGinnis, M.S., Sehring, S., & Papedo, G. (1983). Survival and outcome of infants 501 to 750 gm.: A six-year experience. *Journal of Pediatrics, 102,* 741–748.

Hunt, C.E., & Deddish, R.B. (1983). Medical and neurobehavioral outcome in low birthweight infants. *Birth Defects, 19,* 103–110.

Hunt, J.V. (1981). Predicting intellectual disorders in childhood for preterm infants with birthweights below 1501 gm. In S.L. Friedman & M. Sigman (Eds.), *Preterm birth and psychological development* (pp. 329–351). New York: Academic Press.

Illingsworth, R.S. (1983). *The development of the infant and young child: Normal and abnormal* (8th ed.). New York: Churchill Livingstone.

Knobeloch, C., & Kanoy, R.C. (1982). Hearing and language development in high risk and normal infants. *Applied Research in Mental Retardation, 3,* 293–301.

Kurtzberg, D., Vaughan, H.G., Jr., & Daum, C. (1979). Neurobehavioral performance of low birthweight infants at 40 weeks conceptual age: Comparison with normal full-term infants. *Developmental Medicine and Child Neurology, 21,* 590–607.

Lipper, E., Lee, K., Gartner, L.M., & Grellong, B. (1981). Determinants of neurobehavioral outcome in low birthweight infants. *Pediatrics, 67,* 502–505.

McCormick, A. (1977). Retinopathy of prematurity. *Current Problems in Pediatrics, 7,* 3–28.

Morante, A., Dubowitz, L.M.S., Levene, M., & Dubowitz, V. (1982). The development of visual function in normal and neurologically abnormal preterm and full-term infants. *Developmental Medicine and Child Neurology, 24,* 771–784.

Nickel, R.E., Bennett, F.C., & Lamson, F.N. (1982). School performance of children with birth weights of 1,000 gm. or less. *American Journal of Diseases of Children, 136,* 105–110.

Olson, G.M. (1981). The recognition of specific persons. In M.E. Lamb & L.R. Sherrod (Eds.), *Infant social cognition: Empirical and theoretical considerations* (pp. 37–59). Hillsdale, NJ: Lawrence Erlbaum Associates.

Orgill, A.A., Astbury, J., Bajuk, B., & Yu, V.Y. (1982). Early development of infants 1000 g. or less at birth. *Archives of Disease in Childhood, 57,* 823–829.

Paine, P.A., Pasquali, L., & Spegiorin, C. (1983). Appearance of visually directed prehension related to gestational age and intrauterine growth. *The Journal of Genetic Psychology, 142,* 53–60.

Palmer, P.G., Dubowitz, L. M. S., Verghote, M., & Dubowitz, V. (1982). Neurological and neurobehavioural differences between preterm infants at term and full-term newborn infants. *Neuropediatrics, 13,* 183–189.

Pape, K.E., Buncie, R.J., Ashby, S., & Fitzhardinge, P.M. (1978). The status at two years of low birthweight infants born in 1974 with birth weights of less than 1,001 gm. *The Journal of Pediatrics, 92,* 253–260.

Parmelee, A.H., Jr. (1981). Auditory function and neurological maturation in preterm infants. In S.L. Friedman & M. Sigman (Eds.), *Preterm birth and psychological development* (pp. 127–155). New York: Academic Press.

Peacock, W.G., & Hirata, T. (1981). Outcome in low birthweight infants (750 to 1500 grams): A report on 164 cases managed at Children's Hospital, San Francisco, California. *American Journal of Obstetrics and Gynecology, 140,* 165–173.

Phelps, D.L. (1981). Retinopathy of prematurity: An estimate of vision loss in the United States—1979. *Pediatrics, 67,* 924–925.

Poland, R.M., Wells, D.H., & Ferlauto, J.J. (1980). Methods for detecting hearing impairment in infancy. *Pediatric Annals, 9,* 31–44.

Prechtl, H.F.R., Fargel, J.W., Weinmann, H.M., & Bakker, H.H. (1979). *Developmental Medicine and Child Neurology, 21,* 3–27.

Rose, S.A. (1981). Lags in the cognitive competence of prematurely born infants. In S.L. Friedman & M. Sigman (Eds.), *Preterm birth and psychological development* (pp. 255–269). New York: Academic Press.

Rose, S.A., Gottfried, A.W., & Bridger, W.H. (1979). Effects of haptic cues on visual recognition memory in full term and preterm infants. *Infant Behavior and Development, 2,* 55–67.

Rothberg, A.D., Maisels, M.J., Bagnato, S., Murphy, J., Gifford, K., & McKinley, K., Palmer, E.A., & Vannucci, R.C. (1981). Outcome for survivors of mechanical ventilation weighing less than 1,250 gm. at birth. *The Journal of Pediatrics, 98,* 106–111.

Rubin, R.A., Rosenblatt, C., & Salow, B. (1973). Psychological and educational sequelae of prematurity. *Pediatrics, 52,* 352–363.

Ruff, H.A., Lawson, K.R., Kurtzberg, D., McCarton-Daum, C., & Vaughan, H.G., Jr. (1982). Visual following of moving objects by full-term and preterm infants. *Journal of Pediatric Psychology, 7,* 375–386.

Saigal, S., Rosenbaum, P., Stoskopf, B., & Milner, R. (1982). Follow-up of infants 501 to 1,500 gm. birth weight delivered to residents of a geographically defined region with perinatal intensive care facilities. *The Journal of Pediatrics, 100,* 606–613.

Saint-Anne Dargassies, S. (1966). Neurological maturation of the premature infant of 28 to 41 weeks gestational age. In F. Falkner (Ed.), *Human Development* (pp. 306–325). Philadelphia: W.B. Saunders.

Saint-Anne Dargassies, S. (1972). Neurodevelopmental symptoms during the first year of life. *Developmental Medicine and Child Neurology, 14,* 235–246.

Saint-Anne Dargassies, S. (1979). Normality and normalization as seen in a long-term neurological follow-up of 286 truly premature infants. *Neuropadiatric, 10,* 227–244.

Salamy, A., Mendelson, T., Tooley, W.H., & Chaplin, E.R. (1980). Differential development of brainstem potentials in healthy and high risk infants. *Science, 210,* 553–555.

Schulman-Galambos, C., & Galambos, R. (1975). Brainstem auditory-evoked responses in premature infants. *Journal of Speech & Hearing Research, 18,* 456–465.

Siegel, L.S., Saigal, S., Rosenbaum, P., Morton, R.A., Young, A., Berenbaum, S., & Stoskopf, B. (1982). Predictors of development in preterm and full-term infants: A model for detecting the at risk. *Journal of Pediatric Psychology, 7,* 135–148.

Stewart, A.L., Turcan, D.M., Rawlings, G., & Reynolds, E.O.R. (1977). Prognosis for infants weighing 1,000 gm. or less at birth. *Archives of Disease in Childhood, 52,* 97–104.

Teberg, A.J., Wu, P.Y.K., Hodgman, J.E., Mieh, C., Garfinkle, J., Azen, S., & Wingert, W. A. (1982). Infants with birth weight under 1500 gm.: Physical, neurological, and developmental outcome. *Critical Care Medicine, 10,* 10–14.

Usher, R.H. (1981). The special problems of the premature infant. In G. B. Avery (Ed.), *Neonatology: Pathophysiology and management of the newborn* (2nd ed.) (pp. 230–261). Philadelphia: J.B. Lippincott.

Vohr, B.R., Bell, E.F., & Oh, W. (1982). Infants with bronchopulmonary dysplasia: Growth pattern and neurologic and developmental outcome. *American Journal of Diseases of Children, 136,* 443–447.

Vohr, B.R., & Hack, M. (1982). Developmental follow-up of low birthweight infants. *Pediatric Clinics of North America, 29,* 1441–1454.

Part II

CLINICAL ISSUES: INSULT, IDENTIFICATION, ASSESSMENT, AND PROGNOSIS

Modern techniques for identifying and monitoring medical conditions of the high risk infant have played a major role in the primary prevention of developmental problems. Today, there is an increasingly healthy awareness among physicians, therapists, and educators that while many neonates suffer severe complications that place them at risk for central nervous system damage, such events do not inevitably lead to negative outcome. Newer, more thorough strategies for developmental screening and assessment, as well as long-term follow-up of the tiniest infants into the adolescent years, are positive steps that begin to answer some important questions about prognosis and most vulnerable populations. At present, there is ample justification for cautious optimism.

7

Neurology of the Newborn

Potential damage to the developing central nervous system is a substantial concern with the ever-increasing survival of the very low birthweight infant. The overwhelming numbers of articles and chapters now appearing in the literature make it clear that many investigators are exploring the subtleties of the neurologic examination with the hope of predicting the neonate's developmental outcome. Since Chapter 6 has covered the sensory and psychological development of the high risk infant, this discussion will concentrate primarily on the medical neurologic examination and on insults to the central nervous system.

NORMAL NEUROLOGIC EXAMINATION

The neurologic examination is limited in the newborn. The neonate obviously can offer no verbal input as to the subjective function of the central nervous system, and the integration of sensory processes such as vision and hearing are also not possible. Consequently, the evaluation must be restricted to the general neurologic condition or level of alertness of the child, an examination of the specific cranial nerves, neuromotor development, and primary neonatal reflexes. As previously mentioned, portions of the neurologic examination of the newborn are included in the assessment of gestational age.

Behavior

Responsiveness or level of alertness varies considerably with gestational age and with recent life experiences. Infants beyond 28 weeks have distinct periods of wakefulness and can be stimulated to open their eyes and be alert. Beyond 30 weeks gestation, responsiveness and periods of wakefulness increase and occur without external stimulation. By 36 weeks, the infant is attentive to both visual and auditory stimuli. In general, the extent of alertness is crucial to evaluating the quality of the newborn's responses, especially the reflex reactions (Saint-Anne Dargassies, 1974).

More specific dimensions of the newborn neurologic examination entail an assessment of behavior controlled by the 12 cranial nerves that are connected directly to the brain, without involvement of the spinal cord. The *first cranial nerve*, the olfactory neuron, is responsible for the sense of smell. Since relatively little work has been done on olfactory perception in the newborn to date, this sense is usually not tested as part of the routine examination (Sarnat, 1978). The *second cranial nerve* is the primary neuron of visual function. It connects with the retina of the eye and transmits electrical impulses to the posterior portion of the brain. Appropriate function is evidenced by the fact that full-term newborns typically have a preference for the color red, patterns with heavy contrast, and facial features (Fantz, 1963; Fantz & Miranda, 1975; Peeples & Teller, 1975). The *third, fourth*, and *sixth cranial nerves* govern muscle movements of the eyes. Since most newborns do not fix on and track an object, changes in the baby's head position must suffice for adequate evaluation of movement. The *fifth cranial nerve* controls sensation to the face and also provides motor input for the facial muscles. The *seventh cranial nerve* directs the muscles of the face and is important to symmetry and expression that can be best estimated by facial movement in a crying state. The *eighth cranial nerve* connects the inner ear to the brain and directs the sense of hearing. Recent sophisticated auditory testing has demonstrated that most healthy newborns can discriminate sounds by intensity and pitch (Bower, 1974). Sucking, swallowing, and tongue function are integrated through the *fifth, seventh, ninth, tenth*, and *twelfth cranial nerves*. The sucking, rooting, and gag reflexes are most often tested to ensure that the functions of these neurons are appropriate. The *eleventh cranial nerve* provides motor tone to the major muscles of flexion in the neck (sternocleidomastoid muscle). However, these responses are difficult to test in the newborn with any degree of reliability.

Muscle Tone and Reflexes

The motor system can be examined by observing the resting posture of the infant and various spontaneous movements, along with several newborn reflexes that can be elicited specifically. General observation alone reveals that there is a progression of development of muscle tone by gestational age. Although lower extremity flexor tone is well established by 32 weeks, it is not until approximately 36 weeks that upper extremity flexor tone is apparent (Menkes, 1984). When manipulating the baby, muscle tone can be assessed subjectively by the resistance of the extremities, trunk, and head with changes in position. In various items of the Dubowitz examination, recoil of the extremities, foot and head flexion, head lag, back extension, and ventral suspension are all useful in estimating muscle tone (Dubowitz, Dubowitz, & Goldberg, 1970).

In addition to more generalized observations, several reflexes including the Moro, tonic neck, walking, and grasp responses have been found helpful in the neurologic evaluation. Perhaps most familiar among these is the Moro reflex, which should be integrated and disappear by four months of age. Typically in the newborn, several reactions initially are present. In sequence, these consist of arms and legs abducting (drawing away) from the body, followed by an adduction of the arms, as if the new baby were hugging, and once the arms return to the body, the infant typically cries. Characteristically, asymmetric responses are seen in children with birth injuries or in those with fractures of the clavicle or upper arm bones (Parmalee, 1964). The tonic neck reflex, a second commonly observed response in the newborn, often is referred to as the reflex of the fencing position. As the infant's head is turned to one side, the arm and leg are flexed. If the baby's head then is passively turned in the opposite direction, a reversal of position of the extremities usually occurs. The reflex tends to disappear in the first few months although some of the responses may persist for several years. If the reaction continues and is easy to elicit, this behavior usually is a sign of serious central nervous system pathology (Paine & Oppe, 1966). The walking or placing and stepping responses can be elicited if the infant is held so that the sole of one foot touches a smooth surface. Reciprocal flexion and extension occurs, simulating walking. This reflex usually dissipates by approximately four weeks. The palmar and plantar reflexes are prompted readily by placing a finger in the palm or on the sole of the baby's foot. In response, the fingers or toes curl around the finger. This reflex occurs naturally in the infant, indicates normal neurologic development, and generally disappears at approximately three months (Hogan & Milligan, 1971). Numerous other neonatal reflexes have been described; yet most of these seem to have limited value in the evaluation of the newborn.

MAJOR NEUROLOGIC INSULTS

Birth Asphyxia

As we have discussed previously, birth asphyxia is a major metabolic insult to the brain. There may be insufficient oxygen and elevated tissue acid concentrations, along with poor blood flow. Any portion of the brain may be affected with birth asphyxia, and there may be many causes (Brann & Dykes, 1977). However, infants born prematurely are more prone to have intraventricular hemorrhage than are full-term neonates. The staging of damage to the brain can be estimated fairly accurately. Obviously, the more prolonged the asphyxia, the more severe the manifestations. In such instances, there may be a progressive loss of consciousness, proceeding to coma. Muscle tone may range from normal through hypotonia to flaccidity. The primitive reflexes as well as the complex reflexes, may be absent. In the more severe states, respiratory effort may be diminished or absent and the heart rate may slow.

Management of the asphyxiated infant includes adequate correction of blood pressure, blood oxygen, and carbon dioxide. The baby should receive temperature support, and blood glucose should be maintained. Those infants that develop seizures obviously should be treated with an anticonvulsant.

Surprisingly, the developmental outcome of newborns with birth asphyxia is not as grim as might be expected. Neonates are particularly resistant to the effects of acidosis and hypoxia (DeSouza & Richards, 1978). In absolute numbers, more children with moderate to severe cerebral palsy have been full-term babies than low birthweight or premature. It is therefore critical that all infants suffering birth asphyxia be carefully and serially evaluated for developmental disability (Volpe, 1981b).

Intracranial Hemorrhage

Intracranial hemorrhage refers to bleeding in or around the brain tissue. Until the mid–1970s when new technology became available, such insult seldom was recognized. Now as a result of sonography and computerized axial tomography (CAT) scanning, new information has come to light indicating that as many as 50 percent of small premature infants have some variety of intracranial hemorrhage. The ultimate prognosis, of course, depends on the type and severity of the bleeding (Pape & Wigglesworth, 1979).

Basically, there are two major subgroups within this primary category of insult; i.e., bleeding into the brain tissue and hemorrhage in and around the membranes that cover the surface of the brain (Volpe, 1981a). Accordingly, *subdural hemorrhage* is a collection of blood that results from tearing of the vessels between the brain and the dura (the outermost thick membrane covering the surface of the brain). This is a traumatic lesion found predominantly in the full-term baby. Subsequently, the collection of blood results in the compression of the brain, which may progress to a compromise of the controlling centers of respiration in the brain stem. Once properly identified, the only available therapy is surgical decompression and removal of the clot. By comparison, *subarachnoid hemorrhage* refers to bleeding beneath the arachnoid membrane, which is the center layer covering the brain. This condition is most commonly seen with asphxia, and minor degrees may be completely asymptomatic. On the other hand, blood on the surface of the brain may result in local irritation and seizures. At an extreme, damage may be massive and acute, resulting in death. Unfortunately, since the blood generally extends over the surface of the brain without a localization that would be amenable to surgical removal, no specific therapy is presently available.

The second major subgroup involves bleeding into the brain tissue (parenchymal hemorrhage), which also includes the ventricular system deep inside the brain. By way of explanation, the ventricles comprise an interconnected system of reservoirs that contain spinal fluid. The two lateral cavities, one on each side of the brain, are slitlike and extend from the anterior to the posterior portion of the brain. Cerebrospinal fluid first is produced from collections of blood vessels (choroid plexus) found within the lateral ventricles, and then circulates to a midline third cavity. From this point, the fluid flows through the Aqueduct of Sylvius, a very small canal less than the size of a pencil lead (even in an adult), to the fourth ventricle. Subsequently, the cerebral spinal fluid passes from deep inside the brain tissue through these sequential connections, over the surface of the spinal cord and brain, and finally is reabsorbed by another complex of blood vessels located between the two halves of the brain. This continuous process of circulation results in an exchange of spinal fluid approximately four to five times per day.

With the above description in mind, let us now proceed to a discussion of some specific examples of the parenchymal hemorrhage. A *periventricular* insult refers to bleeding adjacent to the lateral ventricles inside the brain where spinal fluid is produced (Grade 1 hemorrhage). Such bleeding then may break into the ventricular system, developing into Grade 2. If an enlargement of the ventricular system occurs following this damage, a Grade 3 hemorrhage may result. As blood increases the viscosity of the spinal fluid from its normal watery consistency, such a condition can lead to an obstruction of the Aqueduct of Sylvius, either mechanically or by secondary inflammation, by the blood in the cerebral spinal fluid. If this blockage is not relieved, *hydrocephalus*, an enlargement of the ventricular system, then occurs. Most serious is bleeding into the brain tissue itself, which is considered to be a Grade 4 (Hambleton & Wigglesworth, 1976).

In terms of the clinical presentations or manifestations of the insults that we have described, these of course vary a great deal with the amount and location of the bleeding. Recent studies have reported evidence of periventricular hemorrhage to be as high as 50 percent among infants with birthweights of 1,500 grams or less, and frequently Grade 1 damage is "silent." However, as the severity of hemorrhage increases, the presentation tends to be more catastrophic and may involve rapid deterioration progressing to coma, hypoventilation, and respiratory arrest within a very short period of time (Goldstein, 1979). Occasionally in conjunction with intra- or periventricular bleeding, newborns suffer *intracerebellar* hemorrhaging, which is thought to be primarily a result of asphyxia. Often these insults are fatal or, among the survivors, are manifested in uniformly poor developmental prognoses.

In conclusion, it is important to make a distinction here that bleeding alone is not the primary issue, since the blood is broken down and reabsorbed into the body within a week after the hemorrhage. Local changes in blood flow to the brain and the initial pressure effects in the brain are much more critical. Since brain tissue has a high metabolic rate that must be maintained by adequate provision of nutrients through appropriate blood flow, those portions of the organ that are deprived may be irreversibly damaged (Hill & Volpe, 1981).

Seizures

Seizures resulting from abnormal transmission of electrical impulses in the brain are a fairly frequent occurrence in the neonatal period (Craig, 1960; Volpe, 1977a). Tremors similarly may result from minor metabolic disturbances or from catastrophic central nervous system insult. In essence, abnormal electrical activity that may emerge from any portion of the brain is communicated much more rapidly in the newborn than in later life. In part, this condition arises because of an incomplete myelinization (myelin is the fatty material that surrounds the mature nerves and functions as an insulator to electrical impulses). The manifestations thus are seen in the form of abnormal motor movements or seizures.

In general, neonatal seizures have been described according to four varieties of clinical presentation. The first of these, *subtle seizures*, are the most frequent and often are overlooked. They may include staring, lip smacking, sucking, a swimming/rowing motion of the arms and legs, apnea, rapid heart rate, or a change in blood pressure. They may last only a few seconds and may not be harmful to the infant. Their relationship to long-term disability has not been clearly established. The *generalized tonic seizure* includes extension of the trunk, neck, and extremities and has been likened to decerebrate posturing of older individuals. This condition is found primarily in the premature infant who has suffered periventricular or intraventricular hemorrhage. In such cases, it is difficult to distinguish whether the seizures are merely a manifestation of the insult or whether they themselves add to the poor developmental outcome of those babies with the most serious impairment (Freeman, 1970; Volpe, 1973, 1977b, 1981b).

In contrast with the subtle and generalized tonic varieties, the *multifocal clonic seizure* is found more commonly in full-term infants, usually characterized as repetitive jerking movements of one or two limbs; the seizure then may migrate to other portions of the body. The etiology is thought to be primarily birth asphyxia, and the electroencephalogram (EEG) in these infants commonly shows abnormal repetitive spikes. Finally, *myoclonic seizures* are seen in both the premature and full-term infant and are symptomatic single or repeated synchronous jerks of the entire body or limbs, with an EEG pattern that often is abnormal. Although numerous causes of seizure disorders have been identified, in the latter case no specific etiology has been readily ascertained.

Virtually any insult to the brain may precipitate seizures. The single and most frequent origin is an asphyxial event, where brain tissue is compromised as a result of inadequate oxygen, excess acids, and changes in blood flow—with or without overt evidence of hemorrhage (DeSouza & Richards, 1978). In the first week of life, metabolic disturbances such as hypoglycemia, hypocalcemia (low blood calcium), hypomagnesemia (low blood magnesium), and elevated blood phosphate commonly have been cited as responsible agents. Usually, these problems are very amenable to therapy that corrects the metabolic disorder, and it is rare that long-term developmental disabilities emerge. However, other metabolic disturbances may have a much more serious and lasting prognosis. For example, seizures associated with a deposition of abnormal compounds in the brain tissue seldom have a favorable outcome. Included in this group are genetic defects resulting in inborn errors such as amino acid disorders (e.g., phenylketonuria) and lipid (fat) metabolism disturbances (e.g. Tay-Sachs disease) (Volpe, 1981b).

Another large group of problems well known for altering or disrupting brain development are perinatal infections such as toxoplasmosis, herpes, and rubella. Whether or not seizures are a prominent part of the presentation, developmental outcome is poor. Likewise, malformations of the central nervous system that include seizures rarely are associated with typical patterns of growth and maturation.

One very old problem, witnessed with increased frequency, is the delivery of infants born to mothers taking drugs (Zelson, Rubio, & Wasserman, 1971). Babies addicted to narcotics or barbiturates frequently have withdrawal symptoms including a high-pitched cry, high muscle tone, increased activity, vomiting, respiratory distress, and loose stools. Overt seizures may be seen in approximately three percent of these newborns. The judicious use of medication can control the symptomatology and thus allow for gradual drug withdrawal. The little information that is available on the long-term development of these infants, including social and environmental factors, unfortunately precludes any firm prognosis (Wilson, McCleary, Kean, & Baxter, 1979).

The diagnosis of seizure disorders is accomplished by careful observation in conjunction with an electroencephalogram. While an abnormal EEG in the full-term infant more likely portends future developmental difficulties, serious sequelae at the same time may be seen in newborns with seizures but a normal EEG. Thus, it is no surprise that studies generally have failed to demonstrate the prognostic value of the EEG in premature infants (Volpe, 1981b). In any event, the treatment of seizures must be tailored to the specific etiology. In most cases, for example, correction of metabolic disturbances leads to prompt resolution of the pathology. Today, the primary medication for neonatal seizures is phenobarbital, which is not only safe and effective but relatively inexpensive. Less frequently, additional medications such as diphenylhydantoin (Dilantin) or diazepam (Valium) may be necessary. Although most infants are treated for a minimum of six months, the duration of therapy again is dependent upon the severity of seizures, their recurrence, and periodic reevaluation (Menkes, 1984).

Apnea

As many as 50 percent of all premature newborns experience irregular respiratory patterns, often characterized by 10 to 15-second pauses in the breathing cycle (periodic breathing). Subsequently, if these hesitations last more than 20 seconds or are accompanied by a slowing of the heart rate or cyanosis (low blood oxygen), they are termed *apnea* (Parmalee, Stern, & Harris, 1972).

Two centers in the brain stem control the respiratory cycle. These receive cues for inspiration and expiration not only from a constant monitoring of their oxygen and carbon dioxide levels, but also from stretch and pressure receptors within the lungs and chest wall. In the immature central nervous system, the peripheral signals may not be of sufficient magnitude, or the central receptor may not be adequately sensitive to coordinate the respiratory cycle. Damage to the central nervous system—hemorrhagic, metabolic, or infectious—also may affect the centers for control of respiration.

The treatment of apnea is relatively straightforward. If a specific metabolic basis can be determined, the problem may be resolved easily with its correction. On the other hand, if no specific etiology can be ascertained, tactile stimulation may be effective. In the event that these therapies alone are inadequate, several medications including theophylline and caffeine may be helpful in reducing the frequency of apnea. With a few infants, none of the foregoing modes of treatment is sufficient; such children may require intense intervention with intubation and mechanical ventilation (Aranda, Sitar, & Parsons, 1976; Kazenko & Paala, 1973).

In retrospect, apnea per se has not been responsible for poor developmental outcome and, with time and maturation of the central nervous system, the frequency of apnea generally decreases. Those infants who do not seem to respond to therapy or mature with development require continuous monitoring, even after discharge to home.

Developmental Abnormalities

The mature central nervous system is a highly complex and organized network. At approximately three to four weeks gestation, the neural tube is formed. On the back portion of the embryo, crests of nerve tissues on each side of an open nervous system meet and then progressively close, by fusion, in both cephalic (toward the head) and rostral (toward the tail) directions. Failure of this tube to join is referred to as a *neural tube defect*. These problems are the most common developmental abnormalities of the central nervous system, and include anomalies such as *anencephaly, meningomyelocele* (See Figure 7–1), and *spina bifida occulta* (Volpe & Koenigsberger, 1981). The first of these disorders occurs where the *anterior* neural tube fails to grow closed, and any or all of the brain may have failed to develop. Most babies with this type of defect die within the first several days of life.

Failure of the *posterior* neural tube to join may be manifested as a myeloschisis (open nerve tissue) or as a meningomyelocele, which usually is a sac composed of the meninges (the outer membranes of the brain), with nerve tissues (myelo-) in the lower portion of the back. This impairment frequently is associated with a developmental defect of the lower portion of the brain where there is an obstruction to the flow of spinal fluid through the Aqueduct of Sylvius or a blockage to its path from the lower portion of the brain. In over 90 percent of the children with meningomyelocele, hydrocephalus (See Figure 7–2) is present (Lemire, Loeser, Leech, & Alvord, 1975). Although intellect often is spared, profound motor effects can be seen, depending on the level of the spinal malformation. Most lesions of the lower back have accompanying loss of nerve function to the legs, resulting in paralysis and a lack of innervation to the sphincters for bladder and bowel control. Early repair of the meningomyelocele minimizes the risk of the infection in the central nervous system. However, progressive hydrocephalus (enlargement of the ventricles in the central nervous system) does lead to abnormal head growth and nearly always requires a shunting procedure where such fluid can be drained through a catheter from the head, underneath the skin, and into the abdominal cavity in order to relieve the pressure (Volpe, 1977b).

Spina bifida occulta differs from meningomyelocele in that the lesion consists of a defective bony formation of the lower back, without exposed nerve or meningeal tissue. The impairment is very common and may be seen in as much as 25 percent of the population. Although the majority have no associated disability, deficits such as a gait disturbance, muscle weakness, or problems with bowel and bladder sphincter control may occur in early childhood (Volpe & Koenigsberger, 1981).

Many other developmental abnormalities of the central nervous system have been described. These include disordered growth of brain tissue with

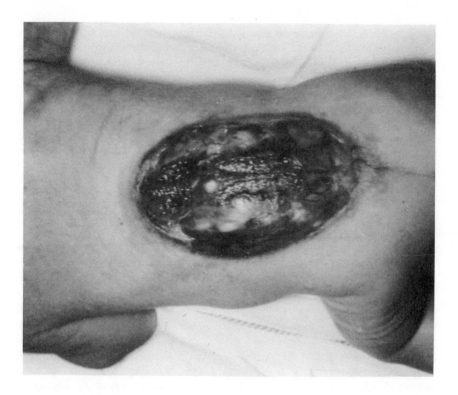

Figure 7-1 Infant with Meningoshisis

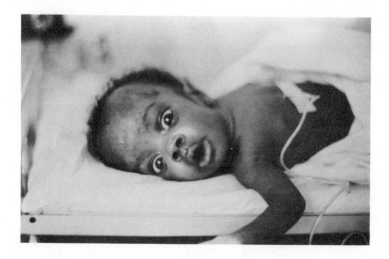

Figure 7-2 Newborn with Early Hydrocephalus, Manifesting the Setting Sun Sign

both the nerve cells themselves or with the supportive tissue, the glial cells. Abnormal growth of blood vessels too may occur. Depending on the portion of brain affected, these children may have increased or decreased muscle tone, abnormal posturing, seizures, and persistence of the primitive reflexes. As might be expected, the developmental outcome is usually poor.

In summary, the brain is a marvelously complex organ that integrates all of our body functions. Unfortunately, relatively little can be done once serious damage has taken place. The magnitude of the insult, its duration, and the location within the brain all determine the severity of residual dysfunction. In these instances, careful sequential evaluation is necessary to determine the degree of developmental disability and to intervene so as to minimize the impact of such impairments.

REFERENCES

Aranda, J.V., Sitar, D.S., & Parsons, W.D. (1976). Pharmacokinetic aspects of theophylline in premature newborns. *New England Journal of Medicine, 295,* 413–416.

Brann, A.W., & Dykes, F.D. (1977). The effects of intrauterine asphyxia on the full-term neonate. *Clinical Perinatology, 4,* 149–161.

Bower, T.G.R. (1974). Development of infant behavior. *British Medical Bulletin, 30,* 175–178.

Craig, W.S. (1960). Convulsive movements occurring during the first 10 days of life. *Archives of Diseases in Childhood, 35,* 336–344.

DeSouza, S.W., & Richards, B. (1978). Neurological sequelae in newborn babies after perinatal asphyxia. *Archives of Diseases in Childhood, 53,* 564–569.

Dubowitz, L.M.S., Dubowitz, V., & Goldberg, C. (1970). Clinical assessment of gestational age in the newborn infant. *Journal of Pediatrics, 77,* 1–10.

Fantz, R.L. (1963). Pattern vision in newborn infants. *Science, 140,* 296–297.

Fantz, R.L., & Miranda, S.B. (1975). Newborn infant attention to form of contour. *Child Development, 46,* 228.

Freeman, J.M. (1970). Neonatal seizures—diagnosis and management. *Journal of Pediatrics, 77,* 701–708.

Goldstein, G.W. (1979). Pathogenesis of brain edema and hemorrhage: Role of the brain capillary. *Pediatrics, 64,* 357–360.

Hambleton, G., & Wigglesworth, J.S. (1976). Origin of intraventricular hemorrhage in the preterm infant. *Archives of Diseases in Childhood, 51,* 651–659.

Hill, A., & Volpe, J.J. (1981). Seizures, hypoxic-ischemic brain injury and intraventricular hemorrhage in the newborn. *Annals of Neurology, 10,* 109–121.

Hogan, G.R., & Milligan, J.E. (1971). The plantar reflex of the newborn. *New England Journal of Medicine, 285,* 502–503.

Kazenko, J.A., & Paala, J. (1973). Apneic attacks in the newborn treated with aminothylline. *Archives of Diseases in Childhood, 48,* 406.

Lemire, R.J., Loeser, J.D., Leech, R.W., & Alvord, E.C., Jr. (1975). *Normal and abnormal development of the human nervous system.* Hagerstown, MD: Harper & Row.

Menkes, J.H. (1984). Neurologic evaluation of the newborn infant. In M.E. Avery & H.W. Taeusch (Eds.), *Diseases of the Newborn* (pp. 652–661). Philadelphia: W.B. Saunders.

Paine, R.S., & Oppe, T.E. (1966). Neurological examination of children. *Clinical Developmental Medicine, 20,* 1–8.

Pape, K.E., & Wigglesworth, J.S. (1979). *Haemorrhage, ischemia and the perinatal brain.* Philadelphia: J.B. Lippincott.

Parmalee, A.H., Jr. (1964). A critical evaluation of the Moro reflex. *Pediatrics, 33,* 773–788.

Parmalee, A.H., Stern, E., & Harris, M.A. (1972). Maturation of respiration in prematures and young infants. *Neuropaediatric, 3,* 294–304.

Peeples, D.R., & Teller, D.Y. (1975). Color vision and brightness discrimination in two-month old human infants. *Science, 189,* 1103.

Saint-Anne Dargassies, S. (1974). Confrontation neurologique des concepts: Maturation et development, chez le jeune. *Revue Neuropsychiate Infant, 22,* 227–235.

Sarnat, H.B. (1978). Olfactory reflexes in the newborn infant. *Journal of Pediatrics, 92,* 624–626.

Volpe, J.J. (1973). Neonatal seizures. *New England Journal of Medicine, 289,* 413–416.

Volpe, J.J. (1977b). Normal and abnormal human brain development. *Clinics in Perinatology, 4,* 3–30.

Volpe, J.J. (1977a). Neonatal seizures. *Clinics in Perinatology, 4,* 43–63.

Volpe, J.J. (1981a). Neonatal intraventricular hemorrhage. *New England Journal of Medicine, 304,* 886–891.

Volpe, J.J. (1981b). *Neurology of the newborn.* Philadelphia: W. B. Saunders.

Volpe, J.J., & Koenigsberger, R. (1981). Neurologic disorders. In G.B. Avery, (Ed.), *Neonatology: Pathophysiology and management of the newborn* (2nd ed.) (pp. 910–963). Philadelphia: J.B. Lippincott.

Wilson, G.S., McCleary, R., Kean, J., & Baxter, J.C. (1979). The development of preschool children of heroin-addicted mothers: A controlled study. *Pediatrics, 63,* 135–141.

Zelson, C., Rubio, E., & Wasserman, E. (1971). Neonatal narcotic addiction: 10 year observation. *Pediatrics, 48,* 178–189.

8

Jaundice

Jaundice is the most prevalent problem that pediatricians confront in dealing with newborns, full-term as well as premature. The familiar yellowish tone results from a deposition of *bilirubin* in the skin when the blood level of this chemical becomes elevated in the neonate. Though it is not common knowledge, all babies are jaundiced and, of course, the condition is more difficult to detect in dark-skinned infants. The perception of yellow also varies from observer to observer, and thus children with mild elevations of serum bilirubin may not appear overtly affected. Basically, the major concern in the newborn period is not the evidence of discolored skin but the elevated blood level of bilirubin, which clearly has been associated with developmental problems in infants. Since jaundice is a treatable, yet main, insult to *all* high risk babies, it is important that educational and clinical staff have a basic understanding of this condition.

UNDERSTANDING JAUNDICE

Production

Bilirubin is a pigmented complex that results from the breakdown of the hemoglobin pigment in red blood cells (hemoglobin in the red blood cell aids in oxygen transport from the lungs to the body tissues). As an old red blood cell is destroyed, hemoglobin is released and catabolized (See Figure 8-1). The *globin* portion of hemoglobin is a protein that can be metabolized to amino acids that, in turn, are reused in the body chemistry. The iron within the *heme* ring also can be recycled into new red blood cell production. When the heme ring is broken, the enzyme *oxygenase* converts the heme to a harmless substance called *biliverdin*. This compound subsequently is altered by another enzyme, reductase, to bilirubin. Both of these enzymatic steps occur in the *reticuloendothelial system*, which includes the liver and spleen. Approximately 75 percent of the total amount of bilirubin is formed by the breakdown of old red blood cells, but as much as 15 percent may result from ineffective red cell formation within the bone marrow. There are also several other heme-containing substances in the body that must be degraded in a similar fashion (Gartner & Arias, 1969).

Transport

Leaving the reticuloendothelial system, bilirubin is transported in the plasma, tightly joined to albumin (a circulating protein). As the solubility of unbound bilirubin is extremely low, this link to albumin is essential and may relate to the potential toxicity of bilirubin (Brodersen, 1979). When the bilirubin-albumin complex reaches the hepatocyte, bilirubin is passed into the liver cell—presumably by a receptor protein. The albumin is then free to recirculate and perhaps bind with bilirubin or some other chemical.

Conjugation

Within the cytoplasm (the protoplasm of a cell outside the nucleus) of the hepatocyte (a parenchymal liver cell), the bilirubin is transformed into a compound that can be excreted. This process is termed *conjugation*. Through enzymatic processes, two glucose molecules are attached to the bilirubin molecule. Prior to this step the chemical is termed *unconjugated bilirubin* and following this process is considered to be *conjugated bilirubin*. After conjugation, the bilirubin is discharged rapidly into bile by the hepatocyte, which consumes energy for the act of transport (Wolkoff, Ketley, Waggoner, Berk, & Jakoby, 1978).

Elimination

Once in the small intestine, conjugated bilirubin is not reabsorbed. In the adult, intestinal bacteria convert the bilirubin to stercobilin (a brown pigment derived from bile), which is lost in the stool, and urobilinogen (a colorless derivative), which is absorbed from the intestine and excreted in the urine. In the newborn, however, an enzyme within the intestinal tract can strip the glucose from the bilirubin molecule and thus allow for absorption of the unconjugated bilirubin. In addition, bilirubin may be excreted in stools without alteration by the bacteria (Maisels, 1981).

Physiologic versus Pathologic Jaundice

Earlier in this chapter, we noted that virtually all newborns have elevated levels of serum bilirubin. Several elements account for this situation. First, we know that a much higher percentage of the total blood volume of the fetus is composed of red blood cells. In utero, this state allows the unborn to extract oxygen from the mother in sufficient amounts to meet the demands of growth and development. Following birth, there is an increased breakdown of red blood cells, yielding greater quantities of hemoglobin and therefore bilirubin. Prior to birth, some of the bilirubin produced by the normal destruction of red blood cells is cleared across the placenta and conjugated in the mother's liver (Maisels, 1972). Following birth, there is a gradual rise in serum bilirubin in the healthy full-term baby until approximately three to four days and then a general lessening, with clinical jaundice usually resolving by seven to ten days after delivery. In term babies that are small-for-gestational age,

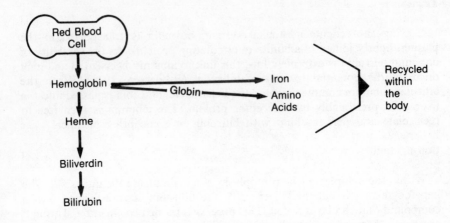

Figure 8–1 Schema of Bilirubin Production within the Newborn

the mean peak level is approximately seven milligrams/deciliter (mg/dl), occurring near three days after birth. In preterm babies, the mean peak level is approximately nine mg/dl, breaking at approximately four to five days. These data have been determined during the course of a National Collaborative Perinatal Project, which examined the clinical progress of over 35,000 newborns (Hardy, Drage, & Jackson, 1979). This study also demonstrated that Caucasian infants are likely to have slightly higher levels of serum bilirubin than black children.

Since jaundice is so common in newborns, researchers have sought to distinguish normal physiology from pathologic conditions. For this reason, criteria that help to establish the diagnosis of pathologic jaundice have been developed. These have been identified as follows:

1. clinical jaundice within the first 24 hours of life
2. a total serum bilirubin concentration that increases by more than 5 mg/dl per day
3. a total serum bilirubin concentration exceeding 12.9 mg/dl in a full-term infant or 15 mg/dl in a preterm infant
4. conjugated serum bilirubin concentration exceeding 1.5 mg/dl
5. clinical jaundice persisting more than one week in a full-term infant or two weeks in a preterm infant.

In light of the above, it is important to recognize that the absence of the pathologic criteria still does not necessarily guarantee that the jaundice is physiologic (Maisels, 1981).

With respect to the normal processes and resolution of physiologic jaundice, numerous theories and explanations have been postulated. For example, it has long been believed that breast-fed infants have higher bilirubin levels than do bottle-fed babies in the first week of life. Over 50 percent of the studies directed toward this question have not been able to verify this association. Rare is the newborn with prolonged jaundice that unquestionably is identified with breast milk feeding. More accurately, such conditions probably arise from increased free fatty acids in the serum that displace bilirubin from albumin, or from deficient glucuronyl transferase activity that interferes with the hepatocyte's ability to conjugate bilirubin (Drew, 1978; Maisels, 1981). Increased bilirubin load on the neonatal liver (the result of normal increased red cell destruction), some limitation in the hepatocyte uptake of bilirubin from albumin, and the enterohepatic circulation of bilirubin now are believed to contribute to the occurrence of physiologic jaundice.

CAUSES OF JAUNDICE

Increased Bilirubin Production

An increase in bilirubin production or a decreased clearance obviously may result in jaundice (yellow skin) or a condition termed *hyperbilirubinemia* (increased blood level of bilirubin). There are numerous processes that can precipitate a breakdown of red blood cells (hemolysis) and therefore increased hemoglobin catabolism, yielding an elevated bilirubin level. One of the best understood mechanisms is the Rh problem. In particular, the Rh antigen is a protein found on the surface of red blood cells. Although there are numerous proteins within the Rh system, the one most commonly associated with neonatal hemolytic disease is the *D antigen*. This specific protein resides in the red blood cell membrane and is inherited from the mother or father. Fetal red blood cells may escape into the maternal circulation, especially at delivery. If the mother is Rh negative (which means that she does not possess the protein in her red blood cells), her body recognizes that this substance is foreign and begins to produce proteins of her own (antibodies) that attempt to neutralize and eliminate the alien protein. In repeated pregnancies, this antibody response may be increased. As a consequence, antibodies then may cross the placenta and attach to the red blood cells of the newborn, where they become misshaped and are removed from circulation by the spleen. This condition causes a greater hemoglobin degradation and heightened bilirubin production. In some pregnancies, the problem may be very severe and the fetus is compromised by such rapid destruction of red blood cells that there are insufficient numbers to carry oxygen to the body tissue. Such cases may result in fetal death or *hydrops fetalis*, wherein the infant is born with excessive body water and severe respiratory distress (Oski & Naiman, 1982).

Within the last ten years, the problems described above have become less frequent. Mothers now can be given Rhogam (a gamma globulin, virtually identical to the protein that the mother produces in response to fetal red blood cell protein) following delivery or abortion of an Rh positive infant. The fetal *D antigen* then is bound by the Rhogam antibody, and the mother thus does not develop her own antibodies. As a result, in subsequent pregnancies she is not sensitized to the fetal red blood cell protein and, therefore, no antibody crosses to the fetus. The administration of Rhogam does not guarantee lack of maternal antibody response. There are situations where mothers have been sensitized during pregnancies by early transfer of fetal red blood cells, such that Rhogam given at delivery does not prevent the response. There sometimes are large fetal-to-maternal transfusions at the time of delivery, and the Rhogam administered may be insufficient to cover the antigen exposure the mother has received (Queenan, 1977).

There are many other etiologies of hemolysis in the newborn period. These include ABO incompatability or additional minor blood group incompatabilities (Oski & Naiman, 1982). Various drugs, especially sulfa, in susceptible infants may induce hemolysis. Anatomic malformations in the fetus and newborn such as cavernous hemangiomas (a vascular tumor with many large spaces) and abnormalities of the cardiovascular system (e.g., severe coarctation or compression of the aorta) may also accelerate hemolysis. Furthermore, anomalies of the red blood cell itself can serve to encourage rapid destruction. In the latter instances, there may be specific deficiencies of enzymes in the red blood cells that are crucial to maintaining its integrity. In other disorders that are hereditary, the red blood cell is altered in shape and, no longer a biconcave disk, is obliterated more readily within the reticuloendothelial system. Likewise, abnormalities of hemoglobin, including thalassemia (a hereditary anemia), are the origin of poor red cell survival (Oski, 1981).

Finally, devastation of normal red blood cells can be hastened by infections. These include bacterial diseases, usually acquired at or just after birth, as well as congenital infections, such as syphilis, rubella, and toxoplasmosis, that have been transmitted transplacentally to the fetus (Nahmias, 1974).

Decreased Bilirubin Clearance

Once bilirubin is produced in the reticuloendothelial system, its clearance may be subject to delay by several factors. The first of these is a decreased transport of the chemical in the blood. If the serum protein, albumin, is diminished, as is the case with premature infants, less bilirubin can be carried efficiently to the liver (Brodersen, 1979). As we have indicated, there are multiple compounds that may compete with bilirubin for the binding sites on albumin. These range from salicylates (any salt of salicylic acid), sulfa drugs, vitamin K, and fatty acids to the heme pigment itself from the red blood cell. Moreover, once the bilirubin has been excreted into bile, a portion of it in the newborn may be reabsorbed from the intestinal tract. This condition is called *enterohepatic circulation*, which implies a necessary reprocessing of bilirubin through the liver. Thus, anything that delays intestinal motility, as with a lack of feeding or hypothyroidism, may result in elevated serum bilirubin levels (Johnson, 1975; Thaler, 1977).

Several types of hereditary disease are responsible for inducing a congential, nonhemolytic, unconjugated form of hyperbilirubinemia (Colon &

Sandberg, 1973). The most common of these is a mild condition known as Gilbert's syndrome, an autosomal dominant disorder that may affect as much as three to five percent of the population. Bilirubin clearance is decreased to approximately 30 percent of the normal process. The syndrome never has been associated with neurologic disease. By comparison, the most severe form of hereditary jaundice is the Crigler-Najjar syndrome, where bilirubin clearance is markedly impaired as a result of the complete absence of the enzymes necessary for conjugation. Blood levels in such cases typically reach greater than 20 mg/dl, and bilirubin encephalopathy (damage to the brain) usually is present.

BILIRUBIN TOXICITY

A direct association has been established between *elevated unconjugated hyperbilirubinemia and neurologic damage.* This connection was first described in 1875 and the link was well documented in work by Mollison, Hsia, and colleagues in the 1950s, where correlations were made between the yellow staining of the brain and hyperbilirubinemia (Hsia, Allen, Gellis, & Diamond, 1952; Mollison & Walker, 1952). While bilirubin itself is responsible for the brain damage, the precise biochemical mechanisms still are not known (Odell, 1970). Circulating bilirubin may be deposited in the basal ganglia and hippocampus of the brain. *Kernicterus* is a histologic description of the impairment. A term more frequently used now for neurologic disease with elevated serum bilirubin is *bilirubin encephalopathy.* The clinical syndrome here includes a high pitched cry, lethargy, poor feeding, and hypotonia. In later stages, irritability, seizures, and opisthotonus (an arching of the body) may occur. Long-term sequelae include athetosis, spasticity, sensorineural hearing loss, and dental dysplasia (Perlstein, 1960).

From the research of the 1950s, it was determined that kernicterus was more likely to occur in infants with serum bilirubin levels of greater than 30 mg/dl and unlikely to occur in newborns with levels of less than 20 mg/dl (Mollison & Cutbush, 1954). However, as with many diseases of the newborn, there have been numerous case reports of infants with elevated levels of bilirubin who have not developed kernicterus, and of low birthweight ill neonates with levels much below 20 mg/dl who have manifested neurologic associations with bilirubin encephalopathy (Gartner, Snyder, Chabon, & Bernstein, 1970).

TREATMENT

The treatment of hyperbilirubinemia is directed toward a reduction of serum bilirubin levels. In 1958, Cremer and others observed that exposure of infants to light produced a decline in blood bilirubin concentrations (Cremer, Perryman, & Richards, 1958). This development has led to widespread use of phototherapy in the United States as an adjunct to exchange transfusion, a procedure that is performed when serum bilirubin levels reach levels unacceptable to the physician caring for the neonate (Tan, 1976).

Several processes need to be understood in order to comprehend the effectiveness of phototherapy in resolving problems of hyperbilirubinemia. First, bilirubin is a photoactive molecule that absorbs light at 440–460 nm. Blue lights provide the greatest energy in the wave length, where bilirubin is most susceptible, and are much more effective than white lights. Either light, however, typically is used at approximately 16–20 inches from the unclothed baby (See Figure 8–2). A plexiglass shield is placed between the light source and the infant to absorb potentially harmful ultraviolet light and to guard against lamp explosion (Maisels, 1981). Second, bilirubin is thought to be cleared from the body by means of two mechanisms. In the *photo-conversion* pathway, the energy of light changes the bilirubin molecule into a photoisomer, which reaches a stable concentration in two to four hours in a high protein solution. This compound can be eliminated through the liver without conjugation (McDonagh & Palma, 1983). *Photo-oxidation* is another pathway (Ostrow, 1972) in which water soluble products are formed and can be excreted in urine and bile. Of course, once phototherapy is stopped, the liver alone again becomes responsible for clearance of bilirubin.

There may be problems with phototherapy. For example, the treatment increases insensible water loss, and therefore infants are more prone to dehydration. Newborn stools tend to become looser and more frequent, and dark-skinned babies pigment more rapidly. Since phototherapy usually is applied to newborns in incubators, a "greenhouse" effect may occur, with babies becoming overheated. In addition, there is animal evidence for degeneration of the retina of the eye with exposure to bright lights, although this problem may be averted by placing eye patches on infants. White phototherapy may produce a mild lowering of the blood calcium level. Blue phototherapy has been shown to lower levels of photoactive compounds such as riboflavin (vitamin B$_6$). Overall, however, white phototherapy is used more commonly than blue phototherapy in view of the fact that the latter tends to limit observation of the child and cyanosis is less easily observed. Finally, long-term effects of phototherapy still are not known. In recent years, several investigators have expressed concern over possible endocrine effects or alteration in sexual maturation (Behrman, 1974).

Exchange Transfusion

When phototherapy does not prevent the rise of bilirubin to an unacceptable level, the blood level alternatively may be lowered by an exchange transfusion (Allen & Diamond, 1958), which is donated by an adult and anticoagulated. At least one catheter is placed into a major blood vessel in the infant and then, over the course of an hour or more, small aliquots of blood are removed from the baby and replaced with that of the adult donor. In general, there is approximately a 50 percent reduction in the serum bilirubin level immediately following an exchange transfusion. With this procedure, metabolic, vascular, and infectious complications may occur, but these are rare occurrences (Maisels, 1981).

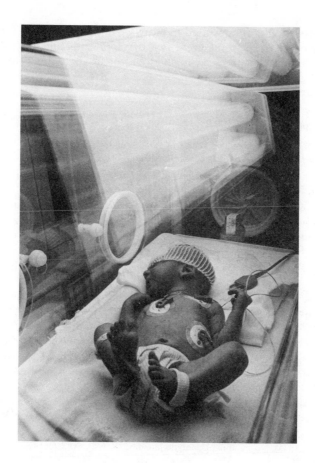

Figure 8–2 Preterm Infant under Phototherapy Lights

Medications

Many pharmacologic agents are capable of stimulating hepatic conjugation and excretion of bilirubin. Phenobarbital is the drug most widely used in newborns (Wallin, Jalling, & Boreus, 1974). In the United States, medications seldom are given to infants to aid in bilirubin clearance. The primary exception to this trend is seen with jaundice resulting from Type II Crigler-Najjar syndrome, that can be managed effectively with phenobarbital (Yaffe, Levy, Matsuzawa, & Baliah, 1966).

In summary, it should be clear that despite the rising tide of technology in medicine, there yet is much that we do not know in terms of long-range and more subtle types of physical and developmental influences of jaundice. Like many other newborn diseases and conditions, hyperbilirubinemia affects each child on a very individual basis. Educators and clinicians responsible for infant intervention programs need to be aware of the possible ramifications of such neonatal histories in the event that developmental and/or physiological difficulties begin to surface with children entrusted to their care.

REFERENCES

Allen, F.H., & Diamond, L.K. (1958). *Erythroblastosis fetalis including exchange transfusion technique.* Boston: Little, Brown.

Behrman, R.E. (1974). Preliminary report of the committee on phototherapy in the newborn infant. *Journal of Pediatrics, 84,* 135–147.

Brodersen, R. (1979). Bilirubin, solubility, and interaction with albumin and phospholipid. *Journal of Biological Chemistry, 254,* 2364–2369.

Colon, A.R., & Sandberg, M.D. (1973). Presently recognized forms of inherited jaundice in infancy. *Clinical Pediatrics, 12,* 326–332.

Cremer, R.J., Perryman, P.W., & Richards, D.H. (1958). Influence of light on the hyperbilirubinemia of infants. *Lancet, 1,* 1094–1097.

Drew, J.H. (1978). Breastfeeding and jaundice. *Keeping Abreast: Journal of Human Nurturing,* January-March, 53–56.

Gartner, L.M., & Arias, I.M. (1969). Formation, transport, metabolism, and excretion of bilirubin. *New England Journal of Medicine, 280,* 1339–1345.

Gartner, L.M., Snyder, R.N., Chabon, R.S., & Bernstein, J. (1970). Kernicterus: High incidence in premature infants with low serum bilirubin concentrations. *Pediatrics, 45,* 906–917.

Hardy, J.B., Drage, J.S., & Jackson, E.C. (1979). *The first year of life: The collaborative perinatal project of the National Institutes of Neurological and Communicative Disorders and Stroke.* Baltimore: Johns Hopkins University Press.

Hsia, D.Y., Allen, F.H., Gellis, S.S., & Diamond, L.K. (1952). Erythroblastosis fetalis: VIII. Studies of serum bilirubin in relation to kernicterus. *New England Journal of Medicine, 247,* 668–671.

Johnson, J.D. (1975). Neonatal nonhemolytic jaundice. *New England Journal of Medicine, 292,* 194–197.

Maisels, M.J. (1972). Bilirubin: On understanding and influencing its metabolism in the newborn infant. *Pediatric Clinics of North America, 19,* 447–501.

Maisels, M.J. (1981). Neonatal jaundice in neonatology. In G. B. Avery (Ed.), *Neonatology: Pathophysiology and management of the newborn* (2nd ed.) (pp. 473–544). Philadelphia: J.B. Lippincott.

McDonagh, A.F., & Palma, L.A. (1983). Why phototherapy works: Identification of bilirubin photoproducts in vivo. *Pediatric Research, 17,* 326A.

Mollison, P.L., & Cutbush, M. (1954). Haemolytic disease of the newborn. In D. Gairdner (Ed.), *Recent advances in pediatrics* (pp. 110–118). New York: Blakiston.

Mollison, P.L., & Walker, W. (1952). Controlled trials of the treatment of hemolytic disease of the newborn. *Lancet, 1,* 429–433.

Nahmias, A.J. (1974). The TORCH complex. *Hospital Practice, May,* 65–71.

Odell, G.B. (1970). The distribution and toxicity of bilirubin. *Pediatrics, 46,* 16–24.

Oski, F.A. (1981). Hematologic problems. In G.B. Avery (Ed.), *Neonatology: Pathophysiology and management of the newborn* (2nd ed.) (pp. 545–582). Philadelphia: J.B. Lippincott.

Oski, F.A., & Naiman, J.L. (1982). *Hematologic problems in the newborn* (3rd ed.) (pp. 83–132, 176–235). Philadelphia: W.B. Saunders.

Ostrow, J.D. (1972). Mechanisms of bilirubin photodegradation. *Seminars in Hematology, 9,* 113–125.

Perlstein, M.A. (1960). The late clinical syndrome of posticteric encephalopathy. *Pediatric Clinics of North America, 7,* 665–687.

Queenan, J.T. (1977). *Modern management of the Rh problem* (2nd ed.). Hagerstown, MD: Harper & Row.

Tan, K.L. (1976). Phototherapy for neonatal hyperbilirubinemia in healthy and ill infants. *Pediatrics, 57,* 836–838.

Thaler, M.M. (1977). Algorithmic diagnosis of conjugated and unconjugated hyperbilirubinemia. *Journal of the American Medical Association, 237,* 58–62.

Wallin, A., Jalling, B., & Boreus, L.O. (1974). Plasma concentrations of phenobarbital in the neonate during prophylaxis for neonatal hyperbilirubinemia. *Journal of Pediatrics, 85,* 392–397.

Wolkoff, A.W., Ketley, J.N., Waggoner, J.G., Berk, P.D., & Jakoby, W.B. (1978). Hepatic accumulation and intracellular binding of conjugated bilirubin. *Journal of Clinical Investigation, 61,* 142–149.

Yaffe, S.J., Levy, G., Matsuzawa, T., & Baliah, T. (1966). Enhancement of glucuronide conjugating capacity in a hyperbilirubinemic infant due to apparent enzyme induction by phenobarbital. *New England Journal of Medicine, 275,* 1461–1465.

9

Respiratory Distress

Respiratory distress is one of the most familiar and critical problems of the newborn period, for both preterm and full-term babies. Without adequate treatment, poor oxygenation of the blood (hypoxia) almost inevitably is the outcome with multiple organ dysfunction, especially of the brain. Understandably in recent years as medical technology has continued to enhance the survival rates of smaller premature neonates, there has been high interest in various forms of respiratory distress, along with much speculation that the incidence of developmental disabilities in this group, in fact, may be on an increase. In this chapter, we will be concerned with normal lung development, an understanding of acute respiratory distress and chronic lung disease, medical treatment, and information regarding outcome.

NORMAL LUNG DEVELOPMENT

Typical development of the lungs proceeds as follows. On approximately the twenty-fourth day of embryonic life, a lung bud appears from the rudimentary intestinal tract (Hodson, 1977; Reid, 1967). This pouch elongates and begins to branch to form what eventually becomes the airways leading to the alveoli (air sacs) where the gases oxygen and carbon dioxide are exchanged. This process is complete by about 16 to 18 weeks of gestation. Subsequently, primitive air sacs evolve, the first functional alveoli appearing at about 24 to 26 weeks gestation. Their activity is limited by the ingrowth of blood vessels, which must closely parallel the development of the air sacs for adequate exchange of gas. The *arterial system* that supplies the lung from the right side of the heart emerges from primitive arch arteries in the embryonic neck. In turn, the *venous system* grows backward from the left side of the heart. These two networks must join to capillaries (the smallest blood vessels) adjacent to alveoli for optimum gas transfer. Prior to 26 weeks of gestation, the aforementioned process is not sufficiently advanced to allow blood to pick up oxygen or to rid the body of carbon dioxide, a waste product of metabolism. Proceeding from 26 to 32 weeks gestation, however, the small terminal air sacs give way to larger alveolar spaces with a very complex branching pattern. Later, between 32 and 36 weeks, further budding occurs and true alveoli, as present in the adult lung, take shape. Lung growth continues even after birth, with the adult volume finally attained in the mid-teens. A full-term newborn has approximately one-tenth of the alveolar surface area available to that of an adult. An infant born at 28 weeks has about one-eighth of the alveolar surface area of a full-term baby. Thus, a neonate delivered 12 weeks prematurely, although approximately one-third the size of the full-term baby, has disproportionately less lung according to body weight.

As the anatomy of the lung is ever changing prior to birth, simultaneously there is an evolving biochemistry (Farrell & Perelman, 1983). Specifically, adult alveoli are lined with an active material called *surfactant*, which reduces the surface tension within the individual alveolus. The presence of this chemical is essential to preventing the air sacs from collapsing during expiration of the breathing cycle. Surfactant is virtually absent before 26 weeks gestation, the primary pathway for its production really not being present until 34 to 36 weeks in most fetuses. Furthermore, recent studies have demonstrated that females biochemically mature approximately two weeks before males. These data help to explain the disparity between sexes, with increased numbers of male premature infants who have respiratory distress.

ACUTE RESPIRATORY DISTRESS

Various types of respiratory distress occur within the newborn period. These are characterized by several different etiologies and may culminate in quite dissimilar outcomes. Certainly, not all respiratory failure in the neonate is caused by intrinsic lung disease. Drugs in the central nervous system may influence the process. Neurological diseases or malformations of the chest may restrict expansion of normal lungs, and massive abdominal distension with ascites (fluid) or tumors may limit diaphragmatic movement and therefore respiratory function. Malformations or tumors of the upper airway also may inhibit air flow to the lungs; however, these impairments are relatively uncommon causes of respiratory distress or failure in the newborn (Avery, Fletcher, & Williams, 1981).

The signs and symptoms of respiratory distress in the neonate do not necessarily help to differentiate specific etiologies. Most infants with respiratory distress evidence an increased respiratory rate (tachypnea), and many are cyanotic (slightly bluish or grayish in color) because of decreased blood oxygenation. Since the musculature and rib strength are not yet well developed, the chest wall is less capable of resisting the strong negative pressure exerted by the diaphragm against diseased lungs. Hence, retractions frequently are seen, which result from the downward movement of the diaphragm, creating a negative pressure within the chest. Under these conditions, the lungs are unable to expand adequately to fill the potential space and thus the more compliant chest wall caves in or collapses. Many preterm infants with poor total body caloric reserve are not able to maintain such labored efforts without serious metabolic compromise.

Transient Tachypnea

Prior to birth the lungs are filled with fluid. During delivery, this liquid must be cleared to allow for adequate exchange of gas in the respiratory system. Recent evidence has suggested that the biochemical activities that initiate labor also may begin chemically to dehydrate the lung in preparation for birth. Most of the remaining fluid then is expelled as the chest is squeezed through the birth canal. The small amount of fluid retained in the lungs is absorbed into the circulatory system and excreted through the kidneys.

Transient tachypnea refers to a relatively mild form of respiratory distress with requirements for some oxygen supplementation. Essentially, this condition results from an increased amount of fluid that has failed to clear from the lung. The problem is seen more often in babies born prematurely, in those delivered by cesarean section, and especially in infants whose mothers have had no labor. In the typical course of the illness, the respiratory symptoms disappear in the first 24 to 48 hours after birth, as the lung fluid is absorbed and excreted (Avery, Gatewood, & Brumley, 1966; Halliday, McClure, & McCreid, 1981).

Hyaline Membrane Disease

Hyaline membrane disease is the specific term for the respiratory distress syndrome seen in premature infants that arises from a deficiency of surfactant in the alveoli (Avery, 1984; Avery, Fletcher, & Williams, 1981; Scarpelli, 1975). As a consequence of this condition, the air sacs (alveoli) collapse and the total area for absorption of oxygen into the body and elimination of carbon dioxide is reduced. The disease tends to be a progressive illness that becomes worse over the first three to four days of life, as the little surfactant remaining in the lungs is degraded faster than it can be replaced. Proteins leak from weakened small blood vessels in the lung into partially or completely collapsed air sacs, and this material (the hyaline membrane) then further limits the exchange of gas from the alveoli to the capillaries. The disease begins to resolve as the lungs synthesize the adult form of surfactant, which provides for stability of the air sacs. Reabsorption of the proteinaceous hyaline membranes then follows over the next several weeks.

Most newborns with hyaline membrane disease require a minimum of supplemental oxygen, and many need mechanical ventilatory support. Fortunately, the majority of infants run a typical course leading to gradual recovery and essentially normal lung function within a few weeks after birth. A few infants, however, may go on to develop chronic lung changes as a result of the intensity of life-supporting therapy.

Aspiration

Aspiration refers to the physiological reactions to abnormal or foreign material that has gained access to the lungs (Avery, Fletcher, & Williams, 1981; Gregory, Gooding, Phibbs, & Tooley, 1974; Stahlman, 1981). The two most common substances that are aspirated around the time of birth are amniotic fluid and meconium. In terms of the first, when amniotic fluid is drawn into the lungs, proteins and cellular debris may provoke an inflammatory reaction that resembles pneumonia. The course is variable and depends, in large measure, upon the characteristics and amount of the fluid ingested and upon its distribution within the lungs. More serious is the condition that occurs when the amniotic fluid contains meconium (a dark green, sterile, viscous material found in the intestine of the fetus). Approximately five percent of babies delivered beyond 34 weeks gestation have sufficient fetal distress to shed meconium reflexively. Severe complications may result. Normally, as we inhale the airways expand and as we exhale they contract. If meconium is aspirated, air is passed beyond the thick material through the dilated airways, but then is trapped in the lung as passages collapse in exhalation. Such obstructions may progress and eventually cause compression of surrounding lung or overdistension and rupture of alveoli. Subsequently, over a period of several days, the diverse components of meconium provoke a severe response in the lungs with inflammation and excess fluid. Obviously, all of these changes interfere with the respiratory process.

Air Block Syndromes

There are three major types of *air block syndromes*, which basically involve conditions where air is lodged in the chest and unavailable for gas exchange (Madansky, Lawson, Chernick, & Taeusch, 1979; Stahlman, 1981). The insults vary with the specific location of air in the chest, which can be seen by x-ray. The first, *pneumothorax*, occurs with air that is present within the chest cavity, but external and usually compressing a lung. By insertion of a chest tube to drain the air and reinflate the lung, the problem is easily treated. The second form of air blockage, *pneumomediastinum*, refers to air trapped around structures in the center of the chest. If this gas is under tension, vessels returning blood to the heart and branching passageways to the more peripheral lung may be compressed or contracted. Third, when air in the medianstinum is confined to the pericardium (the sac surrounding the heart), illness termed a *pneumopericardium* appears. Under tension, a pneumopericardium does not permit adequate filling of the heart with blood. Without immediate relief, such infants die.

Among these air block syndromes, pneumothorax is seen with the greatest frequency, in as high as five percent of all newborns. Only one percent of these babies are symptomatic, requiring medical or surgical intervention. Aside from the initial neonatal period with the rapid expansion of the lungs, the various types of air block syndromes are manifested primarily in babies requiring positive pressure inflation of the lungs with mechanical ventilation or in any of the previously noted acute respiratory diseases.

Hemorrhage and Infection

Babies who suffer from congenital heart disease or severe respiratory distress are at risk for overdistended and weakened pulmonary blood vessels that may rupture. Pulmonary hemorrhage more often is seen in neonates who have experienced significant birth asphyxia. With such illnesses, blood may fill the normal functioning lungs, thus preventing the exchange of gas. As with other forms of bleeding, the disease may be sufficient to reduce the blood volume and result in shock and death, even with aggressive intervention (Avery, 1984; Esterley & Oppenheimer, 1966).

Typically, infection of the lungs is seen in those instances when there has been a prolonged rupture of the membranes surrounding a baby. Under these conditions, bacteria and viruses ordinarily colonizing in the vagina may gain access to the amniotic fluid and invade the lung. The clinical presentation of babies who are infected is quite variable, with x-ray changes ranging from mild to severe and outcomes that are much less predictable than the prognosis of most other acute respiratory diseases managed throughout the newborn period (Hanshaw & Dudgeon, 1978).

CHRONIC LUNG DISEASE

Several forms of chronic lung disease can be distinguished in the neonate, and each of these illnesses implies a long-term dependence on supplemental oxygen (Fox, Murray, & Martin, 1983; Tooley, 1979). In addition, these conditions frequently are characterized by elevated blood carbon dioxide levels resulting from an inadequate surface area for gas exchange in the lung. In the very low birthweight infant (less than 1,000 grams), most common among these problems is *chronic pulmonary insufficiency of prematurity* (CPIP) (Krauss, Klain, & Auld, 1975). Herein, the alveoli are forced to mature under the constant stress of the oxygen content of room air, which is approximately six times greater than that of the developing air sacs when the lungs are fluid-filled in utero. Lung growth therefore is delayed and leads to a long-term oxygen dependency. Gradually, as the nutritional status of the baby improves, the alveoli grow and most children are weaned from oxygen within the first six months of life.

Bronchopulmonary dysplasia (BPD) is another variation of chronic lung disease that emanates from life-saving, therapeutic maneuvers in the treatment of children with acute respiratory illnesses. Combinations of the supplemental oxygen required (especially in amounts of greater than 40 percent), positive pressure, and the trauma of mechanical ventilation inevitably lead to changes in the airways, which become thickened with increased mucous production. In addition, alveolar growth is retarded, and these babies have a prolonged oxygen requirement (Northway, 1979).

Babies with CPIP and BPD may have insufficient pulmonary repair and growth to sustain life. Those that do recover and are removed from oxygen continue to have diminished pulmonary reserve throughout the succeeding year of life. Hence, they are more susceptible to infection and often must be rehospitalized. However, assuming no major intervening illness, the majority of survivors acquire relatively normal lung function by the time they reach the elementary school years.

TREATMENT OF RESPIRATORY DISEASE

It should be quite obvious from the foregoing discussion of respiratory illnesses that the main goal of therapy is the maintenance of adequate blood oxygen and the concurrent limitation of the blood carbon dioxide level. The latter diffuses more readily from blood vessels to the alveoli; therefore, the higher the blood carbon dioxide, the greater the severity of the pulmonary disease. Supplemental oxygen is given in order to sustain blood oxygen levels in the range of 60–80 TORR (the pressure of 1 mm of mercury under standard conditions of temperature and atmospheric pressure). If adequate oxygenation cannot be maintained in 100 percent oxygen or if the blood carbon dioxide exceeds 60 TORR with poor respiratory effort, assisted ventilation is necessary. The first step in this therapeutic process is the use of constant positive airway pressure (CPAP). This treatment involves a low pressure against which the baby breathes, by which alveoli are stabilized for gas exchange. In the event that the infant still is unable to achieve adequate oxygenation, mechanical ventilation is utilized. With this procedure, the concentration of oxygen, respiratory rate, and inflation pressure are individualized to the child and directed specifically toward the form of respiratory distress that is being managed.

Throughout the duration of therapy, general supportive care—apart from respiratory management—is very important. Blood pressure must be carefully monitored, as well as the blood levels of various minerals such as sodium and calcium. Nutrition also is a priority, but often the child is unable to suck and thus must be fed intravenously. In addition, adequate temperature support is essential to conserve calories for repair and growth.

OUTCOME

Outcome data for newborns with respiratory disease are available in several areas of inquiry. While information on survival rates is abundant, long-term developmental evidence is much more sparse. In general, the mild types of respiratory distress are associated with fewer and less persistent delays. Babies with the more severe illnesses, especially those requiring prolonged periods of ventilation, are more apt to manifest developmental problems. At present, however, it is extremely difficult to distinguish the severity of the disease from the intensity of intervention and related medical complications including nutrition, any of which may impinge upon development.

REFERENCES

Avery, M.E. (1984). Hyaline membrane disease. In M.E. Avery & H.W. Taeusch, (Eds.), *Schaffer's diseases of the newborn* (pp. 133–147). Philadelphia: W.B. Saunders.

Avery, M.E., Fletcher, B.D., & Williams, R.G. (1981). Lung development. In M.E. Avery, B.D. Fletcher, & R.G. Williams (Eds.), *The lung and its disorders in the newborn infant* (4th ed.) (pp. 3–48). Philadelphia: W.B. Saunders.

Avery, M.E., Gatewood, O.B., & Brumley, G. (1966). Transient tachypnea of the newborn. *American Journal of Diseases of Children, 111*, 380–385.

Esterley, J., & Oppenheimer, E. (1966). Massive pulmonary hemorrhage in the newborn: I. Pathologic and clinical considerations. *Journal of Pediatrics, 69*, 3–20.

Farrell, P.M., & Perelman, R.H. (1983). The developmental biology of the lung. In A.A. Fanaroff & R.J. Martin (Eds.), *Neonatal-perinatal medicine* (pp. 404–418). St. Louis: C.V. Mosby.

Fox, W.W., Murray, J.P., & Martin, R.J. (1983). Chronic pulmonary diseases of the neonate. In A. A. Fanaroff & R.J. Martin (Eds.), *Neonatal-perinatal medicine* (pp. 467–476). St. Louis: C.V. Mosby.

Gregory, G.A., Gooding, C.A., Phibbs, R.H., & Tooley, W.H. (1974). Meconium aspiration in infants—A prospective study. *Journal of Pediatrics, 85*, 848–852.

Halliday, H.L., McClure, G., & McCreid, M. (1981). Transient tachypnea of the newborn: Two distinct clinical entities. *Archives of Disease in Childhood, 56*, 322–325.

Hanshaw, J.B., & Dudgeon, J.A. (1978). *Viral diseases of the fetus and newborn.* Philadelphia: W.B. Saunders.

Hodson, W.A. (1977). *Development of the lung.* New York: Marcel Dekker.

Krauss, A.N., Klain, D.B., & Auld, P. (1975). Chronic pulmonary insufficiency of prematurity (CPIP). *Pediatrics, 55*, 55–58.

Madansky, D.L., Lawson, E.E., Chernick, V., & Taeusch, H.W. (1979). Pneumothorax and other forms of pulmonary air leaks in newborns. *American Review of Respiratory Disease, 120*, 729–737.

Northway, W.H., Jr. (1979). Observations on bronchopulmonary dysplasia. *Journal of Pediatrics, 95*, 815–818.

Reid, L. (1967). The embryology of the lung. In A.V.S. de Reuck & R. Parker (Eds.), *CIBA Foundation symposium on development of the lung* (pp. 109–124). London: Churchill Livingstone.

Scarpelli, E.M. (1975). Perinatal respiration. In E.M. Scarpelli & P.A.M. Auld (Eds.), *Pulmonary disease of the fetus, newborn, and child* (pp. 116–139). Philadelphia: Lea & Febiger.

Stahlman, M.T. (1981). Acute respiratory disorders in the newborn. In G. B. Avery (Ed.), *Neonatology: Pathophysiology and management of the newborn* (2nd ed.) (pp. 371–397). Philadelphia: J.B. Lippincott.

Tooley, W.H. (1979). Epidemiology of bronchopulmonary dysplasia *Journal of Pediatrics, 95*, 851–858.

10

Nutrition and Metabolism

NUTRITION

Digestion and Absorption: General Considerations

As we discussed in Chapter 2, nutrition prior to birth is provided by the passage of nutrients from the mother across the placenta to the fetus. Waste products of the high fetal metabolic rate then are returned to the mother for excretion. Following delivery, the newborn intestinal tract assumes a permanent role in this process. Since many serious illnesses of the neonate limit the type and quality of feeding, the intravenous route to nutrition (IV nutritional therapy) may become a necessity. The intestinal tract of a full-term infant is approximately 100–110 inches in length, and at birth most of the enzymes required to digest sugar, protein, and fat are present. However, this is not the case in the severely premature baby with restricted digestive capabilities (Avery & Fletcher, 1981). Still, despite our present level of sophistication, IV nutritional therapy remains a poor alternative to a healthy, properly functioning intestinal tract. It is expensive and hazardous, and its use should be limited to those situations where it is absolutely essential (Heird, Driscoll, Schallinger, Grebin, & Winters, 1972).

Each portion of the intestinal tract has a specialized function in the digestion and absorption of nutrients. The breakdown of sugar and starch begins in the mouth and generally is completed by the first portions of the small intestine. Protein and fat digestion starts in the stomach and again terminates within the small intestine. Vitamins and minerals, including sodium and calcium, are absorbed along much of the small intestine. Final salt and water absorption occurs in the large intestine as waste products are being concentrated prior to evacuation (Grand, 1984). In order for digestion and absorption of nutrients to take place properly within the intestinal tract, there must be a continuous movement from the mouth to the anus. This process is referred to as *intestinal motility* and begins with the suck reflex, which is limited in the less than 34-week infant. Consequently, most premature infants must be fed primarily by a tube that is inserted through the mouth or nose into the stomach (gavage feeding). Many hormones are secreted within the intestinal tract, serving either to increase or to decrease motility of the intestine and thus allow for more efficient digestion (Avery & Fletcher, 1981). Dietary components, in isolation or in combination with hormones they stimulate, also may modify intestinal motility. For example, a high fat meal tends to slow intestinal movement, especially the emptying of the stomach, presumably permitting more time for the very complex digestion of fats.

Aside from the problem of a weak suck reflex, prematurity causes other difficulties with the digestion and absorption of specific nutrients. Although digestion of carbohydrates begins in the mouth with the action of saliva on starch, it is quite uncommon for the newborn to be receiving such food ingredients. Therefore, this process in the neonate is initiated in the small intestine. In particular, integral components of the intestinal cell wall alter more complex sugars to simple sugars, which then can be absorbed across these tissues into the bloodstream. The predominant sugar of breast milk is lactose, which is composed of the simple sugars glucose and galactose. The enzyme, lactase, splits the bond between these two simple sugars, allowing adequate absorption of each. In infants born less than 34 weeks gestation, the ability to handle the disaccharide (two-sugar) lactose is somewhat limited. The lactose from breast milk or formula, when undigested, may be utilized by the bacteria within the large intestine and, in some cases, may cause adverse effects, including diarrhea (Grand, 1984).

The digestion of protein is much more complex than that of sugar and primarily depends on the type of compound that the baby is fed. Milk contains two basic groups—*casein* proteins that precipitate and form a curd in the presence of acid and the stomach enzyme renin, and the *whey* proteins that do not form a curd but remain in solution at a low intestinal pH (for those fans of little Miss Muffet, casein and whey are the curds and whey of the poem). Further breakdown is effected by numerous enzymes, some being secretions of the pancreas and others components of the wall of the small intestine. The resulting simple amino acids are absorbed into the bloodstream (Grand, Watkins, & Torti, 1976). In general, preterm infants digest and absorb the dietary proteins relatively well. The one exception is the casein of cow's milk, which is a main ingredient of commercially available formula.

The digestion of a third nutrient, fat, begins in the stomach, in part with the action of the enzyme lipase, which is secreted from glands in the back of the tongue. In the first portion of the small intestine (the duodenum), this process subsequently intensifies with a combination of bile salts from the liver and lipase from the pancreas. Bile salts emulsify the fats and reduce them to their smallest components, the fatty acids and glycerol (Watkins, Ingal, Scezepanik, Klein & Lester, 1973). Newborns, especially those of less than 34 weeks gestation, digest and absorb fat less effectively than older children.

Like fats, water soluble vitamins (with the exception of B_{12}) are absorbed predominantly in the first portion of the small intestine. The fat soluble vitamins, A, D, and E, are absorbed along with the dietary fats across much of the small intestine. Vitamin B_{12} specifically is absorbed in the distal portion of the small bowel (the ileum) and requires a substance called the *intrinsic factor*, which is secreted in the stomach.

Last, minerals such as calcium, sodium, and potassium are taken in across much of the intestinal tract. In large part, this activity is dependent upon and enhanced by the good digestion of other food substances.

Newborns who require long-term IV nutrition may have delayed development of the intestinal tract, with growth and renewal largely contingent upon oral feeding. Often, such babies evidence abdominal distention, vomiting, diarrhea, and malabsorption as oral intake is begun. Thus, feedings generally are started with dilute concentrations, in small volumes, allowing for the build-up of digestive capabilities of the intestinal tract.

Assuming ideal environmental conditions with minimal stress and activity, a few infants may be able to grow on as little as 80–90 calories per kilogram per day. Typically, an estimated 120 calories per kilogram daily has been demonstrated sufficient for good growth in most newborns. In infants who have had intrauterine growth retardation, the caloric requirement may be as high as 160–180 calories per kilogram per day to achieve adequate progress. Unfortunately, despite impressive strides in nutrition research over the last decade, the approximation of intrauterine development has not yet been accomplished. Today, there remains a great debate whether neonatal growth paralleling intrauterine growth should be a goal, and what the approximate compositions of various body tissues should be (Fomon, 1974). Table 10–1 presents the estimated caloric requirement in a low birthweight infant.

While all of the nutritional components are essential, protein is the most important. Tissue growth and restoration are tied directly to adequate protein intake, since this is the basic ingredient of all cells. Moreover, while the body may convert many amino acids, nine such amino acids in adults and an additional two in newborns are critical and cannot be synthesized. The amino acids in proteins are utilized in specific proportions. An absolute deficiency of any of the primary amino acids results in poor cell reproduction and growth.

Table 10–1 Estimated Caloric Requirements in an Active "Growing" Low Birthweight Infant

Item	Kcal/Kg/Day
Resting Expenditure (includes calories for temperature maintenance)	50
Specific Dynamic Action*	10
Fecal Calorie Loss	10
Intermittent Activity	15
Growth Allowance (~ 5 Kcal/Gram Tissue Deposited)	60
Total	145

*Specific Dynamic Action is the difference between the resting expenditure of the fed infant and the fasted infant.

Adequate protein intake has been calculated to be approximately three to four grams per kilogram per day. Quantities less than this do not permit adequate growth, and higher amounts lead to excess toxic breakdown products such as ammonia and urea. These substances cannot be adequately eliminated by the relatively immature kidneys and liver of the newborn. In essence, although the other constituents of breast milk may not be the best for the very preterm infant, the quality of the protein with respect to digestibility and amino acid constituents has no equal (Raiha, Rassin, & Gaull, 1976).

Carbohydrate is the prime, rapidly utilized fuel for the body, with glucose essential to brain metabolism. Fortunately, there are biochemical pathways wherein glucose can be formed in the body from proteins and fats. Although there is no specific dietary requirement of glucose, low blood sugar or *hypoglycemia* may result in brain damage.

Dietary fat contains a little over twice as much energy per weight in comparison with sugar and protein. Fats are vital elements of the walls of cells and also provide the sheathing insulation (myelin) of cells in the central nervous system. Specific syndromes of poor growth and skin lesions may be seen with inadequate intake (Avery & Fletcher, 1981). Diets can be devised with only protein and fat as the caloric sources. On the other hand, they are basically impalatable, and the breakdown products may be difficult for the newborn, especially the premature baby, to handle.

Vitamins are cofactors that, though they provide no calories, assist in body metabolism. With the exception of vitamin K, it is quite rare for newborns to be deficient. Babies born prematurely may rapidly consume vitamin D and E stores present at birth; as a result, deficiencies may surface several weeks after delivery. A lack of vitamin D may impair bone development. Likewise, insufficient vitamin E allows an accelerated destruction of red blood cells. As a general guideline, routine supplementation and treatment of vitamin deficits should proceed with extreme caution. Surplus administration has been known to produce specific toxicities. In example, excess vitamin D can cause constipation and renal failure. Brittle bones, irritability, and increased intracranial pressure may be the effects of too much vitamin A.

Minerals important to the body include calcium, magnesium, sodium, potassium, iron, phosphorous, and iodine. In addition, zinc, copper, manganese, chromium, fluoride, molybdenum, and selenium all are considered prominent trace elements (Sandstead, Burk, Booth, & Darby, 1970). Potassium and sodium are the primary minerals found respectively within and outside the cells in the fluids of the body. Differential concentrations of these two minerals inside and outside the cells are crucial in maintaining polarization or electrical activity, which moves nutrients into and waste products from cells. Such polarity also facilitates transmission of electrical impulses throughout the body and triggers muscle activity of the heart.

Calcium and phosphorous are responsible for appropriate bone growth. Approximately 50 percent of the calcium content of the bones of a full-term baby is deposited in the last trimester. Therefore, infants born prematurely are much more prone to abnormal bone growth, known as *rickets*. Regulation of calcium and phosphorous metabolism is accomplished through the parathyroid glands, the kidneys, and in the case of vitamin D synthesis, the liver. Magnesium metabolism is closely linked to that of calcium, and it is thought that many transport mechanisms in the body may be magnesium-dependent (Tsang, Donovan, & Steichen, 1976).

Iron, essential to hemoglobin formation (American Academy of Pediatrics, 1976), is absorbed primarily in the upper small intestine. *Iron deficiency anemia* commonly is mentioned in the lay press. Signs and symptoms of the condition are manifested in the form of irritability, listlessness, inadequate growth, and feeding difficulties.

Assuming that the intestine is intact, selection of foods should follow a diet that contains sufficient calories that are distributed appropriately across the essential nutrients. For maximum infant growth, this range should include carbohydrates at 35–45 percent, fat at 35–55 percent, and protein at 7–16 percent. Breast milk and the proprietary newborn formulas all satisfactorily meet these requirements (Fomon, 1974). Overall, breast milk still is considered the ideal feeding for healthy, full-term infants, as well as for babies born as early as six weeks prematurely. Still in question is the adequacy of breast milk for neonates delivered at less than 34 weeks gestation. Specifically, the lactose content of breast milk may not be digested appropriately, fats may be too complex for the immature pancreas, and there may be insufficient amounts of the minerals calcium and sodium for the typical premature baby (Avery & Fletcher, 1981).

Apart from the nutritional benefits, advantages of nursing include the fact that it is bacteriologically safe and evidence that there are numerous compounds within breast milk that help the intestinal tract to resist infection. In the event of insufficiencies, various dietary supplements of protein, sugar, carbohydrate, vitamins, and minerals are available to correct these deficits. Obviously, too, the physical contact with breast-feeding is mutually satisfying to both mother and child.

INBORN METABOLIC AND ENDOCRINE DISORDERS

Metabolic Errors

Most developed countries have screening programs for metabolic errors that are amenable to dietary restriction or therapy. In large part, problems emerge from inherited diseases, wherein a normal nutritional component cannot be handled properly in the body. As a consequence, a metabolic block causes damage in one of several ways. Either there are insufficient amounts of a substance critical for body growth and metabolism, or an excessive amount of material that should have been metabolized accumulates in the body, depositing in tissues and preventing their appropriate function. Many such conditions are not amenable to therapy and culminate with severe mental retardation. Thus, with ample justification, routine screening of all newborns for *treatable* inherited diseases is extensive. As Table 10–2 shows, the incidence of identifiable conditions in New York State is low. Still, programs surely have been cost-effective since long-term care, in the aggregate, would far exceed expenditures of preventing mental retardation associated with these illnesses.

Though metabolic blocks may exist, these do not interfere with development prior to birth because excess materials can pass freely back to the mother and she can excrete them. However, after delivery, these nutritional by-products begin to accumulate in the body, resulting in damage to the tissues. Three such diseases are sufficiently common to warrant individual discussion. These include phenylketonuria (PKU), galactosemia, and hypothyroidism.

Phenylketonuria is the prototype of inherited conditions for which screening is justified. Dietary restriction, starting within the first several months of life, has been proven effective in preventing most impairments associated with the excess accumulation of phenylalanine (an amino acid) in the body (Berry, 1981). More specifically, the disease is caused by the absence of an enzyme or protein, which should be found in the liver, that fails to convert phenylalanine to other amino acids. As a result, material in the body increases and disrupts the central nervous system. Although there are several variations of the condition, damage can be minimized by limiting dietary phenylalanine (the substance cannot be removed entirely, as it is an essential component of proteins in many body tissues).

Galactosemia is an inability to convert galactose in the blood to glucose that can be utilized within the body. Glucose and galactose are the two simple sugars that combine to form the primary sugar of milk, lactose. As a consequence, galactose accumulates in the body and causes damage to the liver (cirrhosis). Affected infants become jaundiced and have concomitant bleeding difficulties. Several months into the course of the disease, babies frequently develop cataracts from the deposition of the galactose in the lens of the eye. On the other hand, if lactose is removed from the diet and there are

---

Table 10–2 Incidence of Metabolic Diseases in the New York State Metabolic Screening Program

Inherited Disease	Incidence
Phenylketonuria (PKU)	1:16,700
Galactosemia	1:73,000
Branched Chain Ketonuria	1:600,000
Histidinemia	1:160,000
Homocystinuria	1:480,000
Adenosine Deaminase Deficiency	1:1,200,000
Hypothyroidism	1:4,000

Source: From New York State Health Department, 1982, unpublished newsletter.

no other available sources of galactose, such newborns can grow and develop normally (Nicholson, 1983).

There are many causes of congenital hypothyroidism, including genetic disease, poor thyroid tissue formation, and environmental factors. In each there is an insufficient production of the thyroid hormone that results in a general slowing of tissue metabolism throughout the body. Early hypothyroidism is characterized by a range of symptoms including prolonged jaundice, poor suck, poor feeding, decreased intestinal motility, lethargy, and respiratory difficulties. The more classic manifestations of cretinism appear later, where progressive edema, enlarged tongue, hoarse cry, lethargy, and hypotonia are prominent (Fisher & Klein, 1981). Diagnosis of hypothyroidism can be confirmed by assessing serum thyroxine levels (a hormone produced by the thyroid gland). Other tests are carried out to confirm the particular type of hypothyroidism. Almost all forms are treatable with the oral administration of thyroxine, which is inexpensive. Ultimately, the prevention of mental retardation has been closely correlated with the onset of therapy. For example, Klein, Meltzer, and Kenny (1972) found that children treated before three months of age had substantially higher IQs than those identified thereafter. Obviously, however, given the individuality of families and variations of the disease, no firm predictions can be made. Children need to be followed developmentally and their therapy monitored carefully.

In summary, we know that nutrition plays a major role in the adequate development and function of the various organ systems of the body. Growth disturbances should lead to proper evaluations for possible unrecognized metabolic illnesses that are amenable to therapy. The ideal dietary composition for the preterm infant is still controversial. Yet, further research undoubtedly will illuminate the particular nutritional needs and vulnerabilities of these newborns.

REFERENCES

American Academy of Pediatrics Committee on Nutrition (1976). Iron supplementation for infants. *Pediatrics, 58,* 765–768.

Avery, G.B., & Fletcher, A.B. (1981). Nutrition. In G.B. Avery (Ed.), *Neonatology: Pathophysiology and management of the newborn* (2nd ed.) (pp. 1002–1060). Philadelphia: J.B. Lippincott.

Berry, H.K. (1981). The diagnosis of phenylketonuria. *American Journal of Diseases in Childhood, 135,* 211–213.

Driscoll, J.M. (1973). Parenteral therapy. In R.E. Behrman (Ed.), *Neonatology* (pp. 118–120). St. Louis: C.V. Mosby.

Fisher, D.A., & Klein, A.H. (1981). Thyroid development and disorders of thyroid function in the newborn. *New England Journal of Medicine, 304,* 702–712.

Fomon, S.J. (1974). *Infant nutrition.* Philadelphia: W.B. Saunders.

Grand, R.J. (1984). Disorders of the gastrointestinal tract—General considerations. In M. E. Avery & H. W. Taeusch (Eds.), *Diseases of the newborn* (5th ed.) (pp. 310–318). Philadelphia: W.B. Saunders.

Grand, R.J., Watkins, J.B., & Torti, F.M. (1976). Development of the human gastrointestinal tract. *Gastroenterology, 70,* 790–810.

Heird, W.C., Driscoll, J.M., Schallinger, J.N., Grebin, B., & Winters, R. W. (1972). Intravenous alimentation in pediatric patients. *Journal of Pediatrics, 80,* 351–372.

Klein, A.H., Meltzer, S., & Kenny, F.M. (1972). Improved prognosis in congenital hypothyroidism treated before age three months. *Journal of Pediatrics, 81,* 912–915.

*New York State Health Department. (1982). Unpublished newsletter.

Nicholson, J.F. (1983). Inborn errors of metabolism. In A.A. Fanaroff & R.J. Martin (Eds.), *Neonatal-perinatal medicine* (3rd ed.) (pp. 815–844). St. Louis: C.V. Mosby.

Raiha, N.C.R., Rassin, D.K., & Gaull, G.E. (1976). Milk protein quantity and quality in low-birthweight infants: Metabolic responses and effects on growth. *Pediatrics, 57,* 659–674.

Sandstead, H.H., Burk, R.F., Booth, E.H., Jr., & Darby, W.J. (1970). Current concepts on trace minerals. *Medical Clinics of North America, 54,* 1509–1531.

Tsang, R.L., Donovan, E.F., & Steichen, J.J. (1976). Calcium physiology and pathology in the neonate. *Pediatric Clinics of North America, 23,* 611–626.

Watkins, J.B., Ingal, D., Scezepanik, P., Klein, P.D., & Lester, R. (1973). Bile salt metabolism in the newborn. *New England Journal of Medicine, 288,* 431–434.

11

Abnormal Physical Development

Approximately 5 percent of all children have major birth defects, and many others are delivered with minor variations of physical development. The late physician David Smith devoted his life work to describing the various etiologies of physical impairment. His schema, still generally accepted today, includes three main categories of atypical development. These are *deformations, disruptions,* and *malformations* (Smith, 1982). While admittedly such distinctions may overlap in the same baby, they do help to clarify anomalies resulting from unusual mechanical forces, genetic defects, and infections and toxic agents. Thus, the present chapter is organized around these three classifications.

DEFORMATIONS

The first of Smith's major categories of impairment, deformations, follows the impact of an abnormal mechanical force on tissue that initially was developing normally. Uterine pressure on the rapidly growing fetus in the late stages of gestation is the primary cause of such abnormalities (Smith, 1981). Thus, deformations are found primarily in the individual parts of the body that are most malleable in utero, most commonly involving the head and extremities. The former, atypical physical growth of the head, may include deformation of the nose, folding and ridging of the ears, asymmetry of the mandible, and variations in shape and symmetry of the skull. Impairment of the extremities usually affects the legs and may be manifested as equinovarus (a form of club foot), deformed toes, dislocated hips, and dislocated knees. In addition, if there has been prolonged compression of a peripheral nerve, paralysis may be seen in the distribution of that nerve.

While several etiologies exist, one noteworthy and often catastrophic deformation sequence is precipitated by insufficient amniotic fluid (oligohydramnios), particularly in the second and third trimesters (Thomas & Smith, 1974). This problem may occur as a result of maternal hypertension, severe toxemia of pregnancy, a poorly functioning placenta, or an inadequate flow of fetal urine (a major contributor to amniotic fluid by the second trimester). The last insult also may arise from an early, chronic leak of amniotic fluid. Under these circumstances, the fetus is compressed, limiting movement; the umbilical cord is shorter and cord accidents are more common in such newborns. Fetal compression, too, may lead to multiple defects of the hands and feet, usually with joint stiffness. Abdominal and chest growth frequently are constrained, interfering with adequate alveolar growth. At birth, most babies thus affected do not have satisfactory lung development for survival.

Apart from insufficient lung development, ordinarily the prognosis for resolution of a defect is quite favorable, given the fact that the problem is a deformation of normal tissue rather than a malformation. Therefore, once the infant is released from the uterus, growth and the judicious use of general mechanical forces frequently can reshape the abnormality toward a more normal appearance.

DISRUPTIONS

Tissue disruptions that cause physical defects are likely to take place when the normal fetus is subjected to a mechanical, infectious, or toxic insult. One example of the first is the development of an amniotic band when a portion of the amnion (the innermost membrane surrounding the amniotic fluid) separates from the outer membranes and protrudes into the fluid. This tissue then may wrap around any portion of the body, constricting the blood supply, preventing further growth, and in extreme cases, resulting in amputation of the affected part. Transplacental infections such as rubella and cytomegalovirus, which will be discussed in the next chapter, also adversely affect physical development.

MALFORMATIONS

In contrast with the insults described above, which basically involve some alteration of normal processes of development, malformations emerge with poor production of tissue. These problems may originate from abnormal numbers of chromosomes or genes (the fundamental structures of chromosomes), or they may have no identifiable genetic etiology (Warkany, 1971). In the evaluation of any child found to have a defect, historical data are very important. The obstetrical background of the mother may provide valuable information, especially if there is a history of frequent spontaneous abortions. The use of alcohol, illicit drugs, or medications should be noted. In addition, data on the family may be useful in making a diagnosis, especially if there is a record of mental retardation, a malformation, chromosomal abnormalities, or other unexplained neonatal illnesses. Moreover, several principles should be kept in mind when assessing infants with multiple defects. First, rarely is a single defect sufficient to make the determination of a specific syndrome. For example, there are many healthy individuals in the normal population who have a simian hand crease but do not have Down syndrome. Second, among babies with an identifiable condition, there frequently is a great deal of variation. Again in example, slanted eyes and low muscle tone are evident in only eight percent of the newborns with Down syndrome (Smith & Wilson, 1973). In other situations of intrauterine drug exposure, the timing, duration, and amount are critical factors influencing the severity of the defect. Added to the complexity of issues is the fact that similar features or malformations may arise from different etiologies. For instance, hydrocephalus has been associated with over 20 distinct syndromes. For these reasons, the evaluation of a malformed infant must be done carefully to include all possible anomalies. The constellation of findings then may be used in combination with chromosomal analysis to provide an explanation to the parents during genetic counseling.

It is well beyond the scope of this text to present a detailed discussion of the many types of physical impairment. Several excellent texts are available for in-depth information (Bergsma, 1979; Smith, 1982; Warkany, 1971). However, we would like to describe briefly several congenital malformations that emerge from chromosomal abnormalities. In doing so, we will explain the various types of genetic inheritance and pay brief attention to some of the most common disabilities.

Chromosomal Abnormalities

Normally, humans have 23 pairs of chromosomes, 46 total in each cell of the body. Along with environmental influences, genes on these chromosomes determine body structure in detail. An excess or deficiency of chromosomes often causes poor formation of tissues and recognizable malformations. Excess material is most often evidenced in the trisomy syndromes, where there is a full additional chromosome. The most frequent condition exemplifying such problems is Trisomy 21, which is characterized by an additional chromosome 21 (historically, this also has been termed *Down syndrome* or *mongolism*). In these instances, the excess chromosome is passed from parents, in the formation of either the sperm or egg, wherein two of chromosome 21 are transmitted rather than one. It is well known that infants with Down syndrome are generally born to older women, recent evidence suggesting that these mothers are more likely to tolerate an abnormal fetus. While many different physical abnormalities have been associated with Trisomy 21 syndrome (See Figure 11–1), the most prevalent features include hypotonia, poor reflexes, hyperflexible joints, excess skin, flattened face, slanted eyes, abnormal ears, an atypical pelvis, and abnormalities of hand development. Virtually all, children and adults, have some degree of developmental disability, which generally slows with age. In addition, approximately 40 percent have serious cardiac defects. Abnormalities of the intestinal tract are found with increased frequency in comparison with the general population, and growth retardation is also common (Penrose & Smith, 1966; Smith & Wilson, 1973).

While Trisomy 21 is seen with an overall incidence of 1 in 660 newborns, Trisomy 18 occurs with much less frequency and affects approximately 1 in 3,500 infants. The condition is manifested as a constellation of malformations that are caused by an additional chromosome 18. Although the physical

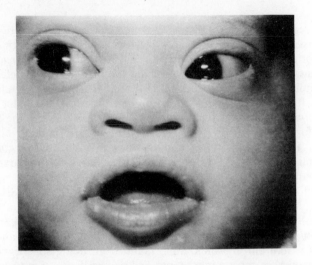

Figure 11–1 Facial Characteristics of a Baby with Trisomy 21 Syndrome

findings are somewhat variable, most babies are distinguished by low birthweight, a weak cry, decreased skeletal tissue, abnormal ears, a small mouth, clenched hands, undergrown fingernails, a short sternum (breast bone), and an abnormal pelvis (see Figures 11–2, 11–3, and 11–4). These infants have a limited capacity for survival. Most have a very weak suck, making feeding extremely difficult; thus even with aggressive management, they often fail to thrive. The 10 percent who do live throughout their first years invariably are severely mentally delayed (Smith, 1982; Warkany, Passage, & Smith, 1966).

Trisomy 13, which is caused by an additional chromosome 13, is even less common than the two conditions described above. The incidence is about 1 in 15,000 births. The most obvious characteristics are defects of the midface (including cleft lip and palate [See Figure 11–5] and a widening of the eyes), and poor development of the internal structure of the brain. Frequently, these infants have skin defects on the scalp (See Figure 11–6), and skeletal abnormalities are seen in the form of prominent heels and extra fingers and toes, often with fusion. Less than 20 percent of these severely retarded infants survive the first year of life, and those that do almost always have seizures and severe failure to thrive (Patau, Smith, Therman, Inhorn, & Wagner, 1960; Smith, 1982).

In contrast with malformations that arise from excess genetic material, monosomy defects are caused by the presence of too few chromosomes (specifically a total of only 45 in each cell). Most fetuses thus affected die early in gestation. One example of such conditions is Turner's syndrome, found in approximately 1 in 5,000 newborns and only in females, where one of the sex chromosomes is missing. Small stature, congenital edema of the extremities, a broad chest with widely spaced nipples, a low posterior

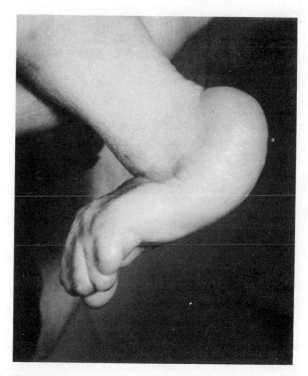

Figure 11-2 "Rocker-Bottom" Foot Characteristic of Babies with Trisomy 18 Syndrome

hairline, and webbing of the neck are typical characteristics (See Figures 11-7 and 11-8). Twenty percent of these children have cardiac defects. Unlike the syndromes already discussed, such youngsters do survive and many have normal intelligence, with a mean IQ of approximately 95. Beyond the newborn period, they tend to be relatively healthy, with the exception of continued small stature and a tendency to become obese. Since the ovaries are underdeveloped, infertility and the absence of secondary sexual characteristics also are later manifestations. The condition is felt to be a sporadic event, and there is no information on the risk of recurrence (Bergsma, 1979; Lindsten, 1963; Smith, 1982).

There are numerous other chromosomal abnormalities where portions of an individual chromosome may be missing (chromosomal deletion) or where portions of a given chromosome may have broken off and become attached to another (translocation). These are much rarer events. Although some specific associations have been made, the amount of material missing or duplicated leads to a wide variability of expressions. The majority are associated with abnormal brain development, mental retardation, and abnormalities of facial development. Furthermore, since relatively few cases have been reported, it is

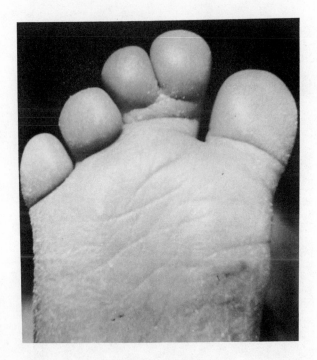

Figure 11-3 Syndactyly (Fused Toes) Seen in Babies with Trisomy 18 Syndrome

difficult to make any broad generalizations with respect to the natural history of these syndromes (Bergsma, 1979; Warkany, 1971).

Types of Inheritance and Genetic Disease

Genetic disease refers to inherited abnormalities that can be attributed to abnormal genes that have exerted an effect on development. Four different patterns of gene inheritance have been defined over the past several decades. These include autosomal dominant inheritance, autosomal recessive inheritance, X-linked inheritance, and polygenic or multifactorial inheritance (McKusick, 1978; Smith, 1982). The term autosome relates to the 22 pairs of chromosomes that do not determine sex. Therefore, an *autosomal dominant* gene is found on one of the non-sex chromosomes that, if present, effects a physical or developmental characteristic. There is no carrier state. If the gene is present, the individual is susceptible. These manifestations, however, may not be obvious in the newborn. Autosomal dominant inheritance usually emerges from a dominant gene passed from one parent to the child. Assuming that either the mother or father has that dominant gene, there is a 50 percent chance that any future child will be similarly affected. If neither parent has the abnormal gene and the newborn still shows indications, it is most likely that this is a fresh gene mutation. An example of an autosomal

Figure 11-4 Clinodactyly of Baby with Trisomy 18 Syndrome

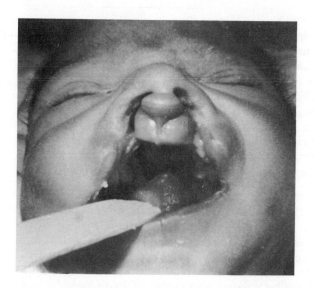

Figure 11-5 Severe Bilateral Cleft of Lip and Palate Seen in Babies with Trisomy 13 Syndrome

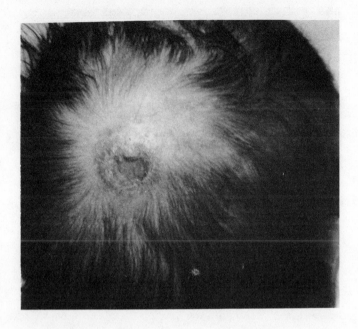

Figure 11-6 Scalp Defect in Newborn with Trisomy 13 Syndrome

dominant illness that has variable manifestations is von Recklinghausen's disease (neurofibromatosis). As can be expected from the name, these individuals have multiple subcutaneous and connective tissue tumors that are fibrous and frequently contain neuronal (nerve) tissue. Over 90 percent of affected individuals have areas of increased or decreased pigmentation of the skin. Although cutaneous lesions are the most common findings, nearly half will develop some evidence of neurologic impairment as a result of nerve compression within their lifetime. The estimated incidence is approximately 1 in 3,000 newborns. Approximately 50 percent of such infants are found to be a fresh gene mutation (Fienman & Yakovac, 1970).

A second genetic condition, *autosomal recessive* inheritance, implies a less potent gene that, though again found on the non-sex chromosomes, must be present in a paired condition in order to result in an atypical state. Most inherited diseases that have been defined have an autosomal recessive pattern of inheritance. Commonly, both parents are carriers and have no features of the illness. One-quarter of their children will be completely normal genetically; one-half will be carriers, but have no obvious physical abnormalities; and one-quarter will be affected. Examples of autosomal recessive inheritance include cystic fibrosis and virtually all of the inborn errors of metabolism, e.g., phenylketonuria. Many autosomal recessive carrier states now can be

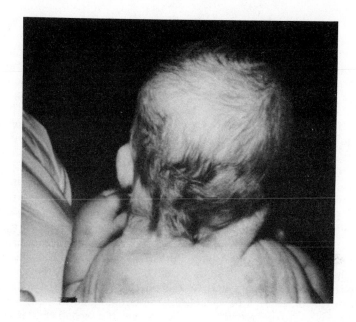

Figure 11–7 Webbing at the Neck of Baby with Turner's Syndrome

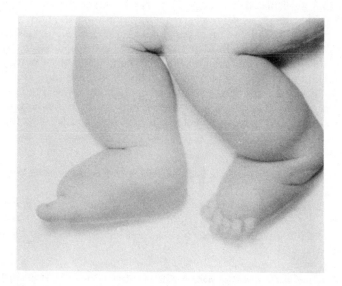

Figure 11–8 Edema of Legs and Feet Seen in Babies with Turner's Syndrome

detected and these determinations, of course, are extremely helpful with family planning (McKusick, 1978).

X-linked inheritance conditions have their origin with an abnormal gene present on one of the female sex chromosomes (the X chromosome). This gene is recessive and therefore the normal gene on the second X chromosome prevents expression of the disease. Every male has an X chromosome from his mother and a Y chromosome with very little genetic material from his father. If the male inherits his mother's X chromosome with the abnormal gene, he will be affected. Instances of such occurrence include adult onset baldness, hemophilia (factor VIII deficiency), and Duchenne type muscular dystrophy. With each pregnancy, there is a 50 percent chance that the male child will have the inherited condition, and 50 percent of the female newborns will be carriers, capable of transmitting this gene to their offspring.

Thus far, we have discussed only the contribution of genes in a single location, resulting in an identifiable illness. In the event of *polygenic* (multiple genes) inheritance, many genes are necessary from both parents before the child will be affected. This type of inheritance has been associated with numerous malformations, including cleft lip and cleft palate, neural tube defects (meningomyelocele), and various congenital heart defects. If parents have a single child with a polygenetically inherited malformation, the risk of recurrence is approximately three to five percent. If a second child is affected, the risk respectively increases to approximately 15 percent (Smith & Aase, 1970).

There are a number of additional malformations that may be present in the newborn. These include abnormalities of the intestine, the abdominal wall, the genitalia, the kidneys, and the extremities. For the majority of these conditions that are isolated instances, there is no known genetic predisposition. On the other hand, as soon as any malformation or anomaly has been detected, very careful examination of the child must be made. Normative data now are available not only for head circumference, length, and weight by age, but also for detailed measurements of the face, hands, and other body parts. In those situations where syndromes have been defined but the initial descriptions included very few patients, it is difficult to be predictive in counseling a family. Therefore, continuous and cautious evaluation and conservative advice for parents generally is the best course of action.

REFERENCES

Bergsma, D.S. (1979). *Birth defects atlas and compendium* (2nd ed.). Baltimore: Williams & Wilkins.

Fienman, N.L., & Yakovac, W.C. (1970). Neurofibromatosis in childhood. *Journal of Pediatrics*, 76, 339–346.

Lindsten, J. (1963). *The nature and origin of X chromosome aberrations in Turner's syndrome.* Stockholm: Almquist & Wiksell.

McKusick, V.D. (1978). *Mendelian inheritance in man: Catalogs of autosomal dominant, autosomal recessive and X-linked phenotypes* (5th ed.). Baltimore: Johns Hopkins Press.

Patau, K., Smith, D.W., Therman, E., Inhorn, S.L., & Wagner, H.P. (1960). Multiple congenital anomaly caused by an extra chromosome. *Lancet, 1,* 790–793.

Penrose, L.S., & Smith, G.F. (1966). *Down's anomaly.* Boston: Little, Brown.

Smith, D.W. (1981). *Recognizable patterns of human deformation* (pp. 97–144). Philadelphia: W.B. Saunders.

Smith, D.W. (1982). *Recognizable patterns of human malformation* (3rd ed.) (pp. 1–23). Philadelphia: W.B. Saunders.

Smith, D.W., & Aase, J.M. (1970). Polygenic inheritances of certain common malformations. *Journal of Pediatrics, 76,* 653–659.

Smith, D.W., & Wilson, A.C. (1973). *The child with Down's syndrome.* Philadelphia: W.B. Saunders.

Thomas, I.T., & Smith, D.W. (1974). Oligohydramnios, cause of the nonrenal features of Potter's syndrome, including pulmonary hypoplasia. *Journal of Pediatrics, 84,* 811–814.

Warkany, J. (1971). *Congenital malformations.* Chicago: Yearbook Medical.

Warkany, J., Passage, E., & Smith, L.B. (1966). Congenital malformations in autosomal trisomy syndromes. *American Journal of Diseases of Children, 112,* 502–517.

12

Infection

Newborns may be infected by a variety of agents. Some of these infections may pass from the mother to the baby during pregnancy and others are acquired by exposure to organisms that are present in the vagina or in the environment after birth (Blanc, 1961). *Sepsis*, a more common term for any viral, bacterial, or parasitic infection in the newborn, is seen in approximately 1 in every 1,000 full-term births. Among infants born at less than three pounds, the incidence may rise to as high as 15 percent. Infections may have profound effects on development, early in the pregnancy altering the growing fetus and in later stages of pregnancy and after birth, disrupting the normal formation of tissues and organs (Klein, Remington, & Marcy, 1983). In this last chapter dealing with newborn medical insult, we will consider the diagnostic features of infections, discuss frequent conditions, and comment upon prevention, treatment, and prognosis.

DIAGNOSTIC FEATURES

The signs and symptoms of infection are diverse, and many can resemble or be disguised by other illnesses of the newborn. Although respiratory distress may be caused by infection, more frequently it occurs as a result of retained lung fluid or a deficiency of surfactant in premature infants. Irritability may arise from an inflammation of the membranes surrounding the brain (meningitis), but is seen more often with birth asphyxia, drug withdrawal, or central nervous system hemorrhage. Jaundice may result from the accelerated breakdown of red blood cells with infection; yet it can occur with bruising and prematurity. Hypoglycemia, while evident with infection, more often is manifested in babies born preterm, growth retarded, or large-for-gestational age as a result of maternal diabetes. In short, many of the features of infections overlap with other problems and illnesses of the neonate (Feigin & Callahan, 1983).

If the above patterns seem to predominate, what characteristics do serve as indicators? A few signs and symptoms are relatively useful in suggesting the possibility of infection (Gotoff & Behrman, 1970). These factors include poor temperature control and the early onset of apnea. Older children and adults generally respond to infection with a fever; however, this is very uncommon among newborns. Typically, full-term babies have a decreased body temperature; premature infants, on the other hand, usually require intensive temperature support. Thus, if the effects of overheating and maternal medication can be ruled out, apnea in the first several days of life commonly is associated with infections (Ablow, et al., 1976).

DECREASED RESISTANCE TO INFECTION

Prior to birth, the fetus has a limited capacity to ward off disease. For most babies, the intrauterine environment is sterile. Once delivered, however, newborns are exposed to numerous viruses and bacteria with which they must cope. The ability to respond successfully to infection is severalfold and includes the function of the white blood cells and circulating proteins.

Basically, the white blood cells of the body are divided into two components, agranulocytes (without granules) and granulocytes (containing granules). The agranulocytes include lymphocytes, small white blood cells that produce antibodies or proteins that are directed against infectious agents. The other primary agranulocyte is the monocyte, which aids in that process and also functions as the main white blood cell involved in the clearing of the debris of infection. The granulocytes are white blood cells that contain granules located outside of the nucleus. Those that primarily fight bacterial infection are the *neutrophils*, containing powerful enzymes (Miller & Stiehm, 1979). For bacterial infection to be managed effectively, the neutrophil must be attracted to the site of the infection, must be capable of ingesting the bacteria, and then must be able to destroy the bacteria once it is inside the white blood cell. In the newborn, while the killing process approximates that of older children and adults, the mobilization of neutrophils to the site of an infection and the subsequent ingestion of the bacteria is somewhat restricted (Miller, 1969).

Circulating blood proteins, primarily the antibodies (immunoglobulins) aid in this process of neutralizing and eliminating bacteria and viruses. One variety, immunoglobulin G (IgG), is a protein that can be transmitted from the mother across the placenta to the fetus. If the mother has been exposed to infection and has responded appropriately to this illness, some protection can be afforded the baby by these proteins. This helps to explain the rarity of chicken pox, mumps, strep throat, and rheumatic fever in newborns. On the other hand, if the baby, after birth, is exposed to an organism that the mother never has coped with effectively, the infant is more likely to contract that disease. The few infants who become infected with agents their mothers have contracted usually have much milder illnesses (Bellanti, 1978). A second immunoglobulin, IgM, is a protein much larger than IgG and is, in general, the first compound produced by the body in response to infection. This substance does not traverse the placenta in either direction, so that the maternal IgM is distinct from the baby's IgM. Thus, if the IgM is elevated in the blood of the newborn, this suggests that the child has been exposed and is responding to an infectious agent (Bellanti & Boner, 1981).

A supplementary complex of proteins found in the blood, the complement system, aids the function of white blood cells and the immunoglobulins in fighting infection. Unfortunately, this mechanism also may be deficient especially in the premature infant (Gotoff, 1974; Miller & Stiehm, 1979). In addition to the foregoing complications, babies also are more prone to infection after birth because of major differences in their anatomy as compared with that of adults. In particular, their skin is much thinner and, therefore, cutaneous infection is more common. Preterm infants frequently are unable to feed and, during the process of placing a tube into the stomach to provide adequate nutrition, the limited antibacterial and antiviral capabilities of the tonsils and adenoids are bypassed. Many invasive procedures such as the placement of tubes down the trachea for respiratory support and catheters into blood vessels increase the potential risk of infection. One of the more prevalent sites of infection, even in healthy full-term babies, is the umbilicus when the cord is shed.

TRANSPLACENTAL INFECTIONS

As we have indicated, the fetus can be infected prior to birth by a variety of different organisms that initially infect the mother, then are passed transplacentally to the fetus. The most common diseases infecting the newborn have been given the acronym TORCH infections (Nahmias, 1974), which denotes toxoplasmosis (TO), rubella (R), cytomegalovirus (C), and herpes (H). Frequently an S is added at the beginning to produce STORCH, with the S standing for syphilis. These agents do not produce a homogeneous group of illnesses; their characteristics are very different and include three viruses (rubella, cytomegalovirus, and herpes), a parasitic infection (toxoplasmosis), and a parabacterial infection (syphilis) (Overall & Glasgow, 1970).

Rubella

Rubella (German measles) is the prototype of viral infections, with much information having been obtained in the decade preceding 1970. Such illness in the mother may be very mild. Only maternal infection with subsequent fetal affliction in the first four months of gestation is likely to produce any abnormal physical finding or developmental disability. It is most important to realize that the infection is well established before the baby's own immune defenses are developed. Therefore, virtually every organ system of the body may be involved. Some of these effects may be transient; others may be long lasting.

The four most common persistent problems of newborns with rubella are hearing loss (approximately 87 percent); visual problems, primarily cataracts and glaucoma (34 percent); heart disease (46 percent); and mental retardation (approximately 40 percent). Two decades ago, the cost of the care of these infants to the government was excessively high as a result of the combination of physical and developmental problems. A concerted effort in the late 1960s culminated in a rubella vaccine that was licensed in 1970. Within several years of that accomplishment, the number of identifiable cases of both rubella and congenital rubella were cut to one-fifth. Presentation of a child with congenital rubella typically includes low birthweight, bruising, a large liver and spleen, abnormalities of bone development, meningitis, hearing loss, cataracts, abnormal retinal development, various forms of cardiac disease, mental retardation, behavior disorders, central language disorders, undescended testes, hernias, and microcephaly. Less commonly seen are jaundice, glaucoma, myopia, hepatitis, generalized enlargement of the lymph nodes, pneumonia, diabetes, thyroid dysfunction, seizures, and degenerative brain disease. Infants infected tend to excrete the virus for prolonged periods of time and as many as 10 percent still actively shed the organism up to one year. These newborns are potentially dangerous to women in the childbearing age group (Cooper, 1975; Modlin & Brandling-Bennett, 1974; Sever, Hardy, Nelson, & Gilkeson, 1969).

Although much has been done to elucidate the transmission and infection-induced malformations of rubella, there remains no specific therapy to eradicate the illness in the newborn. Surgery may help to correct some of the cardiac and visual problems, but only early developmental evaluation and persistent follow-up can blunt the detrimental effects on the central nervous system.

Cytomegalovirus

As the incidence of congenital rubella began to decrease with the introduction of the immunization programs, a new virus rose to the top of the list of newborn infections, cytomegalovirus. (See Figure 12–1.) This is one of the herpes viruses and, like all other members of the group, the infection once acquired remains throughout life. The individual may have no obvious symptomatology, but in periods of decreased resistance the organism may reoccur much like chicken pox, another in the herpes virus group, which may reactivate as shingles or herpes zoster. Cytomegalovirus (CMV) may be passed transplacentally but also may infect the newborn as an ascending infection from the vagina. Manifestations of the virus in the newborn are similar to those of rubella. Infection in the mother, however, is much more difficult to recognize clinically, where she may evidence little more than flu-like symptoms. While maternal illness in the first trimester may produce fetal anomalies, later infection tends to produce much more subtle manifestations in the newborn. Hearing loss, secondary to a viral infection of the inner ear, may be one of the most subtle presentations of cytomegalovirus (Hanshaw, 1975; Kuman, Nankervis, & Gold, 1973).

At present there is no specific therapy available for cytomegalovirus. Current research is focused on developing a reliable and safe immunization that can be used prior to pregnancy and thus avoid the infection that might be passed to the fetus.

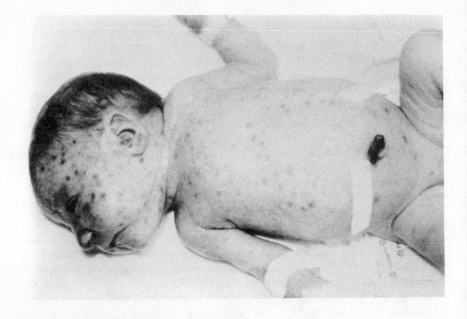

Figure 12–1 Infant with Congenital Cytomegalovirus (CMV) Infection

Toxoplasmosis

Toxoplasmosis differs from most of the other infectious agents in that it is one of the few parasites that may be transmitted directly from the mother to the fetus. The mother again is usually asymptomatic with this infection. Man is an aberrant host for this infection that primarily infects cats but also may infect dogs. The small eggs produced by the parasite may be inhaled by the mother as she changes cat litter. Once in the human, the developing embryos complete their development within the intestinal tract and then seed to various organs throughout the body by means of the blood. Wherever a cyst forms, tissue disruption occurs (Feldman, 1968).

Mothers with infection in the first trimester tend to produce infants with severe congenital disease. Third trimester infections may be subclinical. Manifestations of the more severe conditions include microcephaly, deafness, retinitis, blindness, jaundice, seizures, large lymph nodes, pneumonia, and enlarged liver and spleen. Of greatest concern is the tendency of the parasite to travel to the brain with subsequent tissue disruption. These cysts may be seen by a simple x-ray of the skull since they quite commonly calcify. Antibiotics are available to help limit the extent of the disease. However, areas of brain or other tissue that have been affected generally do not recover adequately. The neurodevelopmental outcome of these babies is variable depending on the distribution and number of parasites that infest the brain or other vital organs (Alford, Stagno, & Reynolds, 1975; Desmonts & Couvreu, 1975; Remington & Desmonts, 1983).

Syphilis

Neonatal syphilis is much less common than it was 30 years ago as a consequence of the aggressive screening of mothers during pregnancy. The treponema is a small wormlike organism that can invade and infect any organ of the body. The severity of the disease manifestation depends on tissue disruption and body response to the invasion of the organism (Taber & Huber, 1975). The typical presentations of congenital syphilis are a dry skin rash, bruising, large liver and spleen, hypotonia, jaundice, anemia, and a profuse rhinorrhea (Nabarro, 1954). The illness may show very subtle symptoms and thus go unrecognized. One of the more common characteristics of the disease now is seen in the baby brought for medical care at several months of age who may have swelling of the joints or limited movement of extremities. Child abuse frequently is suspected; however, x-rays do not reveal fractures but rather an elevation of the outermost layer of the long bones, resulting from infection by the organism. Even this relatively late presentation, if recognized and treated, may lead to relatively minimal long-term developmental disability.

The therapy of syphilis, once recognized, is comparatively simple. It is readily cared for with penicillin or one of many other antibiotics. These medications may be given in several doses, and the child's hospital course may be very short. If there is involvement of the central nervous system, however, the treatment must be more aggressive and prolonged. Once infection is recognized in the child, the mother also should be examined and treated, and her sexual contacts should be found.

Other Infections

Numerous other infections, primarily viral, can cross the placenta and infect the newborn. The signs and symptoms of many of these illnesses tend to overlap and, therefore, may be very confusing. Those affecting the mother, that in turn infect the newborn, include Epstein-Barr virus (the virus of mononucleosis), polio, mumps, chicken pox, and influenza. In each case, an aggressive approach to the diagnosis is important, in large part in order to counsel the parents and to prevent the spread of that infectious agent to other children in the facility caring for the child. Although many of the presenting symptoms of neonatal infections are similar, subsequent developmental disabilities differ with the types of viruses and their predilection for certain portions of the central nervous system (Overall & Glasgow, 1970).

ASCENDING AND NEONATAL INFECTIONS

Ascending infections are those that reach the fetus by passing through the cervix, generally after rupture of the membranes. The infant first may be exposed to these organisms in the process of vaginal delivery. *Neonatal infections*, on the other hand, are acquired after birth. These can be transmitted by family members, hospital personnel, or various materials used with the baby.

Herpes

One of the most serious and virulent illnesses in the newborn, most often acquired as an ascending infection, is herpes. There are several strains of the virus. Type 1 is predominantly an oral organism responsible for cold sores, fever, and blisters. Type 2 herpes is primarily a genital organism. However, the sexual liberation of the last 20 years has led to increasing Type 2 oral infections and Type 1 herpes genital infections. The fetus and newborn may be affected by either form of the disease (Whitley, Nahmias, Visintine, Fleming, & Alford, 1980). The most frequent presenting symptom, found in approximately 80 percent of the cases, is lethargy. Respiratory distress is evidenced in approximately 60 percent. The typical rash of herpes is seen in generally less than 50 percent of affected newborns. Other signs of the disease are those usually evident with generalized infections of the newborn, including temperature instability, enlarged liver and spleen, poor coagulation of blood, and jaundice. Herpes, however, is an aggressive virus and what commonly appears to be localized infection may progress to systemic disease, especially targeted toward the central nervous system. The generalized form of the disease is devastating. Although survival is better with the localized form of the disease, as much as 40 percent of the survivors have serious sequelae, including seizures, mental retardation, and other forms of severe developmental disability (Nahmias, Keyserling, & Kerrick, 1983).

Although newer antiviral agents now are available, they are as yet no panacea for neonatal herpes. They are most beneficial when used for children with localized disease, with the hope of preventing generalized disease. Further, while the treatment of newborns with generalized illness has resulted in an increase in survival, many of the survivors still have serious sequelae (Brunell, 1980). The prevention of herpes is difficult. Mothers who previously have had herpes may be asymptomatic at the time of delivery, but their infants still may become infected. Some evidence today suggests that when there are active herpes lesions in the mother, cesarean delivery may be helpful in limiting the exposure and subsequent illness in the baby.

Gonorrhea

Gonorrhea is a sexually transmitted disease. Adult males usually have a penile discharge, whereas females may be relatively asymptomatic. Babies born to mothers with active gonorrhea are at greatest risk for eye infection. Early in the 1900s in New York State, visual impairment resulting from neonatal eye infection was the most common single cause for children requiring schools for the blind. As a result, all states now mandate eye prophylaxis against this infection.

Generally, the baby is exposed to the bacteria at the time of descent through the birth canal. Less commonly, the bacteria may ascend into the amniotic fluid surrounding the infant after rupture of the membranes. In either case, the organism penetrates the anterior cell layer of the eye, and within five days a purulent infection results. If untreated, disease in the eye progresses to meningitis or other systemic infection. Once established, it may be treated with antibiotics. Unfortunately, although treatment may eradicate the organism, the damage has been done (Handsfield, Hodson, & Holmes, 1973). Therefore eye prophylaxis is very important. As we have discussed in the chapter on typical newborn care, the most commonly used solution is .1 percent silver nitrate solution. This is instilled into each eye shortly after birth and kills the organism. Treatment should not be delayed more than one-half hour after birth since after that time the organism penetrates the outer layer of the eye and the silver nitrate thus would be ineffective. Several topical antibiotics are now being used, including erythromycin and tetracycline. They are equally as effective as silver nitrate with the killing of the gonorrheal organism; yet, their cost is as much as 20 to 30 times greater.

Necrotizing Enterocolitis

Necrotizing enterocolitis is a disease that results in distention of the abdomen, feeding intolerance, and bloody stools. X-rays of the abdomen reveal distended intestine and a classic presentation of gas trapped in the bowel wall. Often the clinical course culminates with hemorrhagic destruction of the intestine, metabolic abnormalities, respiratory insufficiency, and infection progressing to death. While numerous epidemiological associations have been suggested, only a few consistent underlying factors have been identified. These include prematurity, feeding, and bacteria within the intestine. Outbreaks of neonatal illness, in addition, suggest an infectious component. In part, some of these indications are based on analysis of the intestinal contents of babies with the disease that contained sugar, protein, organic acids, and bacteria (Clark et al., 1985).

Infants fed formula are at greater risk for developing the disease than those babies receiving breast milk. The etiology of these differences is complex but, in part, it may be attributed to a selective inhibition of the bacteria most capable of producing the organic acids that are most destructive in the lower intestinal tract. More specifically, as the pH in the intestine is lowered, dietary proteins change their shape and, in combination with calcium, promote the secretion of various chemicals by cells lining the intestinal tract. Local changes take place in blood flow, and white blood cells used to fight infection and platelets (a portion of the clotting mechanism) are brought to the site of the initial injury. In many newborns, especially the more mature babies, this process suffices to repair the damage. In the more premature infant with an immature intestinal tract, the process may accelerate—even to the destruction of portions of the intestine. Bacteria then may gain access to the bloodstream, resulting in more generalized infection. Other etiologies of intestinal damage have been documented in the newborns, including those babies who have not been formula fed or nursed. The majority of these intestinal diseases arise from a period of inadequate blood flow to the intestine, again causing destruction and hemorrhage.

Outbreaks of necrotizing enterocolitis may be partially explained by slight differences in the metabolic capacities of bacteria that normally grow within the intestinal tract. Here, there are bacteria capable of fermenting sugar faster and producing more acid, which subsequently leads to triggering the disease. These bacteria may retain this ability for only a limited period of time. One very important concern with babies suffering from necrotizing enterocolitis is that their bacteria may be passed inadvertently from one infant to another in an intensive care nursery.

The primary therapy for necrotizing enterocolitis remains supportive. Feedings are stopped and IVs are begun to provide sufficient fluid for the newborn. Cultures are taken, and the baby is put on antibiotics for the possibility of systemic infection that originates within the intestine. Up to one-third of such newborns require surgical intervention to remove dead necrotic intestine. With medical or surgical management, approximately 50-60 percent of the afflicted newborns survive. The remaining group succumbs to the disease early, as a result of a massive bowel destruction or surgical removal of the intestine. In the latter case, these babies may have an insufficient length of intestine for digestion, causing long-term failure to thrive and increased susceptibility to infection.

Systemic Infections

Any organism in the mother's vagina or in the baby's environment after birth may infect the newborn. The symptoms usually are those of systemic disease with temperature instability, respiratory difficulty, and other evidence of organ involvement. One common bacterial organism acquired, in some cases at birth and in other instances from family and hospital staff, is *Streptococcus*. There are many varieties of *Streptococcus*. In particular, Group A is predominant with strep throat, and the organism also has been associated with rheumatic fever and severe kidney disease. It is quite rare for the newborn to be infected with this bacteria, since protective antibodies (proteins) from the mother have crossed the placenta, usually limiting the bacterial proliferation. Group B strep infection, on the other hand, is a serious threat to the newborn. Basically, it has two forms of presentation. The early type is marked by severe respiratory distress, simulating hyaline membrane disease in the newborn. Despite aggressive respiratory support and the use of antibiotics, the mortality rate remains high, approximately 50 percent in most intensive care nurseries. A second, more subtle form of the disease is meningitis, generally caused by a different subgroup of Group B strep. Typically the illness becomes manifest two to three weeks after birth, but may present as late as several months after birth. Early symptoms include poor feeding and lethargy. Fortunately, once identified, this form generally is more amenable to therapy (Baker, 1979; Franciosi, Knostman, & Zimmerman, 1973).

The most recurrent environmentally acquired infection in the newborn is *Staphylococcus*. Its mildest form is skin pustules that can be managed topically without the use of antibiotics. Bacteria can infect any portion of the body, including breast (abscess), umbilical cord (omphalitis), and circumcision site, as well as pneumonia. One of the more severe manifestations of staph infection is the *Staphylococcus* scalded-skin syndrome. This type results from a toxin produced by a local colonization of the bacteria. In these instances, shedding of the skin and major problems with fluid losses, much like that of burn patients, occur. With aggressive supportive therapy, these infants generally survive (McIntosh, 1984).

There are many other potentially harmful infections. The more preterm infants and those requiring the greatest therapeutic manipulations generally evidence the more serious manifestations.

PREVENTION AND TREATMENT

Prevention of neonatal infection resides largely with a high index of suspicion and concern among the health team responsible for caring for the pregnant mother. She should be encouraged to avoid sexual contact with anyone with vesicles or a discharge. Meat, a potential source of parasitic infections, should be cooked thoroughly. The mother should avoid animal feces (kitty litter), especially that of little kittens, by which she may become infected with toxoplasmosis. She should be given no live vaccines such as rubella, polio, or mumps during the pregnancy. On visits to the health team, the vaginal examination should include a surveillance culture for gonorrhea. Serologic testing for syphilis during the pregnancy is mandatory. Once an infection has been identified, it should be treated promptly to minimize the potential risk to the fetus.

Treatment of the neonate with infection is relatively straightforward. If the illness is bacterial, antibiotics for that specific organism should be used. If the child has signs and symptoms of infection but no etiology is identified, the choice of antibiotics then is based upon a decision relative to the organisms most likely to be infecting the baby. Apart from general supportive therapy, other treatments that may be useful include transfusing the infant with fresh frozen adult plasma or concentrated adult white blood cells. These therapies may offer essential elements, which the baby has in short supply, in order to cope with infection.

The viral and protozoal infections are much more difficult to remedy. The antibiotics available for their care generally are quite toxic and have limited application. For viral infections such as cytomegalovirus and rubella, there is presently no form of therapy available.

The prognosis for any newborn with an infection is dependent on the responsible organism and its predilection for certain body organs. Overall, viral infections—especially herpes, cytomegalovirus, and rubella—have a stronger tendency to cause damage to the central nervous system and, therefore, are apt to produce more devastating developmental problems. Unfortunately, with many of the perinatal infections, much of the impairment has been done even if therapy is instituted immediately. Understandably, every child who has been infected should be monitored closely for developmental delay.

REFERENCES

Ablow, R.C., Driscoll, S.G., Effmann, E.L., Gross, I., Jolles, C.J., Uauy, R., & Warshaw, J.B. (1976). A comparison of early-onset Group B streptococcal neonatal infection and the respiratory distress syndrome of the newborn. *New England Journal of Medicine, 294,* 65–70.

Alford, C.A., Stagno, S., & Reynolds, D.W. (1975). Toxoplasmosis: Silent congenital infection. In S. Krugman & A.A. Gershon (Eds.), *Infections of the fetus and newborn infant* (pp. 133–157). New York: Alan R. Liss.

Baker, C.I. (1979). Group B streptococcal infections in neonates. *Pediatrics, 64,* 5–15.

Bellanti, J.A. (1978). *Immunology II* (pp. 370–436). Philadelphia: W.B. Saunders.

Bellanti, J.A., & Boner, A.L. (1981). Immunology of the fetus and newborn. In G.B. Avery (Ed.), *Neonatology: Pathophysiology and management of the newborn* (2nd ed.) (pp. 701–722). Philadelphia: J.B. Lippincott.

Blanc, W.A. (1961). Pathways of fetal and early neonatal infection. *Journal of Pediatrics, 59,* 473–496.

Brunell, P.A. (1980). Prevention and treatment of neonatal herpes. *Pediatrics, 66,* 806–808.

Clark, D.A., Thompson, J.E., Weiner, L.D., McMillan, J.A., Schneider, A.J., & Rokahr, J.E. (1985). Necrotizing enterocolitis: Intraluminal biochemistry in human neonates and a rabbit model. *Pediatric Research, 19,* 919–921.

Cooper, L.Z. (1975). Congenital rubella in the United States. In S. Krugman & A.A. Gershon (Eds.), *Infections of the fetus and newborn infant* (pp. 1–22). New York: Alan R. Liss.

Desmonts, G., & Couvreu, J. (1975). Epidemiologic and serologic aspects of perinatal infection. In S. Krugman & A.A. Gershon (Eds.), *Infections of the fetus and newborn infant* (pp. 115–132). New York: Alan R. Liss.

Dudgeon, J.A. (1975). Congenital rubella. *Journal of Pediatrics, 87,* 1078–1086.

Feigin, R.D., & Callahan, D.L. (1983). Postnatally acquired infections. In A.A. Fanaroff & R.J. Martin (Eds.), *Neonatal-perinatal medicine: Diseases of the fetus and infant* (pp. 650–691). St. Louis: C.V. Mosby.

Feldman, H.A. (1968). Toxoplasmosis. *New England Journal of Medicine, 279,* 1370–1375, 1431–1437.

Franciosi, R.A., Knostman, J.D., & Zimmerman, R.A. (1973). Group B streptococcal neonatal and infant infections. *Journal of Pediatrics, 82,* 707–718.

Gotoff, S.P. (1974). Neonatal immunity. *Journal of Pediatrics, 85,* 149–154.

Gotoff, S.P., & Behrman, R.E. (1970). Neonatal septicemia. *Journal of Pediatrics, 76,* 142–153.

Handsfield, H.H., Hodson, W.A., & Holmes, K.K. (1973). Neonatal gonococcal infection. *Journal of the American Medical Association, 225,* 697–701.

Hanshaw, J.B. (1975). CNS sequelae of congenital cytomegalovirus infection. In S. Krugman & A.A. Gershon (Eds.), *Infections of the fetus and newborn infant* (pp. 47–54). New York: Alan R. Liss.

Klein, J.O., Remington, J.S., & Marcy, S.M. (1983). Current concepts of infections of the fetus and newborn infant. In J.S. Remington & J.O. Klein (Eds.), *Infectious diseases of the fetus and newborn infant* (pp. 1–26). Philadelphia: W.B. Saunders.

Kuman, M.L., Nankervis, G.A., & Gold, E. (1973). Inapparent congenital cytomegalovirus infection: A follow-up study. *New England Journal of Medicine, 288,* 1370–1372.

McIntosh, K. (1984). Bacterial infections of the newborn. In M.E. Avery & H.W. Taeusch (Eds.), *Diseases of the newborn* (5th ed.) (pp. 729–747). Philadelphia: W.B. Saunders.

Miller, M.E. (1969). Phagocytosis in the newborn infant: Hormonal and cellular factors. *Journal of Pediatrics, 74,* 255–262.

Miller, M.E., & Stiehm, E.R. (1979). Host defenses in the fetus and neonate. *Pediatrics, 64,* 705–833.

Modlin, J.F., & Brandling-Bennett, A.D. (1974). Surveillance of the congenital rubella syndrome, 1969–1973. *Journal of Infectious Diseases, 130,* 316–318.

Nabarro, D. (1954). *Congenital syphilis.* London: E. Arnold.

Nahmias, A.J. (1974). The TORCH complex. *Hospital Practice, 9,* 65–72.

Nahmias, A.J., Keyserling, H.L., & Kerrick, G.M. (1983). Herpes simplex. In J.S. Remington & J.O. Klein (Eds.), *Infectious diseases of the fetus and newborn infant* (pp. 636–678). Philadelphia: W.B. Saunders.

Overall, J.C., & Glasgow, L.A. (1970). Virus infections of the fetus and newborn infant. *Journal of Pediatrics, 77,* 315–333.

Remington, J.S., & Desmonts, G. (1983). Toxoplasmosis. In J.S. Remington & J.O. Klein (Eds.), *Infectious diseases of the fetus and newborn infant* (pp. 143–263). Philadelphia: W.B. Saunders.

Sever, J.L., Hardy, J.B., Nelson, K.B., & Gilkeson, M.R. (1969). Rubella in the collaborative perinatal research study. *American Journal of Diseases of Children, 118,* 123–132.

Taber, L.H., & Huber, T.W. (1975). Congenital syphilis. In S. Krugman & A.A. Gershon (Eds.), *Infections of the fetus and newborn infant* (pp. 183–190). New York: Alan R. Liss.

Whitley, R.J., Nahmias, A.J., Visintine, A.M., Fleming, C.L., & Alford, C.A. (1980). The natural history of herpes simplex virus infection of mother and newborn. *Pediatrics, 66,* 489–501.

13

Describing Behavior and Analyzing Competence

Historically, screening and assessment of infants has been an ill-defined process, often wanting in application to educational practice. Identifying risk, describing behavior, and determining the prognosis for future development are integral steps to evaluation in the early months and should be intimately connected to the plan of intervention. More frequently than not, however, this has not been the case with the narrow ranges of behavior sampled.

Some of these difficulties have evolved by nature of the population served, some result from imprecise techniques of evaluation, and still others emanate from unfounded interpretations. Though parents and professionals have long searched for early indicators of competence and delay, projections sometimes have caused both family and child more harm than benefit. Sensitive and thoughtfully applied evaluations with acknowledged reservations of time, error, and instrumentation could resolve some of the dilemmas of assessment.

New initiatives in screening and diagnosis in the years ahead will need to depart from known and accepted convention. Professionals need to become more clinically astute, more eclectic, and less comfortable with plan-for-plan measures. Time, follow-up, and a range of settings, caretakers, and teachers eventually may become routine in the course of evaluation, and multiple criteria according to a spectrum of behavioral inventories may become common practice rather than the exception. Finally, we may learn that the real task of screening and assessment is the disclosure of competence, not deficiency, and that this goal is carried out most wisely with a willingness to abide with realistic and inevitable uncertainty. This chapter will reflect recent trends and growth in these directions.

IDENTIFYING RISK AND THE PREDICTION OF FUTURE DEVELOPMENT

Screening and Diagnosis

It is well documented that conditions of risk and impairment during the first and middle months of infancy that lead later to developmental delay are difficult to identify and assess (Keogh & Kopp, 1978; Kopp & Parmelee, 1979; Meier, 1976; Parmelee, Sigman, Kopp, & Haber, 1976; Scott & Hogan, 1982; Thoman & Becker, 1979). For instance, it is not unusual to find that newborns with substantial medical insult, given the advantage of caring home environments, show far fewer problems than initially anticipated. By the same token, infants with mild symptoms of distress after birth, seen in follow-up clinics at 12 and 18 months, may lag in development, likely a result of inadequate or inappropriate family interaction. Indeed, some authors have held the view that socioeconomic status and parent education are the most accurate predictors of developmental outcome among both typical and high risk populations (Brazelton, 1981). On the other hand, such accuracy, successfully claimed with groups, often breaks down upon closer examination of the qualitative differences among families and their offspring. Thus for many children, educational ability appears to be a function of not one but several continuous and cumulative vulnerabilities or benefits that interact to depress or enhance intellectual potential. Further complicating screening and diagnostic efforts are the common transient infant delays or atypical patterns of behavior; e.g., high muscle tone sometimes emerges between 4 and 8 months, yet disappears by the end of the first year to 18 months. Rapidly changing skills and competence throughout the first and second years of life also contribute to the ambiguities. Infants also vary over time in temperament, behavior, and performance, and assessment of optimal response requires highly skilled and sensitive diagnosticians.

In light of the foregoing conditions, a meaningful plan for infant screening and assessment ought to address several questions. In particular, the following deserve direct consideration.

1. Is the design for screening broad based to the degree that the census of infants of a given region who are at risk for developmental delay are included in systematic, periodic follow-up through the first 18 months to two years?

2. Does the screening program allow for follow-up and expectable delays, in the instance of prematurity, without recourse to labeling?

3. Does the screening program encompass information about child, family, and overall home environment?

4. Does the diagnostic phase take place over time sufficient to obtain flexible, reliable, and valid assessments of the infant in formal and natural settings and to determine problems that may not be manifest in the newborn period?

5. Does the assessment process reflect a consensus of diverse professional expertise?

6. How does the plan evaluate the quality of responses in infants and changes in coping and adaptive behavior of child and parent?
7. Does the diagnostic process include a range of age-appropriate behavioral and environmental indicators?
8. How is evaluation clinically tied to the intervention program, and do both activities allow for ongoing assessment that forms the basis for change in the educational plan?
9. How does assessment accommodate the systematic evaluation of different strategies of intervention with family and child?
10. Does the team responsible for screening and assessment offer regular feedback to other involved professionals about infant progress so as to maintain open avenues for communication?

As reflected in the issues above, there are points where screening and diagnosis converge and, obviously, areas where they serve different purposes. By necessity, the screening of infants and young children is directed toward a large but select population that, because of real or potential risk conditions in family and child, more likely has developmental problems. Table 13–1 presents examples of defined handicapping conditions, biomedical insults, and high risk-for-parenting factors that, in the past, have been associated with developmental delay. As we have emphasized throughout this text, however, newborns with similar medical and environmental histories may have very different outcomes. It is therefore crucial that screening and child-find programs, while appropriately being organized around the concept of risk, must fully recognize other considerations and their implications. For example, since many infants discharged from either intensive care or regular nurseries typically do not show delay until some time in the first year or possibly at school age, monitoring and screening efforts need to afford periodic checks. Among highest risk groups, some researchers have recommended that these should be on the order of three to four times during the first year, twice during the second, and once every year thereafter until completion of the second grade of formal schooling (Fitzhardinge & Pape, 1981). This course also seems supported by studies of change and continuity of behavior in infancy (Kagan et al., 1971). These suggest stability within short periods of three to four months, but low correlations between early patterns of motor and psychological development and subsequent characteristics of children in their preschool and school years.

Reaching and identifying target populations is a second major concern in the development of adequate, cost-effective screening programs. Identification by referral (Scott & Hogan, 1982) is a well established approach, and at first glance is more manageable and delineated than large-scale enterprises, which are focused on primary prevention. Indeed, recent statistics allude to the enormity of the task of early identification. At present, it is estimated that infants of 31 to 36 weeks gestational age comprise 6 to 7 percent and infants of 24 to 30 weeks gestation approximately 0.8 percent of the total live newborn population (Usher, 1981). These figures, of course, do not begin to account for the myriad of other neurologic and metabolic disorders, infectious diseases, neuromotor difficulties, congenital malformations, prena-

Table 13-1 Examples of Conditions Placing Newborns at Risk for Developmental Delay

Neonatal Conditions		Environmental Conditions	
Defined Handicap	Biomedical Insult	High Risk for Parenting Factors	Other
Fetal alcohol syndrome	Birthweight <2,000 grams	Poor history of caretaking by own parents	Extended separation of parents from infant
Hydrocephalus	Birth asphyxia	Inadequate parenting of other children	Family instability resulting from catastrophic situations
Myelomeningocele	Chronic lung disease associated with mechanical ventilation longer than two weeks	Limited education	Community reaction to infant
Neurological impairment		Teenage pregnancy	
Trisomy 21	Intracranial hemorrhage	Poor system of support; e.g., few family and friends, marital problems	Adverse interactions between parent and infant, of whatever etiology
Visual and hearing impairments	Small-for-gestational age	Evidence of emotional problems; poor attitude toward pregnancy	
Seizures	Congenital infections; e.g., CMV, herpes, toxoplasmosis	Evidence of developmental disabilities; e.g., mental retardation, physical impairment affecting child care	
	Hyperbilirubinemia		
	Postmaturity	Poor seekers of medical care	
	Congenital heart disease	Inadequate economic resources	

tal and perinatal complications, and conditions of unknown origin that may affect term and post-term infants and thus result in impairment and delay.

Based on educated projections, carefully established criteria and prudent decisions are essential to the feasibility and benefit of the program. Among risk populations, the main goal is to determine infants and families in greatest jeopardy. In this regard, the concept of *levels of risk or vulnerability* is useful. Infants may move up the ladder of service, receiving more frequent and comprehensive evaluations and intervention as necessary and appropriate to their needs and those of their families. Likewise, children may move down the cascade of services, having had their early needs met, their primary disabling conditions treated in normalizing educational programs, and secondary handicapping conditions prevented altogether. Full development of this concept and cautious implementation on a widespread scale could resolve many problems of screening, identification, and diagnosis that continue to thwart efforts of early intervention.

In large measure, educational programs for infants and young children, until recently, have been organized around the premise that rather discrete deficits can be identified in the early months and appropriate therapy can be employed in the name of prevention and amelioration. On several accounts, this tenet has proven unworkable. Despite a strong and pervasive commitment to the value of early programming, several authors (Keogh & Kopp, 1978; Kopp & Parmelee, 1979; Parmelee, Sigman, Kopp, & Haber, 1976) have articulated the serious limitations to accurately defining eligibility criteria in the absence of massive insult.

Developmental screening techniques for newborns are, at best, general in estimations of current functioning and largely have fallen short of the goal of predicting greatest need or future potential. The number of children leaving intensive care nurseries who have eluded identification yet later manifested moderate to severe disabilities is confirmation that, even in the face of significant impairment, more often than not evidence is speculative. It also is clear that any valid risk indices appropriate to the newborn period must encompass both biomedical criteria relative to the child and environmental conditions of the family and community. In terms of the magnitude of impact, it is obvious that certain factors are more critical to development than others and that duration and time of insult are important factors. Last, there is no substitute in the early identification process for astute clinical acumen. Carefully drawn criteria applied en masse and without attention to individual child and family characteristics may prove to be of little benefit, leading to neglected opportunities and eventual untoward developmental consequences.

In short, whatever the differentiated criteria, there are few absolutes in terms of the presence, absence, or extent of disability. Some children, because of the nature of their medical course and home environments, need to be observed more frequently with hands-on evaluations. Others are less suspect and worrisome. Table 13–2 sums up information on a few of the liabilities of medical and environmental insult and concurrent recommendations for follow-up.

At least one more prominent question requires close attention: What setting and professional group should carry out the initial screening program?

Such services in terms of time, effort, personnel, and funding easily may become overwhelming. Partially as a result of initiatives in 1975 by the Robert Wood Johnson Foundation to develop regionalized programs for reproductive medical care (Swyer, 1981), follow-up of infants discharged from intensive care units largely has remained the province of hospital-based perinatal centers. Increasingly, however, recent trends sponsored by state education departments and public schools are beginning to surface. Over the past five years, for example, Preschool Direction Center Programs in New York State, serving as referral and information resources for parents and professionals, have been strongly encouraged to establish close linkages with obstetrical and discharge follow-up services of regional perinatal center programs. The approach has several advantages. While it takes into account the importance of continued medical care and follow-up of infants who have been critically ill, it also acknowledges the educational impact of social and environmental influences. The plan allows for the establishment of well baby public school follow-up systems in collaboration with perinatal centers, which have the capacity to include infants born at risk who have not been admitted to intensive care units. It offers the combined expertise of educational, clinical, and medical staff sufficient to accomplish long-term follow-up without duplication of service. In the latter context, the approach provides opportunities for ongoing communication among professionals.

Standard Approaches

In recent years much research on infant assessment has concentrated on more natural approaches (Als, Lester, & Brazelton, 1979; Parke, 1978; Prechtl, 1981; Sigman & Parmelee, 1979; Uzgiris & Lucas, 1978; Zelazo, 1982), but developmental evaluation in medicine and education continues to rely on standard, traditional practices. Frequently, screening and referral of infants have been based on brief visits, with parent and child in strange situations, with unfamiliar professionals, under sometimes strained and difficult circumstances. The net result is a less than optimal response from both parent and child.

Formal assessment almost always involves standardized instruments, sometimes uses informal measures, and rarely involves systematic, data-based observations. Ideally, infant evaluation combines all three techniques. Documentation of child and family characteristics in relation to other infants and their parents, as established by normative data, is important. Yet routinely, developmental assessments fall short of including the very information that may be most connected to the planning of intervention. Reinforcing this point, researchers in human development, the social sciences, and special education over the past decade have endorsed the need for more dynamic and process-oriented findings in understanding families with typical, high risk, and handicapped infants. (Bronfenbrenner, 1979; Horowitz, 1981; Keogh & Kopp, 1978; Parke, 1978). In situations of social and cultural retardation that continue to escape definition and prevention among large groups of children in this county, such alternatives are mandatory. In addition, genuine concern over the presumed inappropriateness of conventional tests widely used with developmentally delayed infants and young children (Lewis & Taft, 1982; Zelazo, 1982) should not be dismissed lightly. This position is reflected in contemporary efforts to seek expanded concepts of sensory motor intelligence and in new ventures toward assessing neonatal and infant behavior (Als, 1981; Lipsitt, 1979; Miranda & Hack, 1979; Saint-Anne Dargassies, 1981).

It has long been a familiar theme in special education that problems of test interpretation arise not from the nature of standardized instruments but from the ways in which these measures have been used. There are myths and truths on both sides of the controversy. Despite the enormous contributions of Piaget, Bruner, Erickson, and other theorists to the understanding of development, much of our knowledge and recent research on learning and behavior in the early years has remained, in practice, unconnected to planning, methodology, and procedures of evaluation. This shortcoming is especially apparent in measures for the severely impaired, which may consist of infinite minute steps and tasks that seldom resemble approximations and expectations for typical growth and development. This is disturbing because of not only the restrictions placed on evaluations of infants and young children with significant delays, but also the underlying assumptions made about *abnormal* patterns of change, learning, and behavior of such youngsters. From their earliest days and weeks of life these children are perceived as different, and one must wonder whether the assessment instruments themselves reinforce in parents the notion of "looking for trouble" and, in a sense, become synonymous with disability. By contrast, we have seen the opposite effect with healthy term and preterm babies during the first 12 months, where month-by-month evaluations have served as a positive influence with families as they look forward to participating in new skills and behaviors. This phenomenon—witnessed with parents of markedly premature infants of 26 to 28 weeks gestation and across all levels of income and education—has taught us a great deal about the powerful ways in which assessment can be used for incidental teaching, competence building, and home intervention with both families and children.

In closing, two final points should be emphasized. With few exceptions, traditional approaches to infant evaluation have assumed a unidimensional model of behavior. While standard infant scales and inventories include diverse items of motor, language, cognitive, and behavioral response, rarely do they provide tasks within the context of varying situations of social interaction, with alternate testing procedures and materials. Moreover, parallel information is seldom amassed about the developmental home environment, primary caretakers, and siblings. Once again, our experience suggests that all of the variables above deeply affect the quality of responsiveness of the infant and that without planned variability in assessment, some infants are severely penalized.

New Thinking about Assessment

Assessment is a progressive and rapidly growing scene. Over the past 15 to 20 years, there have been dramatic shifts in philosophy, and the decade ahead

Table 13–2 Levels and Conditions of Risk in Undifferentiated Infant Populations and Recommended Follow-Up in the First 18 Months

	Levels and Conditions of Developmental Risk		*Frequency and Mode of Follow-Up*
	Infant	**Family**	
	Presence of One or More Conditions	*Presence of Two or More Conditions*	
III Severe	Persistent atypical patterns of neurologic behavior. Severe respiratory distress requiring mechanical ventilation. Intracranial hemorrhage. Gestational age between 26 and 30 weeks. Small for gestational age, with a birthweight of less than 1,750 grams. Congenital infections.	History of developmental disabilities. History of drug addiction or alcoholism. Inadequate parenting of other children. Evidence of emotional problems; self-destructive behavior; poor attitude toward pregnancy. Teenage parents. Limited education. Poor support system.	Direct screening every 3 months
II Moderate	Birthweight of less than 1,750 grams. Hyperbilirubinemia. Congenital heart disease. Respiratory distress without mechanical ventilation. Post-maturity. Metabolic disorders not associated with mental retardation.	Poor history of parenting by own family. Inadequate housing and caregiving facilities; inadequate economic resources. Poor utilization of medical care and other community resources. Unrealistic and/or inappropriate expectations.	Follow-up by phone and/or mail every 6 months
I Mild	Birthweight of 1,750–2,500 grams.	Extended separation of parent and infant.	Follow-up by mail every 12 months
Typical Growth and Development	Birthweight of 1,750–2,500 grams, without complications.		*Further evaluation with positive findings*

should bring to fruition some of the methods and procedures that still remain in formative stages of planning and investigation. A number of factors including our basic understanding of newborn behavior and its variation and malleability have shaped the direction and newer ways of thinking about assessment (Brazelton, 1981; Keogh & Kopp, 1978). These observations have been made in light of a range of studies from general early intervention programming where short-term gains have been demonstrated (Scarr-Salapatek & Williams, 1973) to more narrowly focused types of stimulation where change in specific infant skills such as visual hand regard has been noted (White, 1971), to evaluation or teaching situations where more transient flexibility of behavior has been common. As Brazelton (1981) has pointed out in a roundtable discussion on infants born at risk, such variability, in contrast with former thought, "demonstrates the recuperability that we have available to us, and it suggests that early testing might well be used to mobilize resources for the baby rather than just to make a static prediction" (p. 69).

By extension, recognition of the diversity and changing quality of infant behavior holds important implications for the types of measures needed for appropriate developmental screening and diagnosis. Most researchers in the field today would agree that assessment ought to be carried out on the basis of multiple predictors. Considerable work continues toward the refinement of "cumulative risk scoring systems" (Parmelee, Sigman, Kopp, & Haber, 1976). To date, these indices largely have been designed to take into account prenatal and perinatal information, as well as neonatal biological events and infant performance on various scales of cognitive, motor, perceptual, and sensory behavior. Such constellations or clusters of factors could reveal how different conditions impact on the lives of young children to retard or facilitate development. Examples of the individuality among term and preterm infants underscore additional requirements of assessment measures. Als (1981) affirms this point in the following comment:

> In a pilot study comparing the behavior of ten preterm and ten term infants at the same post-conceptual age, we found the preterms to be more sensitive to environmental inputs, more easily stressed and overstimulated, and more likely to overreact. They seemed to need more finely tuned environmental structuring and support than the term infants in order to free up their best performance on our test items. Their individual capacities, such as visual tracking, were often as good as those of the term infants, but the organization of their behavior was consistently different. (p. 27)

Als's observation matches much of our experience with high risk and handicapped infants over the past five years. Specifically, we need creative measures of behavioral patterns such as the balance of temperament, social responsiveness, levels of irritability, tolerance for frustration, self-quieting capabilities, play, alertness and attentiveness to the environment, and other characteristics that very early may establish ways of typical interaction with primary caregivers and cognitive styles of learning.

Mounting questions about the appropriateness of standard techniques of evaluation with impaired and high risk populations have prompted still another dimension of activity, the development of process-oriented measures of cognition (Gallagher, 1980; Johnson, 1982; Uzgiris & Hunt, 1975; Zelazo, 1982). In large part, alternative paradigms have taken one of two directions; i.e., efforts to create measures, similar to traditional tools, that accommodate varying conditions and degrees of developmental delay (CAPE, 1980), or the construction of entirely different modes of assessment that, for example, use behavioral change and heart rate to observe infant capabilities to process visual and auditory information (Zelazo, 1979). The Uzgiris and Hunt Ordinal Scales of Psychological Development, based on Piaget's sensory motor stages of infant development, is a third illustration of different ways of thinking about assessment. The instrument departs substantially from traditional approaches in terms of both the content of items and methodology for administration. While the scales initially were not conceived for high risk and handicapped groups, they are employed extensively by some programs.

All of the above-mentioned instruments and other like approaches await rigorous requirements of data collection and standardization with appropriate groups of typical and high risk infants, but they promise to tap potential in very young children that has gone unrecognized or were perceived unimportant. At the same time, they challenge us to avoid pitfalls of the standard tool and traditional program. As Johnson (1982) has aptly noted, "If assessment of cognition is focused only on concepts that develop readily in the absence of motor behaviors, it may be incorrectly concluded that cognition is intact when, in fact, some aspects of cognition are seriously impaired and in need of intervention" (p. 68).

This discussion of contemporary themes would be incomplete without acknowledgment of major work now under way on naturalistic observational methodologies and research on parent-infant interaction and the ecology of home environments (Parke, 1978; Thoman, Becker, & Freese, 1978; Vietze, Abernathy, Ashe, & Faulstich, 1978). Early childhood educators, as well as human service and medical personnel, have been increasingly interested in patterns of family interaction surrounding periods of infant hospitalization and observations of later development in such children. In addition, current study in human development, unlike previous work concentrated almost exclusively on the mother-infant attachment process, is beginning to reflect a more balanced view (Lamb, 1982) in recognizing the importance of father, siblings, and extended family and the influence of home environment on growth and outcome. Sameroff (1979) has summarized the issue as follows:

Cognitive competence during the early years depends, for much of its continuity, not on the unfolding of innate capacities, but on environmental constraints. We can assess the contemporaneous competencies of infants on many sensory, perceptual, and cognitive dimensions. Yet these measures do little to help us determine the child's later cognitive competencies. Inefficient predictions are not the result of methodological problems but of conceptual ones. As long as one conceptually isolates children from their environments, the inefficiencies will continue. Only when development is appreciated as a complex interplay between the child's changing competencies and temperament and the changing attitudes and behavior of the important socializing agents in the environment can the prediction problem be squarely faced. (p. 147)

New attempts to measure the developmental environment of infants and young children are evident in formal instruments for home observation (Caldwell & Bradley, 1979; Ensher, Bobish, Michaels, Gardner, & Butler, in press), structured inventories of parent behavior (Bromwich et al., 1981), and paradigms for informal observation of parent-infant interaction (Parke, 1978). These instruments and methodologies are a positive step toward differentiating specific characteristics of home settings and family interaction, which Sameroff (1979) and others have deemed so crucial to the well-being and healthy development of young children.

Despite contemporary education and intervention programs, infant evaluation predates the 1930s (Lewis, 1976). In the subsequent discussion, we describe a sampling of tests, scales, inventories, and other measures that represent major trends and directions in the field, from earliest initiatives to efforts of our present decade.

SPECIFIC TECHNIQUES AND THEIR APPLICATION WITH HIGH RISK AND HANDICAPPED POPULATIONS

Screening and Assessment with Standardized and Norm-Referenced Measures

Gesell's Developmental Schedules

One of the most familiar and widely used standardized instruments for developmental diagnosis of problems in the young child is the series of *Developmental Schedules* constructed by pediatrician Arnold Gesell (1925, 1929, 1940). The scales, first organized at the Yale Clinic of Child Development, provide for observation and evaluation in four major areas of development including gross and fine motor, language, adaptive, and personal-social behavior. The schedules are formulated around key stages of maturity from birth to six years, focusing on "behavior patterns for diagnostic application" (Knobloch & Pasamanick, 1974, p. 26). In terms of specific tasks, motor portions of the scales consist of items that assess postural and balance response, locomotion, prehension, drawing, and the manipulation of toys and objects. Language behavior is evaluated on the basis of visual and auditory forms of communication, articulation, vocabulary, adaptive use, and comprehension, and both spontaneous and responsive language behavior is observed (Knobloch & Pasamanick, 1974). The adaptive behavior tasks are designed to evaluate how the infant or child, given a variety of simple objects and problem-solving situations, reacts to environmental change. Finally, levels of personal and social behavior are ascertained by observation and interview; these items include inquiries about self-help skills, interactions with primary caretakers and other individuals in the home setting, temperament, play, initiative, and independence. Like a number of measures of development appropriate to infancy and the preschool years, the Gesell schedules vary in emphasis, with initial scales from birth to eight months largely comprised of motor items, and latter dimensions of the series concentrated more heavily on personal-social, language, and adaptive skills.

The schedules overall are highly clinical and offer astute judgments about normative levels of development (Lewis, 1976; Yang, 1979). By Gesell's intent, however, the scales never were conceived to serve as a test of intelligence. This point is repeatedly emphasized by the author (who was interested in the general concept of "mental growth") and by his colleagues (Knobloch & Pasamanick, 1974).

There have been several attempts to standardize the schedules (Gesell, 1940; Gesell & Thompson, 1938) and numerous studies of predictive validity with diverse populations including the high risk infant (Drillien, 1961; Knobloch & Pasamanick, 1960). Yet, with the exception of some modifications by Knobloch and Pasamanick, Gesell's *Developmental Schedules* have remained basically intact since their origination in 1925. Moreover, because of the restricted sample size, clinicians and researchers over the years have considered standardization of the scales to be inadequate (Lewis, 1976).

The most recent and extensive edition of the schedules amassed by Gesell's students, Hilda Knobloch and Benjamin Pasamanick, titled *Gesell and Amatruda's Developmental Diagnosis: The Evaluation and Management of Normal and Abnormal Neuropsychologic Development in Infancy and Early Childhood* (1974) is a seminal work that discusses the application of the scales with high risk and developmentally delayed populations. While individual items may vary by age and detail of task, Gesell's enormous contribution to the formulation of later standardized instruments such as the Bayley and the Cattell is clear. Many activities have been drawn from the schedules and thus have been judged appropriate for assessment with diverse groups.

To a large extent, the scales suffer the shortcomings of other formal instruments that are difficult, if not impossible, to administer with youngsters having moderate to severe impairment or particular types of sensory and motor problems. In such cases, since alternate modes of task presentation are not provided, the schedules are not sufficient to accomplish Gesell's primary purpose, to understand patterns of maturity or development. Similarly, use of the schedules with markedly premature or small-for-gestational age infants during the newborn period also are seriously limited, where evaluation of alertness and attentiveness, quality of response, feeding, and other subtle indicators of temperament and adaptability are critical. Moreover, the schedules are not finely tuned to the degree required for clinical assessments of infants at highest risk for developmental delay, prior to their adjusted or corrected age.

Intelligence Scales Developed by Bayley and Cattell

Despite the fact that both Cattell's *Scale of Infant Intelligence* (1940) and Bayley's *Scales of Infant Development* (1969) borrowed substantially from

Gesell's *Developmental Schedules*, these latter endeavors largely were designed to measure infant mental ability and to rectify some of the preceived dissatisfactions with the descriptive scales. Thus, in purpose, format, and process of standardization, the *Cattell* and *Bayley Scales* depart in several important ways from the pioneering efforts of Arnold Gesell.

Cattell's Scale initially was conceived as an "extension downward" of the *Stanford-Binet* to afford a continuous measure from infancy to maturity (1940, p. 24). As part of a comprehensive study at the Department of Child Hygiene of the Harvard School of Public Health, the scale was standardized on the basis of 1,346 examinations conducted consecutively with 274 children at the ages of 3, 6, 9, 12, 18, 24, 30, and 36 months. The final version of the instrument consists of five regular test items, with one or two alternate tasks, at each of 19 designated age levels from 2 to 30 months. Alternate items are used to accommodate errors or problems in administration. Materials, procedures, and scoring instructions are laid out for each observation or activity. The scale includes a range of items from simple attention to the examiner's voice, visual tracking of a suspended moving ring, and localization of a bell to more complex problem-solving tasks such as securing a covered toy, placing blocks in a formboard, identifying parts of a doll, and identifying pictures named. Essentially, the test draws upon all areas of sensory, motor, perceptual, language, and cognitive functioning. Conspicuously absent from the scale, by intention, are types of items characterized as personal, social, emotional behaviors; such was Cattell's decision since she believed this kind of material to be unrelated to assessment of native intelligence.

The predictive value of the scale varies according to age. Cattell admitted that "the low reliability and validity coefficients of the test for very young infants make it obvious that the individual numerical ratings must not be taken at their face value" (1940, p. 45). Reliability of the scale at 6, 9, 12, and subsequent months she considered to be significantly better, although for unexplained reasons a lower reliability coefficient between the *Stanford-Binet* and the *Cattell* was evident at 30 months.

Differing in format from the *Cattell*, the *Bayley Scales of Infant Development* were conceived to provide "a tripartite basis for evaluation of a child's developmental status during the first two and one-half years of life" (1969, p. 3). Standardization of the instrument spans a period of more than 40 years; the earliest version, the *California First Year Mental Scales*, appeared in 1933. The test is organized into three parts that are considered complementary. Two sections, the *Mental and Motor Scales*, require direct administration, while the third, the *Infant Behavior Record*, is completed after hands-on assessment. The *Mental Scale*, which yields a standard score (the *Mental Development Index* or *MID*), was designed to evaluate sensory and perceptual acuities and discriminations, object constancy, learning, problem-solving abilities, communication, and early skills to generalize and classify. The *Motor Scale* measures both fine and gross motor functioning, which is expressed in the form of a second standard score, the *Psychomotor Index* (*PDI*). The *Infant Behavior Record* (*IBR*) adds a dimension that assists the clinician in assessing such characteristics as general emotional tone, fearfulness, goal direction, attention span, and endurance.

Like the *Cattell* scale, the *Bayley* was standardized with a population of typical children ranging in age from 2 to 30 months. With few exceptions, all children were living at home. Institutionalized youngsters with severe behavioral and emotional problems, infants born more than one month prematurely, and children from bilingual homes were excluded from participation. The present edition, which has sustained several major revisions throughout the course of Bayley's research, contains 163 items on the *Mental Scale* and 81 items on the *Motor Scale*. Carefully designed standardization efforts notwithstanding, Bayley was forced to conclude a low predictive value of her test, once again confirming findings of her forebears. In describing the use of the scales with typical and exceptional children, she wrote:

> The indexes derived from the Mental and Motor Scales have limited value as predictors of later abilities, since rates of development for any given child in the first year or two of life may be highly variable over the course of a few months. The primary value of the development indexes is that they provide the basis for establishing a child's current status, and thus the extent of any deviation from normal expectancy ... . The BSID provides a basic set of instruments for use in identifying mental and motor retardation as well as in gathering clues which the clinician may employ in formulating hypothesis regarding etiology. (1969, p. 4)

It is apparent from this statement that Bayley never conceived her scales as a diagnostic tool, employed exclusively in the planning of intervention programs. It is somewhat ironic that both the *Cattell* and the *Bayley* have been utilized so widely toward this end.

Despite the precedence of history, the degree to which the scales should be used with infants and young children with special needs is a paramount issue. In general, both tests are more designed for obtaining a holistic view of intellectual performance than for determining individual differences and processes of affective and cognitive functioning. Second, while the predictive value of the scales overall is questionable, both tests appear to be considerably less valid and reliable during the first six months of life. Hence, in the event that the instruments were used as a measure of delay or progress in response to intervention, teachers and clinicians should be guarded in placing undue credence in such scores. Third, there is little doubt that the administration of either scale to severely or profoundly delayed children or motor-impaired youngsters is inappropriate. One can easily identify obvious limitations; however, strengths hidden by disabling conditions may be difficult to ascertain. Fourth, teachers and clinicians always must answer for themselves why tests are being given. The *Cattell* and the *Bayley* offer estimate scores of present performance in relation to others of similar ages, and these approximations are of some value to parents and program staff in establishing an exceptional educational need. On the other hand, if the primary intention is centered more directly on the monitoring of progress in high risk or handicapped infants, measures that can be given appropriately on a more frequent basis, that are sensitive to subtle changes, are more connected to programming and constructive in providing guidelines to parents.

The Denver Developmental Screening Test

In contrast with tests described above, the *Denver Developmental Screening Test* was designed as a simple-to-administer screening tool, rather than a measure of intelligence or definitive predictor of future adaptive or intellectual ability (Frankenburg, Dodds, Fandal, Kazuk, & Cohrs, 1975, p. 1). The *Denver*, which is appropriate for young children from birth to six years, covers four main areas of cognitive and affective development including personal-social behavior, fine motor-adaptive, language, and gross motor abilities. The total 105 items provide for repeated administration of three trials per task and allow for adjustment or correction for prematurity. The authors also recommend that where a child's performance is "abnormal or questionable," or when the youngster is "untestable" with the first screening, she or he ought to be reevaluated two or three weeks later. Each item of the test is presented with specific instructions for administration and scoring, with each task assessed as Pass (P), Failure (F), Refusal (R), and No Opportunity for Performance (NO). Results are scored on a one-page, easily read protocol, organized by age, primary areas of functioning, and individual items. Guidelines and examples represent varying profiles of behavior and patterns of questionable or atypical performance. In order to accommodate more rapid changes in growth during infancy, tasks are grouped into one-month intervals from birth to two years and thereafter by six-month periods. Like the standardization samples of the *Gesell*, the *Cattell*, and the *Bayley*, certain groups of children were excluded: those who had serious impairment or who were adopted, premature, twins, or breech deliveries (1975, p. 62).

Since its initial publication in 1967, the *Denver Developmental Screening Test* has received wide usage by pediatricians and other child development and human service professionals in the United States, Canada, and several European countries. In particular, the test has been recognized for its usefulness in perinatal center follow-up programs as a quick measure of performance among large groups of nondifferentiated, high risk children during the first 18 months of life. In view of its acknowledged utility, it is imperative to consider the sensitivity of the instrument in distinguishing, as early as possible, those infants who need further evaluation and intervention. In 1971, Frankenburg and his colleagues (Frankenburg, Camp, & van Natta, 1971) evaluated the validity of the test. The instrument was compared with outcome on four criterion tests; the *Stanford-Binet*, the revised edition of the Gesell *Developmental Schedules*, the *Cattell*, and the revised edition of the *Bayley*. Final comments by the authors are informative in light of current perceptions of the test and findings of previous investigators. Making reference to a degree of disagreement between the *Denver* and the *Bayley*, they wrote:

> Thus, the observation of a great amount of disagreement in classifying the youngest age group is not surprising. Depending on

how the test is used, this finding may or may not be of great concern. One might say that best results are obtained after 30 months of age. If, however, one is concerned with picking up children with developmental deviations in the first year, one must be prepared for the finding that a normal classification on the DDST will, in approximately 13 percent of the cases, conceal a child who would have obtained an abnormal rating on the Bayley. (p. 484)

The authors' statement is an honest appraisal and, for the most part, one must agree that the screening tool does accomplish its major goals for the child of 30 months or older. At the same time, however, the comment leaves the reader with a disquieting sense of concern. If the *Denver* is used in follow-up programs at 4, 8, 12, and 18 months, as is common practice, the problems that Frankenburg and his colleagues raise warrant careful scrutiny.

The Brazelton Neonatal Behavioral Assessment Scale

With respect to almost every dimension of purpose, theoretical orientation, content, method of administration, and statistical analysis, the *Brazelton Neonatal Behavioral Assessment Scale* (1973) differs from the *Denver* and other infant screening and intelligence tests. The scale has evolved from a number of years of research and development and is designed to evaluate the newborn's interaction with his/her environment, and thus indirectly his/her effect upon family or primary caretakers (1973, p. 4). The test is not a neurological examination, though such responses are assessed during the course of evaluation. Moreover, although efforts currently are under way to modify the scale for preterm infants (Als, 1981), the measure is intended primarily for use with the "normal" baby. Brazelton points out also that, in contrast with most standardized instruments, scoring is based on optimal response, not average performance.

In total, administration of the scale entails about 20 to 30 minutes and involves about 30 different observations and tasks. Items are carried out as the infant moves from sleep to awake-alert states, where the examiner is at liberty to vary the order of presentation to achieve optimal response. The concept of "state" is a central theme of the instrument. Such observations, as Brazelton has commented, may offer important information about the newborn's "receptivity and ability to respond to stimuli in a cognitive sense" (1973 p. 5). Behaviors such as hand-to-mouth facility, tremulousness, amount of startle, vigor, and activity, and the number of state changes are assessed continuously throughout the examination.

The scoring of the evaluation, which is completed largely at the close of the session, again departs from conventional procedure. The instrument is constructed so that no single summary score may be interpreted as optimal performance in the newborn. Instead, the author has attempted to capture the essence of individual difference with groupings of items so that "for each baby optimal behavior may be represented by an entirely different cluster of scores" (1973, p. 11).

The content of the *Brazelton* basically covers three main areas of newborn behavior.

1. Neurological integrity is evaluated on the basis of 20 elicited responses scored on a four-point continuum.

2. The neonate's repertoire of interactive behavior is described in light of 26 diverse tasks or observations, each distinguished within a range of nine behavioral descriptors. On a four-point scale, the examiner assesses four general qualities of newborn responsitivity:

   • *attractiveness*, a measure of the infant's overall social appeal

   • *need for stimulation*, a measure of the newborn's use of and need for stimulation in order to respond

   • *interfering variables*, which determine the amount of environmental stimuli that prevents a quiet examination

   • *analysis of behavioral strategies* used by the infant to self-quiet; e.g., hand-to-mouth, sucking, postural changes (Als, Tronick, Lester, & Brazelton, 1979, pp. 188–189).

3. The 26 behavioral items, paralleling ways in which mothers facilitate infant adaptation to the environment (Tronick & Brazelton, 1975), are intended to assess four dimensions of newborn behavior including interactive processes, motor abilities, state control, and physiologic responses to stress (Als, Tronick, Lester, & Brazelton, 1979).

The scale has been standardized with a sample of 54 healthy full-term newborns, delivered at the Lying-In Division of the Boston Hospital for Women, who were screened for "pediatric and neurologic normalcy." Repeated assessments of each infant were made on days 1, 2, 3, 4, 5, 7, and 10. During the course of these and other studies, the reliability of the instrument, as well as its predictive value, have received careful consideration by Brazelton and his colleagues. In view of substantial changes that emerge throughout the first 10 days of life in the newborn, it is no surprise that the establishment of reliability in the traditional sense has been relatively unsuccessful. In addition, attempts to determine the predictive value of the measure, while more accurate than typical neurological examinations, have been somewhat disappointing, with a false alarm rate of 24 percent (Tronick & Brazelton, 1975).

The *Brazelton Neonatal Behavioral Assessment Scale* is a diagnostic tool that continues to attract the attention of many researchers and clinicians involved with high risk infants. In the past, the instrument has been used to study such problems as the behavior of drug-addicted mothers (Soule, Standley, Copans, & Davis, 1974), the behavioral patterns of low birthweight babies (Williams & Scarr, 1971), the effect of poor nutrition on newborn performance (Brazelton, Tronick, Lechtig, & Lasky, 1977), and the functioning of small-for-gestational age infants (Als, Tronick, Adamson, & Brazelton, 1976). Yet despite this diversity of purpose, Brazelton and others have concluded that the scale is best used with full term infants (Als, Tronick, Lester, & Brazelton, 1979).

In conclusion, although the Brazelton still requires further research to establish test-retest reliability and validity with typical, high risk, and handicapped populations, the scale presently incorporates a number of extremely appealing features that have been absent in other measures. The focus on interaction and process-oriented qualities of behavior combines dimensions of cognitive and social capacities essential to understanding the complexities of newborn behavior and the kinds of environmental disruptions and insults that may build to cumulative deficit during the first 18 months of life. Some of the organizational and behavioral differences noted later in school populations with defined handicapping conditions, as compared with youngsters without such learning problems, are not unlike the types of characteristics the Brazelton seeks to distinguish. Second, the scale assesses infant behavior frequently elicited by mothers in helping their newborns to accommodate environmental change. This fascinating concept could be used to develop an important companion measure of the interactive environment of the home. Third, the emphasis of the scale on repeated assessment for optimal response and the evaluation of certain changing behavioral qualities is a positive and creative approach. Last, recent efforts to develop an adaptation of this scale for preterm infants may address some of the unresolved issues concerning the use of the instrument with populations of high risk and premature infants. Such research is currently being carried out in some intensive care nurseries where the *Assessment of Preterm Infant Behavior (APIB)* is being used as a basis for the development of intervention programs (Cole, 1985; Cole & Frappier, 1985).

The Syracuse Scales of Infant Development and Home Observation

In August 1979, the New York State Office of Developmental Disabilities and Mental Retardation awarded a three-year contract to the School of Education, Syracuse University, to offer home-based services to infants discharged from a regional intensive care nursery. One of the immediate tasks facing the staff during the first year of the project was the creation of a simple-to-administer scale that could be used by home visitors to monitor the development of infants in the intervention program.

The *Syracuse Scales* (Ensher, Bobish, Michaels, Gardner, & Butler, in press) is designed to assess preterm, developmentally impaired, and other high risk infants. The tool, currently in the sixth phase of revision, includes items for evaluation of four key areas of child behavior covering neuromotor, sensory-perceptual, language-cognitive, and social-emotional competence, and a separate section to assess the home environment. The instrument affords easily scorable protocols for parents, physicians, and educators. Based on observations of the primary caretaker, infant performance, and information obtained by parent interview, each item of the scales is assigned a rating from 1 to 5, according to specified criteria. Provision, too, is made to record direct observations and parent comments. The evaluation kit includes:

1. a manual with brief discussions of development in preterm and other high risk infants, data on the standardization of the instrument, instructions for administration and scoring, pictures illustrating various developmental stages in preterm and term babies, items covering the first 12 months of life, items relevant to the home environment, a glossary of clinical reflexes and responses indicative of developmental problems, and long- and short-form protocols, each of which yields a Cumulative Index of Development (CID) and four profile scores of competence

2. a kit of toys and materials

3. a series of four 30- to 40-minute videotapes for training and administration

4. a booklet of suggested intervention strategies.

We, the authors, seek to contribute to infant assessment in light of the lack of published standardized instruments for evaluation of high risk populations throughout the first 12 months of life. Existing scales, in most instances, are not refined enough to distinguish potential problems in high risk infants. The *Syracuse Scales* include a section to assess the home environment, a critical dimension heretofore absent from most developmental instruments. Reliability and validity studies currently are being conducted with populations of both term and preterm infants.

Like other measures described above, the *Syracuse Scales* have limitations. The current edition of the instrument is difficult to use in assessing children with motor or sensory impairments. Future efforts are planned for the construction of a second measure, which would provide alternative strategies for evaluation of multiply impaired youngsters. In addition, though we have had few problems in securing adequate numbers of term infants for standardization purposes, the size of the preterm sample has remained relatively small. Standardization studies ought to be carried out with other developmentally delayed populations.

Nonstandardized Measures, Inventories, and Other Methods of Systematic Observation

Standardized or norm-referenced measures for screening and diagnosis have many inherent problems when they are applied to high risk and developmentally delayed populations under 30 months of age. Sensitivity to these issues and difficulties among researchers have served as the impetus for alternative approaches to evaluating infants and very young children. In their own right, these have been designed to address several purposes believed lacking in traditional procedures. In reality, however, while they may resolve some shortcomings of the standard test, they pose other obstacles to the process of assessment. The following discussion will highlight disadvantages and advantages of several newer approaches.

Uzgiris and Hunt Scales of Infant Psychological Development

The *Uzgiris and Hunt Ordinal Scales of Psychological Development* share with traditional approaches the primary goal of determining current developmental levels of functioning and a secondary purpose of establishing relative strengths and weaknesses of ability during the infant sensory motor period (Dunst, 1980). The *Scales* are a direct outgrowth of Piaget's theoretical construct of the origins of intelligence, and differ a great deal from existing procedures.

The test is organized into six developmentally related branches of cognition:

1. The Development of Visual Pursuit and the Permanence of Objects
2. The Development of Means for Obtaining Desired Environmental Events
3. The Development of Imitation: Vocal and Gestural
4. The Development of Operational Causality
5. The Construction of Object Relations in Space
6. The Development of Schemes for Relating to Objects.

Each of the *Scales*, to be administered in total or in part, consists of a series of 4 to 15 items that provide suggested positions of the infant and physical space, recommended objects to be used, instructions, the number of repetitions allowed, and examples of elicited child behaviors likely to be observed. "Critical actions," which are identified for each item, indicate that "an infant has attained a particular level of functioning in a given branch of development" (Uzgiris & Hunt, 1975, p. 49).

Throughout the construction process, the *Ordinal Scales* have had several revisions; yet, by design they never have been standardized. This decision was based on the authors' concern as to whether such norms could be established with any meaningful purpose or validity. Nonetheless, Dunst (1980) has noted that there has remained a need to create a basis from which to decide whether a given infant is advanced, average, or delayed within each of the defined branches of development (p. 10). For this reason, the concept of *Estimated Developmental Age* (*EDA*) placement was added to the *Scales*. These guidelines are assigned to each step within a particular scale. Even though they carry no predictive value, the guidelines serve to help the teacher or clinician in determining an infant's relative, current developmental status. A second landmark guideline, the *Developmental Age* placement, is used to distinguish comparative functioning and classifies each scale step within Piaget's six stages of sensory motor development. Thus, it is possible to obtain a profile of infant behavior according to either developmental index, within and across the six *Ordinal Scales*. The authors indicate that the instrument offers "a novel approach" to the assessment of infant psychological development. They propose that since comparisons, independent of chronological age, can be made across the *Scales*, information derived "cannot help but be substantially greater than that obtained from a mental age or an IQ" (Uzgiris & Hunt, 1975, p. 18). They also emphasize a direct relationship between infant developmental status and childrearing environments and a corresponding utility of the *Scales* in planning for intervention. Like the *Brazelton*, the *Ordinal Scales* are focused on achieving the optimal state of rapport, cooperation, interest, and therefore the highest level of competence. This assumption is fundamental to the authors' strategy to permit a variable order of eliciting situations and scale presentations, suggested rather than required objects and toys for administration, options for repetition of tasks and activities, and resistance to the convention of establishing a single score to represent an overall level of cognitive development.

The *Uzgiris and Hunt Scales* present a unique and imaginative approach to infant assessment, which has an added advantage of a clearly defined theoretical base. The flexibility in administration and the process content of the instrument are viewed, by these authors, as a valuable contribution to new trends and directions in the field. As Uzgiris and Hunt point out, however, "the provisional character" of the *Scales* warrants further investigation with all populations of children. One should use caution in the interpretation of evaluations of high risk and handicapped groups. Age norms have not been established for the scale steps and, if teachers and clinicians wish to determine relative levels and profiles of development on the basis of the scales alone, that objective may be questionable. On the other hand, the tool has considerable worth if used for periodic assessments of progress in cognitive growth, particularly if these are combined with other clinical data. Such a goal is congruent with one of the primary intentions of the scale.

Koontz Child Developmental Program

Many educators and clinicians increasingly feel that traditional techniques of evaluation do not lend themselves readily to intervention. Thus it is not surprising that several recent efforts have centered on the development of packaged programs of assessment and training. The *Koontz Child Developmental Program* (Koontz, 1974) exemplifies this approach. The instrument is appropriate for infants and young children from birth to 48 months and covers four functional areas of gross motor, fine motor, social, and language behavior. Items and activities have been drawn largely from the *Gesell Scales*, the *Bayley*, the *Cattell*, and other independent resources (Koontz, 1974). Activities thus are organized by months into 22 levels, with training strategies specified by age for each performance area. Increments of one month are identified for the first 12 months, intervals of two months for the next three levels, three months for the next four levels, and six months for the last three levels. Activities range from five to eight items for each performance evaluation. Tasks that are inappropriate for youngsters with sensory impairment are so noted.

In many respects, the *Koontz* program is organized for use on a daily basis, with suggestions for regular monitoring of child progress. When new behaviors are observed, these and the respective dates of achievement are entered on the program record card. Koontz suggested that teachers, clinicians, and parents using the instrument exercise temperance and judgment in the interpretation of approximate age levels, which are not grounded in extensive statistical analysis. In point of fact, the genuine asset of the program does not lie in the brief screening task of the performance evaluation items nor in any particular originality of the assessment portion of the instrument. The combination of screening paired with training, on the other hand, is a useful plan and may serve as a step toward quality developmental programming.

The Early Learning Accomplishment Profile for Developmentally Young Children, Birth to 36 Months

This instrument, commonly referred to as the *Early LAP*, was developed as one of several materials created by the demonstration project in Chapel Hill, North Carolina, established in 1969 through federal funding of the Handicapped Children's Early Education Program. The profile was initiated with the expressed purpose of generating "instructional objectives and task analysis programming for the young handicapped child" (Glover, Preminger, & Sanford, 1978). The *Early LAP* is an expansion of an earlier instrument developed by the Chapel Hill Project personnel, the newer edition being targeted for more severely impaired children from birth to three years.

The profile covers six areas of development, including gross motor, fine motor, cognitive, language, self-help, and social-emotional behavior. The instrument is arranged so that performance can be recorded on a continuing basis. Activities are drawn from approximately 20 different standardized and nonstandardized referenced resources. Procedures and criteria for accomplishment are indicated for each item. Up to 18 months, items are provided on a month-by-month basis, while intervals thereafter are spaced with greater lapses of two or more months. Child behavior on individual tasks is indicated with a pass/fail rating and opportunity for examiner comments. Profiles of achievement may be compiled, reflecting pre- and post-intervention performance from birth to 36 months, across the six appointed areas of early learning.

The *Early LAP*, like the *Koontz*, represents contemporary efforts to construct instruments for ongoing assessment that are related to program planning. In that regard, the profile and its intent deserve recognition. However, since many items have been excerpted from standardized instruments that are of questionable relevance to intervention, it is doubtful whether the instrument can be used to accomplish fully the goals for which it was developed. The instrument might have had a stronger basis had the authors utilized a scale or continuum of responses similar to that designed by Uzgiris and Hunt.

The Milani-Comparetti Motor Development Screening Test

Recognizing the need for early identification of developmental problems and the inappropriateness of most traditional approaches for screening purposes, Milani-Comparetti and Gidoni designed the present test to assess motor competence in young children from birth to 24 months (Kliewer, Bruce, & Trembath, 1977). The authors recommend repeated evaluations of infants under 12 months or children who show evidence of consistent delay or other atypical patterns of motor development.

One of the special features of the test is the graphic profile used for scoring the young child's level of motor development. The first 12 months are divided into two-week intervals; the period of 12 to 24 months is collapsed into fewer intervals of time. The scoring profile makes provision for recording both spontaneous behavior and evoked responses, as the instrument is used specifically to examine primitive reflexes; righting, parachuting, and tilting reactions; active movement; and postural control. General milestones of development are provided on the profile as guidelines in the scoring process. Examples of typical, delayed, and atypical responses are described throughout the test manual, and the testing package also makes available a color videotape for training purposes.

In general, the *Milani-Comparetti* appears to fulfill its major intentions and offers a helpful tool for personnel basically untrained in child development and clinical assessment. Its recommended use on a frequent basis in the early months is a clear asset in the screening of preterm infants, who often manifest transient delays in motor ability. In this regard, the authors request that corrections for prematurity not be made in order that actual courses of chronological age development might be followed. In light of the narrow scope of the test, the tool should be used in conjunction with additional measures of language, cognitive, and social-emotional growth and behavior.

Criterion- and Curriculum-Based Assessment

As we have emphasized throughout this chapter, one of the major concerns about the exclusive use of norm-referenced instruments has been the perceived lack of applicability to direct teaching situations. Current efforts to develop criterion- and curriculum-based measures represent an attempt of early childhood specialists to address this issue. *The Carolina Curriculum for Handicapped Infants and Infants At Risk* (Johnson-Martin, Jens, & Attermeier, 1986) and the *Hawaii Early Learning Profile* (Furuno, O'Reilly, Hosaka, Inatsuka, Allman, & Zeisloft, 1979) are two examples of such instruments that are being utilized by increasing numbers of early education programs to supplement more traditional approaches to the evaluation of high risk and handicapped infants and young children.

Though there are some differences, several commonalities are shared by the above measures. While the *Hawaii* (*HELP*) extends developmental assessment one year beyond that of the *Carolina* (*CCHI*) (3 to 36 months rather than 24 months), both instruments basically include skills that may be categorized into six areas of cognition, communication and language, self-help and adaptation, social-emotional, fine motor, and gross motor. Both tests were designed to be used with infants and young children with a diversity of developmental problems and may be appropriately administered by professionals, paraprofessionals, and parents. Individual tasks and skills vary in format; however, the two instruments offer a wide array of carefully sequenced items that allow the clinician to establish a detailed profile of developmental performance and behavior. Most helpful are the correlated, suggested activities that may be used by educators, therapists, and others in creating and implementing intervention programs. Reliability and validity data are available from the authors of the *Carolina Curriculum* and special adaptations are made for children with hearing and visual impairments.

In terms of the overall objectives and purposes specified for both of these instruments, one of the central strengths lies in the fact that they do afford excellent assessment and activity guides to the typical development of infants and toddlers. Such information may be highly meaningful for primary caretakers, for example, in day-care centers, who initially may require assistance with sequencing and content. Indeed, these kinds of criterion- and curriculum-referenced guides could serve as an important means toward on-site training for day-care personnel working with typical, high risk, and handicapped young children.

Other Paradigms of Observation and Informal Assessment

As researchers for over a decade have weighed the advantages and shortcomings of traditional and nonstandardized techniques of assessment, there has been mounting interest in different paradigms of infant observation. Some of these are designed for the evaluation of cognitive abilities in special laboratory settings (Zelazo, 1979, 1982). Others are oriented toward understanding the infant in his or her *natural* environment and the impact of primary caretakers on development (Parke, 1978). These approaches were formulated from entirely different perspectives and with diverse purposes. Yet, each has possibilities for new insights and alternative strategies in evaluating difficult-to-understand infants and young children.

Assessing the ecology of the home setting and parent competence has been approached with several different methodologies. More structured efforts are exemplified by Caldwell and Bradley's *Home Observation for Measurement of the Environment* (1979), the *Parent Behavior Progression* (Bromwich et al., 1981), and the home environment portion of the *Syracuse Scales* described above. Each of the measures is designed to evaluate the quality of the young child's developmental environment and the instruments stand in marked contrast with widely held, traditional views that low income level, minimal education, and inadequate learning are necessarily synonymous. For instance, the current edition of the *HOME* inventory, which is appropriate for use with families of infants and toddlers, originally was developed to provide "a more sensitive measure of environmental influence than gross socioeconomic indices" (Caldwell & Bradley, 1979, p. 27). Over the past several years, an extensive array of studies has been conducted with the screening instrument. Comprised of 45 items, the birth to three section of the *HOME* includes six major subscales, reflecting various dimensions of the physical and interpersonal milieu of the primary caretaking setting.

The *Parent Behavior Progression* and the home environment portion of the *Syracuse Scales* are not unlike the *HOME*, focusing on parent attentiveness and sensitivity to the infant, quality and quantity of parent-infant verbal interaction, parent stimulation of play and infant activity, parental affect and temperament with the infant, and quality of caretaking behavior. In addition, a preschool portion of the HOME for the three- to six-year-old consists of eight subscales, extending into stimulation with toys and games, reading, language experiences, physical and affective environment, development of social maturity, and use of physical punishment.

While an impressive amount of research has been carried out already to establish reliability and validity of these measures and undoubtedly will continue, the present unique contributions of these instruments to the field of infant evaluation need to be recognized. Admittedly, the subject of environmental influence is fraught with bias and misinterpretation. However, the screening and monitoring of home environments of vulnerable infants could reveal as much as, if not more than, any specific developmental evaluation.

Ever-increasing paradigms for studying naturalistic parent-infant interaction, though lacking formal standardization, have yielded "early clues to the general problem of social and cognitive development" (Parke, 1978, p. 69). Some models have studied broad levels of parent functioning in relation to infant behavior and development; others have examined specific caretaking activities, such as feeding and infant responsivity. Parent perceptions of infant competence, impairment, or developmental delay, and the subsequent effect on child growth and behavior, has occupied a great deal of interest over the past 10 to 15 years and remains a priority concern among many researchers today. For example, we need to understand how parental attitudes toward congenital problems influence the quantity and quality of verbal interaction between parent and child. Numerous sociological and psychological studies have described the various effects of terminologies such as "premature" or "high risk" on parent behavior and explored the possible implications for longitudinal development in children. Still another important topic is the influence of fathers within the context of families of healthy newborns or in crisis situations with critically ill infants, and the impact of separation on the family unit. The main goal of such studies is a more enlightened appreciation of those regulatory factors among families that enhance the emotional, social, and cognitive development of high risk and impaired infants and young children (Parke, 1978). To this time, educational personnel have not fully used and endorsed these strategies.

The "alternative assessment strategy" of a group of researchers at the Center for Behavioral Pediatrics and Infant Development of the Tufts University School of Medicine, an innovative, nonstandardized approach to evaluation of high risk and impaired infants, deserves discussion here. In comparison with more holistic, ecological sources of study, Zelazo, Kearsley, and others have focused their efforts on the development of an information processing approach that provides insight into the ways in which infants seem to comprehend and respond to varied auditory and visual sequential events. Specifically, Zelazo (1982) has suggested that such results yield "broad classifications of ability rather than month by month profiles" (p. 117). The approach has been used typically with learning infants and young children from 3 to 36 months, as well as youngsters with cerebral palsy and Down syndrome. Zelazo and his colleagues have indicated that the procedures, unlike other methodologies of assessment, are not biased against children with neuromotor, productive language, or behavioral handicaps (1982, p. 118). That quality and the process orientation of the approach are worthwhile characteristics that attempt to address major shortcomings of more traditional techniques. Given these benefits, at least three paramount questions remain. First, is the strategy applicable within local educational settings? Second, how valid and reliable are the measures? Third and last, how comprehensive are the strategies in terms of tapping multiple areas of infant behavior?

OPTIMAL SCREENING AND DIAGNOSIS: THE INTERACTION OF CHILD, FAMILY, PROFESSIONAL, AND SETTING

Describing behavior and analyzing competence in high risk and developmentally delayed infants is a complex process that has prompted much study and debate and has shown substantial progress toward more balanced views and techniques of implementation. Having examined a few of these issues in detail, we close this discussion with some speculations and suggestions about future directions in this important area of early childhood education.

We are convinced that all aspects of infant evaluation—screening, diagnosis, and long-term monitoring—must reflect interactions of child, family, professional. and setting. Selections of methodology and procedure need to be governed less by individual preference, availability, and ideology, and more by a genuine sense of immediate problems. Innovative measures must survive valid and reliable standardization with diverse populations for whom they are intended, in addition to exploring new dimensions of learning and play that were previously outside the realm of accepted assessment. At a minimum, these areas should include infant endurance and states of alertness, responsiveness to new tasks and unfamiliar situations, unstructured discovery, spontaneous activity, levels of frustration and irritability, and interaction with varied objects and toys. Some strategies should be defined with limited ranges of expected behavior; others ought to be open-ended, allowing for response and novelty beyond the information given. Finally, those committed to the understanding and well-being of newborns, infants, and toddlers must adhere tenaciously to a more integrated view of assessment.

In closing, we would like to underscore a point: It is ironic that those most intent on evaluating young children so often have neglected to think about one key element in the total assessment process with whom they hold most influence; i.e., the examiner or clinician, who by intent, attitude, understanding, and deed may discover the optimal level of interaction for infants and families. That can make the difference of a lifetime in the first 12 months.

REFERENCES

Als, H. (1981). Assessing infant individuality. In C.C. Brown (Ed.), *Infants at risk: Assessment and intervention—An update for health care professionals and parents* (pp. 24–31). Skillman, NJ: Johnson & Johnson.

Als, H., Lester, B.M., & Brazelton, T.B. (1979). Dynamics of the behavioral organization of the premature infant: A theoretical perspective. In T.M. Field, A.M. Sostek, S. Goldberg, & H.H. Shuman (Eds.), *Infants born at risk: Behavior and development* (pp. 173–192). New York: SP Medical & Scientific Books.

Als, H., Tronick, E., Adamson, L., & Brazelton, T.B. (1976). The behavior of the full-term yet underweight newborn infant. *Developmental Medicine and Child Neurology, 18,* 590.

Als, H., Tronick, E., Lester, B.M., & Brazelton, T.B. (1979). Specific neonatal measures: The Brazelton Neonatal Behavior Assessment Scale. In J.D. Osofsky (Ed.), *Handbook of infant development* (pp. 185–215). New York: John Wiley & Sons.

Bayley, N. (1969). *Bayley scales of infant development.* New York: Psychological Corporation.

Brazelton, T.B. (1973). Neonatal behavioral assessment scale. *Clinics in Developmental Medicine,* No. 50. Philadelphia: J.B. Lippincott.

Brazelton, T.B. (1981). Introduction. In C.C. Brown (Ed.), *Infants at risk: Assessment and intervention—An update for health care professionals and parents* (pp. xv–xix). Skillman, NJ: Johnson & Johnson.

Brazelton, T.B., Tronick, E., Lechtig, A., & Lasky, R. (1977). The behavior of nutritionally deprived Guatemalan infants. *Developmental Medicine and Child Neurology, 19,* 364.

Bromwich, R.M., Khokha, E., Fust, L.S., Baxter, E., Burge, D., & Kass, E.W. (1981). Parent Behavior Progression. In R. Bromwich, (Ed.), *Working with parents and infants: An interactional approach* (pp. 341–359). Baltimore: University Park Press.

Bronfenbrenner, U. (1979). *The ecology of human development: Experiments by nature and design.* Cambridge: Harvard University Press.

Caldwell, B.M., & Bradley, R.H. (1979). *HOME observation for measurement of the environment.* Little Rock, AR: University of Arkansas.

CAPE, Consortium of Adaptive Performance Evaluation. (1980). *Adaptive performance instrument.* Unpublished Assessment Instrument. Department of Special Education, University of Idaho.

Cattell, P. (1940). *The measurement of intelligence of infants and young children.* New York: Psychological Corporation.

Cole, J.G. (April 1985). Infant stimulation reexamined: An environmental-and behavioral-based approach. *Neonatal Network,* 24–30.

Cole, J.G., & Frappier, P.A. (November-December 1985). Infant stimulation reassessed: A new approach to providing care for the preterm infant. *JOGNN,* 471–477.

Drillien, C.M. (1961). A longitudinal study of the growth and development of prematurely and maturely born children: Part VII. Mental development two-five years. *Archives of Disease in Childhood, 36,* 233–240.

Dunst, C.J. (1980). *A clinical and educational manual for use with the Uzgiris and Hunt scales of infant psychological development.* Baltimore: University Park Press.

Ensher, G.L., Bobish, T., Michaels, C.A., Gardner, E.F., & Butler, K.G. (in press). *Syracuse Scales of infant development and home observation.* Syracuse, NY: Syracuse University Press.

Fitzhardinge, P.M., & Pape, K.E. (1981). Follow-up studies of the high-risk newborn. In G.B. Avery (Ed.), *Neonatology: Pathophysiology and management of the newborn* (2nd ed.) (pp. 350–367). Philadelphia: J.B. Lippincott.

Frankenburg, W.K., Camp, B.W., & van Natta, P.A. (1971). Validity of the Denver Developmental Screening Test. *Child Development, 42,* 475–485.

Frankenburg, W.K., Dodds, J.B., Fandal, A.W., Kazuk, E., & Cohrs, M. (1975). *Denver developmental screening test: Reference manual* (Revised 1975 ed.) Denver, CO: LADOCA Project & Publishing Foundation.

Gallagher, J.J. (Ed.). (1980). *New directions for exceptional children: Young exceptional children.* San Francisco: Jossey-Bass.

Gesell, A. (1925). *The mental growth of the preschool child.* New York: Macmillan.

Gesell, A. (1929). *Infancy and human growth.* New York: Macmillan.

Gesell, A. (1940). *The first five years of life.* New York: Harper.

Gesell, A., & Thompson, H. (1938). *The psychology of early growth.* New York: Macmillan.

Glover, M.E., Preminger, J.L., & Sanford, A.R. (1978). *EARLY-LAP: The Early Learning Accomplishment Profile for Developmentally Young Children, Birth to 36 Months.* Winston-Salem, NC: Kaplan Press.

Horowitz, F.D. (1981). Toward a model of early infant development. In C.C. Brown (Ed.), *Infants at risk: Assessment and intervention—An update for health care professionals and parents* (pp. 31–40). Skillman, NJ: Johnson & Johnson.

Johnson, N.M. (1982). Assessment paradigms and atypical infants: An interventionist's perspective. In D. D. Bricker (Ed.), *Intervention with at-risk and handicapped infants: From research to application* (pp. 63–76). Baltimore: University Park Press.

Johnson-Martin, W., Jens, K.G., & Attermeier, S.M. (1986). *The Carolina curriculum for handicapped infants and infants at risk.* Baltimore: Paul H. Brookes.

Kagan, J., McCall, R.B., Reppucci, N.D., Jordan, J., Levine, J., & Minton, C. (1971). *Change and continuity in infancy.* New York: John Wiley & Sons.

Keogh, B.K., & Kopp, C.B. (1978). From assessment to intervention: An elusive bridge. In F.D. Minifie & L.L. Lloyd (Eds.), *Communicative and cognitive abilities-Early behavioral assessment* (pp. 523–547). Baltimore: University Park Press.

Kliewer, D., Bruce, W., & Trembath, J. (1977). *The Milani Comparetti motor development screening test.* Omaha, NE: Meyer Children's Rehabilitation Institute, University of Nebraska Medical Center.

Knobloch, H., & Pasamanick, B. (1960). An evaluation of the consistency and predictive value of the 40-week Gesell Developmental Schedule. *Psychiatric Research Reports, 13,* 10–31.

Knobloch, H., & Pasamanick, B. (1974). *Gesell and Amatruda's developmental diagnosis: The evaluation and management of normal and abnormal neuropsychologic development in infancy and early childhood* (3rd ed.). New York: Harper & Row.

Koontz, C.W. (1974). *Koontz child developmental program: Training activities for the first 48 months.* Los Angeles: Western Psychological Services.

Kopp, C.B., & Parmelee, A.H. (1979). Prenatal and perinatal influences on infant behavior. In J.D. Osofsky (Ed.), *Handbook of infant development* (pp. 29–75). New York: John Wiley & Sons.

Lamb, M.E. (1982). The bonding phenomenon: Misinterpretations and their implications. *Journal of Pediatrics, 101,* 555–557.

Lewis, M. (Ed.). (1976). *Origins of intelligence: Infancy and early childhood* New York: Plenum Press.

Lewis, M. & Taft, L. (Eds.). *Developmental disabilities: Theory, assessment, and intervention.* Jamaica, NY: SP Medical & Scientific Books.

Lipsitt, L.P. (1979). Learning assessments and interventions for the infant born at risk. In T.M. Field, A. M. Sostek, S. Goldberg, & H.H. Shuman (Eds.), *Infants born at risk: Behavior and development* (pp. 145–169). New York: SP Medical & Scientific Books.

Meier, J.H. (1976). Screening, assessment, and intervention for young children at developmental risk. In T.D. Tjossem (Ed.), *Intervention strategies for high risk infants and young children* (pp. 251–287). Baltimore: University Park Press.

Miranda, S.B., & Hack, M. (1979). The predictive value of neonatal visual-perceptive behaviors. In T.M. Field, A.M. Sostek, S. Goldberg, & H.H. Shuman (Eds.), *Infants born at risk: Behavior and development* (pp. 69–90). New York: SP Medical & Scientific Books.

Parke, R.D. (1978). Parent-infant interaction: Progress, paradigms, and problems. In G.P. Sackett (Ed.), *Observing behavior: Theory and applications in mental retardation* (Vol. 1, pp. 69–94). Baltimore: University Park Press.

Parmelee, A.H., Sigman, M., Kopp, C.B., & Haber, A. (1976). Diagnosis of the infant at high risk for mental, motor, and sensory handicaps. In T.D. Tjossem (Ed.), *Intervention strategies for high risk infants and young children* (pp. 289–297). Baltimore: University Park Press.

Prechtl, H.F.R. (1981). Optimality: A new assessment concept. In C.C. Brown (Ed.), *Infants at risk: Assessment and intervention—An update for health care professionals and parents* (pp. 1–5). Skillman, NJ: Johnson & Johnson.

Saint-Anne Dargassies, S. (1981). Neurological examination of the neonate for silent abnormalities. In C.C. Brown (Ed.), *Infants at risk: Assessment and intervention—An update for health care professionals and parents* (pp. 5–12). Skillman, NJ: Johnson & Johnson.

Sameroff, A.J. (1979). The etiology of cognitive competence: A systems perspective. In R.B. Kearsley & I.E. Sigel (Eds.), *Infants at risk: Assessment of cognitive functioning* (pp. 115–151). Hillsdale, NJ: Lawrence Erlbaum Associates.

Sameroff, A.J. (1982). The environmental context of developmental disabilities. In D.D. Bricker (Ed.), *Intervention with at-risk and handicapped infants: From research to application* (pp. 141–152). Baltimore: University Park Press.

Scarr-Salapatek, S., & Williams, M.L. (1973). The effects of early stimulation on low-birthweight infants. *Child Development, 44,* 94–101.

Scott, K.G., & Hogan, A.E. (1982). Methods for the identification of high-risk and handicapped infants. In C.T. Ramey & P.L. Trohanis (Eds.), *Finding and educating high-risk and handicapped infants* (pp. 69–81). Baltimore: University Park Press.

Sigman, M., & Parmalee, A.H., Jr. (1979). Longitudinal evaluation of the preterm infant. In T.M. Field, A.M. Sostek, S. Goldberg, & H.H. Shuman (Eds.), *Infants born at risk: Behavior and development* (pp. 193–217). New York: SP Medical & Scientific Books.

Soule, A.B., Standley, K., Copans, S.A., & Davis, M. (1974). Clinical uses of the Brazelton neonatal scale. *Pediatrics, 54,* 583.

Swyer, P.R. (1981). The organization of perinatal care with particular reference to the newborn. In G.B. Avery (Ed.), *Neonatology: Pathophysiology and management of the newborn* (pp. 17–47). Philadelphia: J.B. Lippincott.

Thoman, E.B., & Becker, P.T. (1979). Issues in assessment and prediction for the infant born at risk. In T.M. Field, A.M. Sostek, S. Goldberg, & H.H. Shuman (Eds.), *Infants born at risk: Behavior and development* (pp. 461–483). New York: SP Medical & Scientific Books.

Thoman, E.B., Becker, P.T., & Freese, M. P. (1978). Individual patterns of mother-infant interaction. In G.P. Sackett (Ed.), *Observing behavior: Theory and applications in mental retardation* (Vol. 1, pp. 95–114). Baltimore: University Park Press.

Tronick, E., & Brazelton, T.B. (1975). Clinical uses of the Brazelton Neonatal Behavioral Assessment. In B.Z. Friedlander & L. Rosenblum (Eds.), *Exceptional infant* (Vol. 3, pp. 137–156). New York: Brunner/Mazel.

Usher, R.H. (1981). The special problems of the premature infant. In G.B. Avery (Ed.), *Neonatology: Pathophysiology and management of the newborn* (2nd ed.) (pp. 230–261). Philadelphia: J.B. Lippincott.

Uzgiris, I., & Hunt, J. McV. (1975). *Assessment in infancy: Ordinal scales of psychological development.* Urbana, Il: University of Illinois Press.

Uzgiris, I.C., & Lucas, T.C. (1978). Observational and experimental methods in studies of object concept development in infancy. In G.P. Sackett (Ed.), *Observing behavior: Theory and applications in mental retardation* (Vol. 1, pp. 187–207). Baltimore: University Park Press.

Vietze, P.M., Abernathy, S.R., Ashe, M.L., & Faulstich, G. (1978). Contingency interaction between mothers and their developmentally delayed infants. In G.P. Sackett (Ed.), *Observing behavior: Theory and applications in mental retardation* (Vol. 1, pp. 115–132). Baltimore: University Park Press.

White, B.L. (1971). *Human infants: Experience and psychological development.* Englewood Cliffs, NJ: Prentice-Hall.

Williams, M.L., & Scarr, S. (1971). Effects of short term intervention on performance in low-birthweight, disadvantaged children. *Pediatrics, 47,* 289–298.

Yang, R.K. (1979). Early infant assessment: An overview. In J.D. Osofsky (Ed.), *Handbook of infant development* (pp. 165–184). New York: John Wiley & Sons.

Zelazo, P.R. (1979). Reactivity to perceptual-cognitive events: Application for infant assessment. In R.B. Kearsley & I.E. Sigel (Eds.), *Infants at risk: Assessment of cognitive functioning* (pp. 49–83). Hillsdale, NJ: Lawrence Erlbaum Associates.

Zelazo, P.R. (1982). Alternative assessment procedures for handicapped infants and toddlers: Theoretical and practical issues. In D.D. Bricker (Ed.), *Intervention with at-risk and handicapped infants: From research to application* (pp. 107–128). Baltimore: University Park Press.

Part III

INTERVENTION: PROCESS AND PRACTICAL APPLICATION

Perhaps in no other era of education have professionals witnessed the magnitude of interest and change that has been so evident over the past 20 years in early childhood. Some intervention projects continue to pursue the precedent of the 1960s, emphasizing the prevention of disability among low-income, less-educated, and minority groups. Current efforts, however, are more broadly based, offering services to high risk and handicapped infants and families that start in intensive care settings and represent the full spectrum of age, ethnic, and socioeconomic groups. To this time, research in hospital, home, and public school suggests that supplemental stimulation and early education do have beneficial effects. On the other hand, the larger questions of lasting influence, appropriate timing, matching of interventions to specific populations, and individualization of programs for a particular infant need to remain open for further investigation. Indeed, limitations of the past have provided an impetus for close scrutiny of the present and should serve as a springboard for further research and the development of comprehensive systems of intervention.

14

Families of at Risk Infants: Need and Development

Gail L. Ensher and Evelyn S. Stevens

No one is more important to any baby than its parent. Klaus and Kennell (1976) and Sameroff and Chandler (1975) have awakened us to the premature infant's enormous need for involved parental caregiving to ensure optimal development. Infant intervention specialists are becoming aware of the importance of knowing more about the characteristics of premature babies that affect parents, characteristics of parents that affect infants, and ways in which parents and newborns interact. From a few studies in the early 1970s when babies were being salvaged as never before, research has burgeoned and examined a wide range of aspects of preterm infant-parent relationships. This chapter presents some of the most recent studies and perspectives that might be useful to professionals working with families.

Remember that investigators still are trying to determine what to measure, how to measure, what to use for evaluation of outcome, and when to measure outcome. Procedures are difficult to understand. Some studies employ very complex designs with a large number of variables and assessments that are hard to sort out and subject to misinterpretation by the reader. Other investigations are too simple or the sample too small to be valid. Most of the studies cannot be readily compared because they are not consistent in the subjects included or excluded, in where the research took place, or in treatment versus control groups. We usually do not know whether infants being studied have been in intervention programs or whether a public health nurse or social worker has been visiting. With all these limitations in mind, however, recent research has some meaningful things to say to us that can sharpen our awareness and skills in working with preterm infants and their parents.

For more than two decades now, professionals in child development, education, medicine, and other areas of human service delivery have sought to define preventive and remedial programming for families at risk and with extraordinary need. In particular, prematurity, unwed and teenage parents,

177

severe poverty, and notable neurological deficit again and again have been cited as contributors to vulnerability and delay in the preschool and later years. By the same token, our attempts to predict those circumstances where significant differences are inevitable have met with scant success. The facts remain that newborns faced with cumulative detrimental insults do mature to escape the ravages of deficit; other children, less traumatized, show signs of failure to thrive and departure from typical patterns of growth and performance.

Our views of families of high risk and handicapped infants need to allow for less conventional expectations and more open-ended possibilities. Timing, nature of medical insult, physical makeup of the infant, resources and support available to parents, span of separation, duration of poverty, breadth of any intervention, and constellation of the family unit will affect outcome. Professionals need to be wary of excessive intrusion at inappropriate points. Too often, our efforts have lead to disillusionment. For example, educators and physicians usually share concerns over the heightened probability of developmental delay among children of teenage parents. On the other hand, at the time of initial referral infants frequently do not manifest impairment or retardation. This dilemma, given the constraints of current funding and service delivery mechanisms, is not easy to resolve. Confusion also has arisen during the separation of families from newborns in regionalized neonatal medical care. Such conditions are far from optimal; yet, follow-up studies consistently have reported that the majority of these children remain unscathed.

Retrospective recognition of biosocial ills is not the same as accurate prospective identification of those families most in need of our services—nor perhaps should it be. Uncertainty breeds an element of honesty and care that should infuse every dimension of our research, training, and education.

PERCEPTIONS OF HIGH RISK PARENTS AND CONTEMPORARY ISSUES

Families in Crisis: Common Themes

Research on families in crisis have followed many tracks, and efforts continue to grow in complexity and volume. Yet, familiar themes have been present since the earliest interest in parents and developmental environments. One recurrent area of study has dealt with attachment and bonding and with the effects of variables such as separation, prematurity, twin births, types of handicapping conditions and congenital problems, chronic illness, and the support of the extended family. Of special importance have been the long-term implications for interactions of individual family members with the infant and their impact on child development. Decidedly, there has been a shift away from the belief that for child and parents the outcome is necessarily damaging.

Second, much of the work on prematurity and high risk births has concentrated on analysis of the stages unique to families as they deal with the sorrow and acceptance of preterm and developmentally delayed infants. Again, contact with mothers, fathers, and siblings has taught us that, in contrast with prior assumptions, all families do not pass through universal stages. To some, for example, intensive care nurseries understandably are frightening; to others, they serve as a comfort and source of consolation. In addition, we should not assume that in the face of difficult circumstances, parents require uniform interventions. Support groups aid the healing process for some; for others, time to be alone needs to be respected. It is a well-established observation that families in most serious need often are the most difficult to reach. For instance, while we have documentation on middle- to upper-income and stable parents, less is known about the feelings and concerns of single, adoptive, or very young mothers and fathers. Low-income families, in the past, have been the target of much inquiry, exposure, and criticism, with little meaningful assessment or resolution. In addition, what happens to families—their stages of grief and coping skills—may be largely a function of outside support. That process of interaction, though now given more credence, has been only minimally scrutinized.

Abuse—increasing in our society among very young and elderly populations—is a third dominant issue. Reportedly, it is more evident among poorer families in those situations where premature, at risk, or developmentally delayed infants have been born. Determining factors probably range from heightened stress, lack of knowledge about young children, and vulnerable or impaired relationships to parental histories of child abuse. Still, the unique combinations of circumstances that finally do precipitate abuse are difficult to document before the fact. Professionals in the field freely acknowledge our present paucity of data on middle- and upper-income families where child abuse is more subtle or hidden. Perhaps the one variable but unifying key resides within the early study of parental interactions. The problem is well stated by Solnit and Provence (1979):

> The weaknesses and intolerance of the infant often serve as a magnet and magnifier for environmental actions and reactions, for parental perceptions of and responses to the baby (Ritvo et al., 1963). Included in this focus are vital past experiences that influence parental behavior and that tend to utilize the newborn and young infant as a screen on which past feelings and attitudes, often inappropriate ones, are projected onto the baby and distort the current reality of infant and parent. Such adult behavior is not only inappropriate for the child but tends to promote the repetition and continuation of the adult's deviant behavior.

> What starts out for the child as a weakness or vulnerability may be magnified and elaborated by the parents' responses either because the parents lack resources or because the parents transfer inappropriate past attitudes or expectations onto the child. (p. 802)

Last and still connected to the aforementioned concerns are issues of optimal developmental environments. Countless studies have examined relationships between infants and their primary caretakers. In the past, this research largely has been restricted to mother-infant patterns. By contrast, contemporary themes recognize the centrality of the total family unit. In the process, several fundamental questions have emerged—some answered, others outstanding. For example, how and why do interactions between preterm or developmentally impaired infants and their families vary from those of term and typical babies and their families? How do perceptions and attitudes of parents and newborn characteristics affect patterns of relating and developmental outcome? What aspects of interaction and the developmental environment delay or encourage cognitive, social, and emotional capacities, and are there stages when vulnerabilities and potentials are more likely to change? Parents of high risk and impaired youngsters often experience chronic sorrow throughout the early years of their children, if not longer; how do they finally come to grips with such trauma and misfortune? Research addresses the damaging interactions of lower income families; are there similarities with middle- and upper-income parents who have lost faith that their children can change and learn? Studies today are looking closely at the visiting patterns and involvements of families with babies in intensive care nurseries. With the greater regionalization of medical facilities, problems of distance and separation, how can parents and infants interact positively?

The questions are unending and demand complicated solutions. Just possibly, fruitful study of interactions may be found in situations that defy the hardened stereotypes of our profession. Numerous infants of overburdened and overpopulated areas of the world such as Calcutta, India, are a case in point. Children are left on the streets, deprived of prenatal care, parenting, home, and country. The International Mission of Hope (IMH) is a registered agency in India and America, dedicated to "bringing hope to abandoned children." As Cherie Clark, executive director of IMH, eloquently stated:

> They come broken and defeated, and oftentimes premature and malnourished, ridden with disease that oftentimes makes the battle for their life a losing one. They come so late and so tired often totally lacking the will to live. They struggle, unaware that there is more than pain involved in being. But the fact that within each tiny child lies the spark and the potential to grow, gives our staff of doctors, nurses, and social workers the strength and the hope to struggle on for each and every new life, so that now far more of the tiny babies who come to our home have lived than died.
>
> They come to us from the jails and streets, uneducated, unknowing, and unloved. What will they grow to be? we are asked with suspicion. How can they adjust? Watching them laugh and run and play and become children is our cause and our goal. To see them become educated, responsible, loving adolescents brings joy . . . .
> They come to us as the survivors, who slowly wind their way through tons of paperwork and seals that must be affixed to documents before they are free. They make their way as photographs and papers through the courts, passport offices and immi-

gration departments and all too often they die before the process can be completed.

The lucky ones go off as tiny ambassadors quietly and with complete trust into a world of love and acceptance. They travel across the ocean through the night to new food, new language and into the hearts and homes of a family who has waited and longed for their arrival. These children teach us that we are more alike than different and that the right of each of us to love, family, and childhood is God given. (Clark, 1984)

This statement underscores the importance of quality parent-infant interactions and their compelling positive influence on social and cognitive development, irrespective of specific time periods, medical histories, and in some instances environmental experiences.

Parent-Infant Attachment

Studies have suggested that preterm infants and newborns with other medical risks are less alert and less responsive to their immediate environments and more chronically irritable than full-term babies (Goldberg, 1978, 1982). These observations have set the stage for numerous investigations of the behavior of premature infants, parental attitudes and behaviors toward their offspring, and subsequent patterns of family interaction. Much of this research has emerged from the work on parent-infant bonding by Klaus and Kennell (1976), which has prompted changes in hospital delivery and visiting practices for newborns and their families over the past ten years (Kennell, Voos, & Klaus, 1979). In their words, "there is a sensitive period in the first minutes and hours of life during which it is necessary that the mother and father have close contact with their neonate for later development to be optimal" (1976, p. 14). Klaus and Kennell have tempered that position, however, in a more recent edition of their book on *Parent-Infant Bonding* (1982) in which they state:

The human is highly adaptable, and there are many fail-safe routes to attachment. Sadly, some parents who missed the bonding experience have felt that all was lost for their future relationship. This was (and is) completely incorrect, but it was so upsetting that we have tried to speak more moderately about our convictions concerning the long-term significance of this early bonding experience . . . .

For some mothers one period may be more important than the other. If the health of the mother or infant makes this impossible, then discussion, support, and reassurance should help the parents appreciate that they can become as completely attached to their infant as if they had the usual bonding experience, although it may require more time and effort. (p. 56)

The authors conclude their discussion with the acknowledgement that parents do not always react in "standard" or "predictable" ways in response to separation immediately following delivery (Leiderman, 1978; Yogman, 1981). Such a judgment is much more in keeping with contemporary views that suggest a more tentative evaluation is warranted. Also, studies have indicated that, while differences for many parents of premature and other high risk infants may be evident initially (Chess & Thomas, 1982; Goldberg, 1978, 1979, 1982; Herbert, Sluckin, & Sluckin, 1982), families usually do not sustain long-term, adverse effects unless there are ongoing developmental problems (Boyle, Griffen, & Fitzhardinge, 1977). In the short run, authors have suggested a need for early intervention that focuses on helping parents to deal with their concerns and anxieties over having a premature or at risk infant, responds to some of their developmental questions, and provides support during the first days and weeks of adjustment at home (Campbell & Taylor, 1979; Siegel, 1982; Sigman, Cohen, Beckwith, & Parmelee, 1981).

Our own experiences during the past five years in working with families of high risk and special needs infants have confirmed that observation. Moreover, as soon as parental concerns over medical problems and development begin to subside—even though an infant may not yet have caught up in weight and size—often there are marked positive changes in the nature of the family interaction. For the severely premature baby and parents, this frequently occurs at about six to ten months and steadily improves as the child makes progress and closes the gap with his or her term counterparts. By contrast, we likewise have shared with parents the disappointments and pain of coming to realize that delays and medical insults may persist. Understandably, the process of attachment in these instances may take a different course; some families need to distance themselves from relationships and others want excessively close bonding in order to protect. All such responses are typical patterns of parent-infant attachment even when no obvious developmental problems are apparent. These may be manifest with different overtones, depending upon the severity of illness, parent perceptions, or infant responses.

Whatever the eventual outcome, we would like to stress the importance of looking at issues of bonding or attachment as a process that begins before delivery, transcends the newborn period, and reflects a series of changes over a lifetime. While some dimensions of that process currently are known, most contemporaries in child and family studies now recognize that the concept is not as simple or narrow as previously thought (Seashore, 1981). The area represents one of the most widely analyzed points of interest in early childhood. Future educators and developmentalists need to focus on defining innovative strategies to promote positive interaction between infants and families under conditions of typical deliveries, crises of premature birth and chronic illness, and situations where impairment is immediately confirmed.

Failure To Thrive and Child Abuse

Failure to thrive in infancy and child abuse are two extreme examples of troubled relationships in families. Recently, these disturbances have received much attention as a result of the severity of the problems, their long-term consequences for the child, and the apparent dramatic rise in their occurrence. The etiology of these difficulties, as well as the effective implementation of preventive and ameliorative programs, have plagued educational, medical, and other health care professionals for decades. Though we are now able to identify some of the causes before the events, in too many instances this has not been the case.

Both parties to broken relationships—parent and child—have been studied fairly extensively (Egeland & Vaughn, 1981); however, the findings still are disparate. Moreover, there is increasing awareness among researchers that problems of abuse and failure to thrive are not mutually exclusive. Evidence of one often reveals additional maltreatment. Given this observation, multiple factors have been linked to impaired or disturbed parent-infant interactions leading to abuse. As several authors note (Elmer et al., 1971; Shaheen, Alexander, Truskowsky, & Barbero, 1968), these include past experiences of one or both parents; problems during pregnancy such as illness or the loss of significant relationships; complications during the perinatal period; and stresses of daily life such as marital problems, financial pressures, and the use of drugs and alcohol. In addition, current studies frequently refer to the theory that in some not entirely understood way the attachment or bonding process has been compromised in its early stages (Altemeier, O'Connor, Vietz, Sandler, & Sherrod, 1982) as a result of multiple transactions among environmental factors, primary caregivers, and infants.

Changing societal forces in the last 15 years, in part, have led to an increase in pregnancies among American teenagers. Approximately one in ten teenage girls in the United States becomes pregnant (1,000,000 adolescents) each year. The 600,000 infants born from these pregnancies represent one-fifth of all births in the United States annually. Within one year of the birth of a first child, 40 percent of all such adolescents deliver a second child, and 7 percent deliver a third child within three years after the first. Ninety-three percent of these mothers now keep their infants. The medical and social consequences of adolescent parenting are currently being examined closely. The focus over the last several years has been the intellectual performance of children born to teenage mothers. Maternal educational achievement varies considerably between younger and older mothers. In a ten-year follow-up period reported by Coll, Vohr, & Oh (1984), only 35 percent of the teenage mothers had completed high school versus 77 percent of older women. As might be predicted, postgraduate education, job skills, employment opportunities, and income were significantly lower among the adolescent mothers. The children of teenage mothers achieved less well in school and repeated grades more often than children of older women. In fact, even in their medically low risk population, these investigators (1984) found lower mental and developmental indices at eight months and one year, correlating with lower *Caldwell Home Scale* scores, less optimal child care support, and a greater number of stressful life events experienced by mothers after delivery. Moreover, while child abuse has been suggested as a possible etiology for the increased mortality and morbidity in children born to teen mothers, carefully controlled studies of this problem are extremely limited.

In response to many of the above issues, researchers today are proposing a "transactional view" of these problems, thus attenuating the credence once given to the importance of single, precipitating events. This perspective has dispelled the popular belief that an event such as prematurity, initial separation of parent from infant, or low income alone is sufficient to bring about abuse or child neglect. To be sure, studies of the past and present have been concerned with high incidences of parent-child disturbances among populations of low birthweight babies (Formufod, 1976; Goldson, Fitch, Wendell, & Knapp, 1978). However, as contemporary researchers point out (Egeland & Vaughn, 1981), most investigations have been retrospective in design. The antecedents of abuse are complex, and often the true sources of difficulty are disguised by superficial symptoms. Egeland and Vaughn (1981) have offered this analysis:

> One might readily argue that it is not an attachment problem per se that is implicated in the etiology of the mothering disorder, but that certain personality characteristics of the mother, prior to the birth of the infant, affect her ability to become bonded to her baby and her subsequent mothering. It is possible that such mothers were more irresponsible concerning prenatal care than other mothers and, as a result, were more likely to have premature or otherwise vulnerable infants. The infrequent visits noted by Fanaroff et al. may have been simply a further manifestation of an immature mother's irresponsible behavior toward her offspring. If this were indeed the case, then the failure to form a bond would simply be another symptom of a more pervasive problem and not necessarily the cause of later mothering disorders. (p. 80)

In the end, whatever the speculations on a theoretical level, the reality is clearly before us on an everyday basis in our news telecasts and can hardly be ignored. Abuse is difficult to identify before it occurs. Maybe there are lessons to be learned from another prominent family problem—divorce. Maybe we should try to determine how families do survive, with all of the responsibilities, pressures, and crises that inevitably are a part of parenting.

FAMILY REACTIONS TO IMPAIRED AND HIGH RISK NEWBORNS

Initial Feelings and Reactions

No one expects to have an infant with problems. Irrespective of parental age, family composition, religion, or socioeconomic background, newborn illness and impairment are traumatic and difficult to endure. Some parents cope better than others; yet all must inevitably confront feelings, attitudes, and anxieties. Initially, parents often experience a sense of shock and disbelief. As one father said in the story about his daughter Becky, which appears in Part IV of this book, babies are not supposed to be born three months early, and babies are not supposed to have handicapping conditions.

Whether children are planned or come unexpectedly, parents anticipate that they will be healthy and beautiful. Mothers, in particular, have a sense of loss in not being able to carry their infants to full term, and quite commonly both parents feel guilty and blame themselves—often unrealistically—for the problems that have taken place. One family that we followed actually attributed the premature birth of their baby daughter to "the strong coffee" that they had made that morning. Parents frequently search for answers when there are none.

Coupled with the pain and shock over the birth of an acutely ill or impaired baby, families also must deal with the unfamiliar and overwhelming environment of intensive care nurseries. Though they may be comforted by the excellence of care and the technology of the facilities, there is much they do not understand. This is a time of mixed emotions and constant change—joy over the survival of their baby, uncertainty about outcome, new learning about premature babies, new acquaintances with other families, and hope that perhaps things will be all right. The necessary shifting of medical caretakers may be unsettling in already volatile circumstances. It is typical that parents feel starkly alone, yet at the same time strongly bonded to other families in a common state of insanity.

If babies are severely premature or suffer serious illness, this period may be an emotional roller coaster. If their babies are "doing well," parents are ecstatic. If they are not responding, their world falls apart. Some parents are able to involve other children in the healing process, and that can be positive for the entire family in sharing thoughts and feelings. On the other hand, the questions that brothers and sisters may ask many times are difficult for mothers and fathers to answer even for themselves. The larger world of family and friends also obviously plays a major part in parent adjustment and feelings of well-being. This is true with the birth of a typical infant and is possibly more so when conditions are less than optimal.

Rarely is anyone prepared for the first glimpse of a 26- or 28-week baby connected to monitors and other equipment where the infant is barely visible. All too frequently parents have reported that neighbors fail to send cards or gifts or in any way acknowledge the birth of their new baby; and relatives—attempting to cope with sorrow themselves—refuse to go back to the hospital after an initial visit. Such experiences tend to heighten the problems of dealing with the family crisis.

Understandably, parents feel angry. They ask themselves why this tragedy has befallen them. Friends and families who respond that it is "God's will" or that they can have other children are little consolation. As one parent put it, "I ate the right foods, got plenty of rest, took care of myself and my baby before he was born. There was no reason for him to have been so sick or to have been in that unit." Living with the fear of developmental problems or even death—however well adjusted the families are—exaggerates the frustration and sense of helplessness. "How ridiculous," one parent explained, "to have to pick up the telephone each night to ask someone else how your baby is doing!" Parents naturally want to take care of their own children, and hospitals today are encouraging that participation as much as possible. When that care and contact are limited because of medical treatment in strange settings, the normal loving cycle of interaction is disrupted.

Resolutions

Eventually, after weeks, months, or perhaps years, order emerges from chaos and most parents begin to take charge of their lives. Surprisingly for many, the pain and hard times bring strength, and families feel that they have grown from the experience. The mother who lost her son Joey the week after his first birthday commented that never again would she take life and everyday events for granted. Having survived, many parents believe they are changed people. And indeed they are!

Resolutions come in different ways. Some parents need to work through their own attitudes and feelings alone before they can share with their partners and additional members of the family. Others need to talk and confirm their thoughts right from the beginning. It is difficult to hear all that is being said about one's baby; that too becomes a process, little by little letting in the information. Situations become relative. Parents themselves sometimes are amazed that they can endure all that they do. Those who have grown through the experience discover within themselves that they are healthier human beings if they are able to dwell less on the negative and let go of their anger. Parents who have continued to harbor feelings of self pity and blame themselves and others for their "misfortune" run the risk of tarnishing the special joy of bearing and raising their children. What brings parents to this point of acceptance is hard to define. Many eventually realize that despite a persistent emphasis on perfection in this country, that is not reality for term, preterm, or handicapped children. We have been with families who have lost their babies during the first year of life and known that that was "inevitable" soon after birth. Their faith and belief in the value of even a short life sets an example for the rest of us who may take such gifts for granted. Again and again, our observations have confirmed that sick or developmentally delayed newborns may bring out the best qualities of love and unselfishness, which otherwise might not have risen to the surface. They have learned that they can love themselves and their children in spite of the terrible blow life appears to have dealt them. Much soul-searching, a trust in God, supportive family and friends seem to be common strengths for many who have shared their feelings and attitudes with us. They begin to live their lives again, with a renewed optimism, hope, and realistic expectations.

The Needs of Families

Most parents do well in spite of professional attempts to assist. There is little that one can say to soften the pain and shock that families initially feel. One cannot remove doubt or cancel grief; time heals those hurts. The greatest injustice that child care professionals bring to families are promises that both know are unfounded.

Parents need to have essential medical information and our honest judgment about the current status of their child's development. They need to have the resources of other parents and knowledge about intervention if they want it. They need to have sensitive, caring professionals who are not afraid to share the pain that families go through, who still can remain distant enough to offer sound guidance to the best of their abilities. Last, families need to know that professionals—in medicine, education, social work, or any of the other helping fields—do not have all the answers. They can provide support, but parents themselves can and should make their own decisions about their children. To the extent that we can foster this goal, even with the most limited parents, that should be our objective.

Long-Term Effects

Ultimately, we need to know how early parental reactions and interactions affect development in young children. Although findings may or may not be generalizable from the specific sample studied, investigations conducted particularly in the last five years seem to be honing in on the important components of good preterm infant-parent relationships. We may not be able to speak with certainty about differences between preterm and term infants, but we know that there are possible differences in activity level, clarity of signals, quality of cries, motoric and physiologic response to stimulation, preference for familiar versus novel objects, fussiness, and levels of vocalization. Knowing this, we can alert parents to the possibilities, and thereby help them to read their babies' behavior and adjust their own to match.

We know that visiting patterns in intensive care nurseries set that stage for later interactions, although we do not yet understand whether it is contact with the infant or support from staff that is important. Our best bet is to keep working on both fronts.

We know that early experience has a significant effect on later cognitive development, if not social development. Intuition tells us that secure attachment, which does seem to influence sociability, must be related to some variables of interaction, whether or not they are mediated by mothers' expectations and childrearing attitudes. Cognitive development is seen time after time to be influenced by caregiver-infant interaction at different ages. Caregiver responses to infant behaviors seem to be most important, as well as appropriate play materials at each stage. Intervention programs are inadequate if they work only with the child and do not work with the parents to help them become aware of their own responses to the infant, and if they provide all the playthings and do not help parents learn how to choose the appropriate toys.

More and more research is examining support systems and how they affect the emotions and adjustment of parents with consequences to preterm infants. This is a rich area for future research, and the most we can say for the present is that professionals need to ascertain the level of support from partners, friends, and community when assessing infant functioning. We can be sure that an exciting decade is ahead in the field of preterm infant-family research.

REFERENCES

Altemeier, W.A. 3rd, O'Connor, S., Vietz, P.M., Sandler, H.M., & Sherrod, K.B., (1982). Antecedents of child abuse. *Journal of Pediatrics, 100,* 823–829.

Boyle, M., Griffen, A., & Fitzhardinge, P. (1977). The very low birthweight infant: Impact on parents during the preschool years. *Early Human Development, 1,* 191–201.

Campbell, S.B.G., & Taylor, P.M. (1979). Bonding and attachment: Theoretical issues. *Seminars in Perinatology, 3,* 3–13.

Chess, S., & Thomas, A. (1982). Infant bonding: Mystique and reality. *American Journal of Orthopsychiatry, 52,* 213–222.

Clark, C. (1984). International Mission of Hope calendar introduction.

Coll, C.G., Vohr, B.R., & Oh, W. (1984). Maternal factors affecting developmental outcome of infants of adolescent mothers. *Pediatric Research, 18,* 97A.

Egeland, B., & Vaughn, B. (1981). Failure of "bond formation" as a cause of abuse, neglect, and maltreatment. *American Journal of Orthopsychiatry, 51,* 79–85.

Elmer, E., Gregg, G., Wright, B., Reinhart, J.B., McHenry, T., Girdony, B., Geisel, P., & Wittenberg, C. (1971). Studies of child abuse and infant accidents. In J. Segal (Ed.), *Mental Health Progress Reports* (Vol. 5, pp. 58–89). Washington, DC: Department of Health, Education, and Welfare.

Fomufod, A.K. (1976). Low birthweight and early neonatal separation as factors in child abuse. *Journal of the National Medical Association, 68,* 106–109.

Goldberg, S. (1978). Prematurity: Effects on parent-infant interaction. *Journal of Psychiatric Psychology, 3,* 137–144.

Goldberg, S. (1979). Premature birth: Consequence for the parent-infant relationship. *American Scientist, 67,* 214–220.

Goldberg, S. (1982). Some biological aspects of early parent-infant interaction. *Reviews of Research: The young child* (Vol. 3, pp. 35–56). Washington, DC: National Association for Education of Young Children.

Goldson, E., Fitch, M.J., Wendell, T.A., & Knapp, G. (1978). Child abuse: Its relationship to birthweight, Apgar score, and developmental testing. *American Journal of Diseases of Children, 132,* 790–794.

Herbert, M., Sluckin, W., & Sluckin, A. (1982). Mother-to-infant 'bonding.' *Journal of Child Psychology and Psychiatry, 23,* 205–221.

Kennell, J.H., Voos, D.K., & Klaus, M.H. (1979). Parent-infant bonding. In J. D. Osofsky (Ed.), *Handbook of infant development* (pp. 786–798). New York: John Wiley & Sons.

Klaus, M.H., & Kennell, J.H. (1976). *Maternal-infant bonding.* St. Louis: C.V. Mosby.

Klaus, M.H., & Kennell, J.H. (1982). *Parent-infant bonding* (2nd ed.). St. Louis: C.V. Mosby.

Leiderman, P.H. (1978). The critical period hypothesis revisited: Mother to infant social bonding in the neonatal period. In F. Horowitz (Ed.), *Early developmental hazards: Predictors and precautions* (pp. 43–108). Boulder, CO: Westview Press.

Sameroff, A.J., & Chandler, M.J. (1975). Reproductive risk and the continuum of caretaking casualty. In F.D. Horowitz, M. Hetherington, S. Scarr-Salapatek, & M. Siegel (Eds.), *Review of Child Development Research* (Vol. 4, pp. 187–244). Chicago: University of Chicago Press.

Seashore, M.J. (1981). Mother-infant separation: Outcome assessment. In V. L. Smeriglio (Ed.), *Newborns and parents: Parent-infant contact and newborn sensory stimulation* (pp. 75–87). Hillsdale, NJ: Lawrence Erlbaum Associates.

Shaheen, E., Alexander, D., Truskowsky, M., & Barbero, G.J. (1968). Failure to thrive: A retrospective profile. *Clinical Pediatrics, 7,* 255–261.

Siegel, E. (1982). Early and extended maternal-infant contact: A critical review. *American Journal of Diseases of Children, 136,* 251–257.

Sigman, M., Cohen, S.E., Beckwith, L., & Parmelee, A.H. (1981). Social and familial influences on the development of preterm infants. *Journal of Pediatric Psychology, 6,* 1–13.

Solnit, A.J., & Provence, S. (1979). Vulnerability and risk in early childhood. In J.D. Osofsky (Ed.), *Handbook of infant development* (pp. 799–808). New York: John Wiley & Sons.

Yogman, M.W. (1981). Parent-infant bonding: Nature of intervention and inferences from data. In V.L. Smeriglio (Ed.), *Newborns and parents: Parent-infant contact and newborn sensory stimulation* (pp. 89–95). Hillsdale, NJ: Lawrence Erlbaum Associates.

15

Intervening in Intensive Care Nurseries

Debra A. DeSocio and Gail L. Ensher

Concern for high risk babies today centers not on medical treatment alone. Over the past 15 years, professionals have expressed keen interest in the developmental environment of newborns hospitalized for extended periods of time. Consequently, significant research has been conducted with a hope of defining the effects of early intervention with preterm infants in intensive care nurseries. While results in this area to date have been contradictory and findings obviously are in need of further replication (Ross, 1984), many benefits have been reported. Indeed, there is some evidence that if small premature infants are given various forms of daily stimulation during their stays, they may have many fewer apneic episodes and may show increased weight gain and advances in some areas of central nervous system functioning that persist at least for a short time after hospital discharge. This chapter reviews some of the major intervention strategies currently being studied in intensive care settings and reflects upon the results of this research.

NEURODEVELOPMENTAL STIMULATION WITH PRETERM INFANTS

Tactile-Kinesthetic Stimulation

Hasselmeyer (1964), an early pioneer in the study of the effects of intervention with premature babies, provided extra tactile stimulation to infants that included haircombing, stroking, cuddling, and rocking before, after, and halfway between feedings. He reported that treatment infants were more serene. Conversely, control infants cried more. Statistics on the Hasselmeyer study and other investigations described in this chapter may be found in Table 15–1.

Table 15-1 Studies on Tactile-Kinesthetic Stimulation of High Risk Newborns

Conditions of the Study and Summary Findings

Investigator	Subject Information	Type of Stimulation	Treatment Conditions	Results
Hasselmeyer (1964)	N = 60 Birthweight 1,500–2,000g.	Stroking, handling, & rocking	Treatment subjects: 260 min./day Control subjects: 95 min./day Introduced between 7th & 10th postnatal day Term: 14 days	Treatment infants appeared more serene. No difference in weight gain.
Neal (1968)	N = 62 (31 treatment, 31 control) Gestational age = 28–32 weeks Birthweight 700–1,600g.	Vestibular (movement in a motorized hammock)	5th postnatal day to 36 weeks total age (gestational age + living age) Term: 4–8 weeks	Greater weight gain. Higher scores on *Graham Rosenblith Test* for maturation, visual alertness, pull to sitting, and movement of limbs
Solkoff & Matuszak (1975)	N = 10 (5 treatment, 5 control) Birthweight <2,000g. Gestational age 28–37 weeks	Stroking & flexing of arms & legs	14th postnatal day to 24th day total age, 7.5 min./hr. for 16 hrs./day Term: 10 days	Better scores on *Brazelton Neonatal Assessment Scale*. No effect on weight gain.
Korner, Kraemer, Haffner & Cosper (1975)	N = 21 (10 treatment, 11 control) Birthweight 2,000g. Gestational age 24–28 weeks	Oscillating water beds	Repeated stimulation 6th postnatal day to 13th postnatal day	Limited effects on infants, vital signs, weight gain or frequency of emesis. Treatment infants had fewer incidences of apnea.
Rausch (1981)	N = 40 (20 treatment, 20 control) Birthweight 1,000–2,000g.	Stroking, head to toe	Three 5-min. phases (15 minutes, 12 strokes/minute) *provided once daily* Term: 1–10 days postpartum	Greater weight gain. Increased feeding intake. Increased frequency of stooling.

Table 15–1 continued

Investigator	Subject Information	Type of Stimulation	Treatment Conditions	Results
Anderson, Burroughs, & Measel (1983)	$N = 27$ Gestational age $\overline{X} = 36.5$ Birthweight <2,000g.	Nonnutritive sucking. Research questions: 1. Can preterm infants suck	Term: 5 min. to 7 days after birth Pressures measured for 2 min., 12 times birth to 8 hours, 3 times days 1 to 7	Suck pressures $\overline{X} = 16.9$ (A score of 17 is an average score) Range 0–24
	$N = 11$ Gestational age $\overline{X} = 31$ Birthweight $\overline{X} = 1,594$g.	2. Safety factors	No available data	Suck pressures were found to be a function of infant condition. Nonnutritive sucking is presumed safe.
	$N = 59$ (treatment & control) Gestational age 23–24 weeks Birthweight 1,000–2,000g.	3. Benefits	Term: 5 min. post-tube feeding Continued until discharge	Readiness for bottle feeding 3.4 days earlier. Discharged 4 days sooner.

Source: From *Infants Born at Risk: Behavior and Development* (pp. 381-386) by T.M. Field, A.M. Sostek, S. Goldberg, & H.H. Shuman (Eds.), 1979, Jamaica, NY: Spectrum Publications, Inc. Copyright 1979 by Spectrum Publications, Inc. Reprinted by permission.

With a somewhat different focus, Neal (1968) examined the impact of vestibular stimulation (movement by a motorized hammock) on the development of premature infants. Neal believed that preterm babies were "deprived" of the continuous movement provided in utero. At the chronological age of 36 weeks, the treatment group exhibited significantly higher weight gains than the control infants. Moreover, on the *Graham-Rosenblith* test the treatment babies achieved higher scores in general maturation, motor development, and visual and auditory responses. In contrast with the findings of Hasselmeyer, irritability did not differ between the two groups.

In still another study, Solkoff and Matuszak (1975) used the *Brazelton Neonatal Assessment Scale* to evaluate changes in performance of newborns who received stroking and controls who did not have such benefits. Their work revealed that the stimulated infants showed positive changes of two or more points on 11 of the 26 *Brazelton* ratings, whereas their counterparts showed changes on only 2 of the ratings. Further results showed that the handled infants were more alert, habituated more quickly to light and sound, had improved tone and better head control in movement from pull to sit, were more easily comforted, reacted with more prompt avoidance to noxious stimuli, changed states more rapidly, and had better hand-to-mouth dexterity.

For over a decade, Korner and her colleagues have carried out a series of investigations on the use of oscillating water beds to provide increased vestibular stimulation for premature infants. Specifically, these researchers intended to offer intervention that was "compensating in nature," that would resemble intrauterine conditions, and that would "supply gentle, passive movements designed to improve the infant's tonus" (Korner, Kraemer, Haffner, & Cosper, 1975). In conclusion, the authors found that there were no significant differences between the treatment group and controls in terms of vital signs, weight, or frequency of emesis (vomiting). Yet, all treatment infants had significantly fewer apneic episodes than the controls. In a follow-up study to test further the reduction of apnea in preterm infants, Korner, Guilleminault, Van den Hoed and Baldwin (1978) investigated the effects of water bed flotation on the sleep and respiratory pattern of eight apneic preterm infants. The subjects served as their own controls throughout the course of intervention. Polygraphic recordings of sleep and respiratory patterns were taken during a 24-hour period. The results confirmed the previous study and demonstrated that apnea was significantly reduced while the infants were on the water beds. Moreover, the research found that the most extended apneic episodes and those associated with severe bradycardia showed the greatest decline. Shorter respiratory pauses and periodic breathing were not found to be significantly reduced.

In a more recent study Korner, Ruppel, and Rho (1982) focused on the influence of water beds on the sleep behavior and motility of theophylline-treated preterm infants. Since sleep levels of theophylline-treated infants often are significantly reduced, the researchers were interested in determining whether water bed flotation would calm and increase the sleep patterns of such newborns. In a carefully designed study, 17 premature infants were assessed on days three and four during treatment and control conditions. As in a prior investigation, infants served as their own controls. The researchers reported that the infants displayed significantly more quiet and active sleep, shorter sleep latencies, fewer state changes, less restlessness during sleep, less waking activity, and fewer jittery movements while placed on the water bed. The length of theophylline therapy positively seemed to affect state changes and reductions in wakefulness while on the water beds. Perhaps most importantly, however, Korner and her colleagues disclosed that theophylline levels, which were considered to be low, did not affect state changes. Specifically, they found that

> flotation did not reduce residual apnea and bradycardia as it had done with two previous samples, composed of infants with uncomplicated apnea of prematurity who were not treated with theophylline. Most of the infants in the present study had protracted ventilator care and had many more medical complications than the infants in the previous study. The infants' failure to respond to waterbed flotation with apnea reduction confirms previous observation that suggests that waterbeds may not be effective in reducing apnea in this type of population. The infants' failure to respond may also have been due to the fact that the incidence of apnea and bradycardia in the theophylline-treated infants was so low that any effects of an additional intervention could not be discerned. (pp. 868–869)

With a somewhat different purpose, Korner, Schneider, and Forrest in 1983 used a neurobehavioral assessment procedure to look at the impact of vestibular proprioceptive stimulation on premature neonates. Twenty infants were tested between 34 and 35 weeks conceptional age. They reported that the treatment group demonstrated better skills in attending and pursuing animate and inanimate visual and auditory stimuli, performed with more maturity on spontaneous motor tasks, showed significantly fewer signs of irritability and hypertonicity, and were twice as likely to be in a visually alert, inactive state. Though the authors' conclusions are qualified, the study did replicate Neal's results (1968), which demonstrated that rocking preterm infants augmented their visual and auditory abilities. In closing, Korner, Schneider, and Forrest wrote:

> We would like to stress that we consider the findings of this study as preliminary. The available sample was small and composed of infants who were critically ill when recruited and who, after selection, had many serious medical complications. Both the test-retest reliabilities and the suggestive evidence that compensatory vestibular-proprioceptive stimulation enhances the neurobehavioral development of preterm infants, are therefore in need of replication with a larger and healthier sample of premature babies. (p. 175)

In 1981, Rausch carried out a program of intervention that varied considerably, in the focus and the population of infants included, from the investigations of Neal and Korner and her colleagues. While the control infants were cared for according to standard nursery procedures, treatment newborns received stroking stimulation once daily (for three five-minute intervals at a rate of 12 strokes per minute) over the entire body. Treatments were administered each morning when babies were in an alert state, for a 10-day period postpartum. The study involved infants for whom access was limited. Head and legs were stimulated if a child had chest tubes. Stroking the trunk area was indicated for infants with several intravenous infusions. Rausch found that the experimental infants had a greater feeding intake on day 10 and gained 73 grams more than the controls by day 10. Similarly, treatment infants increased stooling frequency. Parents were allowed to provide some of the stroking stimulation in this study, and the researchers believed that this procedure helped families to establish early positive relationships with their infants.

Many researchers have regarded interventions as a way to settle and calm the high risk newborn. For example, Anderson, Burroughs, and Measel (1983) were interested in the effects of nonnutritive sucking on behavioral states in preterm infants. The authors noted that "the premature infant is truly an infant who experiences absence of self regulatory mother-newborn interaction" (p. 133). From five minutes to seven days after birth, nonnutritive sucking and representative pressures were measured 30 times in each of 27 preterm infants and 27 controls. Measures were taken with a small portable electronic suckometer with a research nipple. Feeding scores usually ranged from 0 to 24, with a score of 17 signifying an acceptable feeding. Average scores of 16.9 were tabulated for the first feedings and during the next six days. At 90 minutes after birth, full-term and many preterm infants were ready to feed with adequate suction. As to why premature infants were able to suck at one time and not at others, the authors commented:

> Pressures were much weaker with increasing temperature, heart rate, and breathing rate .... these findings indicate that sucking strength is related to condition, as well as to maturity .... One finding was strong and consistent: time after time, we saw adequate suction pressure drop to zero following prolonged activity, invasive therapy, and/or a crying episode. Logically, invasive therapy and vigorous procedures such as chest percussion would be done prior to feedings. To do this between feedings would disturb the infant's rest; to do this after a feeding would invite regurgitation; however, to do this before a feeding, as is commonly done for reasons mentioned, appears to compromise the infant's sucking ability, and thus the feeding. The important finding remains to be studied systematically. (p. 134)

Within the same investigation, these researchers next concluded that "whatever the energy cost of sucking, it appears to be, somehow, well reimbursed" (p. 139). Specifically, Anderson and his colleagues investigated the effectiveness of nonnutritive sucking on tube-fed premature infants. Fifty-nine premature infants were allowed to suck nonnutritively during and five minutes after tube feedings. Newborns were between 28 and 34 weeks gestation ($\overline{X}$ = 32.3 weeks), and between 1,000 and 2,000 grams in weight ($\overline{X}$ = 1,420 grams). Treatments began when infants were able to tolerate room air and 10cc of full-strength formula by tube and ended when babies were totally bottle fed. The results indicated that fewer and less intensive complications were required for the treatment subjects. Furthermore, they were ready for bottle feeding 3.4 days earlier and were discharged four days sooner than were control subjects. Anderson and his colleagues concluded that "this finding has been replicated by Bernbaum et al. in 1983, and further suggests that nonnutritive sucking during and following tube feeding improved the clinical course for preterm infants" (p. 143). These findings suggest that the calming results of such intervention have far-reaching beneficial effects for the preterm infant and, in addition, appear to be safe.

Finally, for some time researchers have speculated about the longitudinal effect of early handling on preterm and vulnerable populations. Such a study was conducted by Powell in 1974. A control group was given standard nursery care, while mothers or primary caregivers of treatment infants were encouraged to visit the nursery at least three times per week to provide additional handling. Post-test of the infants took place at two, four, and six months, as assessed by the Bayley Scales of Infant Development. Initially, babies who received extra handling regained their birthweight faster; yet, in the follow-up at two, four, and six months, no differences in weight or height were recorded. Scores of the treatment infants were significantly higher on the *Bayley Mental and Motor Scales* given at four months. The experimental group also performed better on the *Infant Behavior Record* at six months. Powell, in addition, commented that "no positive relationship was found between mothers who had the opportunity to visit and touch their babies and their later maternal behavior" (p. 111). On the other hand, he found that parental perceptions were positively enhanced by the intervention procedures. Moreover, Powell clarified his findings, noting that:

> The absence of positive findings on the effect of letting mothers handle their premature infants in the hospital in this and other studies indicated either that not enough was done with the mothers or that any effects were very short-lived. If hospitals were to adopt the practice of letting mothers handle their premature babies, the effects would seem to be greater on the mother's psychological state and on giving some babies extra stimulation in the hospital than on influencing later maternal behavior at home. (p. 112)

Fortunately, such trends—now ten years later—are beginning to emerge during long-term hospitalizations and separations of mothers and their babies in this country.

Auditory Stimulation

Far fewer studies are available on auditory stimulation than on sensory intervention. In part, this lack of research is a reflection of the complexities of conducting such studies with premature babies. In light of the substantial incidence of hearing loss reported among high risk populations, this is an important concern to pursue. The following studies exemplify the types of research that have been done on providing auditory stimulation with premature newborns.

Katz (1971) looked at the effects of tape recordings of mothers' voices on the development of preterm infants. Results indicated that when the newborns reached 36 weeks postconceptual age, the experimental group showed enhanced maturation (on both the motor and tactile adaptive measures) and increased auditory and visual ability on the *Graham-Rosenblith* test. The findings, however, did not indicate important differences in muscle tension and demonstrated no differences between groups in terms of irritability.

In a similar area of perinatal research, Segal (1972) demonstrated the "association between environmental stimulation and adaptive behavior" (p. 16). Again, using a tape recording of the mother's voice, she exposed 30 low birthweight premature babies in a treatment group to such intervention for a total of 30 minutes each day. At 36 weeks gestational age, each infant's cardiac response was recorded when a variety of auditory stimuli were presented. This study disclosed certain advantages of the treatment group over the control group. Presented with a "white noise stimulus," the experimental group showed greater ability to respond while in a quiet state. Segal noted:

> If cardiac acceleration is associated with the organism's attempt to exclude the stimulus, then it seems the experimental group was more successful in shutting out the stimulus . . . . If habituation is a form of learning not to respond, then it would seem that the experimental group, with their increased exposure to auditory stimulation, reacted initially with a greater protective reaction to the novel stimulus . . . The experimental group showed a downward trend in the amount of heart rate response across trials while the control group showed an irregular pattern. (pp. 17–18)

Segal also found that the experimental infants, in an aroused state, had a decreased response to their mother's voice and to an unfamiliar female voice, as compared to that of the control group. The author concluded:

> These findings indicated that the premature infant is responsive to auditory stimuli, has different cardiac reactions to auditory stimuli depending on his behavioral state, and attends to the human voice when crying. The inclusion of auditory stimulation resulted in those premature infants who have a more adaptive response to stimuli than those premature infants who were not exposed to this form of planned environmental stimulation. (p. 19)

Multimodal Stimulation

As is obvious from the title and the series of studies summarized in Table 15–2, multimodal intervention has been extremely diverse, ranging from visual and auditory stimulation to tactile and kinesthetic input. While a few investigations have included two modalities, most studies offer three or four sources of intervention. Water beds, handling, rocking, taped voices and heartbeats, and mobiles have been commonly used to provide such stimulation programs. Table 15–2 summarizes a few of these studies, which receive fuller discussion below.

In a recent investigation by Barnard and Bee (1983), treatment infants received vestibular stimulation (rocking by an oscillating bed) and simultaneous auditory input of a heartbeat recording. Control infants were given standard nursery care. Intervention consisted of one of three treatment approaches. Fixed interval infants were given 15 minutes of rocking and heartbeat stimulation each hour; self-activating newborns were given 15 minutes of rocking and heartbeat stimulation after every 90 seconds of inactivity; quasi-self-activating infants were given 15 minutes of rocking and heartbeat stimulation when inactive for 90 seconds, but received only one stimulation session each hour. This multimodal stimulation was intended to resemble the intrauterine environment and was based on an assumption that the preterm infants "suffer not so much from insufficient stimulation as from inappropriate stimulation" (p. 1156). Follow-up assessment at 8 and 24 months included measures of neurological condition, sleep/wake behavior, mother-infant interaction, and cognitive and motor development. Treatment infants demonstrated a significant drop in activity through the eighth treatment day, less abnormal reflexes, and improved adaptive responses in relation to their control counterparts. Given the *Mental Development Index* of the *Bayley Scales* at 24 months, treatment babies also exhibited greater maturation. Parent-infant interaction patterns were not found to be significantly different. The researchers concluded that "for the moment, however, our best interpretation of the results of our study is that temporal patterning and contingent stimulation have each had a separate contribution to the improved development in the infant, but that the two effects are additive" (p. 1165). The point is an important one in light of the fact that it is very difficult, if not impossible, to separate modes of input within intensive care nurseries.

Kramer and Pierpont (1976) studied the effects of placing infants on water beds and gently rocking them in association with auditory stimuli. Specifically, the authors reported that the program for the treatment group included mechanical rocking of the water bed one hour prior to each feeding, and playing of a taped simulated heartbeat (72 beats/minute) and woman's voice (74 to 84 decibels) during the rocking period. The intervention group revealed accelerated growth for weight and head circumference. In addition, "the stimulated group nippled earlier, ate better, and were more active than the control group" (p. 298). On the other hand, the control group and the treatment infants exhibited similar maturation on neurologic and behavioral

Table 15-2 Multimodal Stimulation with Preterm Infants

Investigator	Subject Information	Type of Stimulation	Treatment Conditions	Results
Barnard & Bee (1983)	N = 88 (treatment: N = 26 fixed interval, N = 23 self-activating, N = 10 quasi-activating) (control: N = 28) Gestational age <35 weeks	Rocking & heartbeat sound recording	Duration: Fixed Interval = 15 min. each hour Self-activating = after each 90 secs. of inactivity, 15 min. stimulation Quasi-activating = after 90 seconds of inactivity, 15 min. stimulation, 1 presentation per 45 minutes	1. Decreased rates of activity 2. Fewer abnormal reflexes 3. Improved orienting responses 4. More optimal scores on *Bayley Scales* at 24 months 5. No difference in parent-infant interaction
Kramer & Pierpoint (1976)	N = 20 (11 treatment, 9 control) Gestational age <34 weeks	Rocking water beds Heartbeat simulation, recorded mother's voice played during rocking	Provided 1 hour before each feeding from 2nd-7th postnatal day during entire stay in isolette	1. Increased weight gain 2. Growth in head circumference and biparietal diameter of the head 3. No significant differences on *Dubowitz* or *Brazelton*
Leib, Benfield, & Guidubaldi (1980)	N = 28 (14 treatment, 14 control) Birthweight 1,200–1,800 g.	Visual stimulation: mobiles Tactile stimulation: body rubbing Kinesthetic stimulation: rocking Auditory stimulation: talking, singing, and music box	Primary care period: visual & tactile stimulation Secondary care period: visual, tactile, kinesthetic, and auditory provided during feeding and rest times	1. Higher scores on *Brazelton (Mental & Motor Scales)* post intervention 2. More optimal score on *Bayley Scales of Infant Development* at 6 months 3. No differences in rate of growth or weight

Table 15–2 continued

Investigator	Subject Information	Type of Stimulation	Treatment Conditions	Results
Powell (1974)	N = 32 Treatment: Group 1, N=13 Group 2, N=11 Care, N=8 Birthweight 1,000–2,000g.	Group 1: handled by nurse Group 2: handled by mother	Group 1: 1. 20 min. period twice daily until birthweight was regained 2. 20 min. period once daily until discharge Group 2: handling by mother provided at an average of once every 4.8 days	Group 1: 1. Regained birthweight faster 2. Weight and height differences were not significant at 2, 4, or 6 months 3. Higher scores at 4 and 6 months on Bayley Scales of Infant Development
Katz (1971)	N = 62 (31 treatment, 31 control) Gestational age 28–32 weeks	Recorded mother's voice	5 min., 6x/day for 2 hour durations 5th postnatal day to 36 weeks postnatal age term: 4–6 weeks	Higher scores on Graham Rosenblith test: - greater maturation - increased auditory and visual ability - better muscle tone No differences in irritability
Segal (1972)	N = 60 (30 treatment, 30 matched controls) Gestational age 28–32 weeks	Recorded mother's voice	30 min./day Term: birth–36 weeks	Increased heart rate and habituation to white noise Decreased in heart rate to unfamiliar females' and mother's voice Increased attention span

Table 15-2 continued

Investigator	Subject Information	Type of Stimulation	Treatment Conditions	Results
LaRossa & Brown (1982)	N = 56 (28 treatment, 28 matched controls) Birthweight: $\overline{X}$=1,665 g. Gestational age: $\overline{X}$=33 weeks	Stroking Rocking Music box Bright objects Talking to softly	Term: 2 periods of stimulation 5 days per week at feeding time	1. Rate of weight gain improved 2. No effect on length of hospital stay
Siqueland (1973)	N = 20 (10 matched twin pairs)	Ten minutes of "mothering" daily, contingent stimulation for evidence of eye opening during feeding	"Mothering" provided 10 min twice per day "Conditioning" 11 min/day Handling provided 2X/day at feeding time	Exhibited better skill at 4 months on visual reinforcements, control of sucking behavior, and auditory reinforcement tasks

Source: From *Infants Born at Risk: Behavior and Development* (pp. 381-386) by T.M. Field, A.M. Sostek, S. Goldberg, and H.H. Shuman (Eds.), 1979, Jamaica, NY: Spectrum Publications, Inc. Copyright 1979 by Spectrum Publications, Inc. Reprinted by permission.

development as measured by the *Dubowitz* and the *Brazelton Neonatal Assessment Scale.*

In a multimodal sensory enrichment program, Leib, Benfield, and Guidubaldi (1980) revealed that early intervention can improve the developmental outcome of high risk preterm infants. The control group received standard nursery care, while the treatment babies were "provided an environment more like the one the infant would receive at home" (p. 85). Treatment infants were stimulated visually with a brightly colored object hanging from a mobile, approximately in line with their optimal focal distance of six to eight inches. Tactile and kinesthetic interventions included rubbing each baby during gavage feedings in the early days of the research program and touching the infants during nipple feedings in the later convalescent period. Kinesthetic stimulation was accomplished while each child was fed by his or her nurse, seated in a rocking chair. An en face position was maintained whenever possible. Auditory stimulation took place during nipple feeding as the nurses sang or talked to the infants. In addition, as the babies were placed back in open cribs, a music box played the song "This Old Man." The nurses were "not specifically instructed concerning the care for the control group" (p. 85). Uniquely, the study was set up to "prevent contamination" of the control infants. In particular, 14 newborns were identified as controls and after their discharge, a subsequent group of 14 neonates was deemed the control sample. Testing at six months revealed that the intervention children showed a marked increase in developmental scores on the *Bayley Scales of Infant Development.* Leib and her colleagues also reported on other benefits of early intervention that were not a focus of formal evaluation. Lieb explained:

> Our intervention program seemed to positively influence nursing attitudes and behaviors. For example, involved nurses appeared more sensitive to the infants' needs and more aware of the uniqueness and behavioral repertoire of each preterm infant. This aspect of early intervention requires further study. (p. 89)

In still another study, LaRossa and Brown (1982) examined the impact of additional stimulation of preterm infants by foster grandmothers, recruited to assist with the stimulation of 28 matched pairs of premature newborns who were past the critical stage of development, yet who needed more time to grow and gain weight. In general, the target group were infants who had feeding difficulties, lacked alertness, or had parents who found it difficult to visit often. Various forms of stimulation were utilized. For example, LaRossa noted that "each infant was stroked, rocked, spoken to gently, shown bright objects, and played melodies on music boxes" (p. 1835). Unexpectedly, the researchers found that there was a higher rate of early discharge of the comparison babies. This outcome led them to conclude that perhaps the treatment babies were "in worse health" than the control babies. The statistical findings of this study were significant. Specifically, the researchers discovered that

> in the 28 matched pairs, we found that the extra stimulation provided by the grandmothers had no effect on the babies' length of hospital stay or on their discharge weight. However, a comparison of the rates of weight gain indicated that the average rate of weight gain prior to the day of onset of stimulation tended to be slower for the babies in the intervention group than those in the comparison group (as calculated from a comparable day), while the rates of weight gain of the two groups after the day of onset of stimulation were similar. In other words, the additional stimulation helped the intervention babies catch up to the comparison group in rate of weight gain. (p. 1835)

The grandmothers made several informal remarks at the end of the study that proved insightful. In particular, they

> believed that their presence had a positive impact on the nursery staff. They said that after they started working in the nursery, the aides began to hold the babies more and interact with them more. The grandmothers also thought that they had a direct impact on the babies; after several days, they saw a difference in their babies. Both reported that the body tone of the babies improved, and that the babies were more alert (especially around stimulation time). The grandmothers were convinced that the babies recognized them after one or two weeks. Both women became infant advocates, unafraid to voice their opinions if they felt a baby should receive better or different care. (p. 1835)

Last, the researchers noted that the foster grandmothers did not affect the visiting patterns of the mothers. This was an important observation because the total program seemed to have a positive impact upon all included—infants, staff, parents, and foster grandmothers.

In a final course of research, Siqueland (1973) investigated the long-term effects of conditional stimulation on premature twins. Treatment twins were handled at two daily feeding times and given additional visual stimulation if they opened their eyes. At four months, the treatment and control groups were evaluated on visual conditioning tasks. Measured by "high amplitude sucking" responses, babies were presented with various visual patterns that differed in complexity and novelty over an 18-minute period. As compared with the controls, the handled babies demonstrated significant improvement in terms of their sucking responses; many of the nontreatment twins failed to exhibit visual reinforcement, as measured by their less effective control of sucking behavior. When additional testing was completed on an auditory reinforcement task, the control twins continued to show a more deficient level of performance.

In conclusion, the basic question that all of the neurodevelopmental programs seek to answer is this: Does additional or special stimulation in neonatal intensive care nurseries make a substantial and positive difference? To date, we believe that the research in most instances has demonstrated beneficial effects. In the face of this evidence, however, it is necessary to determine whether design factors in each study indicate dependable results. Therefore, the reader must closely examine factors such as selection of infants, sample size, birthweight, gestational age, and the quality and effectiveness of interventions with certain populations. Similarly, the research also suggests that the implementation of such strategies has assisted parents of preterm infants, helping them to feel that they have an important role in providing care while their infant is in intensive care. The practical implications of these results are impressive, and continued research seems to support the importance of early parental contact. Perhaps some answers to these issues are contained in a comment by Chaze and Lundington-Hoe (1984):

> Parents enjoy setting developmental goals for their infants and helping them meet the goals. This enables parents to perceive themselves as the authority on their infant's interaction pattern and behavior: the true mark of parenting and a welcome addition to the character of parent-infant relationships in intensive care nurseries. . . . A most significant parental response is a shift of focus from their infant's pathology ("What is the oxygen level today?" or "What's his latest bilirubin?") to developmental accomplishments ("What can he do today?" or "Is she ready for a new picture?").
> (p. 71)

INTERVENTION WITH PARENTS

Ainsworth (1973) has defined attachment as "an affectional tie that one person forms to another specific person or persons, binding them together in space and enduring over time" (p. 1). In other words, the process of establishing a secure bond elicits reciprocal and nurturing behaviors from both partners. Interactions between high risk infants and their parents often are quite different from responses observed in full-term healthy infants and their families. Based upon gestational age, birthweight, respiration, physical variability, and weight gain, preterm infants may be treated in neonatal intensive care units for 2 to 12 weeks, or possibly longer. As we have discussed in the previous chapter, the birth of an ill baby sets up a crisis event for the family. They are faced with not only a developmental crisis in being parents, but also an involuntary situation of becoming parents of an infant unanticipated until the ninth month. Too, when a premature infant is born, the mother and father must adapt their preconceived image of their infant to the actual newborn before them. For parents, the birth of a baby with medical problems arising from prematurity may elicit many feelings of conflict. Table 15-3 depicts some of the common responses of parents at the time of full-term and premature delivery.

Table 15–3 Typical Patent Reactions to Full-Term and Preterm Births

	Full-Term Delivery	Premature Delivery
Perceptions of event	Gain, success	Loss, failure
Reactions to birth	Joy, relief	Grief, concern
Emotional preparation	Complete	Incomplete
Expectation confirmed	"Wished-for" baby	"Feared" baby
Self-esteem	Increased	Decreased
Baby's primary caregivers	Mother, father	Nurses, doctors
Parents and infants	Together	Separated
Baby's social responsiveness	Well-developed	Decreased or absent
Parents go home with	Baby	Empty Arms
Major psychological tasks re-maining	Reconciling real and fan-tasized baby	Grieving for expected baby; anticipatory grieving for baby; individualizing and accepting baby

Source: From *Parent-Infant Relationships* (p. 320) by P.M. Taylor and B.L. Hall, 1980, New York: Grune & Stratton, Inc. Copyright 1980 by Grune & Stratton, Inc. Reprinted by permission.

It is clear that the birth of a sick or premature infant establishes an event with which the parents most often have not had any prior experience. In a state of crisis, ordinary problem-solving abilities frequently are inadequate. Furthermore, in attempting to understand family crisis, it is important to realize that reactions to a crisis event are extremely variable. As Hill (1965) has suggested, "No crisis-precipitating event is the same for any given family; its impact ranges according to the several hardships that may accompany it" (p. 35).

Behavioral Responsivity of Preterm Infants

The preterm infant is deprived of intrauterine stimulation from the last weeks of pregnancy. In addition, long stays in neonatal intensive care units naturally reduce the amount of gazing, handling, and skin-to-skin contact between parents and their newborns. Premature babies sometimes smile much later than full-term infants; this too may have a negative effect on relationships. In the article, "My Baby Was Premature," Pat Iyer (1981) explained that "by the time Raja was three months old and beginning to smile, I felt comfortable enough to cuddle him and talk to him" (p. 306). As we also have pointed out, premature babies often are less alert than full-term neonates, and this condition may persist well into the time period when they go home.

In research by DiVitto and Goldberg (1979), ten firstborn infants were studied during feeding times. This group included full-term, healthy premature, and sick premature newborns. As predicted by the researchers, full-term infants during initial feedings were touched and talked to more than any other group. These differences were not apparent in observations completed at four months. Preterm infants demonstrated more fussy and crying behavior at four months, while the term infants showed a decline. Holding patterns in parents of preterm infants, in addition, were found to be delayed or depressed. Such "distancing" was seen as a protective response to prepare parents of severely ill prematures for possible death. DiVitto and Goldberg thus reflected:

> The differences which were reported indicated that the fewer medical problems the baby had, the more likely she/he was to be alert for prolonged periods, responsive to social stimulation and able to signal distress by crying. Those infants who were most alert and responsive during neonatal examination were also more likely to be alert and available for social stimulation during feedings and were least likely to need functional stimulation during the early feedings. These same infants were likely to spend the greatest proportion of time in the closest feeding position during most feedings. Those infants who had been least responsive to auditory stimulation during the initial examination received more vocal and tactile stimulation from parents during most of the feedings. These findings suggest that prematurely born infants are initially less available for social interactions with their parents. In the early feedings they are less likely than full-term infants to be held nestled in the arms during feedings and are more likely to receive both social (parents vocalize and touch) and functional stimulation during feedings. Hence, parents of prematurely born infants are initially confronted with a relatively unresponsive infant and seem to adapt by working harder to elicit sucking and social response during feedings. These early patterns appear to persist through the first four months. (p. 4)

This study suggests the importance of identifying parents of ill premature infants early, because they may need professional support and guidance.

Parent-Child Disorders—An Open Question

Many researchers, faced with a growing concern that the premature infant is at risk for parenting disorders, have investigated standard medical care and management of such infants and their families. For example, Minde, Marton, Manning, and Hines (1980) studied the relationships between premature infants and mothers during visits in intensive care units and for the first three months at home. Continuous observations during feeding were made for a sample of 32 babies. Infant behaviors included arm, head, leg, and hand-to-mouth movements; open eyes; crying; vocalizing; smiling; and yawning.

Maternal behaviors consisted of looking, verbalizing to babies, holding, smiling, and touching. Furthermore, mothers were rated according to activity level in high, medium, and low activity groups. Overall, mothers who had superior levels of interaction with their infants were found to have higher rates of nursery visitation. This study disclosed that mothers in the low activity groups were "relatively unresponsive and aloof," suggested that perhaps mothers in the latter group were at greater risk for developing parenting difficulties. The researchers also reported on other potential social factors that might affect parent-child interaction. For instance, families that visited less were found to have poorer support systems. In particular, the following individual items were rated in order of importance as high predictors of parenting problems:

1. relationship with own mother
2. relationship with father of infant
3. prior abortions by mother

Minde concluded:

> Our data showed a clear correspondence between the degree of activity a mother exhibited toward her infant and some of her previous life events . . . . Our data also show that prenatal and perinatal medical complications do not predict later parental activity levels . . . . Similarly, our data showed no association between the type of initial contact the mother had with her baby and her later activity pattern. (pp. 12–18)

This research is significant because it implies that there is a serious need to assess family relationships, both past and present, in neonatal settings. The findings of these underlying aspects of parenting disorders likely will generate new research on improving parent-infant interactions in neonatal settings.

Studies by Field (1979) focused on mother-child interactions for preterm, post-term, and full-term infants. Sessions were videotaped using a split screen, with infants three to four months of age. Field found that the mothers of high risk infants tended to maintain higher activity levels during feeding, while mothers of full-term babies quieted during sucking. Too, higher risk preterm and post-term infants were more fussy and averted their gazes more frequently in face-to-face interactions. Field commented on the possibilities for early positive intervention:

> These studies suggest that early interactions can be manipulated in such a way as to increase the attentiveness or decrease the gaze aversion and fussiness of the infant by instructing the mothers to behave even more like mothers typically behave with their infants. Generally, it seems as if the instructions encourage a greater attentiveness on the part of the mother so that she not only becomes less active, but also becomes more sensitive to her infant's signals and more contingently responsive. (p. 337)

Beckwith, Cohen, Kopp, Parmelee and Marcy (1976) investigated preterm infant-parent interactions and the effects on early cognitive development. Fifty-one preterm infants were studied in natural home settings at one, three, and eight months. The researchers administered the *Gesell Developmental Scales* and a sensory motor scale at nine months. Five levels of caregiving also were assessed; i.e., social interaction, responsive holding, verbalization, mutual gazing, and stressful holding. In brief, the authors reported:

> Infants who were assessed at 9 months as more skillful in sensorimotor performance had at one month more mutual caregiver infant gazing, at 3 months more interchanges of smiling during mutual gazing and more contingent response to their fuss cries, and at 8 months experienced greater levels of social interaction including more contingent responsiveness to their nondistress vocalizations. The significant dimension appears to be reciprocal social interactions, that is, transactions that occur contingently to the infant's signals, either simultaneously as in mutual gazing or successively as in contingency to distress or contingency to nondistress vocalizations. (p. 585)

The above research suggests that prematurity is a risk factor and may lead to later cognitive deficits. Moreover, the United States does not stand alone as a country in need of maternal participation in the care of preterm infants. Perinatal research in India, for instance, also has addressed this topic. Karan and Rao (1983) studied the benefits of early parent contact for preterm neonates in a neonatal setting in India. The researchers followed 79 infants for a period of one year after early discharge. The mean weight of the babies leaving the hospital was 1,580 grams. Discharge was contingent upon criteria that babies were free from infection, could maintain temperature within a typical environment, and could suckle satisfactorily. Karan and Rao discovered that allowing mothers early entry into the nursery improved chances of early discharge. This was especially apparent among newborns who were breast-fed, their mean hospital stay being only 12 days. In addition, the incidence of diarrhea in nursed babies was only 5 percent, as compared with 20 percent in artificially fed infants, and was of a much milder nature. In previous years, before early entry and discharge were practiced, only 10 percent of the mothers were able to breast-feed. Thus, allowing the mothers early entry into the nursery proved to be beneficial, both physiologically and psychologically. The findings of this study are significant for a country in which the mortality rate is extremely high. The researchers concluded:

> Our results revealed that 82 percent came for follow-up out of which 53 percent were doing well and gaining weight rapidly while 38 percent fared moderately and only nine percent did poorly requiring readmission with a five percent mortality. One significant factor determining a favourable outcome was the ability of the mother to breast feed her infant. (p. 115)

Parent-Child Interactions

As we have suggested in early discussions of our own research, we have found that sensitive clinical assessments of infants actually can serve as interventions for parents. Widmayer and Field (1981) made similar observations in a study where they analyzed the effects of *Brazelton* demonstrations for mothers with their preterm infants. Using two approaches, the *Brazelton Scale* was administered to treatment infants in the presence of their mothers. These mothers also were asked to administer an adaptation of the *Brazelton Scale* called the *Mother's Assessment of the Behavior of Her Infant Scale* (*MABI*) at birth and each week during the first month. A second treatment group received only administration of the *MABI* scale and did not receive the *Brazelton* demonstrations. A third group served as a control group.

Testing at 1, 4, and 12 months resulted in statistically significant gains in the first and second treatment groups. At 1 month, the *Brazelton/MABI* group infants received better interactive scores than the babies assigned to the control group. Higher fine motor adaptive abilities were recorded among treatment infants on the *Denver Developmental Screening Test* at 4 months. In addition, both experimental groups had higher ratings on face-to-face interactions than control infants. At 12 months, the experimental infants received higher scores on the *Mental Development Index* of the *Bayley Scales of Infant Development*. In short, this systematic program of parent involvement helped to develop "noticing" skills in the parents and to educate them about infant abilities and appropriate developmental goals. Widmayer and Field explained:

> The results of this study suggest that the introduction of an easy, comparatively brief and cost-effective intervention such as the *Brazelton* demonstrated to teenage, low socioeconomic status mothers, may be an effective method of fostering more responsive interactions between these mothers and their preterm infants. The mother, via observation of the *Brazelton* scale or her own assessment on the *MABI* scale, may become more sensitized to the unique abilities of her infant, more interested in observing his or her development, and more active in providing stimulation to facilitate this development. (pp. 713–714) (emphasis added)

Minde et al. (1980) assisted in the development of a self-help group in a neonatal intensive care unit in Toronto and studied its effects. In a controlled study, 28 families met in a group situation with a nurse coordinator and a "veteran mother" who recently had given birth to a premature infant. The treatment group met for a period of seven to ten weeks on a regular basis. The control group was 29 families who did not attend the group sessions. Parent-infant interactions were recorded in the nursery and at home during one, two, and three months following infant discharge.

At a very basic level, group meetings helped parents to voice their feelings and express their needs. The authors indicated that

> during the three to five initial meetings, the parents talked primarily about their intense feelings of depression, fear, and guilt, about having given birth to such a small baby. Their relief about "not being alone in such a state" was usually quite dramatic and led to a great feeling of intimacy among members and the veteran mother. (p. 935)

The mean length of hospitalization did not vary between the two groups. Other results proved to be statistically significant. Parents in the treatment group attended the group meetings at a high rate; 50 percent of the families attended all the sessions, 25 percent missed only one, and the rest came at least one-third of the time. Similarly, the intervention parents visited their infants more often, and interaction patterns were more positive. Following discharge, treatment infants fed longer at two months, and at three months their parents used baby-sitters more often. This finding suggests that families felt more comfortable with leaving their babies with another caretaker. Treatment mothers were found to interact more with their infants at home, looking en face, touching, and talking. This study reinforces the belief that humanistic caregiving is crucial to the development of premature infants. It is therefore appropriate to increase our attention toward implementing programs to facilitate early parent involvement in the care of preterm infants.

Data collected over the past 15 to 20 years on intervention with high risk infants in intensive care nurseries have been immense. Unfortunately though findings seem to suggest positive impact (Schaefer, Hatcher, & Barglow, 1980), reviews on the efficacy of programming leave many questions unanswered and consistently raise the need for refinement of methodologies and designs of such studies (Cole, 1985; Cole & Frappier, 1985; Cornell & Gottfield, 1976; Harrison, 1985; Linn, Horowitz, & Fox, 1985; Meisels, 1985; Oehler, 1985; Ross, 1984). To move us beyond this point of intense questioning, research in the future will have to address many issues about appropriateness and timing of intervention with varying degrees of prematurity, the nature of specific interventions, sensitive measures of developmental change, the diversity of high risk infant populations, best individuals for program implementation, and the guidance that should be offered to parents relative to earlier and later stimulation. In most instances, it is not possible to acquire significant numbers of infants within given categories of risk, define such classifications accurately, or impose controls where babies are denied programming considered to be beneficial. Thus, studies will need to be developed around these constraints. Last, researchers are indicating that even interventions should be varied or made contingent upon "the ability of individual infants to handle particular stimuli" (Linn, Horowitz, & Fox, 1985, p. 417), and, in addition, baseline data should be amassed prior to the implementation of any educational or therapeutic plan.

Currently, more than sufficient research with possibilities for intervention have been developed. At this stage of inquiry, new directions for study might

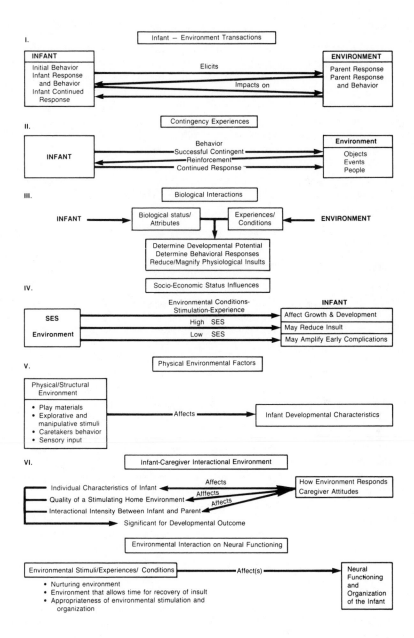

Figure 15–1 Environmental-Interactional Networks (Some Intervention Considerations in the Early Environment of the High Risk Infant)

Source: Reprinted with permission from *Intervention Considerations in the Early Environment of the High Risk Infant* by E. George Bulow (1986).

include careful descriptions of the ecological environments of specific intensive care nurseries, systematic variation of program-givers, and intervention strategies, and perhaps most importantly, the identification of categories of infant states, responsiveness, and developmental change. This approach might help us to more clearly define the subtleties of difference among infants that promote short-term change as a result of educational intervention.

Issues concerning long-term program effectiveness are more complicated problems to resolve. However, a similar method of establishing categories of interaction, family support, as well as child variables, may offer some possibilities for better description and understanding of impact. In conclusion, Figure 15-1 presents some of the environmental-interactional networks that are essential to accurately define research problems as further investigations of intensive care nursery intervention proceed.

REFERENCES

Ainsworth, M. (1973). The development of infant-mother attachment. In B.M. Caldwell & A.M. Riciutti (Eds.), *Review of child development research* (Vol. 3, pp. 1–94). New York: Russell Sage Foundation.

Anderson, G.C., Burroughs, A.K., & Measel, C.P. (1983). Nonnutritive sucking opportunities: A safe and effective treatment for preterm neonates. In T. M. Field & A.M. Sostek (Eds.), *Infants born at risk: Physiological, perceptual, and cognitive processes* (pp. 129–146). New York: Grune & Stratton.

Barnard, K.E., & Bee, H.L. (1983). The impact of temporally patterned stimulation on the development of preterm infants. *Child Development, 54,* 1156–1167.

Beckwith, L., Cohen, S., Kopp, C., Parmelee, A., & Marcy, T. (1976). Early cognitive development. *Child Development, 47,* 579–587.

Chaze, B.A., & Lundington-Hoe, S. (1984). Sensory stimulation in the NICU. *American Journal of Nursing, 84,* 68–71.

Cole, J.G. (1985). Infant stimulation reexamined: An environmental-and-behavioral-based approach. *Neonatal Network, April,* 24–30.

Cole, J.G., & Frappier, P.A. (1985). Infant stimulation reassessed: A new approach to providing care for the preterm infant. *JOGNN, November/December,* 471–477.

Cornell, E.H., & Gottfried, A.W. (1976). Intervention with premature human infants. *Child Development, 47,* 32–39.

DiVitto, B., & Goldberg, S. (1979). The effects of newborn medical status on early parent-infant interaction. In T.M. Field, A.M. Sostek, S. Goldberg, & H.H. Shuman (Eds.), *Infants born at risk: Behavior and development* (pp. 311–332). New York: SP Medical & Scientific Books.

Field, T.M. (1979). Interaction patterns of preterm and term infants. In T.M. Field, A.M. Sostek, S. Goldberg, & H.H. Shuman (Eds.), *Infants born at risk: Behavior and development* (pp. 333–361). New York: SP Medical & Scientific Books.

George-Bulow, E. (1986). *Intervention considerations in the early environment of the high risk infant,* unpublished paper.

Harrison, L. (1985). Effects of early supplemental stimulation programs for premature infants: Review of the literature. *Maternal Child Nursing Journal, 14,* 69–90.

Hasselmeyer, E.C. (1964). The premature neonate's response to handling. *American Nursing Association, 1,* 15–24.

Hill, R. (1965). Generic features of families under stress. In H.J. Parad (Ed.), *Crisis intervention: Selected readings* (pp. 32–54). New York: Family Services Association of America.

Iyer, P. (1981). My baby was premature. *JOGNN Nursing, July-August,* 304–307.

Karan, S., & Rao, S. (1983). Benefits of early maternal participation in care of low birthweight infants leading to early discharge. *Journal of Tropical Pediatrics, 29,* 115–118.

Katz, V. (1971). Auditory stimulation and developmental behavior of the preterm infant. *Nursing Research, 20,* 196–201.

Korner, A.F., Guilleminault, C., Van den Hoed, M.D., & Baldwin, R.B. (1978). Reduction of sleep apnea and bradycardia in preterm infants on oscillating water beds: A controlled polygraphic study. *Pediatrics, 61,* 528–534.

Korner, A.F., Kraemer, H.C., Haffner, M.E., & Cosper, L.M. (1975). Effects of waterbed flotation on premature infants: A pilot study. *Pediatrics, 56,* 361–367.

Korner, A.F., Ruppel, E.M., & Rho, J.M. (1982). Effects of waterbeds on the sleep and motility of theophylline-treated preterm infants. *Pediatrics, 70,* 864–869.

Korner, A.F., & Schneider, P., & Forrest, T. (1983). Effects of vestibular-proprioceptive stimulation on the neurobehavioral development of preterm infants: A pilot study. *Neuropediatrics, 14,* 170–175.

Kramer, L.I., & Pierpont, M.E. (1976). Rocking waterbeds and auditory stimuli to enhance growth of preterm infants. *Journal of Pediatrics, 88,* 297–299.

LaRossa, M.M., & Brown, J.V. (1982). Foster grandmothers in the premature nursery. *American Journal of Nursing, 82,* 1834–1835.

Leib, S.A., Benfield, G., & Guidubaldi, J. (1980). Effect of early intervention and stimulation of the preterm infant. *Pediatrics, 66,* 63–89.

Linn, P.L., Horowitz, F.D., & Fox, H.A. (1985). Stimulation in the NICU: Is more necessarily better? *Clinics in Perinatology, 12,* 407–422.

Masi, W. (1979). Supplemental stimulation of the premature infant. In T.M. Field, A.M. Sostek, S. Goldberg, & H.H. Shuman (Eds.), *Infants born at risk: Behavior and development* (pp. 367–387). SP Medical & Scientific Books.

Meisels, S.J. (1985). The efficacy of early intervention: Why are we still asking this question? *Topics in Early Childhood Special Education, 5,* 1–11.

Minde, K., Shosenberg, N., Marton, P., Thompson, J., Ripley, J., & Burns, S. (1980). Self-help groups in a premature nursery - A controlled evaluation. *Journal of Pediatrics, 96,* 933–939.

Neal, M. (1968). Vestibular stimulation and the development behavior of the small premature infant. *Nursing Research Reports, 3,* 2–5.

Oehler, J.M. (December 1985). Examining the issue of tactile stimulation for preterm infants. *Neonatal Network,* 25–32.

Powell, L.F. (1974). The effects of extra stimulation and maternal involvement on the development of low birthweight infants and on maternal behavior. *Child Development, 45,* 106–113.

Rausch, P. (1981). Effects of tactile and kinesthetic stimulation on premature infants. *JOGNN Nursing, 10,* 34–37.

Ross, E.F. (1984). Review and critique of research on the use of tactile and kinesthetic stimulation with premature infants. *Physical & Occupational Therapy, 4,* 35–49.

Schaefer, M., Hatcher, R.P., & Barlow, P.D. (1980). Prematurity and infant stimulation: A review of research. *Child Psychiatry and Human Development, 10,* 199–212.

Segal, M.V. (1972). Cardiac responsivity to auditory stimulation in preterm infants. *Nursing Research, 21,* 15–19.

Siqueland, E.R. (1973). Biological and experimental determinants of exploration in infancy. In L. Stone, J. Smith, & C. Murphy (Eds.), *The competent infant* (pp. 822–823). New York: Basic Books.

Solkoff, N., & Matuszak, D. (1975). Tactile stimulation and behavioral development among low birthweight infants. *Child Psychiatry and Human Development, 6,* 33–39.

Taylor, P.M., & Hall, B.L. (1980). *Parent-infant relationships* (pp. 315–344). New York: Grune & Stratton.

Widmayer, S.M., & Field, T.M. (1981). Effects of Brazelton demonstrations for mothers in the development of preterm infants. *Pediatrics, 67,* 711–714.

16

Intervention in Home- and Center-Based Programs

Salome A. Arenas and Gail L. Ensher

Throughout history, one of the primary human goals has been protection and education of the young. In most Western cultures, the family traditionally has assumed this responsibility and, when that has not been feasible, society has found other ways to care for its children in orphanages, foster homes, and institutions for the handicapped. Despite good intentions, results in the latter cases invariably have been negative. These findings largely have been a reflection of the custodial approach used in such facilities, which provided physical care yet neglected cognitive development in the infant and preschool years. In the 1940s, with the publication of studies on early development by Goldfarb (1943) and Spitz (1945) and research on individualized care for mentally retarded infants by Skeels and Dye (1939), society and educators in particular began to understand the adverse impact of residential settings.

During the 1950s, kindergarten programs and nursery schools were influenced by educators such as Pestalozzi, Froebel, Montessori, and Dewey, and by the theoretical approaches of Freud, Gesell, and Erickson. Preschools afforded good child care and a supportive environment to middle-class children on fee-paying bases. Subsequently, important social and political changes, together with new attitudes on child development, began to exert a direct influence on American early childhood education. The role of women in the United States changed and work became a major consideration. During the 1960s, more than one-third of the women with children below school age had jobs; by 1970, that figure had risen to 48 percent. In addition, the traditional nuclear family began to break down, and the increase in single-parent households made early education programs an absolute necessity.

Later, the highly charged political climate of the 1960s gave birth to several movements, the most important of which was civil rights. There was a massive attempt to eradicate "class" differences, perhaps most clearly reflected in Lyndon Johnson's "War on Poverty." One noteworthy component was Head Start, the preschool intervention program implemented "in the hope of providing young children with a sort of innoculation against the ill effects of poverty" (Zigler & Berman, 1983, p. 895). Meanwhile, researchers and child development specialists such as Gordon (1969) and Frost (1973) suggested that there were direct relationships between poverty and mental development and that infants in low socioeconomic groups were most vulnerable.

In addition to potent social and political changes, new theories of childrearing have surfaced over the past 30 years. The empirical work of researchers, as well as studies of several educators and developmental psychologists, have indeed confirmed the proposition that environmental experiences play a critical role in intellectual and emotional development and that these experiences are most pervasive during the first two years of life. Bloom (1964) and Hunt (1961) were two early scholars who provided educators with an ideological framework for preschool intervention programs. Coinciding with these positions, Piaget's writings on genetic epistemology focused on the child as an active participant in the learning process, a view that was reinforced by Bruner in his studies on learning and the thinking process. Armed with these theoretical conceptions, early educators thus emphasized structured learning experiences and appropriate stimulation, both inside and outside the home. With such a philosophical position, a new trend emerged in the field of early intervention.

The majority of early childhood programs that were designed and implemented during the 1960s focused on low-income and minority children. Most were compensatory in nature and patterned after a learning deficit model. In contrast, programs in the 1970s based on the difference model placed greater emphasis on prevention. Taking advantage of the past, present early educators are now asking hard questions about the efficacy of early intervention and are attempting to develop innovative programs sufficient to meet the demands of the complex era ahead.

While early education programs may be classified in many ways, we will examine interventions in light of their service delivery (home-, center-, or home-center-based) and their target population (whether they are child- or family-oriented). Any combination of these components is possible. The following section describes each program relative to its theoretical framework, groups served, goals, assessment strategies, and research findings.

HOME-BASED PROGRAMS

Home-based programs offer services in resident settings. Staff members—both professionals and paraprofessionals—visit on a regular basis to interact with parents and/or child, depending on the focus of the program. There are several advantages to this approach. First, home-based programs are cost-effective since professionals work with clients in the natural environment. Not surprisingly, this method is preferred by many educators who insist that infants should not be separated from mothers or removed from their homes. Those who support home-based programs also suggest that there may be a diffusion of effects, and that individuals surrounding target children, such as siblings and even neighbors, may benefit from the intervention. At the same time, these programs may place inordinate stresses on families, who feel that success or failure is entirely dependent upon their doing. Another paramount disadvantage is that most models do not set aside any free time for mothers. Despite these negative points, however, the majority of such projects to date have followed this format and, except for Schaefer's child-oriented study, all have been geared toward parents or the mother-child dyad.

Child-Oriented Programs

The Infant Education Research Project—Washington, D. C.

The Infant Education Research Project, directed by Earl Schaefer, focused on the child as the primary target. The major goal of the program was "to facilitate the intellectual development of disadvantaged children through a period of home tutoring during the second and third years of life" (Schaefer & Aaronson, 1972). Children were selected from two lower-income neighborhoods. A group of 31 babies received the benefit of intervention, and 33 youngsters served as controls. Tutoring sessions began when babies were 15 months old and continued through 36 months of age. This particular period was elected in light of growing evidence that the initial intellectual decline for disadvantaged children seemed to occur at about this stage of development.

Eight college graduates with prior experience with inner-city children were trained as tutors. During a two- to three-month period, they assisted in training sessions that stressed verbal stimulation, readings on Montessori and Russian day-care, and the developmental problems of babies raised in orphanages. Teachers visited homes one hour per day, five days per week for 21 months. During visits, tutors spent time with children, showed pictures, and worked with simple puzzles. Lesson plans were flexible, with an emphasis on verbal development. Materials were developed by individual tutors, and intervention sessions were supplemented by community activities, such as walks to stores, library visits, parties, trips to zoos, and other relevant settings. Participation of family members in these events was encouraged but not required. In order to assess program effectiveness, several scales were used: the *Bayley Scales* at 14 and 21 months, the *Stanford-Binet* at 27 and 36 months, the *Peabody Picture Vocabulary Test* and the *Johns Hopkins Perceptual Test* at 36 months. The final evaluation, at 36 months, rated task-oriented behaviors. The effects of home environment on the emotional development of infants were assessed by measuring maternal attitudes toward children.

In general, Schaefer (1972) found that IQ scores of the controls dropped at 21 months and remained at a depressed level. By contrast, the IQ levels of the experimental children, after a drop at 21 months, rose consistently until 36 months at the end of the intervention program. However, despite these apparent differences between the experimental and control groups, Schaefer explained that these findings were more the result of a decline in the control group than an actual increase in the experimental group. The experimental infants tested at the age of 14 months and again at 36 months continued to be stable with IQs of 106, while scores at 14 and 36 months for the control infants were 109 and 89, respectively (Beller, 1979). The author also disclosed significant correlations between maternal attitudes and measures of child cognitive and emotional functioning. As a result of this study, Schaefer abandoned this strategy of home visitation and adopted a broader approach to early intervention (Schaefer, 1972).

The Structured Tutorial Program for Infants—Urbana, Illinois

The Structured Tutorial Program for Infants, developed by Genevieve Painter, was twofold in purpose: first, to study the effects of intervention prior to the preschool years and second, to prevent anticipated cognitive and language delays among deprived infants. The population consisted of 20 children, 8 to 24 months in age, who were siblings of four-year-olds attending a nursery school for disadvantaged children. Ten children were assigned to an experimental group that received home instruction; a second group served as controls. Babies included in the experimental group received one hour of structured tutoring in their homes five days per week for one year. The program emphasized language, conceptual, and sensory motor development. Sessions were not designed as casual and playful, but they were enjoyable (Painter, 1968). Four female college graduates with varying backgrounds functioned as tutors. They were trained for one week with discussions on readings, home visits, and training continued throughout the program in the form of meetings with a supervisor to discuss child progress. Parents were not involved in the home tutoring sessions. During the initial weeks, home-based teachers focused on establishing rapport with children, playing with gross- and fine-motor toys, and formulating the parameters of the program that included a language curriculum. The latter was subdivided into several components, ranging from development of beginning and elaborative language to breakdown of "giant word units" and facilitation of internal dialogue to fostering concepts of body image, space, number, time, and classification.

Evaluations were "blind," carried out in the homes of children by psychologists who were not informed of subject group identity. While pretest results on the *Cattell* revealed no differences between the experimental and control groups, post-test findings on the *Stanford-Binet* showed an increase of ten IQ points by the experimental group. Children also were assessed by the *Illinois Test of Psycholinguistic Abilities*, the *Merrill-Palmer*, and various items from measures developed by Painter. Again, experimental subjects manifested an advantage over the control subjects on 25 of the 26 variables included.

Painter concluded that infants were capable of intense intervention for at least one hour per day, but that they might benefit even more from group programs away from home and the problems inherent in such visits. It is important to consider that Painter made no attempt to analyze the relationships between parent interaction and infant emotional and intellectual behavior.

Parent-Oriented Programs

The Florida Parent Education Program—Gainesville, Florida

Unlike the approaches of Schaefer and Painter, the Florida Parent Education Program, directed by Ira Gordon, established goals "to find out whether the use of disadvantaged women as parent educators of indigent mothers of infants and young children (1) enhances the development of the infants and children, and (2) increases the mother's competence and sense of personal warmth" (Gordon, 1969, p. 3). One special feature distinguished the program—the employment of paraprofessionals, women from the community who were trained for five weeks in principles of child development. Fifteen women, 12 black and 3 white, were chosen from 75 candidates; all had a high school education. Selection was based on age, marital status, experience with babies, ability to communicate, and expressed interest in the basic aim of the work (Gordon, 1967).

The curriculum of the program was closely tied to Piagetian theory, with an emphasis on experiences to facilitate cognitive development. The first phase of the intervention consisted of games constructed to be sensorimotor, manipulative, and exploratory in nature. At later stages, play included more preoperational activities to develop such skills and knowledge as object permanence.

The study's participants were mothers and their respective babies who had been born between June 1966 and September 1967 at a public health center. Gordon initiated the investigation with 276 mother-infant dyads, which was reduced to a final sample of 193 pairs. The subjects then were assigned randomly to experimental or control groups. Each parent-educator worked with ten mothers and ten babies. The overall plan of the program was the same for all experimental mothers, but the timing was tailored to individual experimental pairs. Parent-educators made home visits once per week. They worked with infants on specific exercises appropriate for their chronological age. In addition, home visitors taught mothers how to construct inexpensive toys. When children turned two, learning or backyard centers were added to the range of program options. These settings were designed to offer group experiences, twice a week for two hours. Sessions were held in the homes of parents involved in the project, and mothers who lived in center homes were employed as aides to the parent-educators.

Over the course of the project, children were divided into eight groups. Group 1 participated in the program during the first three years of life, Group 2 for the first two years, Group 3 for the first year, Group 4 during the second year, Group 5 during the second and third years, Group 6 for the third year only, and Group 7 during the first and third years. Group 8 functioned as a control.

The author collected a massive amount of data. Information about mothers was based on the *Markle-Voice Language Assessment*, the *Rotter Social Reaction Inventory*, the *Mother How I See Myself Scale*, and the *Parent-Educator Weekly Report*. To assess progress of the children, two tests were used, the *Bayley Scales* and the *Griffith Scales*. The final collection of data was completed with the *Parent-Educator Weekly Report* and the *Goldman Race Awareness Test.* In general, the most significant changes occurred in the development of children who received two or three consecutive years of intervention. Those who were involved during the third year only were superior to control children, but not with statistical significance. Groups where intervention was discontinued disclosed no positive effects (Beller, 1979).

DARCEE Infant Programs—George Peabody College

Grounded in the belief that active parental involvement is the most powerful strategy to assure the productive long-term experience of a home visiting program, Forrester (Forrester, Hardge, Outlaw, Brooks, & Boismier, 1971) and Gray (1977) sought to help families become effective educational change agents. Like numerous other intervention programs of the 1970s, the target population of Forrester's study were infants from disadvantaged families. A total of 40 mothers and babies, seven and eight months of age, were assigned to experimental and control groups. Home visits were carried out for one hour weekly, for approximately eight months. The intervention approach was highly individualized, designed in light of the particular backgrounds of families. Home intervention was developed with the general plan of focusing on the parent as the target rather than the infant, including all the family members in the experience, and using inexpensive, easily accessible materials.

The intervention program included six phases. The first session was devoted to training in the areas of physical care and infant growth and development; social and cognitive components of daily routines were stressed. The second was centered on teaching mothers how to observe and record various aspects of infant development such as walking, vocalization, and verbalization. In part, this phase also was designed to educate parents about the construction of toys from inexpensive materials. The third stage goal was helping mothers to become involved in between-visit activities with the infants. Mothers selected toys and games, and home visitors advised families how and when to use reinforcement and discipline. During the fourth session, home visitors encouraged mothers to participate systematically in the selection and implementation of activities. Fifth, families were asked to share their feelings and impressions about what they had observed in terms of motor development, toilet training, eating, social development, response to discipline, construction of materials, father involvement, and other critical information. The final phase was allocated to a review of the program.

To evaluate the effectiveness of the intervention for children, Forrester used the *Bayley*, the *Griffith*, and the *Uzgiris-Hunt Scales.* The developmental environment was rated on the *Caldwell Inventory of Home Stimulation.* In summary, the experimental group achieved higher scores than the control group on the *Mental Index of the Bayley* and on the locomotion and performance scales of the *Griffith.*

In 1976, Gray carried out a second *DARCEE* program. The goals of this project were similar to those established in the Forrester research; however, there were several variations in the ways in which parents were trained. The program included four groups, three experimental and one control: (1) an intensive home-visiting treatment, (2) materials-only treatment, (3) mother-pairs treatment, and (4) nonintervention control group. The first program was carried out by individuals who visited homes once a week for one hour over a one-year period. Teachers served as model, friend, and partner for mothers, with a great deal of support and reinforcement. The theoretical orientation was based on Erickson's first three stages of development—trust, autonomy, and initiative. Specific goals for the children included impulse control, sharing with others, attention to task, development of a positive self-concept, and trust in others. In turn, mothers were encouraged to adjust the environment and their behavior to the temperaments and states of infants and to provide appropriate stimulation.

The second program—the materials-only treatment—was carried out by home visitors selected on a volunteer basis and trained through workshops. Home visitors instructed mothers in the construction and use of play materials and books. Activities were the same for all families; no individual adaptation was offered. Home visitors were assigned to families on a rotating schedule over the course of the project.

Goals of the third program—mother-pairs—were identical to those of the intensive home treatment, with one exception. In the third, families were paired. Specifically, teachers visited families, taking along the children of the other parents. This arrangement provided an opportunity to meet with children twice a week and afforded mothers time alone for themselves once per week. In addition, this phase of intervention offered mothers a minimal amount of training in day-care.

According to Gray (1977), the findings of the study were modest but positive. Results of the *HOME* were favorable for the experimental group on post-tests at 9, 19, and 31 months after primary intervention. Mothers improved the stimulus potentials of homes and their teaching styles and were observed to use more cue labels when talking with their children. Results again were superior for the experimental group on the *Bayley* and *Stanford-Binet*, as well as on a receptive language test devised by Atyas at the Demonstration and Research Center for Early Childhood (Gray, 1977). Assessment with the *Gillmore Basic Concept Test* failed to disclose any significant differences between the experimental and the control group.

The Ypsilanti Infant Education Project—Ypsilanti, Michigan

The Ypsilanti Infant Education Project is another program developed in the 1970s by Weikart and Lambie at the High-Scope Foundation. It was Piagetian in philosophy and operated as a cultural difference model (Epstein & Weikart, 1979), designed to approach families as a unique unit with specific needs. Principal objectives for infants involved the development of emerging cognitive skills, while goals for mothers were focused on the realization of their individual potentials as teachers and effective facilitators of child development.

Eighty-eight families were selected from a total of 150, those meeting two eligibility criteria: having infants of 3, 7, or 11 months upon project entry and having low scores on the *Ypsilanti Socio-Economic Scale*. Families were assigned randomly to one of the three treatment groups, experimental, contrast, and control. The experimental group was visited weekly for 60–90 minute periods by professional teachers trained in a Piagetian curriculum. They worked on tasks relevant to the sensorimotor stage, modeling and helping mothers to develop appropriate child activities. Similarly, the contrast group was seen weekly; however, home visitors were students or women from the community who had experience with young children but were unfamiliar with the program curriculum. Activities focused on gross and fine motor development. The controls were called upon only for testing and data collection. Families within this group were highly motivated and interpreted assessment activities as an intervention. For these reasons, they were considered a "minimal treatment rather than a nontreatment group" by the investigators.

Interventions were evaluated by means of three instruments developed by the Ypsilanti infant program staff. These included the Verbal *Interaction Record*, the *Ypsilanti Picture Sorting Inventory*, and the *Mother's Observation Checklist*. The *Verbal Interaction Record* was used to assess maternal patterns of verbal interaction with children in two different situations—during a period where mothers were asked to elicit verbalizations from babies and sessions of instruction on a block-matching task. The *Picture Sorting Inventory* measured maternal perceptions of the child's development. The *Mother's Observation Checklist* was given simultaneously with the *Bayley Scales* in order to examine maternal behavior toward child performance. The *Stanford-Binet* then was used to retest children one year after the close of the project.

In general, mothers in the experimental treatment scored significantly higher than those in the contrast and control groups on the *Verbal Interaction Record*. However, no differences were found among the three groups with the *Ypsilanti Picture Sorting Inventory* or the *Mother's Observation Checklist*. Moreover, short-term child results of the program were positive. Overall, experimental children performed better than contrast children, who in turn achieved at a higher level than the controls, on the *Bayley Scales* and on a language test developed by the staff. Post-testing with the *Stanford-Binet*, when children were between 31 and 39 months of age, did not offer any significant differences between groups, although all subjects scored above norms. The investigators reported that the treatment effects were the same for infants entering the program at different ages.

The Portage Project—Portage, Wisconsin

Developed by Shearer and Shearer, the Portage Project is perhaps one of the most well-known programs that was originally funded in 1969 as a Title VI grant, under the Education of the Handicapped Act, Public Law 91–230. In contrast with the majority of other early intervention programs conducted during this period, the project was intended to serve parents and multiply-handicapped infants and young children, from birth to six years or school readiness age. Because the program focused on a population residing within a large south central rural area of Wisconsin, intervention was delivered within home settings. In addition, the project directors (Shearer & Shearer, 1972, 1976) believed that such services were most effective when offered in natural environments, when parents were more likely to participate on an ongoing basis.

Eligibility for the program was based on child functioning in five areas of development including self-help, motor, social, cognitive, and language skills. All screening was done in the home. Children qualified if there was clear evidence of a marked discrepancy in any one of the specified areas of development. Babies considered to be high risk also were accepted for intervention. Two instruments were used for initial screening, ongoing evaluation, and curriculum planning: The *Alpern-Boll Developmental Profile* and the *Portage Guide to Early Education*, which was created by the project staff.

The Portage project model relied heavily on a precision teaching approach where target behaviors were identified for weekly home teaching by parents. Specifically, Shearer and Shearer (1972) were convinced that "parents of handicapped children need guidance, but more importantly, they need the experience, satisfaction, and the pleasure of working with their children and seeing them succeed as a result of their own effort" (p. 217). In so doing, families were encouraged to spend a minimum of 15 minutes per day interacting with their children on targeted tasks and recording developmental progress daily. The authors noted that parents considered to be delayed, as well as baby-sitters and other nonparental caregivers, have participated successfully in the teaching process.

In terms of the short-term results, the authors indicated that, on an average, children gained in their development 13 months within an 8-month period. Furthermore, one year later children seemed to be maintaining this advantage. Also, in a follow-up study involving randomly selected children from the project and children randomly identified from local classroom programs for economically disadvantaged youngsters, those who had the benefit of intervention showed statistically significant gains over the comparison group in terms of mental age, IQ, language skills, socialization, and academic performance. The authors concluded from the above evidence that even after the close of the program, families continued home teaching with their children in systematic and effective ways.

Intervention with Teenage Mothers and Premature Infants—Miami, Florida

The more recent intervention project, directed by Field and her colleagues, departed substantially in basic purpose and focus from the studies above. The researchers sought to accomplish two major goals. The first dealt with the developmental follow-up of 150 infants, who consisted of (1) 60 preterm babies born to teenage mothers, (2) 30 full-term newborns delivered by teenage mothers, (3) 30 preterm infants and their adult mothers, and (4) 30 full-term babies delivered by adult mothers. All parents were identified as having low socioeconomic, nonprofessional, and poor educational backgrounds. Teenage mothers were less than 19 years of age, and adult mothers ranged from 20 to 29 years in age. Subject pairs were assigned randomly to intervention and control groups. The second primary objective involved the delivery and evaluation of home-based intervention programs to those preterm infants born to teenage mothers (Field, Widmayer, Stringer, & Ignatoff, 1980). In keeping with the above purposes, home visits began soon after birth, were made biweekly for half an hour, and continued for a period of 18 months. Parent interventions were provided by a two-person team, a trained interventionist and a teenage work-study student. Mothers learned about developmental milestones and childrearing practices, and home visitors taught families exercises and age-appropriate stimulation for enhancing performance in the sensory motor and cognitive development of infants. One especially important thrust of the program was to facilitate mother-infant interactions in order to develop communication skills and strong mother-infant relationships.

During the first weeks after delivery, assessments were made in order to collect demographic, prenatal, obstetric, and neonatal data and to evaluate maternal aptitudes. Developmental follow-up was carried out at four and eight months on the *Denver* and *Bayley Scales*. Ratings of the quality of mother-child interaction also were completed. Field offered this conclusion about her research:

> Being born both preterm and to a teenage mother appears to place the infant at greater risk than simply being born preterm, or to a teenage mother. All preterm infants experienced some developmental delays associated with premature delivery, but in addition, the preterm infants of teenage mothers were exposed to less desirable childrearing attitudes and developmental expectations .... (Field, Widmayer, Stringer, & Ignatoff, 1980, p. 434)

The UCLA Infant Studies Program

The UCLA Infant Studies Program, developed in 1979 by Bromwich and Parmelee (Bromwich, 1981), targeted parent-child relationships, with a particular emphasis on problem-solving. Representing more current interests in the preterm infant, eligibility criteria here included gestational ages of less than 37 weeks and birthweights of less than 2,500 grams. Infants were evaluated using cumulative risk measures developed by Parmelee, Sigman, Kopp, and Haber (1976) and Sigman and Parmelee (1979). The program enrolled families from all socioeconomic and ethnic groups. The project combined a cognitive-developmental curriculum with parent education and parent-infant interaction training (Bromwich & Parmelee, 1979). The infant intervention was formulated to enhance social-affective, cognitive-motivational, and language areas of development. Initial home visits were devoted to establishing rapport with families and assessing infant baseline performance. Subsequently, individualized plans were designed for families.

Progress reports every four months included: (1) assessment of infant behavior, parenting behavior, parent-infant interaction, and the home environment; (2) discussion of changes in areas assessed; and (3) evaluation of the process of intervention, with subsequent programmatic revisions. Bromwich and Parmelee further described several important guidelines central to the program approach. In particular, parents should remain in control, with full recognition of their priorities and concerns. The authority-layman gap should be avoided, and parent goals for infants and individual styles should be respected. Last, parents should be encouraged to participate in planning, building on their recognized strengths.

The effectiveness of the intervention program was determined with two instruments developed by the staff. The *Parent Behavior Progression (PBP)* was designed to analyze parenting behavior in a sequence from a low to high level of functioning. The *Play Interaction Measure (PIM)*, divided into three primary sections, evaluated play-related behaviors, social-affective skills, and language performance. In addition, children were given the *Gesell* and the *Bayley Scales*.

In conclusion, Bromwich and Parmelee reported no significant differences between the one- and two-year *Gesell and Bayley* scores for the experimental and control groups. Nonetheless, they remained convinced that, in the long-term, the program was effective for families in the intervention group.

CENTER-BASED PROGRAMS

In contrast with the home-based model, center-based programs offer services in central locations such as churches or schools, or often are part of a university laboratory or a research center. The *single model* utilizes a control group to study the impact of a specified curriculum. The *multiple model*, on the other hand, analyzes the influence of various curricula, using only one group of children. Originally, most center-based programs focused exclusively on the child but, in recent years, there has been a trend toward securing the active participation of parents. Advocates for center-based programs cite two key advantages: First, the child has more time in an educationally structured environment and, second, mothers have more free time, especially when they are working or single. Opposition to this approach, however, has raised three important issues. For example in most instances, the cost is prohibitive and many communities do not ordinarily have the resources to duplicate the range of services that often have been launched in university settings. Moreover, several authorities realistically have been concerned about the effectiveness of a three to five hour per day program that fails to provide the basic ingredients for home follow-up of physical, emotional, and cognitive development of the child. Perhaps for these reasons, more recent programs have elected an alternative to home- and center-based programs, with an ecological focus that strives to include the child, family, and many resources available within a given community. The programs described below reflect these trends and recent changes in thinking.

Child-Oriented Programs

The Children's Center-Based Program—Syracuse University

One of the most noteworthy center-based projects conceived in the mid–1960s was initiated by Bettye Caldwell at Syracuse University to provide "a research and demonstration day-care center for very young children" (Caldwell & Richmond, 1968). Twenty-five children from low and middle income families attended the program. These were divided by age into two groups—10 babies between 6 and 18 months, and 15 toddlers between 18 and 36 months in another. Children attended the program on a five-day-per-week basis; about one-third received half-day care and the rest attended a full-day program.

While educational requirements for staff were not reported, selections were contingent upon two criteria: a strong commitment to young children and families and some knowledge about child development. For youngsters under three years, a staff ratio of one to four was maintained during waking hours. The same caregiver carried out basic physical needs such as feeding, sleep routines, and dressing in order to maintain consistency for the children. Special emphasis was placed on developing high levels of individual contact between infants and adults in activities such as rocking, holding, talking, and playing. Such events were scheduled for at least 15 to 30 minutes daily. In addition, there was a great deal of deliberate stimulation for learning, coupled with numerous opportunities for self-initiated selection. Services to families encompassed a range of opportunities, involving brief orientations to infant development, staff conferences once per month, social work home visits, and staff home visits to the control families. Parents did not play a role in policy-making but, for those interested, volunteer positions were available at the center.

In the final stages of analysis, 18 children who had attended the program were compared with 23 infants who had been cared for by their mothers at home. Results on the *Cattell* at 12 months of age significantly favored the home-reared group. At 30 months of age, the margin narrowed, but center-based children remained ahead of the control group. These findings were thought to be the result of developmental quotients of the home-reared toddlers and a simultaneous rise in the performance of the center-based children during the 18-month period between the first and second assessment. Caldwell also reported that gains did not appear to be correlated with sex or ethnic background, and that there seemed to be no relationships between the age of program entry and gain in IQ, or between the length of the intervention and final results.

The Infant, Toddler, and Preschool Research and Intervention Program—George Peabody College

The Infant, Toddler, and Preschool Research and Intervention Project, directed at George Peabody College by Bricker and Bricker (1971, 1972, 1973, 1974, 1976), was a noncategorical day-care early education program. Specifically, it was designed to serve children from birth to five years, and the population included both developmentally disabled and typical children. In the authors' words, the program spread "its service base across the preschool development range, across the economic continuum from poverty to affluence and across a broad range of ethnic backgrounds" (Bricker & Bricker, 1976, p. 546). A cognitive-learning model combined developmental theories with operant technology.

Goals were spelled out for each of the various components of the project. For instance, the research phase was intended to explore alternative ways for dealing with the very young child, examine the question of appropriate assessment techniques, develop a model for noncategorical placement of children, and offer a rationale for the involvement of parents in the early education program (Bricker & Bricker, 1974, p. 4).

The infant component obviously centered on programming for children. These objectives thus addressed the development of competence in the areas of gross and fine motor skills, self-help, sensorimotor, and social skills. Individual programs were created with the operation and validation of several Piagetian concepts, the creation of a research and training library of infant behavior videotapes, and the development of curricula for the acquisition of basic skills necessary for adaptive functioning in the toddler unit (Bricker & Bricker, 1976, p. 560). In keeping with the above objectives, the toddler phase offered daily sessions for individual and group language training, gross and fine motor activities, opportunities for self-directed learning, a consistent environment through the application of contingency management techniques, occasions for the development of cognitive skills such as labeling and problem-solving, and time to master adaptive skills necessary for entry into the preschool unit.

Throughout all dimensions, the program maintained a heavy emphasis on parent involvement. Families participated in classrooms at least once a week. Furthermore, staff members were expected to foster parent training and support through resources such as counseling about community services. The mainstreaming strategy and strong commitment to parents as an integral aspect of the program set this project apart from many others during the 1970s.

Family-Oriented Programs

The last two projects to be reviewed in this section have been designed as broad-based programs to include both child and parent dimensions. They have maintained central focus on prevention, and, in scope and duration, their parameters have extended beyond most other interventions toward a more ecological approach.

Milwaukee Family Rehabilitation Project

Like many early programs, the Milwaukee Project was designed to study the possibility of preventing cultural-familial delays among the offspring of families at risk for mental retardation (Garber, 1975, pp. 3–4). The project emphasized both social and educational development for 40 parents residing within an area of Milwaukee that had been characterized in the past by a high incidence of mild to moderate retardation among the school-age population. Subjects were selected on the basis of maternal IQ (all mothers scored less than 75 on the *Wechsler Adult Intelligence Scale*), ethnic background (only black parents were accepted), and the presence of a newborn infant. Families were assigned randomly to experimental and control groups.

The project consisted of two parallel components, an infant and early childhood stimulation program and a maternal rehabilitation program. In total, the combined interventions were designed to modify adverse factors in the environment of the experimental infant (Heber & Garber, 1975, p. 406). More particularly, the main goal of the maternal rehabilitation component was to modify the low IQ performance of mothers (Garber, 1977). In order to reach this objective, the program created several services, including vocational information and counseling, occupational training, and adult education with an emphasis on reading, arithmetic, homemaking, and childrearing training. Classes were scheduled five days per week for the following six months.

Coupled with the above planning, the infant program was designed to commence at three to six months of age and to continue upon the school entry age of six years. Benefits were available year-round on a five-day-per-week basis, with the expectation that the intellectual and social development of high risk infants could be enhanced by means of comprehensive educational intervention (Garber, 1977). While general goals were similar for the cognitive, language, and social curricula, the program was adapted to the needs of individual children in order "to maximize the effects of the educational experiences for each child" (Heber & Garber, 1975, p. 408). The infant curriculum was divided into three areas of development, social-emotional, perceptual-motor, and cognitive-language growth. During the preschool years, the program emphasis was directed more heavily toward cognitive and language development.

At the start of the project, the staff consisted of a curriculum coordinator, two supervisors (one for teachers and one for parents), and several teachers. Staff training entailed a combination of in-service programs, on-the-job training, and instructional meetings. Upon entry into the program, a given infant was assigned to a teacher on a one-to-one basis. This relationship was maintained until the baby reached the age of 15 months; at that point, two infants shared two teachers. At the age of 18 months, all toddlers were grouped together under the supervision of three teachers. The preschool program began when children reached approximately 20 months of age. Teachers of infants worked for the first few weeks in the home until mothers felt enough confidence to allow their babies to attend the center program. This period thus was helpful for teachers to establish rapport with family members.

Evaluation of the Milwaukee Project has been carried out along several dimensions including measures of medical, developmental, and educational variables. In addition, observations assessed mother-child interactions within each family. Components of physical development, which were assessed by periodic examinations from birth to six years of age, revealed significant differences between experimental and control children. In contrast, measurement of intelligence with standardized tests, including the *Stanford-Binet* and the *Wechsler Intelligence Scale for Children (WISC)*, disclosed IQ differences in the range of 20 to 30 points between 24 and 66 months of age, favoring the experimental group. On learning performance tasks, experimental children reportedly were superior to the control children on all assessments between the ages of 30 and 72 months. Likewise, language development, as determined by the *Gesell*, yielded significant differences between experimental and control children by the age of 18 months in favor of the experimental group; by 22 months of age, these children were four months above the norm and six months in advance of the control group. This difference was maintained throughout the program. Evaluation on the *Illinois Test of Psycholinguistic Abilities* administered at four and one-half years of age showed a difference of 18 months in psycholinguistic development, with the experimental children holding the advantage. This discrepancy was still evident when children were assessed at six and one-half years. In terms of mother-child interactions, the experimental group was more informative and communicative than the controls. While there were no differences in maternal teaching abilities between groups, mother-child interactions among the experimental families seemed to be enriched by child performance—by questioning and teaching mothers. According to Garber and Heber, "this finding suggests that the child can become the 'educational engineer' in the dyad where there is a very low IQ, low verbal mother" (1981, p. 80).

Additional long-term effects are noteworthy. In a follow-up study to the age of two years, a *WISC* differential of over 20 IQ points was still present after four years at the end of intervention. The authors suggested a positive diffusion effect that was reflected in a small but significant difference in IQs, benefiting older siblings of the experimental group children. In short, reported findings of the Milwaukee Project have been very impressive. However, positive testable influences on maternal and sibling performance appear somewhat less dramatic. This disparity between the effectiveness of child and parent interventions raises some important issues and questions, which unfortunately to date remain unanswered by the project directors.

Carolina Abecedarian Project—Frank Porter Graham Child Development Center

The Carolina Abecedarian Project was initiated in 1972 at the Frank Porter Graham Child Development Center of the University of North Carolina at Chapel Hill to determine "whether systematic early education can prevent retarded intellectual development in a sample of psychosocially defined high-risk children" (Ramey & Campbell, 1984, p. 515). In 1981, the project directors estimated that the research would be ongoing for at least seven more years, thus final results yet remain tentative (Ramey & Haskins, 1981). Certainly, in view of its magnitude, the study warrants careful scrutiny and high interest over the next several years.

Enrollment of subjects in the project was secured by invitation to patients screened in local prenatal clinics and by survey of a local department of social services. Final determinations were made either before or shortly after the birth of the subject child. Admission to the project was accomplished over a five-year period, with a total of 109 mothers agreeing and 107 babies accepted for participation. These infants subsequently were assigned randomly to educational treatment and control groups. Among the intervention families, 83 percent were headed by females, 67 percent of the children were firstborn, and 94 percent were black (Ramey & Campbell, 1984).

The educational treatment program included opportunities for attending a day-care center as early as six weeks of age. The curriculum was comprehensive in content, consisting of language, motor, social, and cognitive skills development. In addition to the intervention program, ancillary services were available to both the experimental and control groups, including the guarantee of nutritional supplements, regular pediatric care, and social work support as requested. This latter dimension of services offered to all families was provided with the intent of equalizing potentially confounding conditions and assuring that "the primary difference between groups was the systematic infant and preschool curriculum" (Ramey & Campbell, 1984, p. 519). The *Bayley Scales* were administered to infants, and the *Stanford-Binet* and *McCarthy Scales of Children's Abilities* alternately were given to older children.

> Ramey and Campbell offered several findings: No group comparisons reached traditional levels of significance during the first year of life, although the trends consistently favored the educationally treated group even during this early developmental period. From 18 months through 54 months, however, the educationally treated group was consistently and significantly superior to the control group on all full-scale scores of mental development. (1984, pp. 520–521)

While the authors have indicated that such results must be viewed as tentative in light of the small sample size and ongoing nature of the intervention, the project holds considerable promise for revealing the effectiveness of long-term educational investments with high risk populations.

Transactional and Home/Center-Based Programs

In concluding our discussion of specific programs, we have included three contemporary projects that have carried out intervention in a combination of settings or utilized a transactional model of programming.

Carolina Approach to Responsive Education (Project CARE)— University of North Carolina at Chapel Hill

Project CARE, directed by Ramey, Bryant, Sparling, and Wasik (1985) was a study designed to evaluate the effectiveness of two early intervention strategies in the prevention of mental retardation throughout the first three years of life. Sixty-four infants were assigned randomly at birth to one of two treatment groups, i.e., Educational Daycare Plus Family Education, and a less intense condition, Family Education Alone. The intervention groups were subsequently compared to similar samples of high risk children, who received no educational or family education.

Families who had infants placed at high risk for later developmental delays were identified from November 1978 to March 1980. At six months, the base sample consisted of 62 families including a set of twins: 15 assigned to Daycare Plus Family Education, 26 assigned to Family Education Alone, and 23 assigned to the control group. The Daycare component with the most intensive intervention was derived from the Carolina Abecedarian Project, described earlier in this chapter, and basically utilized a curriculum that focused on activities emphasizing cognitive/creative abilities and social/ emotional development (Ramey, Bryant, Sparling, & Wasik, 1985, p. 16). Specifically, the goal of the Daycare Program was the enhancement of skills necessary for public school success. All infants were enrolled in the center-based program by three months of age.

In contrast with the Daycare Plus Family Education treatment, the Family Education aspect of Project CARE was implemented only within the home setting. Family educators typically made home visits every 10 days for the purposes of facilitating child learning activities, information-giving, family problem-solving, and parent education. Infants and young children in the Daycare component, of course, also received the benefit of home visiting and center-based programming.

Control group children existed within their own natural environments, with no known systematic educational intervention. However, these children—like the other two groups—did receive the benefit of an iron-fortified formula until 15 months of age. In addition, the project directors did admit that these families may have had an added advantage with free medical care and social services that might not have been afforded families in similar regions, that were not located near a large university community.

The results of this project have been impressive and point to some important areas for future research. On the basis of performance on the *Bayley Scales,* "the three groups differed significantly at the 12-month assessment occasions and continued to differ at each assessment occasion thereafter" (p.21). Moreover, given the *Stanford-Binet* at 36 months, the Developmental Daycare Plus Family Education group attained a mean score of 104.5, 16.1 IQ points above the comparison treatment of Family Education Alone and 11 IQ points above the control group. The authors noted however that, while the intense intervention group continued to reflect higher performance on these standardized tests, all three groups showed a decline between 18 and 36 months—perhaps a result of increased requirements for language facility on these two measures. Nonetheless, current data indicate that the Developmental Daycare Plus Family Education strategy was effective in preventing the early depression of intellectual development. Long-term results await further follow-up.

Early Intervention Program—University of Oregon

The Early Intervention Program (EIP), directed by Bailey and Bricker (1985), was a three-year demonstration project funded by the Office of Special Education and Rehabilitative Service's Handicapped Children's Early Education Program. For the duration of the project, approximately 100 infants, young children, and their families were involved in the early intervention effort. The program included both a home-based component for babies from birth to 15 months and a center-based unit serving toddlers from 15 to 36 months. The population of children displayed a range of developmental problems, from mild to severe conditions such as Down syndrome, cerebral palsy, sensory impairment, and language delays.

One of the special features of this demonstration project was the attempt of the directors to provide systematic evaluation and documentation of child change (Bailey & Bricker, 1985, p. 53). The evaluation design consisted of four dimensions; i.e., assessment of child change, quantifiable demographic data on children and families, measures of parent involvement and satisfaction, and ongoing records of program operation costs for the home- and center-based components. Child progress was evaluated on the basis of pre-posttest comparisons of performance on the *Gesell Developmental Schedules* and the *Comprehensive Early Evaluation and Programming System (CEEPS)*, an experimental criterion-referenced measure developed for young children from birth to 36 months. Family satisfaction with services was determined by means of a project questionnaire, and program operation costs were computed, per child, for the duration of one year.

Results of this project have disclosed several insights that might be helpful in the establishment of similar early intervention programs. First, the critierion-referenced instrument, *CEEPS*, seemed to be "a meaningful index of program efficacy" (p. 63), indicating that the intervention was effective in enhancing the short-term acquisition of functional skills such as communicative and problem-solving abilities. While comparisons using developmental quotient scores were generally nonsignificant across all groups, the pre-posttest comparisons on the *Gesell*, using MA scores, were significantly different from those for the total groups. Overall, parents indicated satisfaction with the program. Last, records of operation costs revealed a per child expenditure of $1,059 in the home-based component, and an in-class per child allocation of $2,645, including building rent, utilities, and other building maintenance costs. Based on the above data, the directors were optimistic in their conclusions.

Early Home Intervention with Low-Birthweight Infants and Their Parents—McMaster University and Chedoke-McMaster Hospitals, Hamilton, Ontario

Using a "Transactional Model of Early Home Intervention," Barrera, Rosenbaum, and Cummingham (1986) recently studied the effectiveness of training parents to use problem-solving strategies in dealing with their preterm babies. Specifically, the directors "hypothesized that improving parental responsiveness and sensitivity to the child's needs and behavioral cues would result in both environmental changes and developmental gains" (p. 21). The total sample participating in the project included 24 full-term and 59 preterm infants who met specified criteria; i.e., birthweights of less than 2,000 grams, gestational ages of less than 37 weeks, hospital discharge within two weeks of program enrollment, good prognosis as determined by a pediatrician, and residence within a given geographic region. Children subsequently were assigned randomly to one of three treatment groups: a year-long developmental home intervention, a year-long parent-intervention, and a nonintervention control group. The sample of full-term babies functioned as a second control group.

Both intervention programs involved weekly visits by infant-parent specialists, who had prior academic training and practical experience in working with babies and families. In particular, the developmental approach helped parents to assess needs of their infants and, thereafter, to design strategies to enhance positive growth in cognitive, communicative, gross and fine motor, socioemotional, and self-help skills. The second intervention focused more broadly on the improvement of parent-infant interactions, including the development of more sensitive observational skills and greater responsiveness to babies during situation-specific activities such as feeding.

Four measures were used to assess child and family progress, the *Bayley Mental and Motor Scales, Infant and Toddler Temperament Questionnaires* (Carey, 1976; Carey & McDevitt, 1978), the *Caldwell HOME Inventory*, and videotapes of mother-child interactions during 10-minute free play situations. Based on these evaluations, the authors reported "several important findings regarding the effects of home intervention, developmental changes, and overall differences between preterm and full-term infants" (Barrera, Rosenbaum, & Cunningham, 1986, p. 28). Some of these results differed in significant ways from data of other studies by Bromwich and Parmelee (1979), where programming was not initiated until 12 months of age. The authors offered some noteworthy ideas for future research, which are shared by many contemporaries in the field of child development.

The results of this study suggest that home intervention focused mainly on parent-infant interaction within a therapeutic problem-solving model is an effective home treatment for preterm infants and their parents. The effectiveness of the intervention was best demonstrated by measures of the home environment, some behavior changes during mother-infant interaction, and, to a lesser degree, by changes in the cognitive scores. Given the high cost of intervention and the potential for improvement in mental scores in the untreated preterm group, we suggest greater selectivity of high-risk populations in future intervention studies. In particular, we need to be aware of the special needs not only of infants but also of parents who are relatively unskilled in nurturing a difficult baby or a baby who is likely to develop slowly and/or with unusual behavior patterns. (p. 31)

CURRENT TRENDS AND CONCLUSIONS

The illustrative programs described in this chapter exemplify a few of the ways in which early childhood intervention has evolved over the past 20 years. Though the main goal of such projects—to provide maximum opportunities for children to grow and to fulfill their highest potentials—has remained constant, there have been numerous changes in target populations, the form and location of program delivery, the breadth of intervention and community involvement, and the content of curricula that have reflected the theoretical positions of individual researchers and the specific needs of communities where projects have been implemented. Table 16-1, which summarizes pertinent characteristics of projects funded in 1984-85 by the U.S. Department of Education's Handicapped Children's Early Education Program (Assael, 1985), clearly illustrates contemporary directions in intervention research. In essence, such efforts are being focused predominantly on lower age ranges from birth to three years, on populations of children who are categorized as high risk by virtue of medical and/or environmental factors, or on groups who are manifesting clearly identified medical/developmental problems. In particular, at least 50 percent of the programs include intervention with severely and multihandicapped infants and young children. Involvement with intensive care nurseries, in terms of early identification and referral, is beginning to emerge as a new component of service delivery. Representing the blend of problems typically seen in the 0-to-3 age group, multidisciplinary teams have become routine, and while there is considerable variability in the degree of emphasis in program intervention with parents versus children, virtually all projects have some element of family training or participation. The location of projects is fairly evenly divided between home and center, though trends obviously reflect more systematic, community-wide efforts, with some programs being sponsored or based within public school and day-care settings. Last, child and family change and progress are being assessed by means of a variety of norm- and criterion-referenced measures, as well as evaluations of videotaped parent-child interactions.

Findings from previously described studies and a myriad of other projects across extremely diverse populations of high risk, economically disadvantaged, and developmentally delayed populations seem to suggest a cautiously optimistic conclusion that, at least in the short-term, quality education can positively alter the lives of young children. A wealth of information emanating from early studies begun in the 1960s is available (Bronfenbrenner, 1975; Zigler & Seitz, 1980), and these data now have been buttressed with the results from current research. However, controversies persist over issues of long-range impact (Lazar & Darlington, 1982; White & Casto, 1985), program design (Dunst & Rheingrover, 1981), strategies for measuring change (Bricker, 1985; Meisels, 1985; Simeonsson, Cooper, & Scheiner, 1982), and conceptionalizations of intervention (Dunst, 1985; Provence, 1985). Specific populations of parents such as the increasing numbers of adolescent mothers have been a target of concern (McDonough, 1985; Thompson, Cappleman, Conrad, & Jordan, 1982). In their timely article entitled "The Efficacy of Preventive Intervention: A Glass Half Full?," Greenspan and White (1985) have summarized the state of early education research.

> After reviewing the state of the art, should one be optimistic or pessimistic: is the glass half-empty or half-filled? There is a preponderance of positive effect sizes at program termination even for early intervention programs that do not take a comprehensive view of the infant and family. The fact that it cannot yet be demonstrated how long these effect sizes last beyond the end of the program should not suggest that the glass is half-empty. Rather, we should take a rather optimistic, glass half-filled, view toward existing data. Based on rather limited intervention and evaluation technology, such data may well bias results in an unfavorable, rather than a favorable direction. Therefore, any positive effect, particularly one as dramatic as the effect sizes reported above, should lead one to be very optimistic indeed. Energized by such optimism, we must now conduct further research on more challenging questions. In future studies we would be well advised to employ a comprehensive methodology including comprehensive approaches to both intervention and evaluation. That overall efficacy has now been well established as program termination allows us to get to more difficult questions about what kinds of approaches work best with what kinds of children, and with what kinds of effects. (p. 5)

Entering the 1980s, rapid changes in society, political paradoxes, newborn technologies, spiraling family problems, and economic constraints have made it very difficult for educational systems to keep pace with the demands of the day. The scope of infant education no longer can be confined to splintered issues of curriculum content, type of setting, techniques of evaluation, the nature of disabilities, and the orientation of trained personnel in isolation from the context of the environment in which they occur or the combined impact of such factors. In the decade ahead, educators and other human service professionals will need to assume a more imaginative posture toward the direction of research and implementation. Projecting to the future, contemporaries in early childhood have suggested that a primary focus on family networks will be more beneficial overall than individual programming for children; strong supports in terms of respite and quality day-care increasingly need to be an integral part of community intervention for children and families; new energies ought to be directed toward strengthening and supporting families rather than taking over or assuming parental responsibilities (Dunst, 1985); systematic evaluation of family environment and interactions should be as central to the assessment process as the use of norm- and criterion-referenced child measures. Last, in contrast with the accepted tradition in early education research of quantitative projects with large-scale populations, carefully defined in-depth studies of fewer families may disclose variables and relationships currently unrecognized. Early

Table 16–1 Demonstration Projects Funded in 1985 by the Handicapped Children's Early Education Program

Name of Project	Director	Population Served	Involvement with Intensive Care Units or Hospital Setting	Program Focus	Special Features			Measures of Change
					Primary Disciplines Involved	Location of Program	Duration	
Adolescent-Infant Development Program, Department of Pediatrics and Child Health, Howard University Hospital, Washington, D.C.	Eva T. Molnar	Handicapped and high risk infants and young children of adolescent parents	Identification and intervention in NICU	Child and Parent	Parent Educator Social Worker Child Dev. Specialist		Birth to 3 years	Brazelton Neonatal Behavioral Assessment EM1, Bayley Scales of Infant Dev.
Chicago Intervention Project, Institute for the Study of Developmental Disabilities at the University of Illinois, Chicago, Illinois	Arnold J. Sameroff Richard P. Brinker	Economically disadvantaged populations of children developmental delays	Identification from hospital follow-up programs	Child and Parent	Special Educator OT Speech/Feeding Specialist Parent Educator Social Worker	Center-Based	Up to 3 years	Bayley Scales of Infant Dev., Uzgiris-Hunt Ordinal Scales Carolina Record of Infant Beh, Chicago Infant Neuromotor Assess.
Children's Optimal Progress in Neurodevelopmental Growth, John F. Kennedy Medical Center, Edison, New Jersey	G. Gordon Williamson Shirley Zeitlin	Children with neuromotor problems		Child and Family	Psychologist, OT, Special Educator, Speech & Language Clinician, PT, Nurse	Home- and center-based	Birth to 3 years	Coping Inventory, Early Coping Inventory, Milani-Comparetti, Uzgiris-Hunt Ordinal Scales, Hawaii Learning Profile

Table 16-1 continued

Name of Project	Director	Population Served	Special Features					
			Involvement with Intensive Care Units or Hospital Setting	Program Focus	Primary Disciplines Involved	Location of Program	Duration	Measures of Change
Clay County Coordinated Preschool Program, Moorhead State University, Moorhead, Minnesota	Evelyn C. Lunch	Handicapped and high risk infants and young children	None Specified	Children, Parents	Educator Speech & Language Clinician, Social Worker, Public Health Nurse, OT	Center-based integrated preschool setting	Birth to 4 years	*Uniform Performance Assessment Scale, Bayley Scales, Stanford-Binet, Carolina Record of Infant Beh., Adaptive Perf. Instrument, Carey Infant Temperament Scale*
Creating Least Restrictive Options, Jowonio School, Syracuse University, Syracuse, New York	Ellen B. Barnes	Children identified as autistic, emotionally disturbed, or multiply handicapped	None Specified	Primarily child with consultation and training available for parents	Special Educator Psychologist, Speech/Language Clinician	Center-based integrated preschool setting	12 months to 5 years	Developmental Therapy Curr., Early LAP, Videotaping of child interactions
Early Referral and Follow-Up, Meyer Children's Rehabilitation Institute, University of Nebraska Medical Center, Omaha, Nebraska	Cordelia Robinson	Children with longterm hospitalizations who are handicapped or high risk	Referral by attending physician in-hospital	Child and Parent	Medical liaison, Psychologist, Infant/Parent Educator, PT, OT, Speech/Language Clinician, Maternal-Child Health Nurse	Hospital Public Schools	Birth to 3 years	Brazelton Neonatal Behavioral Assessment, Bayley Scales, Uzgiris-Hunt Ordinal Scales, Criterion-referenced assessments

Table 16–1 continued

Name of Project	Director	Population Served	Special Features					
			Involvement with Intensive Care Units or Hospital Setting	Program Focus	Primary Disciplines Involved	Location of Program	Duration	Measures of Change
Family Infant Resource Stimulation Team, Darcy Elementary School, Cheshire, Connecticut	Lois Rho	Children with inadequate home environments Children with significant delay in 2 or more developmental areas	None specified	Child and entire family including siblings and grandparents	Educators, Psychologist, Speech/Language Clinician, OT	Home- and center-based	Birth to 3 years	Early LAP, Parent progress by project questionnaire
Family Involvement with at Risk and Handicapped infants, University of Idaho, Moscow, Idaho	Dale Gentry Jennifer Olson	At risk, premature, chronically ill and handicapped infants	None specified	Child and Parents	Educator Social Worker	Options including home-based, integrated center-based or combination of above	Birth to 3 years	Variety of developmental scales, NCAST Scales, PCIS, Gesell
First Years Together, Wayne County Public School System, Raleigh, North Carolina	Lanelle Taylor	High risk infants hospitalized for at least 2 weeks Economically disadvantaged	Referral from ICU	Child and Parents as primary educators	Nurse Infant Educator, Parent/Infant Specialist	Home- and center-based	Birth to 2 years	Brazelton Neonatal Behavioral Assessment, Bayley Scales
Integrated Family Day-Care Home Model, Pennsylvania State University, University Park, Pennsylvania	Susan Kontos John Neisworth	Handicapped children excluding infants and preschoolers with physical disabilities	None specified	Child and parents	Early Childhood Special Education Intervenors including parents	Integrated day-care homes	Birth to 5 years	Criterion and norm-referenced assessments

Table 16-1 continued

Name of Project	Director	Population Served	Special Features					
			Involvement with Intensive Care Units or Hospital Setting	Program Focus	Primary Disciplines Involved	Location of Program	Duration	Measures of Change
Inter-Reactive Early Child to Adult Exchange, REACH Preschool Development Center, Winfield, Kansas	Ronald R. Pasmore	Infants and toddlers at risk as a result of medical insult and/or environmental factors	None specified	Child and parents	Early Childhood Specialist, Pediatrician, Psychologist, Social Workers, PT, Audiologist, Speech/Language Clinician	Home- and center-based	Birth to 3 years	Bayley Scales, Early LAP, Hawaii, Vulpe Assessment Battery, videotaped observation, Home
Linkage: Infant Special Care Center and Project Hope, UCSD Medical Center, San Diego, California	T.A. Merritt, Suzanne Dixon, Virginia MacDonald	Preterm infants less than 1,500 g. or babies with intraventricular hemorrhage	Identification with NICU	Child with parent support	Infant Education Specialist, OT, Parent Educator, Nurse, Physician	Hospital to home special education program	12 months, adjusted age	Assessment of Premature Infants Behavior Scale, Dubowitz Neurodevelop., Amiel-Tison Bayley Scales, Minnesota Child Inventory, others
Longitudinal Evaluation and Therapy Services, David T. Stiegal Institute, Michael Reese Hospital and Medical Center, Chicago, Illinois	Diana Pien	Infants with learning impairment or other handicapping conditions impacting on language and communication development; Economically disadvantaged	None specified	Child with involvement of parents in treatment plan	Educator, Social Worker, Audiologist, Pediatric Neurologist, Nurse, OT, PT,		6 month periods for evaluation and assessment	Bayley Scales, Gesell, Uzgiris-Hunt Ordinal Scales, Videotapes of parent-child interaction

Table 16–1 continued

Name of Project	Director	Population Served	Special Features					
			Involvement with Intensive Care Units or Hospital Setting	Program Focus	Primary Disciplines Involved	Location of Program	Duration	Measures of Change
Model Early Intervention Program to Develop Linked Evaluation-Programming System, Center on Human Development, University of Oregon, Eugene, Oregon	Diane Bricker	High risk and handicapped young children with mild to severe developmental problems	None specified	Child with educational and support for families	Educator/Parent Specialist	Integrated Center-based classes	15-36 months	Gesell Schedules Evaluation and Programming System for Infants and Young Children
Parent and Toddler Training, Western Pennsylvania School for Blind Children, Pittsburgh, Pennsylvania	Vince VanHasselt	Visually impaired and multiply handicapped infants and young children	None specified	Teaching Parents with supplementary services to children	Child Development Specialist Social Worker	Center-based	Birth to 3 years 10-week intervention	Vision-up, Callier-Azusa Adaptive Performance Instrument, Carey Infant/Toddler Temperament Scale, Parent-child interactions, Home, Other checklists of parent progress

Table 16–1 continued

Name of Project	Director	Population Served	Special Features					
			Involvement with Intensive Care Units or Hospital Setting	Program Focus	Primary Disciplines Involved	Location of Program	Duration	Measures of Change
Parents and Children Together, South Shore Mental Health Center, Brighton, Massachusetts	Geneva Woodruff	Infants and young children whose parents are incarcerated or being treated for alcoholism	None specified	Child and Family	Child Devel. Specialist, Pediatric Social Worker, Nurse	Home Community educational programs	Birth to 5 years	*Michigan Infant Developmental Profile, Hawaii Early Learning Profile, McCarthy Scales of Children's Abilities, Michigan Preschool Devel. Profile*
Sequenced Transition to Education in the Public Schools, Child Development Center Lexington, Kentucky	Rita Byrd	Handicapped children with 1 or more significant delays	None specified	Child and parents through transition process	Social Worker Educator Parent specialist Speech/Language Clinician, OT, PT	Model for transition to public school settings	Birth to 6 years	
Social Communicative Intervention Model, Children's Hospital Medical Center, Akron, Ohio	Philippa Campbell	Term or preterm infants who have suffered birth asphyxia with evidence of developmental delay	Collaboration with NICU	Communication between parent and child	Parent Training Specialist, Psychologist, Speech/Language Clinician, Intervention Coordinator, NDT Trained Clinician	Home	Birth to 3 years	*Brazelton Neonatal Assessment Scales, Bayley Scales,* Medical and neurological assessments, Modification of *A Monaclic Scoring System for Interaction*

Table 16-1 continued

Name of Project	Director	Population Served	Special Features					
			Involvement with Intensive Care Units or Hospital Setting	Program Focus	Primary Disciplines Involved	Location of Program	Duration	Measures of Change
Special Family Support Program, Child Development Center, Children's Hospital Medical Center, Oakland, California	Nancy Sweet Rosamund Gardner	Handicapped infants with disturbed parent interactions. Premature infants less than 1,500 g. or less than 32 weeks gestation with dysfunctional parent relationships. Chronically ill infants, Unserved babies suffering abuse, neglect or problematic environments	In-hospital programs available	Parent and Child education	Infant Development Specialist Parent Educator Social Worker	Home- and center-based	Birth to 18 months (limit not specified)	Bayley Scales, Videotapes of parent-child interaction
Special Program of Infant and Child Education, Department of Exceptional Education, Milwaukee, Wisconsin	Donna Lehr	Range of handicapping conditions represented, with some infants and toddlers with severe developmental problems	None specified	Child with parent training	Primarily Special Education/Child Development Specialist	Home and public school	Birth to 3 years	Learning Accomplishment Profile, Infant Learning Progress Behavioral Repertoire for Handicapped Infants, Observational data

Table 16–1 continued

Name of Project	Director	Population Served	Involvement with Intensive Care Units or Hospital Setting	Program Focus	Primary Disciplines Involved	Location of Program	Duration	Measures of Change
Sunrise Family, Infant, and Preschool Program, Western Carolina Center Morganton, North Carolina	Sharon Lansing, Carl Dunst	Mild to profoundly handicapped infants and young children	None specified	Child with parent training	Child Development Specialist, Parents as Teachers	Center-based parent cooperative preschools	Birth to 6 years	*Griffiths Mental Development Scales, Sequenced Inventory of Commun. Development.* Other instruments as necessary.
Transactional Intervention Program, TOTE-Woodhaven School District, Woodhaven, Michigan	Jacquelyn Pfalzer	Severely handicapped infants and toddlers	None specified	Child and parent	Educators and Therapists trained in areas of visual impairment, emotional impairment, mental retardation, learning disabilities, speech, and OT	Home and parent-center program	Birth to 3 years	Videotapes of parent-child interactions. Child observation.

childhood education in the 1980s will compel us to investigate the notion that levels of intervention are contingent upon child and family needs and competence, as well as structured across multiple components of intensity, types of community support, the nature of medical/clinical/educational staff involved, the sequence and content of program, duration, the nature of transitions to new settings, and follow-up continuity of programming. Of equal importance, these efforts need to be carried out within natural environments and the public domain so that researchers understand the critical realities that eventually diminish or sustain gains throughout the early and later school years.

REFERENCES

Assael, D. (Ed.) (1985). *Handicapped Children's Early Education Program: 1984–85 directory.* Chapel Hill, NC: Technical Assistance Development System (TADS), Frank Porter Graham Child Development Center, University of North Carolina.

Bailey, E.J., & Bricker, D. (1985). Evaluation of a three-year early intervention demonstration project. *Topics in Early Childhood Special Education, 5,* 52–65.

Barrera, M.E., Rosenbaum, P.L., & Cunningham, C.E. (1986). Early home intervention with low birth-weight infants and their parents. *Child Development, 57,* 20–33.

Beller, E.R. (1979). Early intervention programs. In J.D. Osofsky (Ed.), *Handbook of infant development* (pp. 852–894). New York: John Wiley & Sons.

Bloom, B.S. (1964). *Stability and change in human characteristics.* New York: John Wiley & Sons.

Bricker, D. (1985). The effectiveness of early intervention with handicapped and medically at-risk infants. In M. Frank (Ed.), *Infant intervention programs: Truths and untruths* (pp. 51–65). New York: The Haworth Press.

Bricker, D.D., & Bricker, W.A. (1971). Toddler research and intervention project report: Year I. *Behavioral Science Monograph* (No. 20). Nashville: Institute on Mental Retardation and Intellectual Development, George Peabody College.

Bricker, D.D., & Bricker, W.A. (1972). Toddler research and intervention project report: Year II. *Behavioral Science Monograph* (No. 21). Nashville: Institute on Mental Retardation and Intellectual Development, George Peabody College.

Bricker, D.D., & Bricker, W.A. (1973). Infant, toddler, and preschool research and intervention project: Year III. *Behavioral Science Monograph* (No. 23). Nashville: Institute on Mental Retardation and Intellectual Development, George Peabody College.

Bricker, W.A., & Bricker, D.D. (1974). An early language training strategy. In A. Schiefelbusch & C. Lloyd (Eds.), *Language perspectives—Acquisition, retardation, and intervention* (pp. 431–468). Baltimore: University Park Press.

Bricker, W.A. & Bricker, D.D. (1976). The infant, toddler, and preschool research and intervention project. In T.D. Tjossem (Ed.), *Intervention strategies for high risk infants and young children* (pp. 545–572). Baltimore: University Park Press.

Bromwich, R.M. (1981). *Working with parents and infants: An interactional approach.* Baltimore: University Park Press.

Bromwich, R.M., & Parmelee, A.H., Jr. (1979). An intervention program for preterm infants. In T.M. Field, A.M. Sostek, S. Goldberg, & H.H. Shuman (Eds.), *Infants born at risk: Behavior and development* (pp. 389–411). Jamaica, NY: SP Medical & Scientific Books.

Bronfenbrenner, U. (1975). Is early intervention effective? In B.Z. Friedlander, G.M. Sterritt, & G.E. Kirk (Eds.), *Exceptional infant: Assessment & Intervention* (Vol. 3, pp. 449–475). New York: Brunner/Mazel.

Caldwell, B.H., & Richmond, J.B. (1968). The Children's center in Syracuse, New York. In C.A. Chandler, R.S. Lourie, & A.D. Peters (Eds.), *Early child care* (pp. 326–358). New York: Atherton Press.

Carey, W.B. (1978). A simplified method for measuring infant temperament. *Pediatrics, 77,* 188–194.

Carey, W.B., & McDevitt, S.C. (1978). Revision of the Infant Temperament Questionnaire. *Pediatrics, 61,* 735–739.

Dunst, C.J. (1985). Rethinking early intervention. *Analysis and Intervention in Developmental Disabilities, 5,* 165–201.

Dunst, C.J., & Rheingrover, R.M. (1981). An analysis of the efficacy of infant intervention programs with organically handicapped children. *Evaluation and Program Planning, 4,* 287–323.

Epstein, A.S., & Weikart, D.P. (1979). The Ypsilanti-Carnegie infant education project: Longitudinal follow-up. *Monographs of the High Scope Educational Research Foundation* (Vol. 6). Ypsilanti: The High Scope Press.

Field, T.M., Widmayer, S.M., Stringer, S., & Ignatoff, E. (1980). Teenage, lower class, black mothers and their preterm infants: An intervention and developmental follow-up. *Child Development, 51,* 426–436.

Forrester, B.J., Hardge, B.M., Outlaw, D.M., Brooks, G.P., & Boismier, J.D. (1971). *The intervention study with mothers and infants.* Unpublished manuscript.

Frost, J.L. (1973). *Revisiting early childhood education.* New York: Holt, Rinehart and Winston.

Garber, H.L. (1975). Intervention in infancy: A developmental approach. In M.J. Begab & S.A. Richardson (Eds.), *The mentally retarded and society: A social science perspective* (pp. 287–303). Baltimore: University Park Press.

Garber, H.L. (1977). Preventing mental retardation through family rehabilitation. In B.M. Caldwell, D.J. Stedman, & K.W. Goin (Eds.), *Infant education: A guide for helping handicapped children in the first three years* (pp. 63–79). New York: Walker.

Garber, H.L., & Heber, R. (1981). The efficacy of early intervention with family rehabilitation. In M.J. Begab, H.C. Haywood, & H.L. Garber (Eds.), *Psychosocial influences in retarded performance: Strategies for improving competence* (Vol. 2, pp. 71–87). Baltimore: University Park Press.

Goldfarb, W. (1943). The effects of early institutional care on adolescent personality. *Journal of Experimental Education, 12,* 106–129.

Gordon, I.J. (1967). *A parent education approach to provision of early stimulation for the culturally disadvantaged: Progress Report.* Tallahassee: University of Florida, College of Education.

Gordon, I.J. (1969). *Early child stimulation through parent education: Final report to Children's Bureau, Department of Health, Education, and Welfare* (Project PHS-R-306). Gainesville: Institute for Development of Human Resources, University of Florida.

Gray, S. (1977). Home-based programs for mothers of young children. In P. Mittler (Ed.), *Research to practice in mental retardation: Care and intervention* (Vol. 1, pp. 141–147). Baltimore: University Park Press.

Greenspan, S.I., & White, K.R. (1985). The efficacy of preventive intervention: A glass half full? *Zero to Three: Bulletin of the National Center for Clinical Infant Programs, 5,* 1–5.

Heber, R., & Garber, H.L. (1975). Milwaukee project: A study of the use of family intervention to prevent cultural-familial mental retardation. In B.Z. Friedlander, G.M. Sterritt, & G.E.

Kirk (Eds.), *Exceptional infant: Assessment and intervention* (Vol. 3, pp. 399–433). New York: Brunner/Mazel.

Hunt, J. Mc V. (1961). *Intelligence and experience.* New York: Ronald Press.

Lazar, I., & Darlington, R. (1982). Lasting effects of early education. *Monographs of the Society for Research in Child Development, 47* (Serial No. 195).

McDonough, S.C. (1985). Intervention programs for adolescent mothers and their offspring. In M. Frank (Ed.), *Infant intervention programs: Truths and untruths* (pp. 67–78). New York: The Haworth Press.

Meisels, S.J. (1985). The efficacy of early intervention: Why are we still asking this question? *Topics in Early Childhood Special Education, 5,* 1–11.

Painter, G. (1968). *Infant education.* San Rafael, California: Dimension.

Parmelee, A.B., Sigman, M., Kopp, C.B., & Haber, A. (1976). Diagnosis of the infant at risk for mental, motor, or sensory handicap. In T.D. Tjossem (Ed.), *Intervention strategies for high risk infants and young children.* Baltimore: University Park Press.

Provence, S. (1985). On the efficacy of early intervention programs. *Developmental and Behavioral Pediatrics, 6,* 363–366.

Ramey, C.T., Bryant, D.M., Sparling, J.J., & Wasik, B.H. (1985). Project CARE: A comparison of two early intervention strategies to prevent retarded development. *Topics in Early Childhood Special Education, 5,* 12–25.

Ramey, C.T., & Campbell, F.A. (1984). Preventive education for high-risk children: Cognitive consequences of the Carolina Abecedarian project. *American Journal of Mental Deficiency, 88,* 515–523.

Ramey, C.T., & Haskins, R. (1981). The causes and treatment of school failure: Insight from the Carolina Abecedarian project. In M.J. Begab, H.C. Haywood, & H.L. Garber (Eds.), *Psychosocial influences in retarded performance: Strategies for improving competence* (Vol. 2, pp. 89–112). Baltimore: University Park Press.

Schaefer, E.S. (1972). Parents as educators: Evidence for cross-sectional, longitudinal research. *Young children, 27,* 227–239.

Schaefer, E.S., & Aaronson, M. (1972). Infant education research project: Implementation and implications of a home tutoring program. In R.K. Parker (Ed.), *The preschool in action: Exploring early childhood programs* (pp. 410–436). Boston: Allyn & Bacon.

Shearer, M.S., & Shearer, D.E. (1972). The Portage project: A model for early childhood education. *Exceptional Children, 39,* 210–218.

Shearer, M.S., & Shearer, D.E. (1976). The Portage project: A model for early childhood intervention. In T.D. Tjossem (Ed.), *Intervention strategies for high risk infants and young children* (pp. 335–360). Baltimore: University Park Press.

Sigman, M., & Parmelee, A.H., Jr. (1979). Longitudinal evaluation of the preterm infant. In T.M. Field, A.M. Sostek, S. Goldberg, & H.H. Shuman (Eds.), *Infants born at risk: Behavior and development* (pp. 193–219). Jamaica, NY: SP Medical & Scientific Books.

Simeonsson, R.J., Cooper, D.H., & Scheiner, A.P. (1982). A review and analysis of the effectiveness of early intervention programs. *Pediatrics, 69,* 635–641.

Skeels, H.M. & Dye, H.B. (1939). A study of the effects of differential stimulation on mentally retarded children. *Proceedings and Addresses of the American Association on Mental Deficiency, 44,* 114–136.

Spitz, R.A. (1945). Hospitalism: An inquiry into the genesis of psychiatric conditions in early childhood. *The Psycho-Analytic Study of the Child, 1,* 53–74.

Thompson, R.J. Jr., Cappleman, M.W., Conrad, H.H., & Jordan, W.B. (1982). Early intervention programs for adolescent mothers and their infants. *Developmental and Behavioral Pediatrics, 3,* 18–21.

White, K., & Casto, G. (1985). An integrative review of early intervention efficacy studies with at-risk children: Implications for the handicapped. *Analysis and Intervention in Developmental Disabilities, 5,* 7–31.

Zigler, E., & Berman, W. (1983). Discerning the future of early childhood intervention. *American Psychologist, 38,* 894–906.

Zigler, E., & Seitz, V. (1980). Early intervention programs: A reanalysis. *School Psychology Review, 9,* 354–368.

17

Working with Infants and Families in Public Schools and Day Care

Years ago, Martin (1974) noted in a presentation on social policy and early childhood education that the public school system was the most appropriate agency to deliver services to preschool children. Since that statement, several authors have advocated comprehensive implementation of the concept. Yet, public school programming for children under five remains in short supply. At this time, a total of 25 states mandate services for the three- to five-year-old and, among these, only 6 offer a full range of programming to infants and young children, birth to 5 (National Information Center for Handicapped Children and Youth, 1985). In addition, virtually no state, at present, provides an official vehicle for granting early intervention to infants considered at risk for later developmental delay. Certainly, the Handicapped Children's Early Education Program, which continues to fund demonstration, technical assistance, outreach, state implementation grants, and early childhood research institutes (Assael, 1985) has been helpful in bringing the concern for early education services to the public. Such programs have focused on children of diverse social, ethnic, and economic backgrounds, in rural, inner city, and suburban communities, of multi-age groups with various handicapping conditions. Still, the fact that so few states have permanently adopted a legislative position on prevention and educational remediation in the early months suggests a gap in understanding and precedence deserving of parent and professional action. Chapters 15 and 16 have dealt with infant service delivery systems and projects in hospital, home, and center-based settings. This chapter focuses on programming within the public sector.

TAKING CHARGE IN THE PUBLIC DOMAIN

Confronting Issues in the Early Education of High Risk and Handicapped Infants

By common standard, working with infants and families in public schools and day care has been difficult to initiate and sustain. On the other hand, principles of "best educational practice" (Vincent, Brown, & Getz-Sheftel, 1981; Wolfensberger, 1972) increasingly compel us to strive toward service delivery within the public domain. Separate services, as Vincent and her colleagues persuasively have argued, are justified only where typical, ongoing systems cannot be modified to accommodate individual special needs of the child (1981, p. 18). With patience and imagination, educational inadequacies can be dramatically reduced.

While the advantages of public school programming and integrated day-care settings are yet to be fully documented (Guralnick, 1981), available evidence now warrants the investments of educators and other professionals in young populations with known or suspected delays. As we have discussed in earlier chapters, families of preterm and high risk infants often experience stress during the weeks and months following hospital discharge (Parke & Tinsley, 1982). Demands on parents are sometimes excessive, and concurrently, their expectations may be unrealistic. Not infrequently, professionals find themselves coping more with problems of the family, and less with initial presenting difficulties of infant impairment. Thus, intervention is necessary for parent and child and can be accepted most easily through the generic systems within the community, without the trauma and stigma of separate agencies aligned with specific disability groups. Especially during the formative years, an attitude of hope and openness is critical to the well-being and healthy development of all concerned (Bricker, 1978).

Again and again, sociologists and others have found that the nature of family support systems—both internal and external—greatly influence the quality of infant-caregiver interaction (Cochran & Brassard, 1979; Powell, 1979; Unger & Powell, 1980). Of course, strong relationships between mother and father and among immediate relations are basic to the ways that families deal with sorrow, fear, disappointment, uncertainty, and the lifelong responsibilities for children with special needs. With all, parents hopefully come to believe that "in spite of misfortune, life can be full and good" (Murphy, 1981, p. viii). Such coping skills, however, need to extend beyond closest family members to broader networks of the community. Some of these organizations are social; some, religious; some, medical and health-related; and others, predominantly educational. More than any other system, public education represents to parents the commonalities among children, and therein is a sense of belonging. To the degree that services are separately established and programs individualized, images of difference and deviations from the norm may be reinforced among families. Among the myths of special education, professionals continue to believe that special children require one-to-one instruction, homogeneous grouping, and highly specialized programming (Brown, Nietupski, & Hamre-Nietupski, 1976). Such conditions, in most instances, are not needed. Indeed, sometimes, they run the risk of exaggerating impairment and diminishing the likelihood of eventual integration into typical educational and community settings.

The benefit of public school and day-care services in the early years is not limited to children and families with special needs. Bricker (1978) summarizes the point as follows:

> The thoughtful integration of the handicapped and nonhandicapped child may be a strategy that will ultimately assist in changing societal attitudes toward the handicapped child, modifying the handicapped child's self-perceptions, eliminating deleterious effects of segregation, and developing more effective use of the nation's educational resources. Exposure early in life to a handicapped child in an integrated setting may allay many of the fears of peers, parents, and the community in general that form the basis of intolerance and impede progress toward the normalization of the handicapped individual. (p. 11)

In times of escalating competition and pressures to excel academically, all children—whatever their limitations and strengths—can profit from a larger measure of tolerance, compassion, and thoughtful acceptance of themselves and others. By extension, they may discover that "life is the great gift, not for what it gives us, but because of what it allows us to give to others, and by so doing to become our finest self" (Murphy, 1981, p. 32). Such attitudes and values are more likely to grow in those situations where families and children are encouraged to have maximum contact and interaction in the natural heterogeneous groupings of community and school.

In all of the above, the ultimate goal of parents, teachers, and others responsible for young children is the optimal and healthy development of those entrusted to their care. The best ways to facilitate this often are uncertain, but perhaps too frequently our own needs have led us to a tendency "to treat special children too specially" (Murphy, 1981, p. 45). While there are always exceptions, segregated schools and classes for the disabled are prime examples of society's blinded vision and limited expectations. For decades we have made long-term predictions for individual children that are at best tenuous, if not blatantly false. Closer to reality is the view that there is at all times a powerful predisposition toward normal growth, regardless of the circumstances in which the process is begun, and that which is impaired in the developing infant is more often a tarnished reflection of society than an inherent characteristic of the child. This alternative view has important implications for early learning environments for parents and children alike.

We know that the first 18 months of life require involvement that provides for active participation, a play orientation, novel tasks, and an alternating of the old and new, the familiar and the challenging. Such is true for typical children and is no less essential for youngsters with known or suspected special needs. Moreover, professionals (Bricker, 1978; Guralnick, 1978; Vincent & Broome, 1977) increasingly propose that developmental programming with maximum benefit is most likely to be achieved in diverse, high expectancy, integrated, normalized educational environments, where children have daily access to appropriate peer models and are viewed as being less obviously different. Despite their acknowledged shortcomings, the community-based programs are the most permanent, readily available settings to accommodate these requirements.

Setting Priorities

In an age of dwindling resources, lower enrollments, and closing schools, skeptics can and do raise many questions about the appropriateness and feasibility of infant services sponsored by the public schools and day care. How can systems take on greater responsibilities for programs when they already are burdened by current obligations? How can presently overextended budgets be stretched to cover the specialized services for infants and toddlers? Some parents and professionals contend that schools are unable to provide quality services in the primary and secondary grades. How will they deal with infants and families for whom few teachers and therapists are currently trained? Do the advantages of early identification and intervention outweigh the potential disadvantages and harm that may be incurred by labeling children in the first months of life? Are cerebral palsy centers, spina bifida clinics, associations for retarded citizens, and other special service agencies staffed by professionals better trained and experienced to work with very young populations? In short, should infant services be developed and located in the public domain?

Some of the foregoing concerns can be addressed immediately, while others require solutions developed over the next decade. Clearly, training for infant education has not been readily available to professionals until recently. Yet, the cadre of individuals now attending early childhood/special education programs in colleges and universities increases every year and moves us closer to our goal of access to well-qualified personnel. Until the last five to ten years, special service agencies have been the cornerstone of educational and clinical programming for infants. As more and more professionals in public schools and day care gain competence and interest in this area, predictably there may be a shift away from segregated settings and growing associations with the public sector.

Dilemmas of scant resources and mounting costs always will plague public education and constitute a weak argument for restricting the expansion of infant programs. As some systems have realized (Vincent & Broome, 1977), early education opportunities seldom demand greater funding, but rather a reallocation of resources that more than return the benefits when significant numbers of young children later are enrolled in regular kindergarten without special support services (L.J. Vincent, personal communication, December 1982).

Last, taking charge of infant services in the public school domain should not await formal legislation. (See Figure 17–1.) Like the 1972 amendments to the Economic Opportunity Act (La Vor, 1972), which mandated services to disabled children in Head Start, and more recently P.L. 94–142 (*Federal*

Register, 1977), which has prompted the development of appropriate programming for handicapped youngsters in least restrictive environments, implementation at the state and federal levels undoubtedly will evolve long after the immediate need becomes obvious. For many years educators, physicians, and other professionals have faced resistance in this country to establishing nationwide programs for educational prevention and health care, rather than the costly solutions of custodial care and remediation (President's Committee on Mental Retardation, 1980). Technological advances in neonatology, coupled with effective outreach and regionalization programs, have had a dramatic impact on mortality and morbidity rates in recent times. Special/early childhood education need to be equally aggressive in reaching infants with potential and identified developmental disabilities.

A MODEL FOR COOPERATIVE INTERVENTION

Successful early intervention in the community calls for a service delivery system with access to the unified support and participation of staff who are prepared to meet the complex medical, educational, and psychosocial needs of high risk populations and politically wise to the administrative and financial ramifications of such programming. Figure 17–2 represents some of the dimensions essential to establishing a model of cooperative intervention. Basic to the plan are commitments and collaborations among public school and day-care administrators and line staff, and between the program and key medical and human service professionals within communities.

No component alone is sufficient to assure program quality and effectiveness. Further, the system is an evolving one—including core individuals in persuasive positions, who understand primary goals and procedures, who are adept in educating colleagues and the community-at-large. Change is accomplished slowly, proceeding to the degree that personally invested views give way to comprehensive, more unified perspectives of service delivery. In the final analysis, the most convincing argument resides in demonstrated accountability. As illustrated in Figure 17–2, several specific components are integral to the foregoing process. These encompass (1) administrative contributions, (2) medical dimensions, (3) educational and clinical assessment and intervention, (4) psychosocial services with infants and families, and (5) other resources, such as in-service training.

Administrative Contributions

Crucial to the well-being of such enterprises are the aid and understanding of superintendents, principals, directors of special education, and program coordinators who set policy and control staffing patterns, building accommodations, and district budgets. Within and outside the system, their support in the form of active program advocacy is essential to afford stability and to resolve philosophical differences that inevitably accompany innovative efforts. Insight into strategies for funding in the absence of legal mandates likewise falls within their jurisdiction and constitutes an especially cogent

Figure 17–1 Early Education with Babies and Parents in a Public School Setting

responsibility in times of financial and service retrenchment. Those public school and day-care systems that have enjoyed progress in establishing infant programs unquestionably have done so with the participation of administrators willing and able to make these commitments (Vincent, Brown, & Getz-Sheftel, 1981).

Medical Dimensions

In similar ways, medical personnel—while not always involved in direct program implementation—affect service delivery in several ways. As we have noted in earlier discussions, pediatricians routinely are the first professionals to have contact with families and infants, and their influence on referral and identification of youngsters with suspected delays is primary. Equally important is the role of neonatologists and other specialized medical personnel who deal with newborns in intensive care nurseries. In hospitals, they are able to support parents, make vital decisions about continuing service needs of infants and families, and, subsequently, initiate transitions to community programs. Typically, these physicians also take part in perinatal follow-up clinics, which offer medical and developmental evaluations of nursery graduates during the first 12 to 18 months of life. This kind of cooperation and continuity from hospital to school or day care has the potential for building coherence of programs but is often lacking in present, fragmented service delivery systems. Finally, although medical consultation during the diagnostic/evaluation phase is not always warranted, public

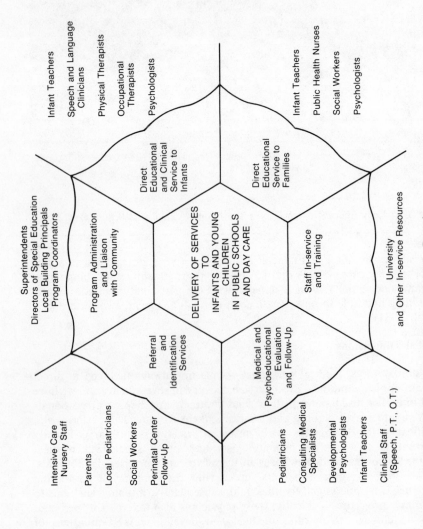

Figure 17–2 A Model for Cooperative Early Intervention in the Public Domain

school and day-care staff should have access to pediatricians and other specialists who can provide guidance about health care concerns related to clinical and educational programming.

Educational and Psychosocial Components

Educational and psychosocial components are complementary dimensions in the system of infant services. Both groups of professionals have investments in developmental assessment; both are integral to child programming activities; and both are directly involved in parent education. Specifically, teachers and ancillary clinical personnel are accountable for the planning, implementation, and evaluation of infant activities in home and school. A central portion of their responsibilities also entails helping families to manage and care for their children in developmentally appropriate ways. In essence, the quality of direct service largely depends on the level of expertise of the educational staff. In their companion roles, psychosocial personnel enhance the intervention process, assisting with diagnosis, monitoring of ongoing child and family progress, and design of program activities. Furthermore, in contrast with traditional approaches, developmental psychologists and family workers need to integrate evaluation and programming along the continuum of educational practice (Keogh & Kopp, 1978). Separation of means and objectives in this latter regard may lead to problems of communication and shallow planning that eventually result in less efficient and less effective strategies for intervention.

To accomplish the above, a systematic plan for coordination is necessary, with goals, methods for programming, and procedures for evaluation clearly understood and maintained by all (Simeonsson & Wiegerink, 1975). For the sake of parents seeking to cope with a myriad of service providers, a consistent message and approach is immensely helpful in dealing with reality in the face of tragedy in order to trust others and themselves. Such is one of the most difficult tasks in the process of education in view of the fact that "every individual situation is unique, and it is a lot of work to keep a healthy balance" (Murphy, 1981, p. 195). For parents and professionals, there are rarely absolute answers or foolproof decisions. Change is the expectable course of events.

Other Resources

Working with infants and families in the public sector ought to include a plan for continuous in-service training. New staff, qualified in their own areas of expertise, need an acquaintance knowledge of the fields of their colleagues. Equally important, as the technology of medical care moves forward, education should be challenged to sharpen strategies for programming and encouraged to pursue new initiatives for prevention and amelioration.

Training that is even modestly influential calls for an organized yet flexible effort. Universities and medical schools are resources, and they can play an important role in the process through degree-granting programs, nonmatriculated work, short-term institutes, and conferences open to the community at large. On the other hand, formats for training need not be limited to institutions of higher education. In-house staff may hold the advantage of daily contact, where the sharing of ideas, knowledge, skill, and values can take place on a sustained basis. In the interest of program development, resources that can be secured with regular support to staff are most likely to have a meaningful and long-range impact.

GOALS AND PURPOSES

The Larger View

While numerous goals might serve as guiding principles for community-based intervention programs, two long-range objectives have received standing priority in previous early childhood efforts and continue to influence future ventures. The first is the provision of quality educational/developmental services to infants to maximize the potential of children in typical home and school settings, irrespective of the nature and level of impairment or risk. The second is a corollary to the first; i.e., the delivery of persuasive educational programs to parents in ways that enhance their abilities to nurture the growth of their children. The concepts are widely supported in the field. Effective application, on the other hand, is less easily claimed.

As we look to the future, we need to think about involving people—professionals and parents, the poor and affluent, the young and older established families, the educated and less schooled—in common yet less traditional public education programs. Skills, so apparently ordinary to families of lower risk children, must be adjusted to unique styles of parenting in lasting ways to strengthen coping and competence in child and family. In contrast with much education, diversity and individualism should become the hallmark of our efforts. Moreover, despite well-established guidelines of parent participation in early childhood, too often intervention has reinforced passive receptivity of goals, which invariably fade with the lapse of time and added responsibility. Indeed, the real test is the extent to which families remain dependent on professionals or, alternatively, become self-directed, personally motivated, and responsive to their young.

Shorter-Term Objectives

It is difficult to conceive of short-range objectives that make the aforementioned goals realistic and possible. It is easy to take the position that achievement is out of reach until schools, day-care centers, society, certain professions—in essence people—change. A more optimistic view, however, recognizes progress in stages and unending ability to evolve toward the greater good, irrespective of what seem to be insurmountable hindrances. We have found the following short-term goals helpful in promoting program development and the central purposes of child and family competence.

1. *A network of strong advocates in positions of knowledge and influence* who are informed and participate in every phase of program planning and development. Minimally, this core group should include at least one individual representing: (a) University faculty with training, research, and service interests in early childhood/special education; (b) pediatricians, neonatologists, neurologists, and other medical specialists (if locally accessible); (c) hospital-based social service staff; (d) public school and day-care administrators; (e) early childhood/special educators; (f) parents of young children with developmental problems; (g) other community resource and child development personnel who have information about local and regional services for children from birth to five. These professionals must disseminate pertinent, accurate program data and assure effective delivery of services specific to areas of expertise and program responsibility.

2. *The maintenance of a flexible service delivery system* with the capacity to provide for families with varying income levels and working schedules; with diverse values, attitudes, capabilities, and knowledge of young children; with varying home situations and support systems; with children suffering a range of risk conditions and impairments. Such accommodations must be adaptable in terms of time, setting, and personnel. For example, some families will require only home intervention; some, center-based programming; and still others, home and school facilities. Some parents and infants need guidance and assistance two to three times per week; others, only brief visits once every two weeks. Families with limited skill and ability may require step-by-step demonstrations of infant care and interaction; for others, support and a chance to talk is sufficient. Moreover, it is always the intent that families will change for the better, needing different and less intense combinations of services. Personnel thus must be sensitive to opportunities to foster such trends.

3. *The establishment of an identification, referral, and intake process* that is clearly defined, widely publicized, and visible to the local community. This objective has several explicit implications. Specifically, criteria for program entry ought to be described and made known to referral sources. Second, a consistent procedure, coordinated by one individual, should be followed from the point of initial contact to the final stage of program enrollment. This strategy is helpful in curtailing misinformation and confusion among community professionals, parents, and program staff. Third, it is essential that members of the cross-disciplinary intake team understand their own individual roles and responsibilities, as well as those of their colleagues, so that disparate advice and conflicting discussions with parents can be avoided. Last, since the primary care pediatrician often is the major professional offering service to parent and child at the time of referral, program staff need to maintain regular communication with such physicians throughout the intake and intervention process.

4. *The development of a multi-faceted educational program* that provides curricula for a wide spectrum of risk and developmental problems in infants and offers equal opportunity for parent teaching. Despite varied techniques, content, materials, and other elements of programming, the central focus for teacher, clinician, parent, and child remains the quality of interaction throughout the home and center or school process. Consequently, much of the contact time with parents and their children should be devoted to enhancing such skills as verbal, physical, and social/emotional relationships. In the long term, these dimensions of interchange transcend the details of any particular curriculum or methodology and all levels or conditions of impairment or delay. They are the most difficult features to teach and sustain; yet they are most likely the factors that distinguish degrees of program effectiveness.

5. *A system of continuous evaluation and longitudinal follow-up* that documents short-term change, existing program methods and curricula, and overall effectiveness in returning children to typical educational situations. Individual assessment is basic to the formulation of child and family goals and should be routine within the course of weekly programming. In addition, there is no better justification than the clear evidence that early intervention has been successful in preventing educational disabilities among significant numbers of young children otherwise destined for specialized services. Family progress is more difficult to sort out and follow, but it is as important as child development. In fact, our analysis of family health and stability may be the key to prediction of long-term outcome for the infant born at risk.

6. *A mechanism for underlying support, feedback, and in-service among all levels of administrative and line staff.* Like the clients they serve, staff benefit from encouragement, a sense of well-being, and opportunities for growth and change. Much of the coherence and continuity of programs depends on this kind of milieu. While large-scale conferences and workshops offer pause for reflection and new ideas, equally valuable are the daily contacts where people teach and come to trust one another in creative environments. Where there are problems, there must be positive alternatives. Where there is apathy and indifference, there must be colleagues willing and able to rekindle the fires of motivation, enthusiasm, and confidence.

7. *Planning for tomorrow.* Viable infant programs require investments in planning not only at the onset of activity but also throughout the stages of implementation. Attention to the future is a demanding obligation. Public funding, family patterns, economic stresses, administrative staff, community services, the survival rate of newborns at risk, and numerous other considerations that affect the need for infant programs are constantly in flux. Those responsible for planning and implementation have a common imperative: to anticipate and prepare creative solutions for the families and young children with whom they work.

TAPPING RESOURCES FOR A BETTER CHANCE

Dealing with Problems in a Positive Context

There are many unknowns in what we recommend and much that is out of our control. Despite the best of intentions, the hard lesson is that circumstances are not always to our liking. For example, families in need—perhaps by default, frustration, or sheer defeat—may decide that they do not want service. Professionals can encourage, assist, and try to help, but parents themselves make the final determination.

Increasing numbers of infants are born to families in their teens or of limited ability. Among experienced professionals, there often is justified concern. Apart from criticism and doubt, the genuine challenge lies in aiding mothers and fathers to maintain charge of their own lives while, at the same time, enabling them to improve their sense of worth, caretaking, and parenting skills. There are few substitutes for time, patience, and sensitive guidance.

Families sometimes consent to programming. Yet, however professionals might seek to intervene, the goal appears unheeded. Excessive or unwelcome patronage is seldom fruitful for parent, child, or teacher.

As communities assume more and more responsibility for infant services, separate agencies inevitably feel the competition and may resist the trend. Predictably, the discord can result in a splintering and duplication of options little understood by the parents we wish to benefit. Broadening the base of public information is a more constructive approach for families. Parents rightfully should make the selection, free from undue pressure and solicitation. Coupled with these sources of tension are differences among professionals still unclear about their own roles and responsibilities.

Again and again, programs and staff from the beginning are challenged in purpose, philosophy, and content. If professionals within the human services would rely less on restricted skills and loyalties to their primary training and more upon the talents of caring human beings, the objectives for all concerned might be more easily secured.

Examples in Action

In order to illustrate some of the principles and guidelines for developing successful early intervention within public school and day-care settings, we have included descriptions of two programs. Both settings have had strong community support for the initiation and maintenance of such services, and have enjoyed a long-term precedence for the inclusion of high risk and handicapped children at very early ages.

The Early Education Program of North Syracuse, New York. Dr. Warren Grund, Director of Special Education for the North Syracuse Central School District, helped launch the first Early Education Program in September 1980, offering services on the basis of a "zero-reject" model to young children from birth to five years of age. Originating with a population of 51 children, the program has grown to a current capacity of 176 youngsters, including 22 infants and toddlers under 18 months of age. In essence, it was the prevailing philosophy of this school district that public education could best serve children with special needs, throughout their educational experiences, by providing continuity of programming within the least restrictive environment—their own school district. Thus, the enormous task of relocating children previously served by other local programs began. There was a great deal of skepticism among professionals outside the school district when this process first was initiated. Advocates weathered the tide of criticism and proved such doubts unfounded with the recruitment of highly skilled professional staff and quality service.

Funding for the North Syracuse Early Education Program is supported through Section 236 of the Family Court Act and Section 4406 of the Education Law. Accordingly, in New York State parents of handicapped children below the age of five may petition the Family Court in their county of residence for the costs of tuition, transportation, and maintenance for special education programs for the school year and summer months. Children delayed as a result of intellectual, sensory, physical, or emotional problems are eligible for this type of funding. Upon receipt of such petitions, a Family Court judge may issue an order to approve costs in appropriate cases. Expenditures then are charged to respective counties. If the Commissioner of Education endorses the order for the Family Court on the basis of review of an individual child's program, the State Education Department subsequently reimburses the counties up to 50 percent of the amount petitioned by the Family Court. The process is a somewhat archaic, yet workable model.

The North Syracuse Early Childhood Program offers full educational and related services to parents and young children, and is committed to working cooperatively with other community agencies that may be involved with families. A full-day, in-school program is available to children between three and five years, although services are flexible to accommodate the needs of youngsters who are better served with part-time intervention. Classes having no more than a maximum of 10 children are heterogeneously grouped across types and severity of handicapping conditions. Such groupings are an attempt of the staff and administration to provide appropriate peer models for children in light of the absence of full integration with typical preschoolers— an approach ideologically supported by the district, which presently lacks a vehicle for adequate funding.

A combined home/school program has been developed for infants and toddlers, birth to three years. Staff responsible for the infant component philosophically are committed to offering service in natural home settings, with either a parent or primary caregiver present. The infant team basically endorses the view that parents themselves are the most significant teachers in the lives of their children; therefore, a majority of the time devoted to the home-based program is allocated to working with parents or primary caregivers on how to play with, stimulate, and interact with babies in optimal ways. For toddlers, two and one-half hours five days per week of educational intervention are provided in school; however, since programming is completely individualized to meet the needs of families and children, services typically extend beyond this minimum time requirement.

Several special dimensions which constitute major strengths of the educational model characterize the infancy to pre-kindergarten age programming in North Syracuse. These include:

- multidisciplinary diagnostic team evaluations conducted by a pediatrician, pediatric neurologist (by referral), psychologist, occupational therapist, physical therapist, speech therapist, and special education teacher
- a review every 10 weeks of child's progress by the program coordinator, school nurse, psychologist, infant or classroom teacher, and relevant clinical specialists involved with a given child's program
- direct services provided daily by speech, occupational and physical therapists, adaptive physical education teachers within, and outside of the classroom setting
- direct consultation services by psychologists, who work with children, teaching and clinical staff, and families
- direct consultation by a home/school resource coordinator, who provides a liaison between home and school
- an active affiliation with the Division of Special Education and Rehabilitation of Syracuse University in the training of undergraduates and Master's degree candidates through student teaching, curriculum courses, and practical experiences
- direct working relationships with all of the major early childhood agencies and networks within the metropolitan Syracuse area and participation of the Director of Special Education in relevant state legislative activities.

At the present time, the Early Education Program is staffed by 18 special education teachers (including 3 home-based infant teachers), 8 speech and language clinicians, 3 psychologists, 2 adaptive physical education teachers, 2 physical and 2 occupational therapists, 35 teaching assistants, 2 teachers of the blind/visually impaired, 2 full-time nurses, one home/school coordinator, and the program director. Currently the program serves a total of 176 infants and young children, variously distributed across age ranges and categories of exceptionality, as presented in Table 17-1. It should be noted that the district also offers service to a number of infants and young children residing outside of the North Syracuse area, who do not have the option of early education in their home schools or day-care centers.

Measures of the effectiveness of the Early Education Program can be seen in several areas of positive change within the Syracuse community, and these are evident far beyond indices of positive change in developmental performance. The North Syracuse Program has more than tripled its enrollment over the past five years, and has continued to enjoy strong support from its school board, in particular, and from the community at large. At its outset, it was an uncommon occurrence to gain referrals from local pediatricians, intensive care nurseries, and other agencies serving young populations; however, such referrals now have become routine to the point that the program has acquired a waiting list because of the lack of physical space.

Table 17-1 Population Served by the North Syracuse Early Education Program

Area of Exceptionality	Age Range		
	Birth–2 Years	3–4 Years	5 Years
Autistic		3	1
Mentally Retarded			2
Visually Impaired	1	1	
Hard of Hearing			
Orthopedically Impaired	2	2	
Emotionally Disturbed		1	1
Multiply Handicapped	20	38	1
Other Health Impaired	6	5	1
Deaf		1	
Learning Disabled		4	24
Speech Impaired	2	21	8
TOTALS	31	76	38

Another dimension that reflects the quality of the program and its reputation for excellence is the continued ability of the staff to recruit highly skilled and motivated teachers, clinicians, and other professionals with advanced degrees, who are committed to working with young populations. Feedback from parents also is a testament to the fact that the program is serving the diverse special needs of families, their babies, and young children. Last, in spite of the fact that the Early Education Program increasingly has enrolled youngsters with more severe impairment and developmental problems, each year the staff returns approximately one-third of those children eligible for regular kindergarten programs. In the absence of New York state legislation mandating services from birth to five years, the North Syracuse school district has demonstrated with strength and leadership the efficacy of early childhood intervention within the public domain. Parents now know that they have options within the least restrictive environments of the public school, whatever the degree or nature of their child's special needs.

The Jewish Community Center of Syracuse, New York. The Jewish Community Center of Syracuse, New York (JCC) is a second agency that has a well established history of integrating mild to moderately handicapped and developmentally delayed children into its Early Education Program. The Center, directed by Diane Rossouw, currently has an enrollment of 260 young children, 18 months to kindergarten age, and includes a staff of 28 highly qualified teachers within 12 self-contained classes. The JCC nursery school/ early education program, which provides day-care accommodations for families, serves a population of approximately 25 children with varying degrees and types of developmental problems such as Down syndrome, cerebral palsy, language delays, and behavioral disorders. Such youngsters with special needs receive close monitoring by the teaching staff and Program

Director—as do all of the children of the Center. Regular consultation with parents is an integral aspect of the Center's activities, whereby families can gain advice as needed about specific problems and concerns. The structured yet flexible program that is tailored to individual developmental levels affords the full participation of special needs children within the day-to-day curriculum. Accordingly, the nursery/intervention program emphasizes the acquisition of cooperative play, problem-solving and discovery, creative language and logical thinking skills, and appropriate social and emotional behavior.

The JCC Early Childhood Program, like the North Syracuse program, is distinguished by several unique characteristics that set it apart from typical day-care settings. All toddlers and preschoolers are afforded a full range of developmental testing which is utilized in the formulation of specific classroom plans and strategies. As needed, consultation with specialists such as speech and language clinicians and pediatricians are available. Secondly, as children approach school age, direct contact is initiated in order to ensure continuity of programming from Center to public school. The Special Kindergarten Enrichment Program is another opportunity offered by the Center that enhances continued associations with the public schools.

One significant problem often experienced by day-care settings, in general, is the lack of staff trained to deal with children with special needs. In this regard, the Jewish Community Center again is unique. The Center's director has educated her staff about the necessity of screening the children at the point of program entry and about the development of appropriate teaching strategies. The focus is on prevention, coping with problems before they develop into secondary insults, and fostering positive growth. In essence, the Center operates with a "zero reject" philosophy, never having turned away a child because of the nature or severity of handicapping condition. In addition, unlike the funding constraints of public schools in New York State, the Center does not resort to labeling and also does not receive financial reimbursement for serving youngsters with handicapping conditions.

The accomplishments of the JCC Early Childhood Program are especially important in light of the substantial numbers of mothers, as well as fathers, of children under five who are now working full-time (a statistic that presently exceeds 50 percent). In view of mounting needs, it seems reasonable to expect that day-care programs increasingly will be called upon to make provisions for high risk and handicapped infants, young children, and their families.

Recognizing the above concerns and the importance of starting intervention as early as possible, the Jewish Community Center again is taking another lead in initiating a new home-based, integrated model of services for babies, 2 to 18 months of age. In its present planning stage, the project will involve the selection of one or possibly two additional day-care centers to participate in a collaborative effort. Accordingly, six to eight families attached to each center will be recruited to provide intervention and day-care within homes for small groups, including one baby with special needs and three typical children under 18 months. Services will be coordinated by JCC, and staff of the Jewish Community Center and the Special Education Department of Syracuse University will be available for training and technical assistance in establishing individual educational plans and implementing programs. Clinical personnel such as speech and language, physical, and occupational therapists will be secured to offer direct service and consultation. In the process, home-based settings will provide major practicum sites for the training of early childhood/special education Master's degree students who are interested in youngsters within this age range. With careful monitoring, this model has significant potential for expanding inservice opportunities to other day-care centers within the region and thus enhancing the quality of programming for special needs and typical children alike.

In summary, much of what has transpired in the North Syracuse and JCC programs is a reflection of the imagination and perseverance of the directors and the staff. Among several advantages of these services is the fact that they are firmly grounded in existing programs that have become known and respected across diverse professional disciplines and among families with infants and young children. Challenges in the future will emanate from the extent to which these programs are able to collaborate with other public school systems and centers to develop similar initiatives close to home.

Using What Is Available and Beyond

In an era of inflation and rampant unemployment, public schools and day-care centers suffer the ills of economic decline along with other businesses and institutions. Programs for children with special needs often are forced to create workable mechanisms for survival within antiquated systems of support. The task of meeting financial, space, and personnel requirements of infant service is difficult. On the other hand, resources are available. As we have suggested earlier in this chapter, much of what is feasible relates to setting priorities and having faith in work that is important. Allocations in public schools and day-care centers can be used differently to accommodate efforts on behalf of infants and young children, and there are ways to foster this.

• Combining the skill and diversity of multiple disciplines and professionals toward a unified goal of service, unlike separate programming with additional consultants, has strong economic advantages and programmatic value.

• Contrary to prevailing views, many specialized materials and excessive numbers of teaching assistants are not necessary for quality programming. In fact, overstaffing may be confusing and may jeopardize independence and competence in families and children.

• As public schools come under increasing pressure to serve more severely impaired children, they are acquiring experienced and qualified personnel from the private sector. Already we see that schools contract less often with agencies for clinical and therapeutic services.

• Separate diagnostic and assessment facilities for infants are rarely warranted and raise the costs of educational programming. In lieu of this approach, teachers, clinicians, physicians, and others associated with services for young children in schools and centers more appropriately should carry out these activities as an extension of ongoing intervention.

- Integrated and heterogeneous grouping of infants and families in public school and day-care settings cost little. Moreover, the benefits for staff, families, and infants in terms of sharing ideas, modeling, and problem-solving can be invaluable. (See Figure 17-3 for an example of a cooperative play environment.)

Working with Infants and Families: The Promise of Fulfillment

In this chapter, we have briefly charted the course of program development for infants and families in need, from newborn nursery to public education. As human service professionals, we have seen its trials, disappointments, stalemates, and joys, which gradually brought us to the conception of this text.

The study of newborns—medical care, parent-infant interaction, intervention, and developmental follow-up—constitutes one of the most fertile and rapidly expanding areas of research and service today. We are convinced that multidisciplinary professionals can work well together in the best interests of children and parents within the context of the public sector.

Figure 17-3 Babies in a Cooperative Play Environment

REFERENCES

Assael, D. (1985). *Handicapped Children's Early Education Program: 1980–81 overview and directory.* Chapel Hill, NC: Technical Assistance Development System (TADS). Division of the Frank Porter Graham Child Development Center.

Bricker, D.D. (1978). A rationale for the integration of handicapped and nonhandicapped preschool children. In M.J. Guralnick (Ed.), *Early intervention and the integration of handicapped and nonhandicapped children* (pp. 3–26). Baltimore: University Park Press.

Brown, L., Nietupski, J., & Hamre-Nietupski, S. (1976). The criterion of ultimate functioning and public school services for severely handicapped students. In M.A. Thomas (Ed.), *Hey! Don't forget about me: New directions for serving the severely handicapped* (pp. 2–15). Reston, VA: Council for Exceptional Children.

Cochran, M.M., & Brassard, J.A. (1979). Child development and personal social networks. *Child Development, 50,* 601–616.

Federal Register (August 23, 1977). Washington, DC: U.S. Government Printing Office.

Guralnick, M.J. (1978). Integrated preschools as educational and therapeutic environments: Concepts, design, and analysis. In M.J. Guralnick (Ed.), *Early intervention and the integration of handicapped and nonhandicapped children* (pp. 115–145). Baltimore: University Park Press.

Guralnick, M.J. (1981). The efficacy of integrating handicapped children in early education settings: Research implications. *Topics in Early Childhood Special Education, 1,* 57–71.

Keogh, B.K., & Kopp, C.B. (1978). From assessment to intervention: An elusive bridge. In F.D. Minifie & L.L. Lloyd (Eds.), *Communicative and cognitive abilities—Early behavioral assessment* (pp. 523–547). Baltimore: University Park Press.

La Vor, M.L. (1972). Economic opportunities amendments of 1982, Public Law 92–424. *Exceptional Children, 39,* 249–253.

Martin, E. (1974). Public policy and early childhood education: A Buddhist garden. In *Implementing child development programs: Report of an August 1974 national symposium.* Washington, DC: Education Commission of the States.

Murphy, A.T. (1981). *Special children, special parents: Personal issues with handicapped children.* Englewood Cliffs, NJ: Prentice-Hall.

National Information Center for Handicapped Children and Youth (1985). *State resource sheets.* P.O. Box 1492, Washington, DC

Parke, R.D., & Tinsley, B.R. (1982). The early environment of the at-risk infant. In D.D. Bricker (Ed.), *Intervention with at-risk and handicapped infants* (pp. 153–177). Baltimore: University Park Press.

Powell, D.R. (1979). Family-environment relations and early child-rearing: The role of social networks and neighborhoods. *Journal of Research and Development in Education, 13,* 1–11.

President's Committee on Mental Retardation. (1980). *Mental retardation: Prevention strategies that work.* DHHS Publication, No. OHDS 80–21029.

Simeonsson, R.J., & Wiegerink, R. (1975). Accountability: A dilemma in infant intervention. *Exceptional Children, 41,* 474–481.

Unger, D.G., & Powell, D.R. (1980). Supporting families under stress: The role of social networks. *Family Relations, 29,* 566–574.

Vincent, L.J., & Broome, K. (1977). A public school service delivery model for handicapped children between birth and five years of age. In E. Sontag, J. Smith, & N. Certo (Eds.), *Educational programming for the severely and profoundly handicapped.* Reston, VA: Division on Mental Retardation, The Council for Exceptional Children.

Vincent, L.J., Brown, L., & Getz-Sheftel, M. (1981). Integrating handicapped and typical children during the preschool years: The definition of best educational practice. *Topics in Early Childhood/Special Education, 1,* 17–24.

Wolfensberger, W. (1972). *The principle of normalization in human services.* Toronto: National Institute on Mental Retardation.

Part IV

A FRAMEWORK FOR THE FUTURE

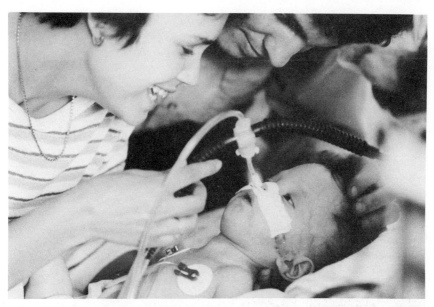

In retrospect, there is little that has been very helpful in our service delivery systems for parents, professionals, or children entrusted to our care. Communication often has been lacking, as well as a genuine understanding of other people. Child care teams frequently have functioned with parallel participants rather than coordinated, interdisciplinary members of a whole. Still, in recent years there have been strong trends toward positive change in reaearch and training programs that hold promise for professionals in the future. These differences will not alter some of what parents inevitably face with critically ill newborns. However, they may have a meaningful impact on family-professional relationships and the nature of services offered as parents in crises progress toward a semblance of normalcy in their lives. In the long term, the things that really matter to professionals and families will depend as much on the simple tasks of every day where all of us can make an ordinary, yet significant contribution as on broader concepts of ecological intervention with high risk infants that take into account hospital, home, school, and community.

18

Physicians, Educators, and the Child Care Team

As we have indicated throughout several foregoing chapters, the increasing survival rate of low birthweight infants over the past decade has heightened the concerns of many professionals about newborn growth and development. The complexity of preventing and remediating handicapping conditions thus demands that we become acquainted with new techniques of screening, identification, and evaluation; new objectives and educational interventions; and new systems of communication among disciplines. Furthermore, early childhood programs must not be merely compensatory or enriching; they must strike at the heart of medical/physical, cognitive, and behavioral insults. Putting this observation into practice, however, often is confounded by inadequate knowledge on the part of specialists who have an immediate influence on child and family. In addition, intervention programs require commitment of parents who—because of ignorance, fear, or apathy—may find it difficult to offer sustained activities conducive to amelioration and growth. Intensive early education, therefore, dictates melding the potential of the child with the responsibility, skill, and confidence of primary caregivers and parents and the expertise of human service and medical personnel in a total, integrated endeavor.

Dramatic changes in social values and public policy, advances in medical technology and primary care of the newborn, a renaissance of interest in child development among multiple disciplines, and an emerging sense of inquiry into biosocial problems are but a few factors which presently shape the direction of service, training, and research about high risk infants. Despite trends in medicine, education, and other human service professions toward higher degrees of specialization, traditional insulated points of view are giving way to more balanced perspectives and cooperative problem-solving. Special education and pediatrics are examples of two fields that have expanded narrowly defined areas of knowledge and expertise with the goal of preventing developmental disabilities among infants born at risk.

Much remains to be learned about medical and educational interventions with newborns and their families and the value of our efforts. Fulfillment of

271

current promising prospects will entail continuing improvement of perinatal care, reductions in morbidity in newborns, effective child find and outreach programs, and appropriate allocation of resources to families and young populations. With increasing economic pressures, such changes undoubtedly will require a close look at our priorities, reexamination of our resources, and a wedding of psychoeducational philosophy, training, research, and clinical practice previously lacking in many fields.

This chapter examines past and present relationships among educators, pediatricians, and other professionals in the early education of infants and young children with special needs. Discussion focuses on the historical context of traditional viewpoints and sources of controversy, recent trends toward cooperation, contemporary roles and responsibilities, the status of current collaborations, and an analysis of unresolved issues.

PHILOSOPHY AND TRAINING

Traditional Points of View and Sources of Controversy

While the link among professions, at first glance, appears essential and self-explanatory, the historical alliance among disciplines has often been strained, if not adverse and counterproductive. Differing philosophies and attitudes, unrealistic expectations, insufficient or erroneous information, and widely variant training experiences have contributed to controversy. Such disparities have been evident in approaches to parent counseling, recommendations for institutionalization, support of early intervention, and maintenance of young children with special needs in public school and community-based programs.

Pediatricians, special educators, and other professionals have shared the error of making biased judgments, with little data and few opportunities for clarification. These problems have had a far-reaching impact on those in need. The responsibility for talking with parents about medical and developmental problems of their infant is an unenvied role. In the past, pediatricians seldom have received preparation or training to assume the task, and thus quite understandably, communication with parents sometimes has been more negative than situations might have warranted (Clyman, Sniderman, Ballard, & Roth, 1979).

Numerous reports are available on the chronic dissatisfaction of parents and other child care professionals with pediatricians and their presumed lack of empathy and support. Surveyed physicians have consistently viewed themselves as inadequate to serving in this role (Dworkin, Shonkoff, Leviton, & Levine, 1979; Wolraich, 1982). Hence, despite widespread misunderstandings attributed to physician insensitivity, one can hardly conclude that the medical profession has been unaware of these shortcomings. Most service providers recognize that family counseling is an extremely complex process—perhaps more so than we have acknowledged (Murphy, 1981). Parents, wrapped in grief for themselves and their newborn, may be incapable of hearing and absorbing the disheartening news of potential disability. By the same token, educational and social service staff—well-meaning in their quest to comfort the family—may offer little assistance for parents or physicians to face reality and to deal constructively with the future. As a result of such confusion, the literature on parent-professional relationships has been replete with cliches, contradictions, and good intentions—frequently with minimal appreciation for other positions or perspectives.

The impact of medical impairment and early risk factors on later development is another area that has been debated vigorously over the years. Limited truths and numberless uncertainties have pervaded efforts to prevent or ameliorate handicapping conditions with early intervention (Bronfenbrenner, 1975; Denhoff, 1981; Ferry, 1981; Howard, 1982). The prevalence of preschool "wash-out" and a paucity of long-term data have been major contributors to the lack of consensus on developmental gains. Several authors in medicine, education, clinical therapies, and other fields have suggested a perennial need for carefully documented clinical and scientific study of biosocial variables and their relationship to favorable outcome (Clarke & Clarke, 1977; Denhoff, 1981; Parmelee, Sigman, Kopp, & Haber, 1976; Yogman, 1981). Professionals in medical and psychoeducational fields have promoted shallow thinking on both sides of the argument. For instance, physicians, nurses, and social workers traditionally have received little background and information on developmental disability, child development, or educational benefits and services for the very young (Anastasiow & Stengel, 1980; Guralnick, Richardson, & Kutner, 1980). It is, therefore, not surprising that certain conditions like mental retardation sometimes have been looked upon as basically unalterable (Springer & Steele, 1980). In the extreme, recommendations of professionals have been based on feelings of blighted hope, anger, and grief surpassing objective appraisal. As a consequence, the perceived incurability of the condition may have given rise to courses of action, such as residential placement, that themselves limit growth and development. Educators and others in the human services have been quick to criticize such judgments and attitudes of medical staff. Yet, the wholesale promotion of unsubstantiated, often short-lived, early education programs has equally raised the rancor and dismay of physicians, and unfairly given some parents expectations for change and normalcy that never can be realized.

Despite lingering disagreements among professions, it is clear that many questions relating to the prognoses for high risk newborns await further investigation. Denhoff (1981) has noted that we need to know more about the effects of intensive medical care, psychosocial factors in nurseries, and the continuum of home intervention on long-term developmental outcome. Such investigation will require cooperation across disciplinary lines if children and their families are to benefit in a cumulative way from the combined wisdom of the child care professions. Moreover, it will demand a level of communication qualitatively removed from the narrow codes that have marked single areas of expertise.

In times of increasing technology, there is a need to set priorities and to define what is efficacious. However, as a result of diverse interests and involvements, historically it has been difficult for special educators, pediatricians, therapists, and other clinical staff to find a common ground for fruitful professional relationships (Guralnick, 1982). The psychoeducational fields have taken the view that "antiseptic" hospital environments too often have exacted an emotional price, and that health care and life support have denied parents their rightful place beside their child in the early struggle for survival. Genuine time constraints and the failure of special education, in training and practice, to capture the attention and support of medical personnel (Guralnick, Richardson, & Heiser, 1982) probably have created distance among professionals. Last, physicians, nurses, and physical and occupational therapists seldom have acknowledged that infants and young children with special needs might be served equally well, or perhaps better, in public schools and day care as opposed to separate, medically oriented settings. These longstanding philosophies, even with the impetus of recent federal legislation and emerging evidence, may be slow to give way to newer thought. While there is surely merit to the concern that medically oriented personnel have had different priorities, the balance will not be righted without equal change and accountability among all professionals. The plea for cooperation and creative ideas alone will not suffice in our efforts to move beyond current procedures and present levels of effectiveness. Knowledge in education is insufficiently assessed and therefore incapable of sound implementation. Only informed practitioners ultimately will set the pace to initiate meaningful action and transform speculation and good intentions into daily practice.

Recent Trends

Changes in primary health care and community service are promising signs for the future of joint endeavors among specialists with diverse backgrounds and clinical experience (Davidson et al., 1984). In recent years, the survival and prognosis for the infant weighing less than 1,500 grams has dramatically improved (Gordon, 1981). Still, serious ethical dilemmas remain. These concerns have both developmental and psychosocial ramifications (Field, Sostek, Goldberg, & Shuman, 1979; Friedman & Sigman, 1981; Smeriglio, 1981), which no discipline can resolve alone. The advantages of modern intensive care nurseries are clear; yet coupled with these benefits are the potential negative effects of greater regionalization and increased likelihood of separation between parent and child. Though the factors contributing to child abuse and other family disorders admittedly are varied and complex, there is a growing consensus that such problems are observed more often among premature and other high risk infants (Sameroff, 1981). Intensive interventions that address inadequate caregiving practices need to begin during the perinatal period and require rigorous follow-up in hospital, home, and community settings. As we have discussed in earlier chapters, child care professionals are interested in the possibility that despite the positive outcome for many newborns requiring intensive care, impairment associated with certain conditions such as chronic lung disease may be on the rise (Gordon, 1981). Longitudinal data specific to medical insult are needed before some of these questions can be answered.

Teenage pregnancy and childbearing—once believed to be an isolated phenomenon—is now recognized in this country as a sobering social problem

(Zellman, 1981). A mounting body of research shows that risk factors are substantially heightened with the birth of an infant to a teenage mother. Potential hazards include more pregnancy complications; greater incidence of premature, low birthweight, and growth-retarded infants; higher newborn mortality rate during the perinatal period; and more environmentally associated difficulties eventually leading to developmental delay. New programs have had some impact on adverse outcome for mother and child. Typically these services have drawn upon a number of disciplines to provide quality prenatal care, educational programs designed to encourage mothers to complete high school degrees, educational programs focusing on good nutrition, child growth and development, and appropriate childrearing practices, and periodic follow-up to monitor child progress. The influence of such services is exemplified in the results of one study initiated in 1974 at Johns Hopkins where, following intervention, teenage mothers showed a reduced rate of prematurity and delivered healthier babies (President's Committee on Mental Retardation, 1980). Time will reveal whether prevention efforts of this nature become routine within the public domain.

For these strategies to be even partially successful, a reeducation of professionals and consumers will need to take place. A major step in this direction was the Task Force on Pediatric Education report in 1978, specifying several areas in pediatric residency programs requiring further development. Based on a survey of more than 7,000 recent graduates of residency programs, the Task Force affirmed that training should include concentrations in child development, community programming, and parent counseling, as well as information about exceptional children, developmental disabilities, and special concerns; e.g., problems of disadvantage, child abuse, and neglect. The report also clearly advocated participation of the pediatrician in a multidisciplinary role.

Predating the Task Force, yet suggesting parallel trends in special education professions, the Education for All Handicapped Children Act, P.L. 94–142 (*Federal Register*, 1977) was passed in 1975. Brought to the forefront with this legislation were several explicit concepts to assure a "free appropriate public education" for all handicapped persons between the ages of 3 and 21 years. To meet this mandate, the regulations emphasized provisions for the least restrictive environment, due process, comprehensive nonbiased assessment, individualized educational programming, and consultation with parents (Cohen, Semmes, & Guralnick, 1979). While the act has shortcomings, leaving service from birth to five years contingent upon state discretion, P.L. 94–142 has created a more favorable climate for children, parents, and professionals. Significant among these conditions are promising possibilities for cross-disciplinary interaction (McCormick & Lee, 1979) and the direct involvement of parents in the decision-making process. The legislation sets the stage for improved communication among primary health care and community service providers, and for the development of training programs concerned with astute diagnosis and effective intervention (Palfrey, Mervis, & Butler, 1978).

Other major themes continue to fuel the thinking of professionals and affect practice. One central philosophy is that the young can change, and that the very young can change most, with the greatest potential for long-term gains. Contemporary newborn sensory stimulation programs in intensive care nurseries are a prime example of this conviction. Although these notions require firmer ground in study and evidence, many medical staffs already have modified the status quo of hospital settings, and some public schools now have opened their doors to infant education. As changes have proceeded, there has been accelerating interest in the ecology of learning environments for children, and these ideologies too have influenced newer perceptions of early intervention (Bronfenbrenner, 1979).

Radical as the trends described above may have appeared a decade or two ago, it is more than conceivable that they will become reality within our professional future. Indeed, in many ways the course for disciplines concerned about the high risk and handicapped infant already has been defined. What remains for solution are workable strategies for implementation.

STANDING ISSUES

Communication

In describing the team approach to early intervention, Caldwell has suggested that "what young, possibly handicapped children and their families need is a group of concerned professionals who can 'de-discipline' themselves and cooperate in the task of answering questions and providing services" (1978, p. xi). Caldwell's statement poses two issues: First, the problem of communication among specialists of different disciplines, and second, the challenge of bridging the gap between profession and service to parents. In both instances, similar difficulties have caused barriers to understanding in the past.

Familiarity and experience with related fields of service deeply affect communication among professionals and with parents. The language and terminologies of our respective areas of expertise are fraught with real and perceived differences, and maturing specializations have not clarified diverse interpretations. Terms such as "mental retardation," "developmental delay," and "neurological impairment" have always pertained to particular audiences. In a genuine sense, terminology reflects our own traditions and esoteric frames of reference. Furthermore, as Murphy has written, "The common ground of interactions with special children ranges from anguished frustration to exquisite tenderness, from moments of despair to those of joy, from the deadly serious to the ridiculous, from feeling pulled apart to feeling whole" (1981, p. viii). Surely this spectrum of experience serves to breed a richness of perspective, but may at the same time cloud perceptions, being less open to alternative points of view. Herein lies the root of some of the divergent thinking and attitudes among professionals and the range of families entrusted to our care.

It is neither possible nor necessary that nonphysicians understand the medical ills of the high risk infant in detail. Likewise, it is seldom necessary for medical staff to comprehend the intricacies of therapeutic and educational intervention. Yet many parents and professionals would profit from a working knowledge across disciplines. Far too many students and practicing teachers responsible for severely and profoundly handicapped youngsters lack the most basic information about medical problems and fundamental daily care. Clinicians and educators, even with the rapidly increasing numbers of infant programs, usually have had little course work or experience with newborns and very young children. Inadequate knowledge about the medical aspects of developmental disabilities will continue to place the community special service provider at an unqualified disadvantage in communicating with pediatricians and other health care specialists until training programs and working relationships positively deal with the issue of terminology and language (Condry, 1981). The imprecision of psychoeducational jargon and pedagogy has more thwarted than aided learning and insight. The goal is simple to state but still escapes our grasp at a widely applied level of acceptance.

Ultimately, to bridge the gap from profession to service we must forgo our academic preciousness and learn new skills in translating areas of specialization into practice. Medical staff and clinical therapists must simplify material and make it relevant to educational and developmental considerations. Social services, education, and child development professionals must redefine and clarify language for greater consistency, substance, and accuracy. Such changes should contribute to a new concept of role that diminishes misunderstanding and rivalry, enhances the personalization with which service is delivered, and helps to focus on the family as the responsible agent in the growth and progress of the child.

Roles and Responsibilities

Success in modifying parallel professional roles and responsibilities, in all probability, will lie in a subtle balance between joining current systems and maintaining a reasonable distance for discovering alternative solutions. Medical and human service personnel can promote growth in their own lives and professional work through progress toward sufficient clarity of roles and functions, largely wanting in many present cross-disciplinary efforts. Vague definitions and overlapping responsibilities, inadequate team leadership, and competition across disciplines are but a few issues that await resolution. Present keen interests of several disciplines in early prevention undoubtedly have served to heighten rather than to diminish such concerns. Too, healthy partnerships—however articulated—are most likely to be formed under conditions of direct communication, tempered with mutual respect (Howard, 1982). The undertaking is difficult in times of rapid change because so few guidelines exist upon which to base decisions of task and responsibility.

Cooperative problem-solving makes essential the independent skills of unique disciplines as well as the blending of expertise. In addition to the obvious importance of quality service, the nature of the client populations, types of service delivery settings, demands of assessment and intervention, and the composition of given teams are key factors in defining specific roles and the substance of professional interaction. The growing involvement of physicians—pediatricians, neonatologists, neurologists, and others—in public schools and new educational enterprises puts them in a prime position to guide parents and professionals through the screening, referral, and diagnostic process. In particular, they must counsel parents in intensive care nurseries and developmental follow-up clinics, advise on medical care and nutritional needs of young children, and interpret pediatric data to educators and other clinical staff even with the current press to serve the severely handicapped and preschool populations within the public sector. While legislation to date has not accurately defined the role of physicians (Palfrey, Mervis, & Butler, 1978), their participation in evaluation and program implementation is critical to effective early intervention. For families of the under-three-year-old, the most frequent and influential contact remains the physician who often makes the initial decision to refer for special services. Present early childhood efforts at times falter as a direct result of scant physician support or skepticism. Our respective fields can greatly profit from specialists who appreciate related fields of human service, give of themselves as well as their skill and knowledge, and understand children and families in need, not simply through training but by having themselves survived the challenges of living. The allied fields of physical and occupational therapy likewise need to specify more clearly their roles and sense of purpose (Beckmann & Peat, 1981). In the drive toward specialization, these individuals will make a rare and genuine contribution by cutting through administrative trivia and the barriers to constructive intervention.

The role of the special/early childhood educator—though explicit in mandated services—also requires a sharpened focus. Traditionally, young high risk populations have not been served in public schools and day-care settings. By extension, lines of demarcation between education and other disciplines, especially with respect to newborns and children under 18 months, are still unclear. Planning and educational programming, monitoring of infant development, assessment, counseling of teenage mothers on growth and development, child and family advocacy, referral to ancillary services, and interpretation of legislation to parents all are appropriate tasks for the knowledgeable and competent educator, child development specialist, social worker, and psychologist. Like physicians, however, these personnel may not be fully qualified to meet the demands of these responsibilities. Moreover, they may be challenged by other staff who view such functions as an infringement on their own areas. Persisting debate over physician roles (Battle, 1972; Bennett, 1982; Howard, 1982) reflects this ambiguity and potential conflict along several dimensions of responsibility including team leadership, diagnostic evaluation, family advocacy, and parent advice.

In the long term, solutions to competition, parochial interests, lack of experience, and awkward communication may be found in flexible models of service based on client need rather than systems with "preordinate requirements" (Martinson, 1982), and in training initiatives concerned not only with autonomy and specialization, but also the synthesis of skill, attitude, and values. While we continue to produce basic knowledge, the times also call for experimentation with new modes of service delivery. Urie Bronfenbrenner (1979), writing in a different but relevant context about the ecology of human development, says, "A transforming experiment involves the systematic alteration and restructuring of existing ecological systems in ways that challenge the forms of social organization, belief systems, and lifestyles prevailing in a particular culture or subculture" (p. 41). New relationships across disciplines hold the potential for confronting the status quo of service delivery systems. The challenge before us is twofold: Can we divorce ourselves from existing programs and procedures to a degree that permits the development of such experiments? Can we convince our colleagues of the need for transformation in order to assume a measure of realistic trial and error, and modestly successful implementation?

PRESENT COLLABORATIONS

State of the Art

While parents and professionals for years have acknowledged the paucity of existing collaborative efforts and widespread deterrents to establishing programs, various disciplines have increasingly recognized the imperatives of cooperation on behalf of vulnerable infants (Derevensky, 1981). To date, changes have been limited (Guralnick, Richardson, & Kutner, 1980), but improvements are evident in small numbers of service delivery programs. Furthermore, modifications now are seen in the professional literature and in training centers, which can affect future directions. Journals in pediatrics and special education (in particular, mental retardation) previously carried physician surveys of attitudes and skills in relation to developmentally disabled children (Kelly & Menolascino, 1975; Todres, Krane, Howell, & Shannon, 1977; Shonkoff, Dworkin, Leviton, & Levine, 1979). While contemporary articles continue to spell out inadequacies of pediatric training, they now focus more constructively on strategies in residency and fellowship programs to address these weaknesses (Richardson, Guralnick, & Tupper, 1978; Richardson & Guralnick, 1978; Wolraich, 1979). Also, discussions on new relationships among disciplines—virtually nonexistent ten years ago—are slowly emerging; a dramatic example is the January 1982 issue of *Exceptional Children*, devoted exclusively to this topic. Recent continuing education programs have disseminated information to pediatricians about developmental disabilities and the care of handicapped children. In 1980, the American Academy of Pediatrics, in cooperation with the Office of Special Education and Rehabilitative Services, developed a 16-hour in-service training package entitled *New Directions in Care for the Handicapped Child*. The curriculum specifically covers material on diagnosis and treatment, family education, and the community, with the expressed purpose of assisting "the primary care physician in recognizing and understanding the problems faced by handicapped children and their parents" (p. i). Similarly, the May 1982 issue of *Pediatric Annals: A Journal of Continuing Pediatric Education* carried a series of feature articles on mental retardation, including papers on early identification, communication between pediatricians and parents, assessment, prevention, service delivery, and medical care.

The trends and changes described above constitute long-awaited beginnings. They represent a revolution of thought in the professional fields and significant progress toward a more integrated service delivery system. By themselves, however, they are not sufficient to accomplish the full range of future developments requisite for optimal collaboration. Existing residency and fellowship programs dealing with disability are still at an experimental stage, and special education training institutions are far from satisfactorily preparing graduates to work effectively with medical staff and clinical therapists in hospital, clinical, and educational settings. In the future, intervention with the at risk infant should synthesize the commitment, expertise, and resources of these and other allied health and human service professionals.

Model/Demonstration Projects

Though many programs have offered training on a sporadic or elective basis for some time (Guralnick, Richardson, & Heiser, 1982), more systematic model/demonstration projects in the medical and psychoeducational fields are currently beginning to surface. Characteristically, these efforts have been prefaced by needs assessments and have included, as integral components, minimal program evaluation of short-term impact. Overall, such assessments should play a more central role in forming the groundwork for more encompassing programs. Those already initiated have involved several major medical and clinical facilities; e.g., the Nisonger Center of Ohio State University, the University of Tennessee, the John F. Kennedy Institute of Johns Hopkins University School of Medicine, Children's Hospital National Medical Center in Washington, D.C., Upstate Medical Center in Syracuse, New York, and the University of Washington in Seattle. While individual curricula vary—depending upon time allotted, the level of residency or fellowship training, and the orientations of particular institutions—commonalities are prominent. For instance, attention often has been focused on the nature of developmental problems, prevention, early identification, assessment, parent counseling, attitudes, interdisciplinary processes, and community services (Bennett, 1980; Guralnick, Richardson, & Heiser, 1982; Wolraich, 1980). Less frequent but analogous projects are being pursued by departments of special education, in cooperation with faculties in pediatrics, to train teachers to deal with the medical aspects of developmental disabilities (Freund, Casey, & Bradley, 1982) and to acquaint preservice graduate students with major medical conditions of high risk newborns (Clark, 1981). Last, public schools and university departments involved in the training of diverse professionals are beginning to participate in collaborative projects with special care nurseries and regional perinatal centers to provide early intervention services to high risk and developmentally delayed infants and their families (Levine, Palfrey, Lamb, Weisberg, & Bryk, 1977; Lacino, 1981; Ensher, Clark, & Williams, 1979). While it is premature to make any definitive statements about the effectiveness of cross-disciplinary approaches, preliminary evaluations suggest that skills and knowledge are relevant to clinical practice, that interactions among various disciplines are feasible and worthwhile, and that empathy for handicapped children and their families is enhanced. By the same token, special education, human development, and social work students in basic medical courses have gained understanding critical to the care of infants and multiply handicapped youngsters. Like their colleagues in the medical fields, they have found communication with other disciplines a beneficial learning experience. The real test and modest success of model/demonstration projects and other similar efforts will be realized in the strong support and routine involvement in early intervention programs of medical personnel and other members of the child care team, who have an abiding faith in the healing power of education. In the process, cross-disciplinary efforts will require an awareness and acceptance of difference not only among children of varying capabilities but also among professionals representing unique disciplines, levels of training, and positions.

REFERENCES

American Academy of Pediatrics. (1980). *New directions in care for the handicapped child* (Vols. 1 & 2). Washington, DC: U.S. Department of Education, Office of Special Education & Rehabilitative Services.

Anastasiow, N.J., & Stengel, A.H. (1980). Educating physicians in child development: Why, what, and how. In M.J. Guralnick & H.B. Richardson, Jr. (Eds.), *Pediatric education and the needs of exceptional children* (pp. 27–52). Baltimore: University Park Press.

Battle, C.U. (1972). The role of the pediatrician in the health care of the young handicapped child. *Pediatrics, 50,* 916–921.

Beckmann, U., & Peat, M. (1981). The physical therapist's role in neonatal intensive care: a survey. *Physiotherapy Canada, 33,* 357–363.

Bennett, F.C. (1982). The pediatrician and the interdisciplinary process. *Exceptional Children, 48,* 306–314.

Bennett, F.C. (1980). A three-month residency curriculum in child development and handicapped children. In M.J. Guralnick & H.B. Richardson, Jr. (Eds.), *Pediatric education and the needs of exceptional children* (pp. 121–128). Baltimore: University Park Press.

Bronfenbrenner, U. (1979). *The ecology of human development: Experiments by nature and design.* Cambridge: Harvard University Press.

Bronfenbrenner, U. (1975). Is early intervention effective? In B.Z. Friedlander, G.M. Sterritt, & G.E. Kirk (Eds.), *Exceptional infant: Assessment and intervention* (Vol. 3, pp. 449–475). New York: Brunner/Mazel.

Caldwell, B.M. (1978). Forward. In K.E. Allen, V.A. Holm, & R.L. Schiefelbusch (Eds.), *Early intervention—A team approach* (pp. xi–xii). Baltimore: University Park Press.

Clark, D.A. (1981). *From newborn nursery to public school: Comprehensive services for infants and young children* (Presentation). Detroit: American Association on Mental Deficiency Convention.

Clarke, A.D.B., & Clarke, A.M. (1977). Prospects for prevention and amelioration of mental retardation: A guest editorial. *American Journal of Mental Deficiency, 81,* 523–533.

Clyman, R.I., Sniderman, S.H., Ballard, R.A., & Roth, R.S. (1979). What pediatricians say to mothers of sick newborns: An indirect evaluation of the counseling process. *Pediatrics, 63,* 719–723.

Cohen, S., Semmes, M., & Guralnick, M.J. (1979). Public Law 94–142 and the education of preschool handicapped children. *Exceptional Children, 45*, 279–285.

Condry, G. (1981). Towards multi-professional co-ordinator: The rationale of an in-service training course. *Early Child Development and Care, 7*, 371–379.

Davidson, P.W., Reif, H.E., Shapiro, D., Griffith, B.F., Shapiro, P. F., & Crocker, A. C. (1984). Direction services: A model facilitating secondary prevention of developmental handicapping conditions. *American Association on Mental Deficiency, 22*, 21–27.

Denhoff, E. (1981). Current status of infant stimulation or enrichment programs for children with developmental disabilities. *Pediatrics, 67*, 32–37.

Derevensky, J.L. (1981). Infant intervention and parent education: The necessity for an interdisciplinary approach. *Journal of Education, 163*, 275–281.

Dworkin, P.H., Shonkoff, J.P., Leviton, A., & Levine, M.D. (1979). Training in developmental pediatrics: How practitioners perceive the gap. *Journal of Diseases of Children, 133*, 709–712.

Ensher, G.L., Clark, D.A., & Williams, M.L. (1979). *Syracuse service and demonstration project: Early education of high risk and handicapped infants.* Albany, NY: Office of Mental Retardation and Developmental Disabilities.

Federal Register (August 23, 1977). Washington, DC: U.S. Government Printing Office.

Ferry, P.C. (1981). On growing new neurons: Are early intervention programs effective. *Pediatrics, 67*, 38–41.

Field, T.M., Sostek, A.M., Goldberg, S., & Shuman, H.H. (Eds.). (1979). *Infants born at risk: Behavior and development.* New York: SP Medical and Scientific Books.

Freund, J.H., Casey, P.H., & Bradley, R.H. (1982). A special education course with pediatric components. *Exceptional Children, 48*, 348–351.

Friedman, S.L., & Sigman, M. (Eds.). (1981). *Preterm birth and psychological development.* New York: Academic Press.

Gordon, H.H. (1981). Perspectives on neonatology—1980. In G.B. Avery (Ed.), *Neonatology: Pathophysiology and management of the newborn* (2nd ed.) (pp. 3–12). Philadelphia: J.B. Lippincott.

Guralnick, M.J. (1982). Pediatrics, special education, and handicapped children: New relationships. *Exceptional Children, 48*, 294–295.

Guralnick, M.J., Richardson, H.B., Jr., & Heiser, K.E. (1982). A curriculum in handicapping conditions for pediatric residents. *Exceptional Children, 48*, 338–346.

Guralnick, M.J., Richardson, H.B., Jr., & Kutner, D.R. (1980). Pediatric education and the development of exceptional children. In M.J. Guralnick & H.B. Richardson, Jr. (Eds.), *Pediatric education and the needs of exceptional children* (pp. 3–19). Baltimore: University Park Press.

Howard, J. (1982). The role of the pediatrician with young exceptional children and their families. *Exceptional Children, 48*, 316–322.

Iacino, R. (1981). Comprehensive care to high-risk handicapped newborn and family. In *1980–81 overview and directory: Handicapped Children's Early Education program* (p. 26). Office of Special Education, Division of Innovation and Development, Technical Assistance Development System, Division of the Frank Porter Graham Child Development Center, University of North Carolina, and Western States Technical Assistance Resource.

Kelly, N.K., & Menolascino, F.J. (1975). Physicians' awareness and attitudes toward the retarded. *Mental Retardation, 13*, 9–13.

Levine, M.D., Palfrey, J.S., Lamb, G.A., Weisberg, H.I., & Bryk, A.S. (1977). Infants in a public school system: The indicators of early health and educational need. *Pediatrics, 60*, 579–587.

Martinson, M.C. (1982). Interagency services: A new era for an old idea. *Exceptional Children, 48*, 389–394.

McCormick, L., & Lee, C. (1979). Public Law 94–142: Mandated partnerships. *The American Journal of Occupational Therapy, 33,* 586–588.

Murphy, A.T. (1981). *Special children, special parents: Personal issues with handicapped children.* Englewood Cliffs, NJ: Prentice-Hall.

Palfrey, J.S., Mervis, R.C., & Butler, J.A. (1978). New directions in the evaluation and education of handicapped children. *The New England Journal of Medicine, 298,* 819–824.

Parmelee, A.H., Sigman, M., Kopp, C.B., & Haber, A. (1976). Diagnosis of the infant at high risk for mental, motor, and sensory handicaps. In T.D. Tjossem (Ed.), *Intervention strategies for high risk infants and young children* (pp. 289–297). Baltimore: University Park Press.

President's Committee on Mental Retardation. (1980). *Mental retardation: Prevention strategies that work.* DHHS Publication No. OHDS 80–21029.

Richardson, H.B., Jr., & Guralnick, M.J. (1978). Pediatric residents and young handicapped children: Curriculum evaluation. *Journal of Medical Education, 53,* 487–492.

Richardson, H.B., Guralnick, M.J., & Tupper, D.B. (1978). Training pediatricians for effective involvement with handicapped preschool children and their families. *Mental Retardation, 16,* 3–7.

Sameroff, A.J. (1981). Psychological needs of the mother in early mother-infant interactions. In G.B. Avery (Ed.), *Neonatology: Pathophysiology and management of the newborn* (2nd ed.) (pp. 303–321). Philadelphia: J.B. Lippincott.

Shonkoff, J.P., Dworkin, P.H., Leviton, A., & Levine, M.D. (1979). Primary care approaches in developmental disabilities. *Pediatrics, 64,* 506–514.

Smeriglio, V.L. (Ed.) (1981). *Newborns and parents: Parent-infant contact and newborn sensory stimulation.* Hillsdale, NJ: Lawrence Erlbaum Associates.

Springer, A., & Steele, M.W. (1980). Effects of physicians' early parental counseling on rearing of Down Syndrome children. *American Journal on Mental Deficiency, 85,* 1–5.

The Task Force on Pediatric Education. (1978). *The future of pediatric education.* Evanston, IL: American Academy of Pediatrics.

Todres, I.D., Krane, D., Howell, M.C., & Shannon, D.C. (1977). Pediatricians' attitudes affecting decision-making in defective newborns. *Pediatrics, 60,* 199–201.

Wolraich, M.L. (1979). Pediatric training in developmental disabilities. *Mental Retardation, 17,* 133–136.

Wolraich, M.L. (1980). A one-month pediatric rotation in developmental disabilities. In M.J. Guralnick & H.B. Richardson, Jr. (Eds.), *Pediatric education and the needs of exceptional children* (pp. 107–119). Baltimore: University Park Press.

Wolraich, M.L. (1982). Communication between physicians and parents of handicapped children. *Exceptional Children, 48,* 324–329.

Yogman, M.W. (1981). Parent-infant bonding: Nature of intervention and inferences from data. In V.L. Smeriglio (Ed.), *Parent-infant contact and newborn sensory stimulation* (pp. 89–95). Hillsdale, NJ: Lawrence Erlbaum Associates.

Zellman, G.L. (1981). *The response of the schools to teenage pregnancy and parenthood.* Santa Monica, CA: Rand.

19

Enhancing the Potentials of Parents and Infants: Portraits of Need and Final Reflections

Over the past six years, more than 300 families have participated in our research and intervention programs for high risk infants and young children with special needs. Many of these babies initially received medical treatment in the intensive care nurseries of Crouse-Irving Memorial and Saint Joseph's hospitals in Syracuse, New York. Upon discharge, they were followed for one to two years in home and/or public school early education programs.

In this concluding chapter, we have drawn excerpts from personal stories written by eight families.* Common to each of these recollections are experiences before birth, descriptions of delivery, details about intensive care, memories of the first weeks and months at home, comments on the greatest joys and disappointments, and suggestions and advice for parents in similar situations. While all of the infants were born prematurely, their medical conditions, hospital courses, and specifics of their developmental outcome varied greatly. Likewise, the parents represent a broad spectrum in terms of income level, ethnic background, religion, education, profession, family size, values, attitudes, and a host of other dimensions. Each family is unique. On the other hand, these accounts strike a responsive chord in every one of us.

In countless ways, the stories are instructive for those in the helping professions involved in the delivery of service to special care infants and their families. Often, we stereotype and generalize in order to understand. The portraits defy such simplistic assumptions and teach us to examine the merits

---

*Excerpts included in this chapter have been drawn from the autobiographical case studies written by Gary and Margaret Brockway, Henry and Effie Buie, William and Pamela Corrigan, Michael and Beth Daly, Fred and Sarah Edelman, Patrick and Linda Fullan, Nicholas and Carol Marsella, Robert and Ann Pratt.

and needs of each situation. For instance, extended hospital stays do not necessarily go hand in hand with adverse developmental problems or lead to permanent difficulties in attachment and family relationships. Likewise, higher levels of income and education do not absolve any parent from coming to grips with an infant born at risk or making hard-pressed adjustments in life at home. In addition, parents react quite differently to information given by hospitals about their babies. Some want to know and remember everything; some prefer less feedback; still others sense the severity of circumstances from the beginning without being told. The developmental outcome of these babies presents another dynamic variable that makes accurate prediction tenuous and difficult. To be sure, each of the ten children—as described by their parents—did show delays throughout the first year. Yet in reassuring ways, most of the babies approached the developmental norm as they reached their second birthdays. Indeed, these observations raise serious issues about the advice to be offered parents and strengthens the wisdom of tentative conclusions.

There are striking similarities among these families, notwithstanding their diverse personalities and unique circumstances. Without exception, each was thrust into crisis with little or no warning and was forced to cope with an unknown world. Fear, doubt, loneliness, and disappointment were shared by most and, not surprisingly, these concerns did not end with hospital discharge. The majority experienced a first year of waiting to see and hoping for the best. In addition, for almost half of the group, the first 12 months brought repeated hospitalizations, and for one set of parents the eventual death of their baby boy one week after his first birthday. Still, despite sorrow, each of the families demonstrated faith, strength, joy, optimism, and will excelled by few. They have deeply touched our lives and surely serve as outstanding examples of the infinite capacities of human beings for positive change and development.

This book, after all, has been written on behalf of families and high risk infants. For this reason we have included, in word and picture, excerpts from these eight autobiographical portraits to celebrate the achievements of parents and those of the helping professions who were willing to participate in a unified effort for the sake of their children. We offer, in conclusion, some reflections about a framework for the future.

BEFORE BIRTH AND AT DELIVERY

There is much that is inevitable about the birth of a high risk infant. On the other hand, professionals need to focus on places where they can make a positive difference, before birth when indications of trouble become evident. Mothers have talked to us about their feelings of loneliness and sensitive concerns that their pregnancies were not progressing normally. Many times, they were able to identify problems before their physicians.

I know my body better than anybody. Unfortunately, mothers often have a tendency to let doctors talk them out of feelings. I knew all through my pregnancy with Jennifer (see Figure 19–1) that something was wrong. Perhaps it was a sixth sense. I counted the days up to the point of my delivery. Every woman needs to listen to her body and needs to believe in her own intuition.

* * * *

I had suspected twins early in the pregnancy because of the rapid growth of my abdomen, as well as the fact that at one point in an exam the nurse had gotten a heartbeat in the lower part of my abdomen, while I had felt a bulk in the upper part. A sonogram at about two and a half months gestation confirmed that I was carrying twins. As the pregnancy progressed, I noticed a different activity level in the two babies. The lower baby, which I now know to have been Anna, made very gentle and subtle movements. By six months gestation, different activity levels could be distinguished. The babies seemed to change positions within their own hemisphere of the womb, but never traded places. By six and a half months, the lower baby, Anna, appeared to be moving less frequently; the activity was less noticeable to a degree that caused me to check several times a day to make sure that she was moving.

* * * *

From the day that I learned I was pregnant, I knew that there was something wrong with my baby. I told Bill constantly that something was not right and that something should be done. Everyone thought that it was just a feeling and that everything would be fine once I had the baby. Finally, when I was about seven months along, I went to my doctor. He could not find a heartbeat and had not felt any life. I was hysterical. I told the doctor that he needed to find out if the baby inside me was dead or alive because I refused to deliver a dead baby. At that point, he did find the baby's heartbeat, which made me feel a little better. Yet, I still had a sense that something was not right. I could not get rid of that worry.

Figure 19–1 Jennifer

Meanwhile, I started to feel life, very faint flutters and a faint kick now and then. That was all! A week before I delivered the baby, my obstetrician sent me for a second sonogram. The day before I had the baby I went in for the results, and the doctor told me that he was going to put off my delivery for another month. At that point, I knew that he was wrong because I was very sure about when I had gotten pregnant. The doctor did not listen to me. Within 24 hours, I delivered Joey.

Parents have reported equally traumatic experiences during and after delivery. They are fearful and naturally confused about the birth of a child two or three months early. They are worried at first about whether the baby will live and, second, about whether the infant will have lasting problems. In the delivery room, frequently little is said because physicians themselves are uncertain about the outcome. As our family accounts show, this period is extremely difficult for parents to handle.

With about two minutes left in the procedure, the anesthesiologist kept telling me, "Okay, she's almost born now; they're getting her; she's almost ready; she's almost out; she's almost out." That time seemed to take an hour; yet it was only a matter of minutes before she was born. I hoped and prayed that she was not dead. As things turned out, Jennifer was born and she started to cry immediately. She sounded like a battery-operated doll—a little tiny voice. Then the doctors brought her over to me. I looked and I could not believe my eyes. There lay this tiny creature with a fur-like covering; all her veins were showing through her skin. Everything was in its proper place. She had all her limbs, toes, and fingers. She was so tiny. It was a real shock. In fact, I was looking at a fetus!

* * * *

They showed me both babies and informed me that Anna would need to go to the intensive care unit because she was so small. I worried some, but she looked good in color. I anxiously awaited the Apgar scores, knowing that they would give me an indication of the babies' condition. Margaret's scores were eight and nine, and Anna's scores were seven and nine. That information somewhat relieved me about Anna. Mike, my husband, brought Margaret to me in the recovery room. I had such after-birth tremblings that I could not hold Margaret; I just touched her. My husband laid her next to me, but I was afraid that my shaking would unsettle her. Mike finally took Margaret to the nursery, and I slept.

The first hours were the worst. The special care nurses told me that Anna was doing well. I also knew that she would not be going home with me, and that knowledge was agony. I was trying to juggle my own recovery from the Caesarean section, breast-feeding with Margaret, and consulting with all the doctors and nurses. I got very little sleep, knowing the entire time that when I left that hospital I would be taking only one of my babies home. No one talked with me about my feelings and I felt very alone. Thank goodness, Margaret was learning to nurse well and gave me no problems. However, having at least one baby home was not the consolation that I thought it might be.

It was ironic that so many people came in to consult with me on breast-feeding, on caring for twins, on my physical care; but no one talked with me about those feelings that were the most painful. I needed someone at that time who had gone through the same kind of situation, who could comfort me and let me know that what I was feeling was not abnormal, that it was okay for me to cry for Anna. (See figure 19–2—Anna and Margaret.)

* * * *

After Joey was born, I can remember hearing very faint cries. I was not even sure whether that was the baby. At first, no one said anything. Finally, when Joey was born, one doctor did tell us, "You have a little baby girl." Then all of a sudden we heard other doctors saying, "No, no," whispering amongst themselves. They wrapped the baby in a blanket, showed us his face quickly, and took him into the nursery—saying that he had to be transported immediately to the intensive care unit. As I went into the recovery room, the transport team brought him to me. To this day, I do not remember what I said. What I recall was a perfectly healthy, beautiful little baby like my firstborn. I saw no tubes, no monitors, nothing unusual. My husband was very upset, listening to me talk about how beautiful and perfect he was.

Meanwhile, the doctor who was taking care of Joey came in to explain some of his problems. I do not remember much of what he said, except that they did not know whether our baby was a boy or a girl, that he or she was 2 pounds and 13 ounces, and that the first 24 to 72 hours were critical.

* * * *

The next morning I was eager to see my baby. He nursed quite well for me in the morning, but as the day wore on he became disinterested and jumpy. I was slightly concerned that evening when one of my visitors asked why he was being kept at the back of the nursery. I decided to question the doctor about it in the morning. Early the

Figure 19–2 Anna and Margaret

next day, Brian's general practitioner told me that they were transferring our son to a neonatal unit in a teaching hospital 120 miles away. He did not know what was wrong with the baby. He told me that Brian was rolling his eyes, twitching, and throwing his head back. I was stunned!

Many of the problems recounted by the parents above arose as a result of crisis circumstances and a rapid turn of events for which they were unprepared. Thus, professionals always face the question of how such situations could be handled better in the future. First, it is important to recognize that parents remember selectively and that, in retrospect, they may believe that they have fully described symptoms during pregnancy when this really is not the case. Second, whenever mothers do have hints of trouble, they should be sent or should refer themselves for second opinions so that their conditions can be monitored more closely. This practice should be followed especially where mothers have had previous complications with their pregnancies. Obstetrical services of regional perinatal centers have been designed specifically to manage such cases, which cannot ordinarily be handled, for example, by rural hospitals. Routinely, mothers now are being transported before delivery to centers that offer newborn intensive care. In recent years, these changes have greatly improved both mortality and morbidity rates.

If problems are identified before birth, early contact can help parents in several ways. Medical technologies can possibly delay or avert premature delivery. Whatever the outcome, the counseling of parents at this stage by the attending neonatologist, who is familiar with the treatment of high risk infants and subsequently might be involved in the care of the baby, can help to prepare families before they confront the reality of a premature delivery. Close collaboration between obstetricians and neonatologists prior to and during delivery is essential to the success of these services in the future.

The point of delivery inevitably is chaotic for physicians and parents alike. Families want to know about the immediate prognosis of their babies. In the majority of cases, it is impossible to give such information without a period of observation and the benefit of additional tests. Parents need to express all of their concerns and address these to one primary individual, namely the attending physician. By their nature, teaching hospitals where intensive care units are located are staffed by large numbers of professionals at different levels of training. It is especially important in the beginning stages of communication with parents that information is provided consistently, simply, and soon after delivery. In addition, attending physicians well know that things said in the delivery room need to be repeated to both mother and father throughout the first days of intensive care because they often do not remember. Also, while time may be limited at delivery, parents need to be prepared by the attending neonatologist for the first introduction to their newborn. The physical appearance of the baby and the collection of monitors and equipment are frightening to many families. Without exception, these communications come when mothers and fathers emotionally are in a state of shock and when the mothers themselves may require medical care.

NURSERY EXPERIENCES

From all of our parent accounts, it is clear that the first days and weeks of hospitalization—whatever the duration—were difficult to face. Families were torn between home and their new babies. Frequently, they received conflicting information about the conditions of their babies from nurses, house officers, and rotating attending physicians. In addition, with the regionalization of intensive care facilities, many families are able to visit only on a weekly basis, or sometimes less. Thus, they are restricted to following the progress of their children primarily by phone. Because of the high costs, technology, and intensity of such centers, the majority of the problems that families face unfortunately are not likely to change in the near future. However, there are services that could aid parents throughout these stressful transition periods. The recollections of families speak to a few of these needs.

The most frustrating part of Jennifer's nursery experience was the fact that I could not see her enough. I could go into the unit 24 hours a day and stay, but I was not able to hold her as long as I wanted because she was on CPAP. Also, with my one-year-old at home, I was limited in the time that I could spend at the hospital. At 10 o'clock at night if I felt like going, I could go in and sit with her, touch her, and talk to her. The nursing staff really made me feel that Jenny was my baby and that I was her mother, even though I knew they had total control over her. Whenever I was there and she needed to be changed or powdered, they always encouraged me to care for her. In that sense, I did not feel that I was left out totally during those two and one-half months that she was in the hospital.

* * * *

As we left the hospital, the nurse handed us a booklet about the neonatal intensive care unit. Pictures prepared us for what we were soon to see. However, little has helped us emotionally to deal with the stress of having our baby in a neonatal ICU. Entering the hospital was like visiting a strange and frightening world.

Brian was sedated, given antibiotics to ward off infection, kept in an incubator, and essentially left to heal himself. The nurses were marvelous, loving toward the babies and so patient with us, the families. We kept in touch by phone and were happy, yet apprehensive, when he was moved out of the ICU. We knew Brian was being transferred because his condition was improving. Yet, until we could visit him in his new surroundings and become accustomed to them, we felt very uneasy. At home, so many miles away from him, we needed the comfort of being able to envision him in his surroundings. The unknown worried us.

* * * *

In the beginning, when Rebecca was in the nursery, I did not want to think about the possibility of what could happen to her. More and more this prospect became a fear. I remember the doctors saying that the first 48 to 72 hours would tell them a great deal; e.g., how healthy the baby was or whether there was something physically wrong with her. I was in the hospital from Tuesday to Friday morning, and it was very convenient for me to go downstairs to the third floor. I did go often. Sometimes I simply felt concerned and worried.

The day that I was discharged from the hospital was very difficult, knowing that I would be away from the baby. I understood that I could call at any time. The nurses were wonderful and constantly assured us that we could call, day or night. I prepared to go home that morning, got my things together, was busy with packing. When I left the hospital, I had a horrible feeling and cried all the way home, wondering what was going to happen to Rebecca.

Rebecca was in the nursery for seven weeks and one day. During this time, Pat and I went through almost every emotion imaginable. It was a period of great stress, worry, guilt, anger, relief when she was doing well, joy and excitement at being parents, yet a terrible fear of losing her. Each morning we received a call from our pediatrician, and he or his associates would let us know how the baby was doing, what her new weight was, how she was progressing, and whether there were any problems. We waited for that call to start our every day.

* * * *

The time that Rebecca was in the nursery was filled with many fears of her being handicapped. It was all such a delicate balance. She needed to have the right oxygen level; that was being monitored and measured. Too much oxygen could be harmful. She needed to have the right blood sugar level; in the beginning she could not regulate that very well. Again, that condition was being monitored. It was scary, relying on all these machines. Temperature was another problem. She was kept warm by a heating system, at first in an open crib and later in the isolette. This had to be checked. Exactly two weeks after the baby was born, Pat lost his job. I was still on leave of absence from my job. This situation added tremendously to our stress. For those who are familiar with the Holmes Stress Scale, we were getting pretty high in our score of traumatic life events! (See Figure 19–3—Rebecca.)

* * * *

It was on that second day that I was able to bring myself to unwrap Anna a bit during my half-hour visit with her. She was like a new little flower petal. Her skin was so translucent that I could see through her fingers. It seemed like every vein in her head was in view. Each day that I left her, I had a dreaded fear that when I returned, she would not be there. This feeling recurred every time that I left her for the next four days. Finally, on the fourth or fifth day—the day that I was going home with Margaret—one of the pediatric cardiologists examined Anna. My husband and I were there. He informed us that the staff had noted some irregular blood pressures between the upper and lower half of her body and would be checking for circulatory or cardiac problems. The day after I came home from the hospital, my fear about Anna's not being there was stronger than it ever had been. Only after the third or fourth day at home did that fear subside. The cardiologists had discovered more about her problems each day and informed us in a fairly matter-of-fact way about their findings.

* * * *

For those first 28 days, she was cared for totally—fed, changed, dressed, warmed, administered medication—by someone else. I went in to visit her, but she did not seem like my child.

Involving parents in the nurturing care of their babies to the extent possible has become routine in most intensive care nurseries over the past decade. While this participation does not resolve all of the irregularities and concerns that families face, it does help to make them a part of the healing process and feel needed. Attachment to newborns who look so fragile and far removed

Figure 19–3 Rebecca

from typical infants takes time for mothers and fathers. Staffs can attempt to enhance such relationships; yet nurses and others need to let parents work out their fears and feelings of distance. Following the progress of families through this period is beneficial in order to determine ways in which professionals can assist prior to hospital discharge.

Communication of information is another continuing source of issues in intensive care settings. Constant changes in staff are difficult because they rarely allow parents to establish lasting relationships with one physician. Obviously, there are wide differences in personality among attendings, some being much more parent-oriented than others. Nurseries need better mechanisms to assist families with these transitions and to facilitate communication among the large numbers of disciplines involved in such units. Nursery teams that meet on a regular basis and include those professionals in primary decision-making roles can be a useful strategy in achieving the above goals. In particular, these groups ought to draw upon the expertise and feedback of the attending neonatologist, head nurse, social worker, pediatric physical or occupational therapists assigned to the nursery, developmental psychologist responsible for the evaluation of babies in associated perinatal follow-up centers, public health nurse coordinator, and an early childhood/special educator associated with a child find or direction services facility who is familiar with intervention programs in the catchment area. This group ought to have the capacity for sharing up-to-date medical and psychosocial information relevant to nursery infants at any given time and for coordinating feedback provided to parents. In addition, professionals from perinatal and community-based education programs offer important linkages to services needed by families following discharge. Deliberations of this nature can fulfill two further purposes: First, to train professionals from a variety of disciplines and, second, to smooth transitions from one attending physician to another, a process beneficial to both staff and parents.

Physicians, nurses, social workers, and other professionals offer one kind of support for parents; yet many families known to us over the years have suggested that they need something more. Nursery discussion groups, directed by parents of babies who have left the hospital as well as infants still receiving care, can provide a critical outlet and source of emotional nurture. Moreover, while every child follows his or her own unique developmental course, the experiences of other families who have survived and resumed normal lives, with or without handicapping conditions, can be a strength to those still in the midst of the unknown.

Finally, as the parents have noted, the point of final discharge is traumatic for most in spite of their longing to have their baby at home. When at last that day arrives, often they hardly can believe that the time has come. Understandably, they are fearful about a tiny baby who may weigh little more than four pounds, who still requires very special care. Consequently, families must cope with another in the long series of transitions—in this instance, from hospital to home. Public health nurses experienced in the care of high risk infants, assigned prior to discharge, offer a continuing resource to families. If initial contacts are made when babies are still in the hospital, parents are better able to cope with the change and are not as likely to feel abandoned. Likewise, if perinatal center developmental follow-up appointments and plans for intervention programming are set in place before discharge, parents have a few of the supports that are critical to their well-being and that of their babies in the first weeks at home.

THE FIRST WEEKS AT HOME

Although many high risk children by 18 months to 2 years seem to approach typical development, in the early weeks and months at home professionals need to maintain a position of cautious optimism. Parents carry numerous worries and uncertainties from hospital to home, and these constitute one of the areas most difficult for them to manage. Recurrent hospitalizations serve to reinforce all of these concerns. In addition, as several families have mentioned, their babies initially were not easy to care for because of excessive irritability, problems with sleeping, and lengthy feedings. Often too, these demands were coupled with the very realistic awareness of parents that they needed to segregate themselves and their other children from normal daily activities outside of the home as a result of the risks of infection. The pressures, as described by the parents, were a considerable burden.

It was a hard time when Jennifer first came home. I could not sleep while she did because I had my one-year-old to take care of, too. Fortunately, I have a very supportive husband who was willing to get up with her at night to help out with the night feedings. Nick would do anything for her. Meanwhile, it was very evident that she went through a transition period when she first came home. At first, she had to sleep with the light on all the time. She was comfortable only with people around and with constant noise. The staff at the hospital had warned us that she probably would have these kinds of problems.

Taking Jennifer out to a store or any public place, having people ask how old she was, was difficult. She still only weighed five pounds or so.

We still did not know if she was going to have any problems as far as her health or development. It was a wait-and-see time. That was hard and made us very tense. In fact, it was quite a while until we felt confident that she was going to be fine. We told ourselves and other people that she did not have problems, but inside we had a lot of doubts.

* * * *

Wayne was growing, gaining weight, and everything seemed to be fine until one night when he was two and one-half months. He became very ill. We were giving him his bottle, and his father started to burp him. He began to spit up and choke. He stopped breathing and turned blue. Gary immediately called the ambulance, while I tried to get him breathing again. I had never had a course in CPR, but I had to try. He was in intensive care for eight days, in critical condition. We came very close to losing him.

Wayne continued to have chronic respiratory difficulties. At six months, he was hospitalized with pneumonia. He remained for a week and was in a mist tent to help him breathe easier. Christmas Eve he finally was released, but three weeks later he was back in intensive care again. (See Figure 19–4—Wayne.)

* * * *

When Brian was nine weeks old, both the public health nurse who had been visiting weekly and I noticed how stiff his muscles were becoming and how he was arching his head. Brain's GP suggested that again we see a specialist 120 miles away. He did not warn us that Brian might be hospitalized. Therefore, we were totally unprepared for this event.

Every three weeks, we drove the 120 miles to see a specialist and physical therapist. We found dealing with the doctor a very frustrating experience. He was an extremely busy person and always pressed for time. Once while Brian was in the hospital, we overheard him speaking to students about cerebral palsy in regard to Brian. It was two weeks before we could question him about that comment at our regularly scheduled appointment. Naturally, in those weeks we imagined the worst and worried incessantly. The doctor gave us no prognosis for the future.

* * * *

One of the most difficult pressures that I, as a new mother, had to cope with was an immediate return to work two weeks after Rebecca's discharge. I felt cheated, knowing that most people are home with their babies for at least six weeks. Indeed, it

Figure 19–4 Wayne

took me a great deal of time to work out these feelings of anger and resentment. I knew that it had to be, but I was not happy. I always had reminders at work. There were other people who were pregnant, and they made me recall that my pregnancy had terminated right at the time when I was enjoying being pregnant; and that it had ended not in a normal way. We had neither the typical nursery experiences nor a typical homecoming.

After a while, we honestly felt as if we had entered "no man's land." We never got more than four hours sleep. I remember getting up one day when Linda had gone to work, starting to get dressed, and putting on my suit to go to work. I had no job and had to take care of the baby, yet almost went out the door. I remember hearing the baby and saying to myself, "My God, what are you doing?" I was confused, disoriented, did not even know what day it was.

* * * *

It should have been a glorious day, the day that Anna came home from the hospital with us, but I had a great deal of apprehension. The doctors had reassured us that she would not lapse into a crisis condition, that if she were to develop a problem with her heart we would have a period of days rather than minutes or hours of warning to get her checked. This was reassuring insofar as her physical condition; however, I soon discovered that the absence of a relationship was a genuine problem for me.

We could not go anywhere as a family unit without exposing Anna. It was bitterly cold during those days, and I could not take her out unless it was for a doctor's appointment or an urgent situation. After a while, the lengthy feedings caused me great agitation. At times, I simply wanted to say to Anna, "Why can't you just be normal?"

* * * *

I could see the frustration setting in with Pam when Joey came home. He did not
want to be cuddled. He was very used to being in the hospital, in his crib, with
someone holding him only when he ate. He was not comfortable being rocked. Joey
really got to her. I tried to talk with Pam, thinking that we ought to let Joey be by
himself.

Then the nightmare came true. They told us that we could bring our son home, as
long as he was on oxygen. With all that equipment in the house—the oxygen tent, the
heart monitor, the oxygen tanks—I was afraid of the whole set-up.

To this time, early intervention programs in most states have been designed
to accept only those babies with identified handicapping conditions. Therefore, infants typically are not eligible for services that could be beneficial on a
home visitation basis. These outdated restrictions should change in the near
future so that babies at greatest risk who meet specified medical and
psychosocial criteria can be seen immediately after hospitalization for
developmental/educational programming. In collaboration with public
health nurses, such opportunities could help to sustain parents through the
earliest stressful weeks. Moreover, the coordination of these activities with
initial follow-up perinatal center visits affords a continuity of planning that is
very important at the outset of parental care. In-service training of physicians
and hospital personnel by unit and perinatal center staff within nursery
catchment areas, with Robert Wood Johnson funding, has been largely
responsible for substantial improvements in the medical care of high risk
newborns over the past ten years. Similar efforts now need to be initiated for
infant educators and therapists who may not have had experience with at risk
populations. Unfortunately, home-based traveling assessment and intervention teams tend to lack both time and funding. Parents need caring
professionals who are close at hand.

While they cannot resolve all problems, primary care physicians interested
in and knowledgeable about developmental issues and education can facilitate
the above process a great deal and can give parents considerable guidance.
They have the clear advantage of seeing families regularly, usually within two
weeks of return home. Furthermore, in terms of presenting consistent
feedback to parents, pediatricians, educators, therapists, and staff of perinatal
center programs need to take responsibility for sharing information and
reaching agreement on optimal courses of action for intervention as they offer
feedback to parents.

We have raised counseling of parents as a central issue throughout this
book. Without question, it continues to be one of the major sources of
controversy among professionals delivering services to young children and
their families. Training institutions of higher education are now paying more
attention to such concerns; yet they ought to receive further emphasis in the
future through direct practice. Parents need to be kept informed and
realistically prepared. If concerns about handicapping conditions must be
discussed, families should be given opportunities and time to raise questions

and to talk about their fears. They should not be left to deal with these problems alone.

THE MIDDLE MONTHS AND END OF THE FIRST YEAR

For most parents, the middle months and end of the first year prove to be a turning point. Many marked delays begin to fade, and families see their babies looking and behaving in more typical ways. Visits to follow-up programs have been made and, through one or more resources, parents have received feedback on their baby's developmental progress. Also very importantly, the difficult periods of early adjustment are behind them, and they begin to feel more rested and comfortable with daily routines. If early intervention was indicated, they have been able to proceed with those decisions. Such are the experiences for the majority of families. However, a small group of parents face continuing struggles that sadly terminate with the losses of their babies. These families obviously require a great deal of support, even after the death of their children. Excerpts taken from the autobiographical stories written by our eight sets of parents represent both sides of this continuum, with very different needs represented:

This was the time when everything started to get better. Jenny did more, and we were less nervous. I think it was around the eighth month, which would have been her fifth month at home, when I finally felt confident that she was going to be all right. She started to sit up, she started to vocalize more, and she was more attentive. With Catherine's development, I remember this period as being a slow and gradual process. With Jenny, it was as if she did nothing one day, and the next day she did everything.

* * * *

When Brian was seven months old, we began to attend a public school twice a week. The program was in its early stages, and the groups were small. Often, we had physical and occupational therapists to ourselves. Having the guidance, expertise, and advice of the professionals on a weekly basis was tremendously reassuring. My major concern was physical therapy, and Brian received a lot of it that year. He also benefited greatly from the infant stimulation activities that the teachers did in school. The therapists thought up more ways for the babies to experience tastes and textures than I imagined possible, most of them too messy for me to consider attempting at home. Gradually, we noticed that Brian was reaching milestones closer to the norm.

It would be wrong for me to instill the false hope in anyone that a handicap can be cured by early intervention. We were very lucky. We have no way of knowing what Brian's development might have been without intervention. I am convinced, however, that without it he would not be the active, bright little boy he is today. I do believe that early education helps a handicapped child to develop to his or her full potential *and* provides immense gratification to the family members working with the child. (See Figure 19–5—Brian.)

* * * *

Figure 19-5 Brian

Things started to smooth out a bit during the middle months. My anger seemed to diminish, although at times it seemed ever present. I still had concerns about whether we were taking proper care of the baby. I felt as if I did not have enough time to do the reading that I wanted to do, take care of Rebecca, and continue my work. I remember the LaLeche counselor saying that it is difficult for people with jobs because they feel that if they are doing their work successfully, they are not giving all they could to their children. If they are doing the most they can with mothering, they feel as if they are cheating their employer. It is difficult to come to a balance, and I was having trouble with that.

My little girl was now 8 months adjusted age, 11 months in actual age. In March, we returned to the perinatal center follow-up program. The staff found what we already knew—that Rebecca was doing well in her fine motor skills, but her gross motor skills (crawling, sitting, and other skills) were a bit behind. The staff reassured us that we should not be concerned. Overall, we were quite happy with her developmental progress, especially that she was fine mentally.

* * * *

We have been pretty fortunate since we have had a great deal of support from our family and friends when we needed it the most. We also have made some new friends, who helped us to understand and deal with all of Wayne's problems. Without them, it would have been very difficult for us. There have been some disappointments and irritations along the way. For example, when Wayne started school at an early childhood center, he was evaluated as physically handicapped. That term bothered both Gary and me a lot. Our son was, and still is, slow in some ways. We were told that being labelled *physically handicapped* did not mean anything. It was just a label. Still to us, it was much more than that. We went along with the decision only because we wanted him to get the help he needed.

* * * *

In total, Anna did not look like a baby; she did not act nearly her age in comparison with Margaret. I was not able to nurse her, as I did Margaret and Peter. Finally, it came as a shock to me one day that I could not say to Anna, very naturally, "I love you." This realization occurred some time in April, when I began to analyze some of my feelings. The recollection that kept coming back to me was an experience that I had as a child—watching a litter of pups, which had been born to our family dog. There appeared to be too many pups for the number of working nipples. I remember finding one little pup tucked under the mother's leg each time the puppies nursed. This puppy was not attached to a nipple, and seemed to grow weaker and weaker. I recall being angry with the mother dog, questioning why wasn't she watching out for this little one, why wasn't she taking special care since it was so weak? Thinking back to this experience, it suddenly occurred to me that this was how I was feeling about Anna. In a sense, she was my "runt of the litter."

Despite the above understanding, I still struggled with myself to feel love for Anna. She was scheduled for surgery in Boston to correct three of her defects on June 8. It was not until two weeks before scheduled surgery that I allowed myself, finally, to admit that I did love her. Once I accepted that feeling, a myriad of other emotions surfaced. I took on a great burden and was almost consumed by it.

* * * *

The middle months were the very hardest, to sit back and watch Joey go from what we thought was healthy to what was just awful. At this point, he was about six or seven months old. He weighed only six or seven pounds. He was still wearing newborn baby clothes. Joey's being on oxygen was the most difficult part of these middle months. No matter where I took him, he had to have his portable oxygen tank. What hurt the most were the eyes of other people who looked at him as if he were some sort of "freak." I could not imagine what they thought. In time, I was able to accept those looks because I knew that my little boy was a part of me and he was beautiful.

After Joey went on the oxygen, he was a very hard child to care for at home. He was irritable most of the time. He never slept through the night and was awake most of the day. He still rarely ate more than three ounces at a feeding, and he refused cereal and fruit. Throughout this period, Joey stayed home possibly a week to ten days at the most, then returned to the hospital for a week or two weeks. He was never with us for more than ten days at a stretch.

Joey's doctor and I went into the conference room to talk. He did not have to tell me anything. I looked at him and said, "I know that my son is never going to come home." He seemed amazed. I explained how I felt. I told him that I knew all along that there was something terribly wrong with Joey. Nobody knew it, except my husband and me. At that point, he said that he did not think that Joey would ever come home and that it was only a matter of time. His heart could not hold out. He said then that if, by some miracle, he did improve a little, he definitely would be back in the same condition very soon.

By this time, Joey was nine months old, and things were not getting any easier. We took a trip to Rochester and spent the day with a pediatric pulmonary specialist. He examined Joey and looked at his x-rays. The doctors had not one bit of advice to offer, except to say that if Joey's pulmonary hypertension did not improve very soon, he would not live to see his second birthday. I was glad that they were so blunt. Again, all of the deep feelings that both my husband and I had since the day Joey arrived home came back. We knew deep down inside that somehow our son would never see his second birthday.

I realized, with Joey's being ten months old, that I could not carry the total burden any longer. I needed help. I decided to take the advice of doctors, hire a nurse to come in a few days and nights a week. Bill and I needed to leave the pressure at home for a few hours. It took a lot to admit that I could not care for my son by myself.

A few days prior to his birthday, I had talked to the doctors. They did not think that Joey (see Figure 19–6) could hold on much longer. It was a matter of a few days because his heart was getting so bad. It was just seven days after his first birthday— exactly one week—that God took Joey to Heaven. As long as I had expected it, I could not accept what had happened. That was the hardest day of my life, saying "good-bye" to my son forever.

As some of the accounts suggest, those babies and families enrolled in educational programs profited immensely from these services. Mothers and fathers benefited from opportunities to share ideas with teachers, therapists, and other parents. Moreover, since all of these children were enrolled between four and eight months of age, they responded well to programming within relatively short periods of time. With both home and center-based

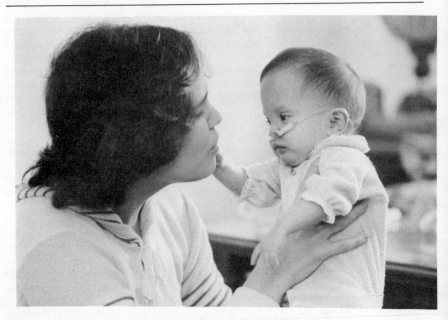

Figure 19–6 Joey

settings, provisions for parent observation and modeling are critical in order that families reinforce and add to the continuity of activities. In our experience when parents have not been centrally involved, progress has not been as readily obvious and prognoses have been less optimistic. In other programs of the past, as well as our own, family commitments seem to have been determined by two factors; i.e., the extent to which parents feel needed and invested in the educational process and the strength of their relationships with primary professionals. In general, our respective fields have been more effective in reaching such goals with middle- to upper-income families, and less so with young, single parents. Broader and more active participation of high school systems in the future will be necessary if we are to achieve success with teenage populations. In all cases, moreover, the support of and ongoing communication with family pediatricians is essential so that parents do not receive divided recommendations. Positive professional relationships thus constitute another goal that will largely be accomplished by cooperative efforts.

It is difficult for parents to acknowledge that their children have developmental problems that necessitate intervention, as each of our families has noted. Present mechanisms for obtaining services do not make that acceptance any easier. In most states, families are required to sign papers that indicate specified handicapping conditions and, in New York State, they must participate in a Family Court process that certifies such delays. Parents obviously are concerned that labels, given in infancy and toddlerhood, will follow their children into the school years. While the main objective of early education is prevention and amelioration of long-term disabilities, profession-als are hard-pressed to offer guarantees. General categories of risk with defined parameters need to be introduced into state regulations that permit the funding of programs for birth-to-five populations. Overall, this approach would be less expensive for communities than present burdens that most school districts carry in terms of special education. The facts are undeniable in those instances where local public schools serving infants and young children have returned at least 50 percent of their early education youngsters to regular kindergartens with few or no continuing special services.

Probably with families in catastrophic circumstances, such as Pam and Bill Corrigan, communities never will be able to meet all of their needs. On the other hand, psychological and educational supports ought to be more readily available than at present. Indeed, the Corrigans do not stand alone in the crises that they faced daily. Respite arrangements, other than developmental centers or costly individual medical care, rarely are found for parents with infants who are difficult to manage. Networks of available families trained in coping with the special needs of severely involved babies are an alternative and, if prescribed by pediatricians, should be reimbursed through state aid or Medicaid. Home and center-based programming through the public schools, in addition, can offer direction to families in the areas of feeding, handling, and general stimulation that are unfamiliar to most parents.

For working families, community day-care facilities need to be an option. At the present time, most centers are far from capable of managing the baby or young child with special needs. In part, this void could be filled with the assistance of corporative ventures between day-care personnel, universities, and public school systems.

THE ADVICE OF PARENTS

While families have shared many suggestions with us over the past several years, the advice that they consistently have delivered centers around the need for communication with professionals and other parents in similar situations. This message may not alter the ultimate course of events; it does help families deal more creatively with their circumstances and does enhance their potentials as teachers and primary caregivers of their children. The following were taken from the final statements of our parents.

My first advice to a parent in this kind of situation is to seek help before leaving the hospital. Ask a social worker, speak with someone who has been through this experience, who can offer to share some feelings. Mothers, talk with your doctors and your baby's doctors about your feelings and about your child. These people may or may not give you comfort in this situation, but the effort is worth a try. You may find others more helpful than you would expect. Most hospitals now are starting parent support groups.

* * * *

Perhaps more important than anything are chances to talk—with your husband, your own parents, and your friends. Our families helped us a lot by being there. Hopefully, if other parents find themselves in circumstances like ours, the situation will turn out as happily as ours did. Seventeen months ago I thought that things were really bad; I could not foresee a bright future. Today, Jennifer is one of the happiest little girls I know.

* * * *

I regret that we were not more demanding of Brian's first physician. We knew he was overworked and therefore did not want to bother him. Had we been a bit more firm, asked more questions, and not hesitated to disturb him, we would have been better informed and perhaps saved ourselves a lot of worry.

One thing that has helped me over the past two years has been talking about Brian's handicap. Everyone I could corner heard Brian's story from beginning to end. The more I talked about it, the more comfortable I became with the fact that he had a handicap. It is very therapeutic for me to share my fears and concerns, even when they seemed trivial or silly. This was especially true with family and close friends.

* * * *

Be as open with each other as you can. For us, it was a benefit to talk with each other about our fears and concerns, to talk with friends and family, anyone who could be understanding and supportive. Take one day, and sometimes one hour, at a time. Focus on what is happening and how the baby is doing. Don't get too far ahead of yourself and think of all the possibilities. You have no way of knowing what is going to take place the next day or next month. Ask the doctors and the nurses about questions or concerns that you have. Maybe they can help you with the information that you need. Read about premature babies so that you can see what other people have gone through and know that you are not alone. Other people have had some of the same feelings, same fears, and concerns. Learn about how they have coped with them. If there is a parent group available, go and get all the information and support that you can. Talk with other parents. If you are able to give them suggestions, that may make you feel good, too. Find ways to acknowledge and release your anger and disappointment. In addition, try to examine your expectations, realize that even though term births look ideal, they also are not perfect.

Go to the hospital, and visit your baby as often as you can and touch the baby. When the staff will let you, hold your baby, feed the baby, become as involved in the care as you can, and be confident that you can give that little one something that the nursing staff cannot offer—the love of a mother and father.

Help may come from several directions. Some people may talk to a professional person, to anybody who can understand what you are saying, someone who is not going to be prejudiced. Anybody who is reading this, who has had a child with developmental problems, surely will understand. Many people rely on their religion to resolve these problems. That can be helpful; yet ultimately, each person must find his or her own peace of mind and strength. Eventually, you start to see things differently. You are more open to things and can share the joyous experience of your child, whatever your situation happens to be.

* * * *

Many mothers and fathers who have gone through the discomfort, disappointment, and fear involving surgery with their young children are capable of giving great encouragement. Seek these people out; you do not have to struggle alone. I suspect that many parents in similar circumstances go through periods of ignoring illness in their children, having difficulties with the bonding, and developing feelings of guilt. I suspect that all of these are very natural reactions. Talking with professionals may help us with factual information regarding our children but we, as parents, need to find comfort and support with each other.

* * * *

One of my greatest joys was watching what Joey did for other people and how he touched their lives. He gave so much love to everybody around him. It seemed almost impossible that this tiny baby could bring such happiness to so many people. As an example of that joy, one of the nurses who took care of Joey wrote a poem for his first birthday. It was entitled just plain "Joey."

Sweet little babe, beautiful boy
You'll never know the wondrous joy
You've brought our hearts in one small year
And all the reasons we hold you dear.

You seem to always understand
Just when we need your smile
And when we feel you hold our hands
That makes our lives worthwhile.

Sometimes we feel it isn't fair
That you should suffer so,
But God knows that your stay with us
Will give us strength to grow.

And so with smiles and happiness
We celebrate today
For the love you give and the love we share
Will never fade away.

C. Lockyer (June 4, 1982)

Despite what we might think, families do not expect professionals to have all the answers to their problems or those of their newborn babies. Any parent who has had a child with special needs knows this. For "experts" in the human and health care services, there should be some consolation in that thought. As Murphy (1981) has written:

> Participating in the lives of special children is frustrating and fascinating. We play many roles in the process, and interwoven are the countless distractions that are part of every life. It is quite a trick to keep from scrambling the roles, to make the quick shift from one to the other—caretaker, teacher, listener, friend. Every individual's situation is unique, and it is a lot of work to keep a healthy balance. Every parent or professional lives, works, and stays vital as long as there is response with spirit and some success to the challenges. If we stop responding we die. We stop responding only if we relinquish the will and the strength to persevere, to make our own decisions, and to abide by our own true conscience. We work with what we have and what we believe. There will be doubt, but doubt will be used as a springboard to more productive reasoning .... (p. 195)

FINAL REFLECTIONS

There are those who have argued persuasively that despite sophisticated technology, current legislation, well-intentioned curricula, and able, committed professionals, benefits to "the disadvantaged" weigh heavily upon changes among "the advantaged." Recent trends in the delivery of services to high risk and handicapped infants and their families are confirmation of this concept. Moreover, the accounts of our eight sets of parents seem to reinforce Urie Bronfenbrenner's thesis of the need for extending research, training, and service efforts "to encompass functional systems within and between settings" (1979, p. 7). Such an approach in the future will obligate us to a perspective very different from widely held views and programs of the past and present. Narrowly focused ventures, over the years, have often restricted our awareness of obstacles and opportunities, serving to confuse rather than clarify central questions and issues. For the infant born at risk or with developmental problems, who may have spent the earliest weeks and months of life in-hospital, a broader, ecological framework for creating research and service is imperative. (See Figure 19–7—Philip and Jessica.) One example that we have discussed throughout this text is that our respective fields now are beginning to recognize the mutuality of interactions within a total family context, which influences the developmental outcome of newborns. These newer concepts stand in marked contrast with previous notions of the exclusive impact of mother-infant relationships. Carefully designed study and intervention in natural home, hospital, and community settings could be very helpful toward a better understanding of the prevention of early childhood disorders. Further, it is clear that larger connections between family, community, hospital networks, and other systems of support during periods of family crises and adjustment are fertile areas for investigation, with both service and social policy implications for intervention. Broader, integrated views will lead us to more frequent applications that maintain a fine balance between rigor, on the one hand, and openness to observation, reinterpretation, and new data, on the other.

There is much to learn about the treatment and education of the high risk newborn. Given the necessary constraints of time and funding, the task of knowing what happens to hospital staff, parents, and infants in the face of critical care will not be easily accomplished. To date, a great deal of psychosocial and developmental intervention with infants and families lacks a solid empirical base. Yet as we discuss in the opening chapter of this book, professionals and researchers are beginning to raise pertinent and timely issues. Specifically, we need to understand what kinds of stimulation are growth-promoting and how these can be matched with infants and parents.

Figure 19–7 Philip and Jessica

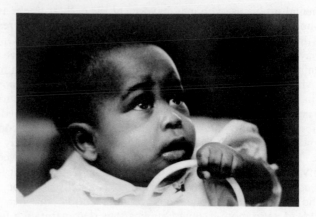

Figure 19–8 Serena

We need to know how to mitigate short-term adverse effects of inappropriate stimulation in hospital units. We need to analyze how the impact of interventions varies with the stage of crisis, educational background, and ages of the parents. We need to examine the underlying processes of early parent-infant attachment and, as our families have emphasized, the kinds of transitions from hospital to home needed by parents as well as infants. (See Figure 19–8—Serena.)

Over the past three decades, neonatology, early childhood, developmental psychology, and other areas of research and study have witnessed countless changes in target populations served, medical technology, assessment techniques, and strategies for intervention, as well as in the theoretical constructs for comprehending what we do. Still, as our families discovered, the medical and developmental sciences often are not as exacting or predictive as we sometimes have imagined. Many of the same basic questions raised by pioneers in our fields persist as variations of common themes. In fact, we have erred at both ends of the continuum in our quest for data and explanation, analyzing minute pieces of behavior only to lose sight of the larger picture, or conceptualizing global issues to the neglect of the finer subtleties of individual differences. Fortunately, continued research, training, and service among professionals has not been diminished by such obstacles. If anything, these efforts have intensified our need to learn more.

REFERENCES

Bronfenbrenner, U. (1979). *The ecology of human development: Experiments by nature and design.* Cambridge: Harvard University Press.

Lockyer, C. (1982). *Joey,* unpublished poem.

Murphy, A.T. (1981). *Special children, special parents: Personal issues with handicapped children.* Englewood Cliffs, NJ: Prentice-Hall.

Index

A

Abnormal physical development
  deformations, 121–122
  disruptions, 122
  malformations, 122–130
  See also individual abnormalities.
Active phase, labor, 22–23
Age of mother
  effects on fetus, 18
  teenage mothers, risk factors,
    274–275
Air block syndromes, 109
  pneumomediastinum, 109
  pneumopericardium, 109
  pneumothorax, 109
Alcohol use, 45
Alternate assessment strategy, 168
Amnion, 16
Amniotic fluid, 16
  deformations and, 121–122
Anencephaly, 92
Apgar score, 26
Apnea, 91–92
  treatment of, 91
Asphyxia, resuscitation, 27–28
Aspiration, 108–109

Assessment, 145–169
  alternate assessment strategy, 168
  *Bayley Scales of Infant
    Development*, 156–157, 209
  *Brazelton Neonatal Behavioral
    Assessment Scale*, 159–161
  *Carolina Curriculum for
    Handicapped Infants and Infants
    at Risk*, 166–167
  *Cattell's Scale of Infant
    Intelligence*, 156–157
  cumulative risk scoring systems,
    152
  *Denver Developmental Screening
    Test*, 158–159, 209
  early identification, 146, 149
  *Early Learning Accomplishment
    Profile*, 165
  Gesell's Developmental Scales,
    154–155
  Hawaii Early Learning Profile,
    166
  home environment factor in,
    153–154
  *Home Observation for
    Measurement of the Environment*,
    167–168
  issues in screening, 145–146

About the Authors

Gail L. Ensher, EdD , is Associate Professor of Special Education at Syracuse University in Syracuse, New York. She is responsible for coordinating the Master's degree program in Educating Infants and Young Children with Special Needs. Her publications have related to curriculum development for the education of the mentally retarded, the integration of handicapped children into Head Start programs, and research on the development of high risk and premature infants. She has directed two major early childhood projects. The first was sponsored in 1972 by the Office of Child Development and evaluated the education of preschool, handicapped children in Head Start. The second was a three-year grant in 1979 by the New York State Office of Mental Retardation and Developmental Disabilities to provide home-based early intervention to high risk babies who had been in intensive care. Dr. Ensher's educational background consists of degrees from Denison University (B.A.), and from Boston University (M.Ed. and Ed.D.).

David A. Clark, MD, is Associate Professor of Pediatrics at New York Medical College and Westchester County Medical Center in Valhalla, New York. In this capacity, he is responsible for teaching, outreach education, research, and patient care. In the past he has held academic appointment at North Carolina Memorial Hospital in Chapel Hill, Rainbow Babies and Children's Hospital in Cleveland, Ohio, and Upstate Medical Center of the State University of New York in Syracuse. In 1983, he received the Young Investigator Award from the American Academy of Pediatrics. Dr. Clark's research interests have focused on neonatal digestion, necrotizing enterocolitis, chronic lung disease, and developmental disabilities. He has published over 50 articles on these various topics.